Living Theater

AN INTRODUCTION TO THEATER HISTORY

Living Theater

AN INTRODUCTION TO THEATER HISTORY

EDWIN WILSON
Hunter College
The City University of New York

ALVIN GOLDFARB
Illinois State University

McGRAW-HILL BOOK COMPANY

New York St. Louis San Francisco Auckland Bogotá Hamburg
Johannesburg London Madrid Mexico Montreal New Delhi Panama
Paris São Paulo Singapore Sydney Tokyo Toronto

Living Theater

AN INTRODUCTION TO THEATER HISTORY

234567890 DOCDOC 89876543

ISBN 0-07-070730-8 SC

ISBN 0-07-070732-4 HC

Library of Congress Cataloging in Publication Data

Wilson, Edwin.
    Living theater.

    Bibliography: p.
    Includes index.
    1. Theater—History. I. Goldfarb, Alvin.
II. Title.
PN2101.W54   1983   792 .09   82-13047
ISBN 0-07-070732-4
ISBN 0-07-070730-8 (pbk.)

This book was set in Trump Mediaeval
by Black Dot, Inc. (ECU).
The editors were Alison Meersschaert,
Marian D. Provenzano, and Barry Benjamin;
the designer was Joan E. O'Connor;
the production supervisor was Dominick Petrellese.
The photo editor was Inge King.
The drawings were done by Fine Line Illustrations, Inc.
The soft cover etching was done by Tom Lulevitch.
R. R. Donnelley & Sons Company was printer and binder.

To our mothers,
Catherine J. Wilson
and
Shirley Goldfarb,
and to the memories of our fathers
E. W. and A. G.

CONTENTS

Part Three THE THEATER FROM 1660 TO 1875—YEARS OF CHANGE

Part Four THE MODERN THEATER

Part Five THE ASIAN AND BLACK THEATERS

APPENDIXES

PREFACE

Living Theater attempts to do what its title suggests: bring theater to life. This entails, on the one hand, demonstrating the liveliness and vitality of theaters of the past and, on the other, showing that the heritage of the past is still with us—that theatrical practices established long ago can be found in productions we see today.

To make theater history clear and comprehensible, *Living Theater* stresses concepts rather than a catalogue of people, places, and events. Crucial developments of the theater are covered, but an overview of events is also introduced. The threads that run through theater history are established and then discussed as they appear in one period after another. For example, the two important forms of dramatic structure found in western theater history—the crisis or climactic structure of the Greeks and neoclassicists and the episodic structure of the English and Spanish Renaissance—are identified early and are traced carefully through succeeding historical periods. The same is done with stage spaces, approaches to acting, critical theories, and so forth. Still another element is an emphasis on the audience: what audiences were like in each period, and what it meant to audience members to go to the theater.

Several important features make *Living Theater* accessible as well as informative to students. The book is divided into historical segments, but there are also broad groupings: The Early Theater (Greek, Roman, Medieval); The Renaissance Theater; the theater during a time of transition (1660–1875); The Modern Theater; and finally, a section on the Asian and black theaters. With this arrangement, the sweep of theater history is within the grasp of every student.

The start of each chapter has a section on the cultural, social, and political history of the era under discussion. In this way, theater is put in the context of the period; it is seen not as an isolated phenomenon but as part of a larger picture. To reinforce this notion, at the beginning of each chapter there is also a dated timeline, giving, on one side, important events in theater history and, on the other, significant events in general history such as wars, inventions, and reigns of monarchs. The time charts provide a graphic, easily understood chronology of every epoch.

Throughout, the book is illustrated with pictures and charts that are carefully integrated with the text. Also, playwrights and other key figures in theater history have been treated in individual boxes which contain a picture of the person and a brief biography. This not only sets the figures apart, it also allows the flow of the main text to continue uninterrupted. There are also several helpful appendixes: a lengthy, comprehensive glossary of technical terms and names; a phonetic pronunciation guide for proper names and special theater terms; and a list of related plays as suggested reading for each period.

It should be pointed out that *Living Theater* can serve several types of courses. The first, as the subtitle suggests, is theater history, either a one-semester or a two-semester course. The book covers the full range of theater history, but the material has been carefully selected so that it can be covered in a single semester. At the same time, *Living Theater* is comprehensive and can serve as the basic text for a two-semester course, especially when supplemented by the study of plays suggested in the Related Plays appendix, and with additional readings from sources listed in the bibliography.

The other popular course for which *Living Theater* is designed is the general introduction to theater. Many teachers and departments prefer the historical approach in teaching the introductory course, and the current text should be ideal for their needs. Some texts for such an introductory course have one section on history and another on the people and functions of the theater: playwrights, designers, actors, etc. In the present work, such elements are covered by being integrated into each historical period.

A word must be said about the countries and cultures covered in *Living Theater*. The second through the fourteenth chapters trace the history of western theater, the theater that forms the basis for most of the theater with which we are familiar. At the same time, it was recognized that other theaters are of great importance and have had a strong influence on western theater. This is particularly true of the Asian and black theaters, and a great deal of thought was given as to how we should deal with these theaters.

Texts that include Asian theater generally introduce the subject before the western medieval period, or after the Renaissance, or in the late nineteenth century (when Asian theater was discovered in the west). None of these dates is satisfactory: first because the introduction of Asian theater at any point interrupts the flow of western theater history, and second—and more important—because Asian theater has it own integrity and chronology. For this reason, it was decided to give a separate chapter to Asian theater—India, China, and Japan—so that it could be given its due. A leading authority on the subject, Prof. J. Thomas Rimer, head of the Department of Chinese and Japanese at Washington University, St. Louis, has provided the material for this chapter.

In the same way, a separate chapter is devoted to the history of black theater. Obviously, the important black figures in the modern theater are discussed in the appropriate sections in the study of western theater, but it was felt that a more detailed study of the background and development of black theater was called for, and hence another expert, Prof. James V. Hatch of the City College of New York, has provided the material for a chapter devoted solely to this purpose.

ACKNOWLEDGMENTS

There are many people to thank for making this book possible. Professor Rita Plotnicki of Southern Illinois University provided all of the material and did most of the writing for the biographical boxes. The one exception is the chapter on black theater for which George C. Wolfe supplied the bibliographies. Sally Small did all of the typing as well as important research, including the preparation of the pronunciation guide. Others who assisted in research are Patricia Stobaugh, Emily Brown, and Gayle Gerard.

We are grateful for the important contributions of the following people who read and commented on the manuscript while it was being developed: Professor June Compton, Sul Ross State University; Professor Robert Gobetz, Pittsburg State College; Professor Robert Graves, University of Illinois at Champaign-Urbana; Dr. E. James Hooks, University of Florida; Dr. Robert Huber, Coastline Community College; Professor Jack McCullough, Trenton State College; Professor James Moy, University of Wisconsin; Dr. Ronald Moyer, University of South Dakota; Professor Gary Schoepfel, Lorain County Community College; and Professor Ann Vliet, North Adams State College.

We wish to thank our wives, Catherine Wilson and Elaine Goldfarb, for their unending patience and understanding. We also thank Elaine Goldfarb for preparing the index. Our associates at McGraw-Hill, who have been exceedingly helpful, include Joan O'Connor, the exceptional and talented designer; Inge King, the resourceful photo editor; Barry Benjamin, the ever supportive editing supervisor; Marian Provenzano, sponsoring editor; and finally, our overall editor, the incomparable Alison Meersschaert.

Edwin Wilson
Alvin Goldfarb

Living Theater

AN INTRODUCTION
TO THEATER HISTORY

Chapter One

The year is 441 B.C., and the place is Athens, Greece. It is a morning in late March and many citizens of Athens—perhaps 12,000 to 15,000—are up early. They have dressed in their best tunics and are making their way to the Theater of Dionysus, an amphitheater placed on the south side of the Acropolis, the tallest hill in Athens. Atop the Acropolis are several temples; the Parthenon, a magnificent temple dedicated to the goddess Athena, is under construction at this very time.

The Theater of Dionysus is carved from the side of the Acropolis. It is a semicircular seating space built into the slope of the hill; at the foot of the seating area is a flat, circular space—called the *orchestra*—where the actors will perform. Behind the orchestra a temporary stage house has been built from which the performers will make entrances and exits.

The people in the audience arrive early, and because they will be

Basic elements of theater   *Whenever and wherever theater occurs, certain elements are always present. Three of the most important are a performance space, the performers, and the audience. These three elements are shown here at the Oregon Shakespeare Festival in Ashland, Oregon. The actual presence of the performers sets theater apart from films and television. (Photo—Hank Kranzler.)*

there all day, they have brought food and wine. The priests of various religious orders sit in special stone chairs at the edge of the circle opposite the stage house. Other dignitaries—civic and military officials—range around them in the first few rows, while above them sit both citizens and slaves. Since the seaport near Athens has recently been reopened after being closed for the winter months, a number of foreign visitors are also present.

Even those sitting on the top row will have no trouble hearing the performers; the acoustics of the amphitheater are so good that a whisper by an actor in the orchestra will carry to the upper reaches of the theater. The plays the audience will see today are part of the City Dionysia festival. During the festival, all business in Athens—both commercial and governmental—comes to a halt and all attention is focused on the festival itself, an annual series of events lasting seven days. On a day before the plays began there was a parade through the city; it ended near the theater with a religious observance at the altar of the temple dedicated to the god Dionysus, for whom the festival is named.

Today is one of the three days in the festival devoted to presenting tragedies. On such a day, a playwright will offer three tragedies and a satyr play. (The satyr play is a short comic piece burlesquing tragic subjects, with actors dressed as satyrs, mythological creatures that were half-men and half-goats.) The three tragedies might be linked to form one long play—called a trilogy—or, as is the case today, can be three separate pieces.

Sophocles, the author of today's plays, announced a few days earlier that one of them will deal with the story of Antigone, and it is this play which the audience is now eagerly anticipating. The subject comes from a myth familiar to the playgoers. Antigone was the daughter of King Oedipus. After her father's death, her two brothers, Eteocles and Polynices, became involved in a war against each other and killed one another. Antigone's uncle Creon then became king of Thebes and issued an edict that Polynices was not to be given an honorable burial. Antigone decided to defy Creon's order and bury the body of her brother Polynices.

Members of the audience, knowing the myth well, are curious to see how Sophocles, one of their favorite dramatists, will deal with the story. As the play begins, two actors, wearing masks and female costumes, appear in the playing area. The audience realizes immediately that they represent Antigone and her sister Ismene. Antigone tells Ismene that she means to defy their uncle, the king, and give their brother an honorable burial. Ismene, who unlike her sister is timid and frightened, argues that women are too weak to stand up to a king, and besides, that Antigone will be put to death if she is caught. Antigone argues, however, that she will not accept such a subservient role for women.

When the two women leave, a chorus of fifteen men enters. They represent the elders of the city, and throughout the play—in passages that are sung and danced—they will fulfill several functions: providing background information, raising philosophical questions, and urging

*T*he Theater Dionysus at Athens   *Set in the hillside of the Acropolis in Athens, Greece, and named after the god Dionysus, this theater was the site of the original productions of the most famous plays written in ancient Greece, including the* Antigone *of Sophocles. The remains of the theater as shown in this photograph, can still be seen today. (Photo—Ned Haines, 1981, Photo Researchers.)*

restraint on the principal figures. The choral sections alternate with scenes of confrontation between Antigone, Creon, and the other main characters.

When the showdown comes, Antigone does defy Creon, and as punishment is put in a cave to die. In the end, not only is she dead, but so too are Creon's wife and son. In the final scene, the audience sees Creon standing alone, wearing his tragic mask, bereft of all those he held dear.

At the close of the day, as the sun sets behind the Acropolis, the audience walks home, recalling highlights of the drama: the scene when Antigone argued vehemently with Creon, standing up to him as his equal, and the final, dreadful tableau of Creon alone.

We move eighteen centuries ahead and half a world away—to Japan. The year is 1413, and the place is the Kitano Temple. A platform stage, with a polished wood floor, has been set up; there is also a wooden walkway, or bridge, on which actors can move to the stage from a dressing

The Noh theater of Japan *This highly stylized theater was first brought to full flower by Zeami in the early fifteenth century. It is still performed today as is shown in a performance in Kyoto, Japan, at the left. In Noh, all characters are played by men, who wear masks such as the traditional one of a young woman shown on the right. (Photos—George Holton, Photo Researches; Frank Wing/Stock, Boston.)*

room set up in one of the temple buildings. The spectators will be on three sides of the platform stage.

The actor performing today is Zeami, a 50-year-old man who has been under the patronage of the shogun since he was 12 years old. Zeami's father had been a renowned actor before him, and Zeami has carried his father's art to even greater heights. He has studied different acting styles, perfected his own technique, trained other actors, and written plays for them to perform. The theater he has fashioned from all this, called noh, has elements of opera, pantomime, and formal, stylized dance.

The main character in noh, who wears a beautifully carved and painted wooden mask, recites his or her adventures to the constant accompaniment of several onstage musicians. Toward the end of the play, the chief actor will perform a ritualistic dance with symbolic head and hand gestures and stomps of the feet on the wooden floor.

The crowd is gathered today for a special reason. Usually Zeami performs only in a restricted environment for the shogun and the members of his court or at a temple for a select audience. But here at the Kitano Temple performances will go on for seven days and will be open to everyone; as one later commentator explained: "All were admitted, rich and poor, old and young alike."

As with all noh performances, several plays will be presented each day. The play the audience is awaiting now is the one in which Zeami plays a woman. (As in the ancient Greek theater, all of the performers are men.) It may be the play called *Sotoba Komachi*, written by Zeami's father, Kwanami. The legend of Komachi is well known to the audience, just as the story of Antigone was to the Greeks. Komachi, a beautiful but cruel woman, was pursued by a man named Shii no Shosho. She told him he must call on her for one hundred nights in a row, and for ninety-nine nights he came, in all kinds of weather. But on the one-hundredth night he died.

As the play begins, the audience sees two priests enter. They are discussing the virtues of following Buddha when they come upon an old woman. This is Zeami in the mask and wig of Komachi as an old woman. She tells how she was once beautiful:

Long ago I was full of pride;
Crowned with nodding tresses, halcyon locks,
I walked like a young willow delicately wafted
By the winds of Spring.
I spoke with the voice of a nightingale that has sipped the dew.
I was lovelier than the petals of the wild-rose open-stretched
In the hour before its fall.[1]

But Komachi has lost her beauty and grown old. She argues with the priests about religion and then reveals who she is. She recounts the story of what she did to Shosho. As the play progresses, the audience watches Zeami's performance with rapt attention. At one point he enacts a possession; the spirit of Shosho takes over Komachi, and Zeami acts this out in pantomime to musical accompaniment. At other times he acts out Komachi's part while a chorus—ten or twelve men sitting at the side of the stage—chants Komachi's lines. Another time, Komachi is dressed as Shosho and becomes him, feeling his death agony in her. Zeami performs this part as a mesmerizing, frightening dance. At the end of the play the spirit of Shosho leaves Komachi, and she prays to Buddha for guidance and for a peaceful life in the hereafter.

The audience which has heard so much about Zeami but never seen him perform, watches in awe. Throughout he has played the various parts with astounding grace, subtlety, and understatement, developed through years of training and performance. The times when he lets go—as in Shosho's death agony—are all the more effective due to their contrast with the stately, measured quality of the rest. For the audience the play is a moment of revelation at how moving a theatrical performance can be. It is an experience unlike any they have had before.

[1]Arthur Waley, *The Nō Plays of Japan*, p. 151. Reprinted by permission of Grove Press, Inc. All rights reserved.

Three-quarters of a century later we return to Europe, a world not known to Japan, and where Japan was equally unknown. The time is 1501 in Mons, Belgium. We are in the large town square where a series of small stage houses, or "mansions," have been erected across one side. They serve as the setting for a series of plays based on the Old and New Testaments—dramatized Bible stories that move from the creation to the crucifixion.

In the biblical plays at Mons this year about 150 actors will perform 350 roles. They have held forty-eight rehearsals, and it will take four days to present all the plays in the cycle.

The mansions set up across the stage area are changed to suit the play being performed. In all, sixty-seven different mansions—representing the garden of Eden, the manger in Bethlehem, the Temple where Christ drove out the money changers, and so forth—will be used during the four days. At each end of the stage are two permanent mansions, symbolic of the two sides of the giant religious drama being played out: one is Heaven and the other is Hell, represented by the large mouth of a monster, out of which devils and smoke pour at the appropriate moments.

The audience has already seen the stories of Adam and Eve, and of Cain slaying his brother Abel. The drama the audience is waiting for just now is the story of Noah, the man ordered by God to build an ark to save his family and the animals when the flood comes. In the play Noah is warned by God that it will rain forty days and forty nights, and that he must build an ark into which he will take his family and two animals of every kind. As Noah begins building, his neighbors make fun of him, and his wife argues with him. The audience enjoys this byplay, but the moment they are waiting for is the deluge itself, which is expected to be spectacular.

At last the moment arrives, and the audience is not disappointed. On the roofs of houses behind the Noah stage area, water has been stored in wine barrels. Men are standing by, waiting for a signal to open the barrels; now the signal is given and the deluge begins with torrents of rain falling on the stage. The audience is overcome; enough water has been stored to provide a steady rain for five minutes. Water rises all around, but Noah, his family, and his animals are safe in the ark.

Soon after, a dove comes, indicating that Noah can leave the ark. When the play is over the next play begins, but afterwards the sensational flood still remains in the minds of the audience.

Moving ahead 450 years, and from Europe to the United States, we arrive in California. The date is November 19, 1957, and the place is San Quentin Prison near San Francisco. In the prison's North Dining Hall, where a stage is set up, a group of actors from the Actor's Workshop is going to perform Samuel Beckett's *Waiting for Godot*. It will be the first performance at the prison in over forty years.[2]

---

[2]Based on an account in Martin Esslin, *The Theatre of the Absurd*, pp xv–xvii.

A modern classic   Waiting for Godot *by Samuel Beckett features two tramps who epitomize the feelings of many people today. The main characters, Gogo and Didi, live from moment to moment, hoping that someone named Godot will come to save them, but he never does. When the play was shown at San Quentin prison, the prisoners felt a strong connection to men waiting to be saved. (Photo—The Juilliard School, Diane Gorodnitzki.)*

The performers are nervous, not only because they are performing in a penitentiary, but also because of the play they are to present. It is a drama without much action, about two tramps who meet each day on a barren plain hoping that an unknown figure named Godot will come. They have the vague expectation that somehow Godot, if he ever comes, will be able to help them. While they wait, they try to break the painful monotony of their boring lives with bickering and occasional vaudeville routines. In addition to having very little action, the play is filled with literary and religious references. It has already baffled intellectuals in Europe and the United States; how, the actors wonder, will a group of restless prisoners react to it?

Shortly after the performance begins they have part of the answer. The audience grows quiet. A group of men sitting on some steps who had planned to leave early become engrossed, and stay. The audience follows closely from beginning to end.

After the performance is over, it is clear that the audience has understood much of what it has seen: perhaps more than other audiences might. The prisoners—who must wait out their sentences in boredom and frustration—intuitively connect with the men on stage who wait for the unknown Godot, who never comes.

THE ELEMENTS OF THE THEATER

These four theater events, spanning three continents and 2,400 years, suggest the nature of theater. Our own experiences of theater probably consist of seeing performances in high school, college, local professional, and Broadway-type theaters. The kinds of plays we see will include revivals of classics—Shakespeare, for example—and modern plays, such as a comedy by Neil Simon *(The Odd Couple)* or a drama by Tennessee Williams *(A Streetcar Named Desire* or *The Glass Menagerie).*

The productions we see, however, and the type of theater we see them in, share certain qualities with all theater. When combined, these qualities—or elements—give theater its unique character and set it apart from other human activities, including other art forms. What are these elements?

A Playing Space

One element of theater is a place where people can come together to watch a performance. Whether it is outdoors (in a Greek amphitheater or the theater in the square at Mons) or indoors (a college playhouse), whether it is a permanent space (a Broadway theater) or a temporary one (the dining hall at San Quentin), a place must be set aside where the spectators can observe and where the actors can perform.

The Audience

The idea of a place for viewing suggests a second element: the audience itself. Unlike some art experiences—reading a book or viewing a painting, for instance—theater requires more than a single spectator; it calls for a congregation of people as observers. It is a communal experience for the audience, and this coming together is one of its essential elements.

In this respect theater is also different from a drama on television or in a film: it is a live exchange between audience and performers. Each theatrical event is unique and happens only once. Even the same play with the same actors will vary from night to night, and one reason is the electricity which passes spontaneously back and forth between actors and audience.

The Performers

Equally important are the performers: the other half of the actor-audience equation. Performance is the essence of theater. A man or woman stands on stage and impersonates another man or woman. This feature of people playing other people gives theater its uniqueness. Music is also a performing art, but in a concert, a singer or an orchestra is producing music. In the theater, people are playing roles. Whether it is a young woman defying a king in *Antigone,* a man building a boat to save his family in *Noah,* or two men coping with the anxieties of daily life in *Waiting for Godot,* the recognition of other human beings struggling with the problems we ourselves face is eternally fascinating.

There is another aspect to performances. As we watch actors and actresses on stage we admire their talent and technique: the precision of a Shakespearean actor delivering the soliloquys from *Hamlet;* the graceful, intricate dance steps in a musical like *A Chorus Line;* the swift, sure movements of two opponents in a sword fight in a swashbuckling drama like *Cyrano de Bergerac.* We know that these feats take great skill and long hours of practice, and as we watch them we admire the accomplishments of the performers on stage.

Visual Elements

Still another element of theater, found in the examples we have cited, is scenery, lighting, and costumes. The scenery may be simple—it may be the architecture of the theater space itself—or it may be elaborate, as in the designs for an expensive Broadway musical, but there is always a visual environment in which the drama occurs. This environment contributes immeasurably to the total experience.

For many centuries, lighting in the theater was largely a matter of being able to see the actors and actresses. For this reason performances were held outside during the day and the sun was the source of light; inside, candles or gas lights were used. With the coming of electricity in the late nineteenth century, however, lighting took on a new dimension. Colors and intensity could be changed at the push of a button; a designer could "paint with light," changing moods by shifting the focus and colors of lights. This became an integral part of most theater productions.

Costumes are probably the oldest visual element, because they are found in the rituals and ceremonies of the earliest civilizations: in Africa, New Guinea, among American Indians, and in the first civilizations of Europe and the Middle East. Costumes not only make performers resemble the persons they are portraying, but they also include decorative and symbolic elements, such as masks and elaborate headdresses.

Subject Matter: Human Concerns

Another element of theater is what the play is about. There are many possible subjects for drama. It can deal with the life of a famous person, such as Joan of Arc or Abraham Lincoln; it can tell the story of a family and family conflicts; it can present a series of episodes that illustrate a theme or argue a point of view; but always it has a subject that centers around human concerns. It does not focus on pure sound, as music does, or on abstract movement, as modern dance often does, but on human beings: their problems, joys, fears, foolishness, and aspirations.

Structure

Finally, the subject of the play must be given a dramatic structure. The story unfolds in one of several frameworks that have evolved through the years. It might be a direct reenactment of scenes from everyday life such as we find in plays like Henrik Ibsen's *A Doll's House* or Eugene O'Neill's *Long Day's Journey into Night;* it might be a structure like that in *Antigone* and other Greek tragedies, in which confrontations between characters alternate with choral sections that are sung and danced. It might be a series of episodes such as we find in the plays of Shakespeare: scenes that move rapidly from place to place and from one time to another, almost the way movies do. Whatever the structure, though, it will be a recognized pattern, a framework within which the story of human adventures can be shown.

Combining the Elements

When theater occurs there is generally a person, or a group of persons, responsible for bringing these elements together: a person who rehearses the actors and interprets the script, and another person who takes care of the financial arrangements and the accommodation of the audience. In the modern theater the person who rehearses the actors and sees that all the elements on stage are coordinated is the director; the person who handles the business and other arrangements is the producer.

When the elements we have listed come together, we have theater. Throughout history there has been such a coming together, and that is the subject of this book: to look at the unfolding panorama of theater over many years and in many parts of the world. By examining the theaters that have emerged in various cultures at different times, we can come to an understanding of the nature of theater. We can learn the common denominators of all theater experiences and the features that make certain periods unique. Before we begin this journey, however, we ought to consider the roots of theater. How and where did it emerge? What does it take to make theater possible?

HOW THEATER DEVELOPS

The impulse toward theater is universal among human beings. In every culture and every historical period there is evidence that people use elements of theater to communicate with each other, to learn from one another, to entertain themselves, and as an important part of their rituals and religion. Imitation, for example, is a universal practice among children. A child sees an older person walking upstairs or opening a door, and learns to do the same by imitation. More than that, children imitate the gestures and the tone of voice of their elders; many of them are excellent mimics, and their imitations are often very funny.

The ritual theater of Africa *All tribal ceremonies—whether in Africa, among North American Indians, or in Southeast Asia—have a strong theatrical component. This includes costumes, masks, repeated phrases, music, and dancing. This photograph shows a "makishi" dancer at Livingston in Zambia performing in a ceremony. (Photo—Marc and Evelyne Bernheim, Woodfin Camp & Associates.)*

Role-playing, another theatrical device, is practiced by everyone too, young and old alike. People assume family roles—father, mother, grandfather, sister, brother—and also social roles, such as doctor, lawyer, social worker. In playing these roles, individuals adopt certain modes of behavior required by the society in which they live. In this sense, they become actors. Judges, for instance, are expected to act in a certain way toward those who appear before them in a courtroom. A sales clerk in a store is expected to act in another way. When people do not act as expected, their behavior is considered inappropriate.

Beyond the imitation and role-playing engaged in by individuals, societies develop group activities that contain dramatic elements. This is especially true of rituals and ceremonies. A ritual is a formal, often-repeated act or series of acts: a ceremony that is carried out the same way over and over again. A ritual can range from a family event, such as an annual Thanksgiving or Christmas dinner, to the elaborate religious ceremonies of a Roman Catholic high mass or a Jewish Yom Kippur service during the High Holy Days.

The ceremonies and rituals that are found in every human society invariably contain important theatrical elements. Throughout central and western Africa, for example, one finds striking and imaginative costumes and masks used in a variety of ceremonies. In a ceremony performed by the Guro tribe in the Ivory Coast, a dancer meant to be an animal figure wears a large mask that is a combination of antelope horns, an abstracted human face, and a large toothed beak. The costume consists of orange netting on the arms and bamboo reeds on the body. Other dancers wear masks and costumes appropriate to their roles.

Among the Bakuba tribe in Zaire there is a dance that marks the initiation rites of young men into manhood. The central figure in the ceremony is the Woot, a mythical hero who taught the skills of weaving and forging, and founded the tribe's royal dynasty. The Woot figure wears an enormous headdress and mask consisting of feathers, plumes, fibers, shells, and beads.

The costumes and masks used for ceremonies in Africa are among the most beautiful found anywhere in the world, but it is not only in what people wear, it is also in the actions of the celebrants that we find theatrical elements. Frequently the participants enact the part of a person or thing: a bird, an animal, or a spirit. In many cases the people who take part in these rituals believe that the performers are actually inhabited by the animal or spirit they portray, that they are transformed during the ceremony and become the figure they are representing.

The Abydos Ritual in Ancient Egypt

The ritual itself—the story or ceremony being acted out—has theatrical elements as well. A good example is the ritual enacted in ancient Egypt for nearly 2,000 years, from around 2500 B.C. to around 550 B.C., at a sacred place called Abydos. Every year thousands of Egyptians apparently made their way to Abydos to see this ceremony.

The ritual performed at Abydos deals with the Egyptian god Osiris, who became the ruler of Egypt and married his sister Isis. Osiris's brother later became jealous of him and killed him, scattering the parts of his body throughout the Egyptian kingdom. Isis recovered the pieces of Osiris and with the aid of a god brought him back to life. Osiris could not remain on earth, however, and so his body was buried at Abydos. His spirit then went to dwell in the underworld, where he became the most human of Egyptian gods, the one who judged people's souls. The tale of Osiris is an almost universal religious story, recurring in societies throughout the world: a story of betrayal, death, and life after death.

We do not have the text from the ritual of the Osiris legend performed at Abydos, but we do have a partial account of it by a person named Ikhernofret, who participated in the ritual sometime between 1887 B.C. and 1849 B.C. It is clear from this account that the ceremony had unmistakable theatrical elements, with people playing the roles of characters in the story and acting out episodes from Osiris's life.

As far as we know, the ritual at Abydos remained a religious ceremony in the same way as the celebration of the Mass in the Roman

*T*heater and religion *Religious celebrations, such as this celebration of the Mass, have many things in common with theater: music, ritual, a form of costumes, exchanges of dialogue. But there is an essential difference: religion is intended for worship and praise of a deity, whereas theater is an end in itself—an art form that focuses on human concerns. (Photo—George Rodger, Magnum.)*

Catholic Church. It is not too large a step, however, from such a ritual to pure theater, and we will see this step taken in the classical Greek period and later in the Middle Ages. In the following section we will look at the difference between theater and ritual.

THEATER AS AN ART FORM

Aspects of theater—imitation, role-playing, costumes, rituals—are universal, but theater itself is not. The difference is that theater is an art form with a life of its own.

For theater to develop as an art form, certain conditions must be met. One is that a dramatic structure, described above, must be fashioned. As a second condition for theater, this dramatization must exist for its own sake, not primarily to serve some other purpose. Theater, as we have suggested, has a close affinity with religion, and in the history of theater we frequently find that theater emerges from religious ceremonies. A good example is the medieval theater—such as that at Mons mentioned above—which developed from elements of the Roman Catholic church service. The Bible stories told in the chants or scriptural readings would be acted out in the church ceremony; priests or members of the choir would take parts. Gradually these little scenes were expanded to become short plays.

At some point, however—and it was a crucial moment—it was recognized that these dramatizations had a life of their own: that they were being enjoyed more for their own value than as an integral part of the religious ceremony. At this point, because of a variety of factors, including the secularization of drama, the performances were no longer held in the church sanctuaries but held outside instead.

The essential difference between theater and religion is a difference in purpose and focus. Religion centers on the worship of a god or some other deity or group of deities. During a religious ceremony, the intent of those taking part is to pray to the deity: asking forgiveness, seeking help, and offering praise.

The focus of theater, on the other hand, is not worship. Theater serves as a mirror or a celebration of life here on earth. Theater can serve a number of purposes: challenging people to think, transporting them to the past, entertaining them, taking them outside themselves, making them cry and making them laugh. But the focus is always on human beings: their suffering, their pain, their frustrations, their hopes, their joys, their laughter. Even when theater deals with a religious subject, it concerns itself with human beings and the way religion affects their lives.

Theater can also derive from activities often associated with religion, such as pagan rites and celebrations. Comedy or farce particularly might begin in this way. The rowdy activities of a festival might develop into a dramatic form. Another source of theater might be storytelling. This ancient art—in which one person tells a tale to a group of listeners—can be transformed into drama if the speeches in a story are not recited by one person, the storyteller, but are actually delivered by performers playing separate parts.

It is important to remember, however, that whatever the source of theater, it must always develop a dramatic structure before it emerges as a separate art form.

ADDITIONAL REQUIREMENTS FOR THEATER

Assuming that a dramatic form is achieved, theater still has other requirements. Theater is a communal art calling for the collaboration of many individuals and groups; in the modern theater these include the playwright, the performers, the director, the scenic, lighting, and costume designers, the stage manager, the backstage crews, and the administrative staff (ushers, box office, and public relations personnel).

These participants must be skilled at what they do, and this requires tradition and practice. The performers, especially, must have the training and skill to stand in front of an audience and pretend to be someone else; to recite lines from a script and to move and speak with authority.

In addition to individual skills, theater production requires organization of a kind that can only be found in a society that has developed a complex social structure. Usually this occurs in population centers, where numbers of people have gathered together.

A population center—a village, a town, or a city—is important, too, in providing an audience. As we have said, the essence of theater is the exchange between the performers and the audience, and therefore both must be present for the event to have meaning. Without a center of population there would not be an audience to attend the event.

Whenever a civilization develops, the situation is ripe for theater to evolve. Despite, however, the extremely strong pull that theater has on people—and despite the tendency to create theater in any fully developed society—theater has not found a place in every civilization.

The Prohibition of Theater

The strongest deterrent to the emergence of theater appears to be religious prohibition. We have noted the close relationship between theater and religion. This could best be described as a love-hate relationship. Just as religion has theatrical elements and theater has frequently evolved from religious ceremonies, so there have been times when religion has bitterly opposed theater. The early Christians, for example, repeatedly denounced the Roman theater and at one point passed an edict that any Christian attending the theater would be excommunicated. When the Puritans in England came to power under Oliver Cromwell and took control of the Parliament in 1642, almost the first thing they did was to close all the theaters in London.

Given the involvement and contributions of Jewish people to the theater in later times, it seems puzzling that the ancient Hebrew nation did not produce theater. There is evidence of poetic and narrative skills in the Old Testament, and we know from the psalms and other sources that there was singing and dancing. But no separate theater developed.

There were political and social reasons why theater did not emerge in ancient Israel. The ancient Jews were a nomadic people, moving from place to place, and did not at first develop the permanent centers of population found in Greece and elsewhere, but they did not develop theater even after they had established their kingdom and settled in urban centers like Jerusalem. This was apparently due to their religious beliefs. David S. Lifson, in a book on the Yiddish theater in America, noted that during the biblical period the Hebrew religion forbade Jews to attend the pagan theater. A prayer from the period illustrated the prohibition: "I thank thee, my Lord, that I spend my time in the temples of prayer instead of in the theaters."

Some commentators feel that this religious injunction against theater stems from the Second Commandment in the Bible: "You shall not make a graven image, or any likeness of anything that is in heaven above or in the earth beneath." According to this theory, the concept of likeness was interpreted to include impersonating a character onstage.

When we turn from the Hebrew to the Islamic religion, the prohibition against theater is even more explicit. Founded by the prophet Mohammed in A.D. 610, Islam became the dominant religion in lands stretching from beyond Persia in the east to Spain in the west. It included all of the Middle East, the eastern Mediterranean, North Africa, and southern Spain.

The Islamic religion forbade the personification of God, that is, showing persons who might embody God. This has remained a steadfast rule from the early days of the religion until the present time. No permanent theater as such has emerged in Islamic lands.

Despite this strong deterrent, however, it is significant that theater crept into Islamic society. There is archaeological evidence of circuses and other entertainments, and indications of popular plays in the eastern part of the Persian Empire.

Even more significant is the *Taziya* "passion play," a religious drama which is performed each year as part of the Muhurran festival in lands where the Shiite branch of Islam prevails. The play recounts the story of the survival of Zain, a grandson of Mohammed, after the remainder of his branch of the family was slaughtered. Zain is claimed by the Shiites to have been the legitimate successor of Mohammed. There are many versions of the *Taziya* passion play; an Englishman living in Persia (now Iran) in the 1860s found fifty-two of them and in 1878 had thirty-seven published.

The *Taziya* has been performed regularly in Baghdad, Teheran, and Isfahan (Iran), as well as in smaller towns and villages. This is because the *Taziya*, though a drama, was considered part of a religious festival through all of its early history. Theater, however, was not allowed to develop independently in Islamic lands. The *Taziya* is an exception, and the firm policy in most Islamic lands is no theater whatsoever.

The ancient Hebrew and the Islamic civilizations are exceptions to the rule that theater has generally accompanied the emergence of civilization. The subject of this study will be those places where theater has evolved, free from outside strictures, to follow a natural course. We will focus mainly on the Western tradition because it is out of that tradition that modern American and European theater comes. But we will look also at the Asian theater, and at the Black theater in America, including important African influences on the Black theater.

THEATER RELATED TO SOCIETY

"The purpose of playing [acting]," Shakespeare wrote in *Hamlet*, is "to hold, as 'twere, the mirror up to nature; to show virtue her own feature, scorn her own image, and the very age and body of the time his form and pressure."

Shakespeare suggests here that acting can reflect society in a given period, and this, in fact, is what theater does: it mirrors the age in which it is written and produced. In every period in history where theater occurs, society and theater are indissolubly linked. The society provides the context—the environment and the soil—in which theater grows. Theater, in turn, presents an image of that society.

If we examine the four productions with which we opened this chapter as examples, we find that distinctive qualities of each culture are apparent in the performances discussed. The Greeks in the fifth century B.C. focused on human beings as the measure of all things; hence, they wrote about heroic figures like Antigone. As can be seen in their architecture, they also admired balance and symmetry, and these are reflected in the way choral scenes in Greek tragedy alternate with dramatic episodes. The Greek concern for moderation is exemplified in the fact that scenes of violence—the death of Antigone and of Creon's son and wife—are carried out not in view of the audience but offstage.

When we turn to the noh drama of Zeami, the indirection and understatement of the Japanese culture of that time is reflected in the play. People did not come out and say what they meant, but rather spoke in circumlocutions, and this finds its parallel in such devices as the chorus speaking the main character's words for her. Also, the plays involve a great deal of politeness and decorum, which even today is found in the Japanese culture in such customs as bowing deeply from the waist when meeting another person.

The biblical plays of medieval Europe typify a society in which the Roman Catholic church played a central role. The most important building in every town was the cathedral: the center of the social as well as the religious life. The sense of order, the communal feeling, and the familiarity with Bible stories found in medieval life are directly mirrored in these theatrical productions.

When we come to the modern age, we see the close affinity between theater and society once again. *Waiting for Godot* presents an image recognized not only by those in prison but by people everywhere who experience today's world as fragmented, alienating, and uncertain. The contrast between the proud Antigone and the pathetic men on an empty plain in *Waiting for Godot* reflects the contrast between the way the Greeks viewed human beings and the way we often do.

This close relationship between theater and society should be a part of any study of theater history, and so as we look at each era in this book, we will also examine the social and political conditions of the time. This will enable us to understand the environment in which theater develops and to relate it to the other arts and to society at large.

Part One

The theaters we refer to as early theaters—the Greek, the Roman, and the medieval—actually cover a period of nearly 2,000 years: from the Greek theater in the fifth century B.C. through the medieval theater, which began 1,500 years later. This is a long time-span, but it is important to remember that for several centuries—from the declining years of the Roman empire until the emergence of the medieval theater—there was no formal theater, and therefore in the Middle Ages it had to begin all over again.

These can legitimately be called early theaters because they established the foundations on which all subsequent western theater was built. Not only in theater, but in virtually every area of life, these cultures formed the basis of western civilization. The list of their accomplishments is monumental: the classical Greeks developed democracy, philosophy, the study of science and mathematics, and architecture; the Romans were great conquerers, architects, and law-makers; the medieval Europeans organized methods of farming and established trade guilds.

It would be incorrect to oversimplify the relationship among the theaters of these three societies, but there are important common elements. One is the significant connection in all three between the theater and religious and civic celebrations. Many argue that the roots of theater lie in religious rituals, and this seems substantiated by the Greek theater's initial connection to rites honoring the god Dionysus, the Roman theater's relation to the festival of Jupiter (Zeus), and the medieval theater's close tie with the Roman Catholic church. At the same time, a strong secular element permeated the three theaters; there was a desire to treat human as well as religious subjects. This was partly the natural evolution of theater in any society; when theater becomes an art form on its own, it concentrates on human problems and aspirations.

In addition to having ties to religion, theater in each of these cultures was a significant civic and social event. This is reflected in the huge open-air theaters of Greece and Rome as well as the spectacular outdoor medieval stage settings. We have large outdoor theaters today—for summer Shakespeare festivals and rock music concerts—but the level of involvement in theater by a large proportion of the population in each of these early societies will never be equaled in modern times.

As we begin to survey the early theaters, we should remember how much of their drama has survived in our own day. Greek tragedies and comedies are still produced; plays of the Roman dramatist Plautus have been adapted into Broadway musicals; and there are modern versions of the medieval morality play *Everyman*. In this section, as we explore the theater from its origins in religious rituals through the close of the Middle Ages, we should not view it as a remote activity; rather, we should search for those conventions that continue to be part of our theater today.

Chapter Two

THE GREEK THEATER

There are times in history when many elements come together to create a remarkable age. Such a time was the fifth century B.C. in Athens, Greece, when there were outstanding achievements in politics, philosophy, science, and the arts. It was at this time, too, that Western theater was born.

THE GOLDEN AGE OF GREECE

A number of events had prepared the way for this. Prior to 500 B.C., impressive civilizations had developed around the eastern part of the Mediterranean Sea: in Egypt, in Persia (which included present-day Iran,

The theater of ancient Greece   *One of the most famous works of the classical Greek theater is* The Oresteia, *three connected plays. The plays are by Aeschylus, considered the father of Western theater. In this scene, from a production by the National Theater of Great Britain, Orestes stands behind the chorus of Furies who pursue him after he has murdered his mother. (Photo—Nobby Clark.)*

The Greek Theater

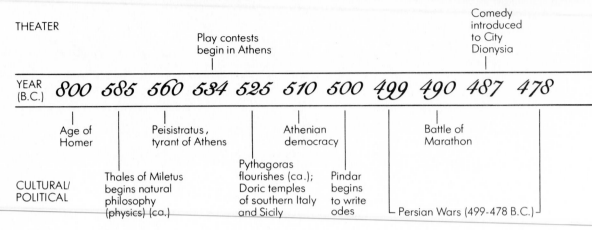

THEATER			Play contests begin in Athens						Comedy introduced to City Dionysia

YEAR (B.C.)	800	585	560	534	525	510	500	499	490	487	478

CULTURAL/POLITICAL

Age of Homer — Peisistratus, tyrant of Athens — Athenian democracy — Battle of Marathon

Thales of Miletus begins natural philosophy (physics) (ca.) — Pythagoras flourishes (ca.); Doric temples of southern Italy and Sicily — Pindar begins to write odes — Persian Wars (499-478 B.C.)

Iraq, Turkey, and other countries), and in Greece. Advances had been made in art—in pottery, for example, and the performances of elaborate ceremonies such as the one at Abydos in Egypt—as well as in science, astronomy, and mathematics. Athens carried forward this tradition.

Greece at this time was not a united country or an empire but a series of independent city-states occupying parts of the Greek peninsula and nearby islands: at the start of the fifth century B.C., the most important city-state was Athens. Early in the century the Persians had attempted to conquer the Greeks, but the Greeks had defeated them. Later in the century—from 431 to 404 B.C.—there was a costly conflict between Athens and Sparta known as the Peloponnesian War. Between these two events, however, Athens enjoyed a period of remarkable achievements. It is known as the classical period and is also referred to as the Golden Age of Greece. There are good reasons for calling it a Golden Age because there were important accomplishments in so many fields.

Athens is credited, for example, with being the birthplace of democracy. In 510 B.C., the rulers of Athens established a semocracy of free citizens, which means that all male citizens—men who were not slaves or of non-Athenian origin—were allowed to have a voice in matters of politics and government. Though there were slaves in Athens, and women were subservient, it should be remembered that the United States, also founded on democratic ideals, once suffered from similar limitations: slavery was not abolished until 1865 and women could not vote until 1920. Despite these drawbacks in ancient Athens, it was still an admirable achievement to establish democracy for such a large portion of the population.

There were advances in other areas as well. Greek philosophers, such

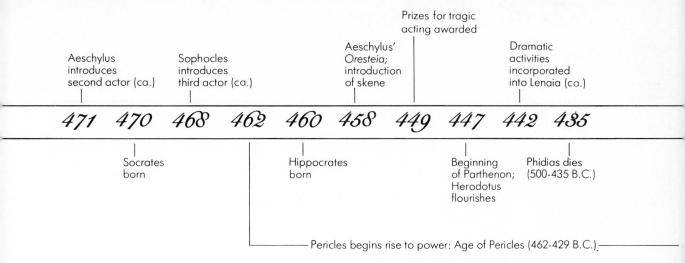

Aeschylus introduces second actor (ca.) — Sophocles introduces third actor (ca.) — Aeschylus' *Oresteia*; introduction of skene — Prizes for tragic acting awarded — Dramatic activities incorporated into Lenaia (ca.)

471 470 468 462 460 458 449 447 442 435

Socrates born — Hippocrates born — Beginning of Parthenon; Herodotus flourishes — Phidias dies (500–435 B.C.)

Pericles begins rise to power: Age of Pericles (462–429 B.C.)

as Socrates and Plato, tried to explain the world around them, while Herodotus transformed history into a social science. A number of important scientific discoveries were made: the Greek mathematician Pythagoras formulated a theory that remains one of the cornerstones of geometry, and the physician's oath written by Hippocrates is the one still taken by doctors. The classical Greeks were also remarkable artists and architects: Greek sculpture from this period is found in museums around the world, and the Parthenon, the temple that sits atop the Acropolis, has withstood time and natural catastrophies and is still visited by multitudes of tourists. Its columns and proportions remain models for architects even today. Obviously this was a time conducive to developments in many fields, and one of the most significant was theater.

THE GREEK THEATER EMERGES

Theater is a complex art, as we noted in the introduction, which requires the coming together of many elements: a story to be told, a dramatization of the story (the script written by the playwright), a meeting place at which performances can be given, performers to enact the drama, costumes for the performers, some form of stage, perhaps scenery, and an audience that gathers to witness a performance.

In different ways, these elements had been developing in Athens prior to the fifth century B.C. Important forerunners were the religious ceremonies that had been an important feature of Greek society in the form of funeral services, festivals celebrating the seasons, and ceremonies honoring the gods.

The Greek Theater

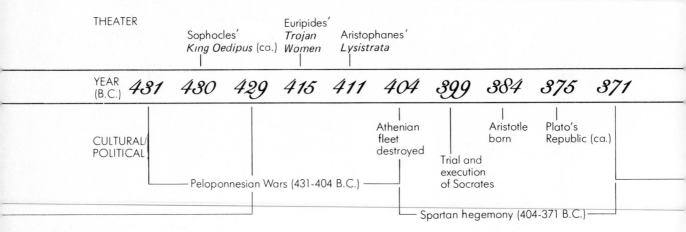

THEATER		Sophocles' *King Oedipus* (ca.)		Euripides' *Trojan Women*	Aristophanes' *Lysistrata*					

| YEAR (B.C.) | 431 | 430 | 429 | 415 | 411 | 404 | 399 | 384 | 375 | 371 |

CULTURAL/ POLITICAL

Peloponnesian Wars (431–404 B.C.)

Athenian fleet destroyed

Trial and execution of Socrates

Aristotle born

Plato's *Republic* (ca.)

Spartan hegemony (404–371 B.C.)

Of particular importance to theater were the ceremonies honoring Dionysus, the god of wine, fertility, and revelry. Later Greek drama was presented in honor of Dionysus, and most historians, though not all, believe that Greek drama originated out of the dithyrambic choruses presented in the god's honor. (The *dithyramb* was a lengthy hymn honoring Dionysus, sung and danced by a group of fifty men. In what may have been similar to a modern-day choral presentation, the leader of the chorus recited or sang an improvised story while the other members sang a popular refrain. By about 600 B.C., the dithyramb became a literary form detailing heroic stories.)

A performer named Thespis, in the sixth century B.C., is customarily credited with transforming the dithyramb into tragedy by stepping out of the dithyrambic chorus and becoming an actor. He delivered a prologue and presented dialogue that required him to impersonate a character: thus a purely narrative, storytelling form became a dramatic form with characters exchanging lines. Thespis is credited with being the first writer of tragedy as well as the first actor; his decisive contribution is reflected in the term *thespian,* a synonym for "actor." The ancient Greek word for "actor" was *hypokrite,* literally "answerer," which further underscores that drama required the verbal give-and-take of dialogue and the interaction of the actor with the chorus.

Greek Theater and Greek Religion

It is important to understand the part religion played in the life of the people of Athens, because Greek theater is intimately bound up with

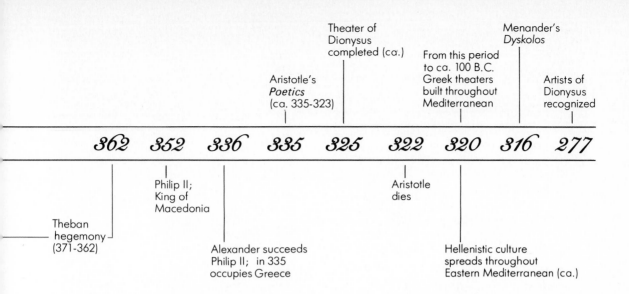

362	352	336	335	325	322	320	316	277

Theater of Dionysus completed (ca.)

Menander's *Dyskolos*

From this period to ca. 100 B.C. Greek theaters built throughout Mediterranean

Aristotle's *Poetics* (ca. 335-323)

Artists of Dionysus recognized

Philip II; King of Macedonia

Aristotle dies

Theban hegemony (371-362)

Alexander succeeds Philip II; in 335 occupies Greece

Hellenistic culture spreads throughout Eastern Mediterranean (ca.)

Greek religion. Through the centuries the Greeks had developed a religion based on the worship of a group of gods, of whom Zeus was the leader along with his wife, Hera. The Greeks did not regard the gods as all-powerful, but they did believe that the gods could protect them and reveal the future. In the cities, annual festivals were held in honor of those gods who the people felt would guide and protect them.

Theater became a part of these events, with plays being the central features of certain religious festivals. Theatrical presentations were both religious events and entertainment for the people. Partly because of theater's religious connections, people of all social classes attended performances. We know that the lower as well as the upper classes participated because Pericles, the great ruler of Athens in the middle of the fifth century B.C., established the Theoric Fund in 450 B.C. to assist those who were too poor to be able to afford admission to the theater.

The significance of the "religious-theatrical" event in Greek society gave theater a far more important place than the one it occupies in our society. Business came to a standstill during the dramatic festivals; wars ceased; political concerns were ignored. The total cessation of a society's activities for religious purposes as practiced by the Greeks has no present-day equivalent.

The City Dionysia

One festival in particular became important for theater in Athens. This was the *City Dionysia*, a festival honoring the god Dionysus. The City Dionysia was a signal event in Athens; it was held toward the end of

The Parthenon Built during the Golden Age of Greece to honor the goddess Athena, the Parthenon (447–432 B.C.) stands atop the Acropolis, the tallest hill in Athens. The symmetry, grace, and classical proportions of the building mirror the ideals of the Greek society of the time. Greek theater, like architecture, reflected the spirit of the age. (Photo—Greek National Tourist Office.)

March, when spring had arrived and the port near Athens, which was closed for the winter, had reopened and visitors began pouring into the city. It was also when trees and flowers began to come to life again. In 534 B.C., tragedy was incorporated into the City Dionysia, and by 489 B.C., two additional forms of drama—comedy and the satyr play—were added to it as well. (The satyr play was a brief comic parody that will be discussed shortly.)

The City Dionysia lasted seven days. On the first day, all the theatrical participants paraded and appeared in the *proagon*, a preliminary presentation designed to announce and advertise the upcoming events. On the second day there were processions, sacrifices, and ten dithyrambic presentations. On one day five comedies, each written by a different playwright, were staged. Three other days were dedicated to tragedies and satyr plays, with three tragedies and one satyr play being presented on each day. The four plays presented on any given day, called a *tetralogy*, were written by one dramatist. On the last day of the festival awards were given, and those persons who had acted improperly or disrespectfully during the festival were punished. We are told, for example, that this was the case with someone who used violence to prevent another person from taking his seat in the theater or who carried a whip and struck an enemy with it while intoxicated.

The Greeks were great proponents of competition; the Olympic Games, for example, originated during the classical era. In drama, at the end of the City Dionysia, the best tragic and comic playwrights were awarded prizes. In 449 B.C., the best tragic acting in the festival was also recognized with an award. The Tony Awards in theater and the Academy Awards in film are modern-day equivalents of these Greek awards.

Since theater was a religious and civic event, the organization of the dramatic presentations was undertaken by the city-state's government. The *archon*, an appointed government official, chose the plays eleven months prior to the festival. The archon appointed a *choregus*, the equivalent of a modern-day producer, for each of the selected playwrights.

In our commercial theater today, the producer raises the funds for a production. In the fifth century B.C., the choregus, a wealthy individual, provided the money himself and underwrote major expenses. The choregus was responsible for all expenses connected with the chorus: rehearsal costs, costumes, musicians, and properties. The city provided the awards, payment for the playwright, payments for the actors, and the theater space. While a stingy choregus could hurt a playwright's chances for winning the contest, most choregoi strove to produce contest winners. Some, when their productions won, erected monuments in their own honor.

Myths: Stories for Tragedies

What about the plays that were written for the festivals? What kind of stories did they tell and where did the writers find these stories? In most cases the answer is Greek myths.

Along with festivals and the move from dithyrambic choruses to drama, other aspects of theater had been developing prior to the fifth century B.C. One was the accumulation of a group of stories on which much of Greek drama, particularly tragedy, was based. In the centuries before the Golden Age, a number of myths had become an important part of the Greek heritage. A myth is a story or legend—sometimes invented, sometimes based loosely on fact—that is handed down from one generation to the next. Frequently myths are an attempt to explain natural and human events: the changing of the seasons, for example, and cataclysmic occurrences like earthquakes or civil wars. Myths often deal, too, with extreme family situations: one branch of a family opposing another, or a difficult relationship between a husband and wife or between parents and children. In every culture certain myths are seized on because they seem

AESCHYLUS
(525–456 B.C.)

Aeschylus is considered the father of Greek drama and therefore of all Western drama because he was the first dramatist whose plays still exist who had developed the drama into a form separate from singing, dancing, or storytelling.

His dramas dealt with noble families and lofty themes and were praised for their superb lyric poetry as well as their dramatic structure and intellectual content. His plays were awarded a number of first prizes in the drama contests, and he was the acknowledged master of the tetralogy: four plays which can stand separately but are also united by a single story or theme.

In developing theater practice, Aeschylus added a second actor—allowing for a true exchange of dialogue—and reduced the size of the chorus, making it more manageable. After the third actor was introduced by Sophocles, Aeschylus incorporated this feature into his plays as well. Aeschylus's theatrical involvement included directing and acting as well as playwriting. He was fond of spectacle in the theater and is credited in some sources with developing new forms of stage scenery, elaborate costumes, and painted scenery.

In the comedy *The Frogs*, Aeschylus was caricatured by Aristophanes as being pompous and rhetorical. In the same play, however, he was also judged a superior dramatist to Euripides.

Born of a noble family in Eleusis near Athens, Aeschylus was highly regarded as a soldier and prominent citizen as well as a playwright and poet. Among other military exploits, he fought for Athens at the battle of Marathon. He died in 456 B.C. at the age of 69.

Aeschylus is said to have written ninety plays. The titles of seventy-nine are known, indicating a diversity of subject matter, but only the following seven plays still exist (the dates indicate when the plays are known or thought to have been first produced): *The Suppliants* (ca. 490 B.C. but may have been considerably later); *The Persians* (ca. 472 B.C.); *Seven Against Thebes* (ca. 469 B.C.); *Prometheus Bound* (ca. 460 B.C.); *The Oresteia* (458 B.C.), a trilogy which contains three plays: *Agamemnon*, *The Choephori* (*Libation Bearers*), and *The Eumenides*.

to sum up the way that society views human relationships and the problems and opportunities life presents to individuals.

In Greece, there were a multitude of these myths. Good examples are the poet Homer's accounts of the Greek war with the Trojans in the *Iliad* and the return from the Trojan War of the hero Odysseus in the *Odyssey*. These and other myths furnished many of the stories for Greek drama, but before they could be performed in the theater, they had to be transformed by a playwright into dramatic form.

ARISTOTLE AND THE TRAGIC FORM

The most admired form of drama presented at the festivals was tragedy, and the three most important writers of Greek tragedy were Aeschylus, Sophocles, and Euripides. The first critic to attempt to pinpoint the characteristics of Greek tragedy was the philosopher Aristotle. Although Aristotle wrote about classical tragedy nearly a hundred years after the Golden Age and thus was describing a type of drama that had flourished prior to his lifetime, his work on the subject, *The Poetics* (ca. 335 B.C.), is the best starting point for a discussion of tragedy.

In addition to being a philosopher, Aristotle was a scientist who described and catalogued the world he saw around him. He brought the same careful, sensible approach to analyzing tragedy that he brought to other fields, and though *The Poetics* is loosely organized and not complete—it may have been based on a series of lecture notes—it is so intelligent and penetrating that it remains today the single most important piece of dramatic criticism we have.

According to Aristotle there are six elements of drama: (1) plot (the arrangement of dramatic incidents), (2) character (the people represented in the play), (3) thought or theme (the ideas explored), (4) language (the dialogue and poetry), (5) music, and (6) spectacle (scenery and other visual elements). The implication in *The Poetics* is that tragedy deals with the reversals in fortune and eventual downfall of a royal figure. In "complex" tragedies, which Aristotle feels are the best type, the suffering hero makes a discovery and recognizes what has led to his or her tragic downfall. There are also a number of what Aristotle calls "simple" tragedies in which there is no such scene of recognition.

Though there are variations in the structures of the thirty-one Greek tragedies that still exist, many follow the same pattern in the unfolding of the scenes. First comes the *prologos*, the opening scene, which sets the action and provides the background information; next the *parodos*, in which the chorus enters; then comes the first *episode*, a scene in which the characters confront each other and the plot starts to develop; next there is a *choral ode* performed by the chorus. Through the body of the play, episodes alternate with choral odes until the *exodos*, the final scene, in which all of the characters exit from the stage. Aristotle suggests that Greek tragedy usually focuses on one major plot without bringing in

The theater at Epidauros *The most perfectly preserved of ancient Greek theaters, which in its present form dates from the Hellenistic age. Note the sloped audience seating for approximately 14,000 spectators, the orchestra where the chorus performs, and the stage house at the left. The remarkable acoustics allow every word to be heard in the top row. Shown here is a scene from the* Oresteia *of Aeschylus. (Photo—United Press International.)*

subplots or unrelated secondary concerns, though some plays have such subplots.

Several points raised by Aristotle have been subject to different interpretations because sometimes it is difficult to know exactly what he meant. An example can be found in the following two translations of his definition of tragedy:

Tragedy, then, is an imitation of an action that is serious, complete, and of a certain magnitude; in language embellished with each kind of artistic ornament, the several kinds being found in separate parts of the play; in the form of action, not of narrative; through pity and fear effecting the proper purgation of these emotions.[1]

Tragedy, then, is an imitation of an action which is serious, complete, and has bulk, in speech that has been made attractive, using each of its species separately in the parts of the play; with persons performing the action rather than through narrative carrying to completion, through a course of events involving pity and fear, the purification of those painful or fatal acts which have that quality[2]

Parts of this definition are clear enough: tragedy presents a complete story (an action) that is serious and important (has magnitude and bulk) and is dramatized for presentation on the stage rather than told by a narrator. When we come to the last part of the definition, though, there is disagreement. Aristotle says that tragedy produces the emotions of pity and fear but that there is a *katharsis* of these emotions. One translator above calls katharsis a purgation of emotions and the other a purification.

The most generally accepted explanation of katharsis, and the one indicated in the first translation, is that the members of the audience feel

[1]S. H. Butcher, *Aristotle's Theory of Poetry and Fine Art*, 3d ed., Macmillan and Company, London, 1902, p. 23.
[2]Gerald F. Else, *Aristotle's Poetics: The Argument*, Cambridge, 1957, p. 221.

pity for the suffering tragic hero and fear that a similar fate could befall them. If a king or queen suffers so greatly, how much easier for a common individual to be confronted by similar tragic circumstances? These emotions, however, are purged by the drama because the audience acknowledges them, and by doing so cleanses itself of the evil effects. There are some critics who disagree with defining katharsis in this way. They suggest that the tragic character, rather than the audience, undergoes the purgation of pity and fear through the discovery of the reason for his or her suffering and downfall. This is the implication in the second translation above. Others suggest that the katharsis occurs in the chorus, as it is confronted with the tragic details of the plot, and that the audience is meant to identify with the emotional impact on the chorus. Despite differing interpretations, Aristotle makes it clear that changes occur due to the strong emotions associated with tragedy.

There is another debate about Aristotle's discussion of the tragic hero, who is usually a royal figure. Why does the tragic protagonist suffer?

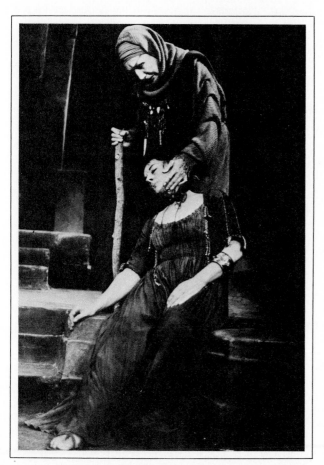

The tragic figure of Medea *The playwrights of the Greek theater perfected tragedy, the dramatic form described by Aristotle in* The Poetics. *One of the best known tragic heroines is Medea, shown here being comforted by her old nurse. In this recent production, Zoe Caldwell played Media while Dame Judith Anderson played the Nurse. Dame Judith had played the role of Medea 35 years earlier. (Photo—Jack Buxbaum, The Kennedy Center, Washington, D.C.)*

ARISTOTLE
(384–322 B.C.)

If Aeschylus is the father of Greek drama, the philosopher Aristotle is the father of dramatic criticism. His analysis of tragedy in *The Poetics* is still considered one of the most important documents ever written on the subject.

Born at Stagria in northern Greece, Aristotle was the son of a doctor who became court physician to the king of Macedon. Aristotle's lifelong interest in the sciences, especially biology, may be a reflection of his upbringing. As a young man he went to Athens to study with Plato at his Academy, where he remained for twenty years. Here he began to develop his own philosophic system, at first by suggesting improvements in Plato's ideas. After Plato died in 347 B.C., Aristotle left the school and spent thirteen years away from Athens, including three years as tutor to the young Alexander the Great in Macedon. Aristotle returned to Athens in 335 and opened his own school, the Lyceum. He remained in Athens until a wave of hostility against Macedon—the region Aristotle was born in—swept Athens following Alexander's death in 323. Aristotle left Athens and died the following year on a nearby island.

Aristotle's *Poetics*, the work in which he outlines his views on literature, is incomplete and may have originally been written as notes for a series of lectures. Most of the treatise is on tragedy; comedy, epic poetry, and other forms of literature are mentioned only briefly. Aristotle's discussion of tragedy, however, is of supreme importance. Aristotle breaks tragedy down into its essential components. Plato had charged that drama, especially tragedy, is a danger to society because it encourages the irrational. As if answering Plato, Aristotle argues in *The Poetics* that tragedy is positive and helpful because it not only arouses pity and fear but also purges these emotions, restoring harmony to the soul.

Logic, metaphysics, psychology, physics, theology, ethics, politics, biology, and literary theory are some of the topics that Aristotle covered in his 170 works. In his writings he stressed the importance of detailed observation and description of a phenomenon before attempting to form a theory, a process that still forms the basis of the scientific method. Aristotle employed the same technique when examining drama. Rather than formulating rules in *The Poetics*, he carefully observed classical Greek tragedy and described it in detail. Ranked with Socrates and Plato as one of the most influential Greek philosophers, Aristotle was the only one of the three to include an analysis of drama in his philosophic writings.

The Poetics was little studied by the Greeks and Romans, but became the basis of dramatic criticism when it was rediscovered by Renaissance scholars. During this period Aristotle's descriptions and suggestions were misinterpreted as inflexible rules for the writing of tragedies, a distortion that Aristotle never intended but that has unfortunately persisted to modern times.

The traditional interpretation of Aristotle's commentary suggests that the hero suffers from a tragic flaw, or *hamartia*, in his or her character. The critics attribute the flaw of *hubris*, or excessive pride, to many of the Greek tragic figures. There is, however, a great deal of disagreement over what Aristotle actually means by hamartia. The term literally translates as "missing the mark," which has suggested to some scholars that hamartia is not so much a character flaw as an error of judgment made by the protagonist. Other recent critics have suggested that the "flaw" is often not in the leading character but in the tragic world represented by the play, a world that is temporarily disordered or "out of joint." The characters themselves may act nobly but are damned by circumstances or fate.

Despite these problems, Aristotle pointed out much that is not in dispute, a good example being his emphasis on plot. The Greeks developed an approach to dramatic structure that became the prototype—in an altered and more rigid form—for plays written in the Renaissance (in Italy and France) and the modern period (the well-made plays of Ibsen, Strindberg, and others). Though not every Greek play conformed to this structure, which we will refer to as *crisis drama*, the elements were first developed in Greece and are evident in a number of dramas, particularly those by Aeschylus and Sophocles.

The Crisis Plot Structure and *King Oedipus*

In a crisis drama the action begins near the climax, or high point, of the action, with the characters already in the midst of their struggles. There are very few characters and one main action; the play occurs in a short span of time (frequently twenty-four hours or less) and takes place in one locale. The dramatic tension, therefore, is increased by the fact that the calamitous events befall the characters in a short span of time. Since the play begins in the midst of the crisis, the audience must be provided with a great deal of background information, which is known as exposition. As a result, the plots of crisis dramas often unravel like a mystery story.

It will help us understand the structure of Greek tragedy if we examine a single play, such as Sophocles's *King Oedipus*, first presented around 430 B.C. Like most Greek tragedies, *King Oedipus* is based on a myth. In this case the story tells how the infant Oedipus, son of the king and queen of Thebes, is put on a mountaintop to die because of a prophecy that he will murder his father and marry his mother. Before he dies, however, he is saved and taken to be raised by the king and queen of Corinth. When he grows up, Oedipus hears the prophecy and, not knowing that he is adopted, leaves home so that he will not kill the king of Corinth, the man he thinks of as his father. On the road he encounters a stranger, argues with him, and subsequently kills him, unaware that it is actually his own father whom he has slain. Later, Oedipus becomes king of Thebes and, still in ignorance, marries the woman who is really

The Chorus from King Oedipus *One of the most famous Greek tragedies is* King Oedipus *by* Sophocles. *Oedipus became King of Thebes after mistakenly killing his father and marrying his mother. When a plague hit the city, the chorus of elders, shown in this production at the Herod Atticus Theater in Athens, complained to Oedipus that he must bring relief to the city. (Photo—Todd Webb, Photo Researchers, Inc.)*

his mother, Jocasta. When a plague hits Thebes, he sets out to find the cause.

Following the pattern of the crisis drama, Sophocles begins his play near the major crisis in the story. He also structures his plot by using the basic elements of the classical Greek tragedy. The play opens with a prologue in which Oedipus learns about the plague and also learns from his brother-in-law, Creon, that an oracle says the plague will be ended when the murderer of the former king is found and punished. Next comes the parodos: the appearance of the chorus of elderly men, who pray to the gods to end the plague. Then begins the first episode. Oedipus proclaims that he will find and punish the guilty party. The blind prophet Teiresias arrives and professes ignorance of past events, but when accused by Oedipus of conspiring with Creon against him, Teiresias hints that he, Oedipus, is the guilty one. Oedipus is incensed at the suggestion. Following this, in the first choral song, the chorus asks who the murderer can be and expresses doubt that it is Oedipus.

In the second episode, Creon defends himself against an angry Oedipus, who accuses him of a conspiracy with Teiresias. Jocasta,

Oedipus's wife, enters to tell her husband to ignore the oracle; it had predicted that her first husband would be killed by his son, she says, but according to all reports he was killed by thieves at a crossroads. Oedipus, remembering that he had killed a man at a crossroads, begins to fear that he is the murderer, but is reassured by Jocasta, who urges him to ignore such fears. (Notice how skillfully Sophocles alternates good news and bad news for Oedipus, carrying him from the heights to the depths and back again time after time.)

In the next choral song the chorus, beginning to have doubts about Oedipus's innocence, says that reverence for the gods is best; prosperity leads to pride, which will be punished. In the third scene, or episode, a messenger comes from Corinth announcing that the king there is dead. Jocasta is jubilant, for this means that the oracle cannot be trusted: it had said that Oedipus would kill his father but the father is dead of natural causes. The messenger then reveals that Oedipus is not the son of the king of Corinth. Fearing the worst, Jocasta tries to persuade Oedipus to cease his search. When he will not, she rushes into the palace. Oedipus sends for a shepherd who knows the full story of his origins and forces him to tell it. Learning the truth, Oedipus then goes into the palace himself.

In the next choral song, the chorus says that all life is sorrowful and bemoans the fall of Oedipus. In the exodos, or final scene, a messenger from the palace describes how Jocasta has killed herself and Oedipus has put out his own eyes. The blind Oedipus reappears to recite his sad story, courageously accepts his fate, and leaves in exile.

The Strong Points of *King Oedipus*

The play of *King Oedipus* is admired for several reasons. One is the masterful way in which Sophocles unfolds the plot; it is like a detective story in which Oedipus is the detective tracking down a murderer. Another admired quality is the beauty of Sophocles's language. Though most modern readers do not understand ancient Greek, even in translation we can often see the effectiveness of Sophocles's poetic expressions. As an example, the following are the words of the chorus just after Oedipus has discovered his fate. The chorus is speaking here of how life is only a shadow and happiness often only an illusion.

Alas, ye generations of men, how mere a shadow do I count your life! Where, where is the mortal who wins more of happiness than just the seeming, and, after the semblance, a falling away? Thine is a fate that warns me—thine, thine, unhappy Oedipus—to call no earthly creature blest.

King Oedipus is also admired because of the religious and philosophical questions it raises. Why does a man like Oedipus suffer? Is it because of some flaw in his character—his pride, for example—or because of an error in judgment? Is it, perhaps, to test Oedipus, as Job was tested by God in the Bible? Or is it because the world is a place in which life is sometimes cruel and unjust to the point where even innocent people must suffer?

$\mathcal{S}$OPHOCLES
(ca. 496 B.C.–406 B.C.)

The tragic playwright Sophocles developed the dramatic techniques of Aeschylus even further. He was particularly noted for the superb construction of his plots. In his plays he introduces characters and information skillfully and then builds swiftly to a climax; Aristotle used Sophocles's *King Oedipus* as the model for his analysis of tragedy. An interest in the exploration of character and a focus on the individual are also characteristic of the plays of Sophocles.

Besides being a playwright Sophocles acted in his early dramas. Aristotle credits him with innovations in scene painting that brought greater realism to the theater, and Sophocles also increased the number of members of the tragic chorus from twelve to fifteen. Sophocles is credited with introducing the third actor to Greek tragedy, thereby increasing the number of characters in the play and enlarging the possibilities for conflict in drama.

In his plays Sophocles told his stories in one drama instead of extending the tale into the usual trilogy of three connected plays, a change that added more action to the plot. From his very first play Sophocles was a popular success, and his plays were invariably first or second in dramatic contests.

As a general, a civic leader, an ambassador, and a priest, Sophocles participated fully in Athenian life during that Greek city's Golden Age. The son of a wealthy Athenian factory owner, Sophocles was so devoted to his native city that he refused many invitations to live at the courts of foreign kings. The aged Sophocles was spared the sight of the defeat of his beloved Athens by Sparta by his death at 90 in 406 B.C. Throughout his long life he was known for his good nature, a fact noted by the comic playwright Aristophanes in *The Frogs*.

Though Sophocles wrote over 120 plays, only seven whole plays have survived: *Ajax* (ca. 450 to 440 B.C.); *Antigone* (ca. 441 B.C.); *King Oedipus* (ca. 430 to 425 B.C.); *Electra* (ca. 418 to 410 B.C.); *Trachiniae* (ca. 413 B.C.); *Philoctetes* (409 B.C.); and *Oedipus at Colonus* (ca. 406 B.C.).

People have been studying the play of *King Oedipus* for over 2,000 years and they still find profound and complex meanings in what its characters do and say. The psychoanalyst Sigmund Freud, for instance, developed a theory that men subconsciously wish to murder their fathers and marry their mothers, and he named this desire the "Oedipus complex." Because of its profundity, and its beauty as a work of art, *King Oedipus* has continued to be read and produced through the years.

SATYR PLAYS AND OLD COMEDY

As was mentioned earlier, on the days devoted to tragedy at the dramatic festival three tragedies by a single playwright were presented. Thus *King Oedipus* would have been performed as one of three tragedies by Sophocles. (When the three tragedies presented in one day were linked to form a connected dramatic whole—for example, *The Oresteia* of Aeschylus—they were called a *trilogy*.) Following the presentation of the three plays, whether they formed a trilogy or were independent, a short play by the same author, called a *satyr play*, was given as an afterpiece.

The satyr play was a comical play involving a chorus of satyrs, mythological creatures who were half-goat and half-man. Structured like Greek tragedies, the satyr plays parodied the mythological and heroic tales that were treated seriously in tragedies. They poked fun at honored Greek institutions, including religion and folk heroes, and often had a vulgar element. The only complete satyr play still in existence is *The Cyclops* by Euripides.

*V*ase painting of satyrs *Because we have few visual records of Greek theater productions, we rely on evidence found on artifacts such as vases. The vase painting shown here depicts satyrs—half men and half goats—who appeared in the short play that followed each set of three tragic dramas. The satyrs are playing harplike instruments known as lyres. (Photo—The Metropolitan Museum of Art, Fletcher Fund, 1925.)*

ℰURIPIDES
(ca. 480–406 B.C.)

Of the three great tragic playwrights of ancient Greece, Euripides is considered the most "modern." There are several reasons for this: (a) his sympathetic portrayal of women characters, (b) the greater realism of his plays, (c) the way he mixed tragedy with melodrama and comedy, and (d) his skeptical treatment of the gods.

For his "modernism," Euripides was often criticized. Euripides's characters were much more realistic than those of other Athenian dramatists; that is, they behaved the way people do in everyday life. But such realism was not considered appropriate for tragedy. His plays were also faulted for other reasons, such as weak plots, a diminished use of the chorus, and sensational subject matter. His mixing of comedy and tragedy, though derided in his time, was the model in later periods for tragicomedy and melodrama. The most controversial element of Euripides's plays was his portrayal of the gods as human and fallible, a treatment that was said to undermine the traditional moral order.

Unlike the playwrights Aeschylus and Sophocles, Euripides took no active part in the political and social life of Athens. The son of a wealthy citizen, Euripides was probably born on the Athenian island of Salamis. Though his family background and education prepared him to take public roles in society, he was, by temperament, reclusive and moody, interested in observing society and in examining the philosophical and scientific movements of the day. It was often claimed that he had marital problems and disliked women. As a dramatist, however, Euripides created believable female characters and showed a greater understanding of women than his contemporaries.

The playwright Aristophanes, who wrote comedies, frequently parodied scenes from Euripides, ridiculing both his philosophy and his dramatic methods. Though only five of the ninety-two plays by Euripides received prizes, his reputation grew rapidly after his death. He came to be much admired for his originality and independence of thought, and many of his dramatic methods were copied by both ancient and modern playwrights.

Eighteen plays by Euripides still exist: among the best known are *Alcestis* (438 B.C.); *Medea* (431 B.C.); *Hippolytus* (428 B.C.); *Andromache* (ca. 424 B.C.); *The Suppliants* (ca. 420 B.C.); *The Trojan Women* (415 B.C.); *Electra* (ca. 412 B.C.); *Iphigenia in Tauris* (ca. 410 B.C.); *Helen* (412 B.C.); *Orestes* (408 B.C.); *The Bacchae* (ca. 406 B.C.); and *Iphigenia in Aulis* (ca. 406 B.C.), as well as *The Cyclops*, a satyr play.

The third type of drama presented at Greek festivals was comedy. The only extant classical comedies are by Aristophanes and they contain certain recurring characteristics. Most Old Comedies, as the comedies of this period are called, do not follow the pattern of the crisis drama. They do not take place in a short span of time, are not restricted to one locale, and contain large casts of characters. Old Comedy always makes fun of social, political, or cultural conditions, and frequently the characters in the plays are recognizable contemporary personalities. In *The Clouds*, for instance, the philosopher Socrates is shown as a character suspended in the air in a basket—in other words, his head is always in the clouds. A present-day equivalent might be the kind of TV variety-show sketch that features caricatures of political figures, such as the President of the United States.

Greek Old Comedy employs fantastical and improbable plots to underline the satire. In *The Birds*, two characters who are unhappy with their earthly existence leave for Cloudcuckooland to observe the lives of the birds. They discover ludicrous parallels between human society and bird society. In *Lysistrata*, Aristophanes condemns the Peloponnesian War raging in Greece at the time. The Greek women in his play go on a sex strike, refusing to sleep with their husbands until the men cease warring. Miraculously, the scheme works.

Greek Old Comedies are broken down into sections similar to those in tragedy: prologos, episodes, alternating with choral odes, and the exodos. There are, however, certain unique episodes in Old Comedy. The *agon* is a scene with a debate between the two opposing forces in the play—each representing an antithetical side of a social or political issue. The *parabasis* is a scene in which the chorus, directly addressing the audience, makes fun of the spectators and specific audience members or satirizes other subjects. It should be remembered that religious and political officials attended the dramatic festivals and were seated in the front row of the theater. The chorus, during the parabasis, would single them out for ridicule in a fashion found today in the style of insult comedians like Don Rickles.

THE CHORUS

The chorus is an integral and unique feature of classical Greek drama. The importance of the chorus is attested to by the employment of a *chorodidaskalos*, a choral trainer, for all festival productions. The chorus in tragedy probably consisted of twelve male members when Aeschylus began writing and then was raised to fifteen by Sophocles. In comedy there were twenty-four chorus members. Greek comedy often employed a double chorus, with the twenty-four members divided into two groups of twelve. In *Lysistrata*, there are choruses of old men and old women. Chorus members probably intoned their lines in unison; on occasion, the choral leader delivered his dialogue independently.

ARISTOPHANES
(ca. 448–380 B.C.)

Aristophanes was the best-known comic playwright of the Greek Golden Age. In his play *The Clouds*, Aristophanes complained that other playwrights were copying his plots and ideas, but this plagiarism indicates the popularity of his comedies. Written in the style of Old Comedy—that is, comedy that poses a problem and then solves it with an absurd resolution—Aristophanes's plays reflect the social and political climate in Athens as it declined in power toward the end of the fifth century B.C..

The son of a wealthy citizen, Aristophanes was a member of the prosperous, conservative middle class of Athenian society. His plays indicate that he came from a cultured but old-fashioned home. Athenian life was changing rapidly as greed for an empire undermined the traditional simplicity, stability, and moral order, and Aristophanes used his plays to ridicule the ideas and people that he felt were leading Athens to ruin. One of his satiric targets was the Peloponnesian War with Sparta, a conflict that drained Athens of wealth and destroyed the social order. His death came after the Peloponnesian War had reduced Athens to poverty and disorder.

In spite of his conservative outlook, Aristophanes's plays are full of bawdy wit—a reflection of the open attitude toward sex in Athenian society. Since Old Comedy did not emphasize plot or character, Aristophanes's plays are distinguished for their inventive comic scenes, witty dialogue, and pointed satire. Because of the many references to people and events of his time, Aristophanes's plays are difficult to translate into playable modern versions.

Besides what we know about Aristophanes from his plays, an incident recorded in Plato's *Symposium* reveals that Aristophanes was very much involved in the daily life of Athens, including attending parties with friends. Plato reports that after outdrinking and outtalking all the guests at an all-night party, Aristophanes left with the philosopher Socrates, debating whether one man could write both comedy and tragedy.

Though he wrote about forty plays, Aristophanes did not feel competent to stage his own works and usually turned his plays over to a producer-director. Eleven of the plays survive. Some of the best known are *The Clouds* (423 B.C.); *The Wasps* (422 B.C.); *Peace* (421 B.C.); *The Birds* (414 B.C.); *Lysistrata* (411 B.C.); and *The Frogs* (405 B.C.). Aristophanes's last plays, in particular *Plutus* (388 B.C.), are often characterized as Middle Comedies. These are transitional works which led to the development of the nonpolitical New Comedy.

Greek choruses performed a number of dramatic functions. They provided expository information, commented on the action, interacted with other characters, and described offstage action. The chorus in Greek tragedy often represented the common people of the city-state ruled by the tragic hero or heroine. Their feelings and ideas represented the feelings and ideas of ordinary people with whom members of the audience could identify. Through singing and dancing, choruses also provided spectacle, as do choruses in today's musical comedies.

In Old Comedy, the chorus was frequently fantastical, its members appearing, for example, as birds in *The Birds* and as frogs in *The Frogs*. The chorus is the most difficult Greek dramatic convention for modern audiences to envision, because the notion of a group of performers speaking in unison, chanting, and dancing is hard for modern spectators to imagine.

THE ARCHITECTURE OF GREEK THEATERS

An important element of Greek theater was the kind of space in which plays were presented. Since tragedies, comedies, and satyr plays were offered at religious festivals, huge theaters were necessary, with the typical Classical Greek theater accommodating 15,000 to 17,000 spectators. The most noted of these theaters was the Theater of Dionysus in Athens. Greek theaters were outdoor amphitheaters with light provided by the sun, and the Greeks were often resourceful in the use of natural lighting in their dramas; if a play required a "sunrise effect," for example, it would be presented as the first drama of the day at dawn.

There were three distinct units in the Greek theater: the *theatron* (literally the "viewing place"), the seating area for the audience; the *orchestra*, or playing area for the actors; and the *skene*, or scene building. These three units were adjacent but unconnected architectural entities.

The audience sat in the theatron. The Greeks ingeniously built their theaters into hillsides which provided naturally sloped seating and excellent acoustics. During the classical period the hillside theatron contained temporary wooden bleachers, which were replaced by stone seating during the later Hellenistic period (336–146 B.C.). Some historians, who believe that a specific seating plan was followed in the Greek theatron, suggest that the various Greek tribes were segregated and that men and women sat separately. Front-row seats, known as the *proedria*, were reserved for political and religious dignitaries. The theaters, though huge, could not accommodate everyone, and therefore in the fifth century B.C. entrance fees and "tickets" were introduced. It is important to remember, though, that unlike a theater event today, a substantial portion of the population saw each play. Today it would be like virtually the entire population of a small town taking part in a single event—truly a communal occasion.

In commercial American theaters, the orchestra is the audience

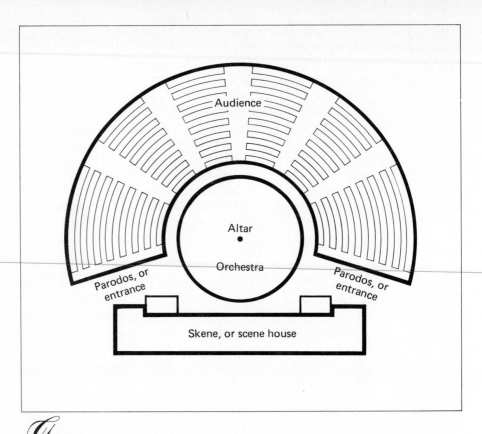

*G*round plan of typical Greek theater   *The theaters of ancient Greece were set into hillsides which made natural amphitheaters. At the base of the seating area was a circular space (orchestra) in which the chorus performed; at the center of the orchestra was an altar (thymele). Behind the orchestra was a temporary stage house (skene), at the sides of which were corridors (parados) for entrances and exits.*

seating area on the ground floor. In the classical Greek theater, the orchestra was the playing area. The first permanent structural element in the Greek theater was the orchestra, a circle paved with stone about 66 feet in diameter. Here again, the theater had evolved from past practices. In ceremonies of earlier days, it is believed, a circle was beaten down in a field of grain to serve as an area for presentations. This circle was the forerunner of the orchestra in Greek theaters.

The acting area was surrounded by audience members on three sides, in a configuration similar to modern thrust or three-quarter-round theaters. In this type of theater the stage juts out into the auditorium and the audience sits in a semicircle or on three sides around the stage. In the center of the orchestra was the *thymele*, an altar. The altar is a reminder

The theater at Delphi Among the theaters from the classic period still standing is this one at Delphi. Note the semicircular seating area in the hillside, the orchestra, and the remains of a stage house beyond. (The stone stage house dates from the later Hellenistic period.) Note also, the grandeur of the view of the mountains in the distance. (Photo—Peter Menzel, Stock, Boston.)

that the Greek drama was a part of religious worship. Some scholars have argued that the thymele may have been employed as a scenic element. For example, in *King Oedipus* Jocasta makes an offering, indicating a possible use of the thymele. Other commentators, however, argue that the altar was too holy a relic to have been used in the dramas.

The third element in the classical Greek theater building was the skene, or scene building, located behind the orchestra. Our knowledge of the skene is sketchy, but we do know that it contained dressing space for actors who needed to change costumes and was used to store properties needed for the presentations. (A property or "prop" in the theater is any object used by the actors during a play, such as a sword or shield used in a battle scene.) It is also believed that the skene building was used as scenic background for all plays after 458 B.C. What the skene looked like is another major point of contention among theater historians: how tall was it, for example, and how many doors did it have? At first, it was a temporary wooden structure, and after the classical period, it became a permanent stone edifice. In the classical period, the building was probably one story, later becoming a two-storied structure. The skene also had side wings *(paraskenia)*. Since the typical background needed for most Greek tragedies is a palace, the skene had to be patterned after such an edifice. There were doorways, probably three, although some argue that there was only one, for entrances and exits.

One additional controversy surrounds the architectural configuration of the playing area of the classical Greek theater. Although some scholars argue that there was a raised stage area in front of the skene and directly behind the orchestra, other scholars vehemently reject the existence of a raised stage. We do know that following the classical period huge raised stages were constructed in the Greek theaters. A scholarly compromise suggests that there may have been a slightly raised platform in front of the skene.

Scenery and Special Effects

The standard setting for Greek tragedy, with its royal heroes and heroines, was a palace, but there are some tragedies with other scenic requirements. The comedies require a wide variety of locales. How, then, did the Greeks transform the facade of the skene so that it might appear to be a different setting for different plays? There is no definite knowledge about the methods employed during the classical period. Nonetheless, many scholars believe that the later Hellenistic Greeks adopted their scene-changing techniques from their classical ancestors. Apparently the two most popular devices used in the Greek theater were the *pinakes* and the *periaktoi.* The pinakes were similar to flats, which are wooden frames covered with stretched canvas and painted. The pinakes were placed against the front of the skene, thereby altering the facade of the building. The periaktoi were three-sided prisms, composed of painted flats, on a pivot. By pivoting the prism a new face would be revealed to the audience, suggesting a scene change. What should be kept in mind is that the scene changes in the classical Greek theater were not realistic. Modern audiences expect the environments of different plays to be markedly distinct, but in the Greek theater there were only hints that the setting of the play had changed. Because of the vast size of the theaters and the limited scenic possibilities in an outdoor space, it was impossible to create unique environments for every tragedy, comedy, and satyr play.

The skene also masked the mechanisms for special effects. If modern audiences are hypnotized by technological wonders in theater, the classical Greeks were no different. The two most popular special-effects devices were the *mechane,* or "machine," and the *ekkyklema.*

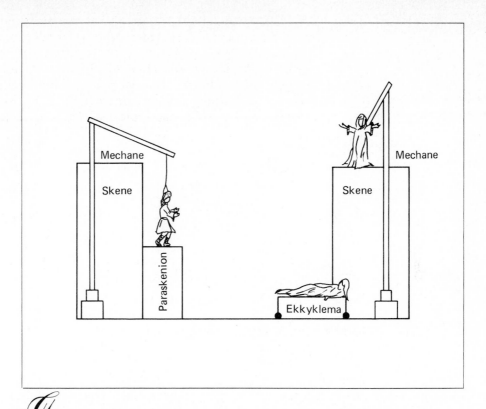

*G*reek mechane and ekkyklema *A conjectural reconstruction of Greek stage machinery: on the left, a crane used for flying in characters located on a side wing (paraskenia) of the scene building. On the right, a mechane higher up on the roof of the skene. The ekkyklema below was a platform on wheels used to bring out characters from inside the building. (Adapted from Margarete Bieber,* The History of the Greek and Roman Theater.*)*

Greek dramas often reached a climax with the sudden appearance of a god or goddess who resolved all the dramatic problems. The mechane, a crane hidden behind the upper level of the skene, was used as a means of effecting the entrance of the actor playing the role of the god or goddess in such a manner as to suggest that he was descending from the heavens; hence the term *deus ex machina*, which means "god from the machine." In subsequent usage the term was broadened, and today any unjustified or arbitrary dramatic device employed to unravel a plot is still referred to as a "deus ex machina." Since the Greeks did not present violence onstage, stage machinery was needed to reveal climactic offstage occurrences. One such machine was the ekkyklema, a platform on wheels that would be rolled out from behind the central doorway of the skene. In one use of the ekkyklema, the bodies of those characters who had been killed or had died offstage were placed on the wagon and strikingly revealed.

ACTING IN THE GREEK THEATER

Even though the actors were paid for their participation in the festivals during the classical period, there were not enough of these events for them to make a living by acting and so they could not have been full-time professionals. At first, when tragedy had only one actor, the role was usually performed by the playwright; both Thespis and Aeschylus wrote plays and performed in them. Sophocles was the first playwright to give up acting.

Aeschylus is credited with introducing a second actor, and Sophocles supposedly introduced a third actor. After Sophocles introduced the three-actor rule in tragedy, calling for no more than three actors, excluding the chorus, it seems to have been followed by other Greek dramatists. (Comedy was not restricted by the three-actor rule.) The rule was bent to allow additional performers to portray mute roles, that is, minor characters who did not speak lines. Since one actor could *double*— play more than one part in a play—it was possible to have more than three characters in a play, though never more than three onstage at one time. The *King Oedipus* of Sophocles, for instance, has seven speaking parts, and the same actor might play several minor parts.

At first, the playwrights chose their own casts and also oversaw the production of their own plays. The tragic playwrights, in particular, functioned as directors; they worked with the chorus and also assisted the actors, conferring with them about roles and scripts. After acting contests were introduced in 449 B.C., leading actors were assigned by lot in order to prevent any dramatist from having an undue advantage in the contest. Greek dramatists, like playwrights, directors, and producers in the modern theater, were aware of how difficult it is to discern the quality of a play when the acting is poor.

To imagine the fifth-century B.C. acting style is almost impossible. It could not have been very realistic, that is, conforming to everyday speech and gestures, for many of the conventions of the classical theater seem to argue against such realism. While many plays require that the audience believe that the female characters are sexually alluring—*Lysistrata*, for example—women were not allowed to perform and men played these parts. All forms of Greek drama required dancelike movement and chanting.

Costumes and Masks

The major element in Greek costuming was the mask. All Greek performers wore masks, which covered the entire head and included hairstyle, beards, and other distinctive facial features. These aided the audience in differentiating characters and allowed the actors to perform multiple roles. During the classical period, the facial coverings were not highly exaggerated, and in tragedies, the masks for all the chorus members were identical. Comic choruses, on the other hand, often required unusual masks, as in Aristophanes's plays, where chorus members sometimes represented frogs or birds.

Greek theatrical costuming, for the most part, was fairly conventional. Our knowledge of costumes comes mostly from scenes painted on Greek vases. Tragic characters of Greek origin, regardless of historical period, probably wore a long, decorated tunic and either a short or a long cloak. Illustrations frequently depict Greek performers wearing a thick-soled boot known as the *kothornus,* but this was not employed until the later Hellenistic period. Soft-soled footwear was worn in the classical period.

Comic costuming was often cut tight to emphasize certain physical features and thereby create a humorous effect. The unique element in comic costuming was the phallus, which was an exaggerated penis worn around the waist of all male characters. It has been suggested that this use of the phallus originated in the fertility rites out of which comedy possibly originated.

NEW COMEDY

For seventy-five years after the close of the fifth century B.C., the Greek theater continued to employ the classical conventions, with the major change in Greek drama in the fourth century B.C. occurring in comedy. By 336 B.C., Old Comedy had given way to a form called *New Comedy.* The only extant example of this later comic form is Menander's *The Grouch,* but there are fragments of a number of other comedies. New Comedy is an extremely important form because most modern comedy continues to employ its dramatic techniques. Instead of the political, social, and cultural satire of Old Comedy, the plots of New Comedy deal with romantic and domestic problems. The typical plot line can be summarized as "boy meets girl, boy loses girl, boy gets girl." A domineering parent usually comes between the young lovers, with the romantic complications resolved by sudden dramatic coincidences and discoveries.

The characters in New Comedy are recognizable stock types, such as the domineering parent, the romantic young lovers, and the comic servant. The chorus is relegated to a minor position. (In tragedy the chorus had also become less important toward the close of the classical period, particularly in the tragedies of Euripides.) Strong parallels can be drawn between New Comedy and today's television comedies, which also focus on domestic and romantic complications.

THEATER IN THE HELLENISTIC AGE

The Hellenistic period in Greece—which followed the classical period—is dated from the takeover of Greece by Alexander the Great in 336 B.C. to the conquering of the Greeks by the expanding Roman civilization in 146 B.C.

Significant changes took place in theater during the Hellenistic age. One was a shift of importance from the playwright to the actor, and another was the emphasis placed on the construction of theaters. Numerous new buildings were built throughout the Greek world. We know of at least forty Hellenistic theaters—doubtless there were more—built in places stretching from Asia Minor in the east to Italy in the west. The remains of a number of these are still standing, in sizes ranging from 3,000 seats to 21,000.

The Hellenistic theaters, which had become permanent stone structures, contained huge raised stages, which were part of the remodeled skene. The scene house was now two stories with the wings removed, and the stage was supported by the lower level of the skene. The upper level provided the background for the stage. In many theaters, ramps led up to the stage, and doorways—12 feet wide and almost as high as the skene's second story—led onto the stage. There were as many as seven of these doorways, known as *thyromata*, in some Hellenistic theaters; other theaters, however, continued to have a single portal.

The stage was much larger than most modern playing areas: between 8 and 13 feet high, sometimes 140 feet long and 6 to 14 feet deep. The relationship between the stage and the circular orchestra has been debated, with some arguing that the orchestra slowly fell out of use as a playing area and others suggesting that the stage was used for new plays and the orchestra for revivals of classical dramas.

The remodeled skene, the huge, raised stage and other changes made in theater structures all indicate a sharp shift of visual focus to the actor.

The Rise of the Actor

Throughout theater history the focus shifts from one element to another: from script to performers to visual effects. Such a shift occurred during the Hellenistic period as new scripts—a prominent feature of the classical era—became less important and the work of performers became more and more prominent. This is like the focus of much of contemporary film and television, which, like the Hellenistic theater, is also actor-centered, with scripts taking second place to star performers.

During the Hellenistic era, there was a general increase in the number and kind of Greek theatrical activities. Worship of Dionysus was no longer the sole reason for staging drama, and plays, therefore, were included in other festivals, such as those honoring military victories. With more productions, there developed the need for professional actors.

The ascendancy of the actor led to the establishing by 277 B.C. of a guild known as the Artists of Dionysus. All actors, chorus members, playwrights, and various other theater personnel were members, and if a local government wished to stage a play, the local branch of the Artists of Dionysus had to be contracted. Wealthy Hellenistic Greeks were no longer expected to produce plays, probably because there was a decrease in personal wealth in Greece at this time. The government became the producing agency, with a government official, the *agonthetes*, in charge of production details. The Artists of Dionysus, an ancient ancestor of Actor's Equity, the union of American professional actors, provided actors with professional security. During times of war, actors, who were not expected to take part in military service, could travel unhindered, and oddly enough, performers were called upon to serve as ambassadors and messengers during wartime.

Developments in costumes also indicate the ascendancy of the actor. Masks exaggerated facial features and were larger than life, which was not the case in classical Greece. Tragic characters wore large, exaggerated headdresses known as the *onkos*, and the shoes worn by tragic characters, the *kothornoi*, were thick-soled and elevated. Because the actor was costumed to look larger than life, and performed on a raised stage, he became the clear focus of the audience's attention.

The Social Position of Actors

Though the actor was the center of the Hellenistic theater, this should not obscure the fact that he was viewed as being less than socially acceptable. In the classical period, the actor was a semiprofessional involved in a religious activity. Yet even in the early fourth century B.C., the philosopher Plato, in *The Republic*, expressed his disapproval of theatrical performers, concluding that they should not be allowed to enter the ideal state. Plato's distrust was rooted in his fear that actors would employ their chameleonlike personalities to harm society.

In the Hellenistic era the distrust intensified, and even Aristotle, a great admirer of drama, viewed actors as disreputable. (The view that actors are "less moral" than the average citizen continues to be believed, and today gossip columnists feed the public's obsession with Hollywood and Broadway "immorality.") Because the Hellenistic performers wished to remind their audiences of their ties with Greek religion and circumvent social hostility, they named their theater guild the Artists of Dionysus.

The adverse reputation of actors was reinforced by the life-style of the *mimes*, who were probably the first real professional performers in Greece. The mimes were not originally involved in religious or official festivals but were traveling players who presented a variety of entertainments, including feats of juggling and acrobatics, wordless dances dramatizing fables, and sketches with dialogue. Greek mimes, because they spoke and engaged in a variety of entertainment activities, were not the equivalent of modern mimes, such as Marcel Marceau, who perform without words. Many of the mime troupes originated in southern Italy, and their most popular dramatic pieces were satires of the great tragedies.

Their life-style seems to have earned them public condemnation. These performers were nomads who entertained at banquets and probably in the streets on temporary stages. After 300 B.C., they were allowed to perform at festivals, but were never accorded recognition in the Artists of Dionysus. The traveling mime troupes were also criticized because they included women. Theater was not viewed by Greek society, or by many succeeding civilizations, as a fit profession for women, and those involved in theatrical endeavors were castigated for being licentious and immoral.

Summary

Greek theater set the stage for all western theater to follow. The dramatic form known as the crisis-play structure evolved during the classical era, and the tragedies of Aeschylus, Sophocles, and Euripides—which dramatize the downfall of a royal figure caught in a difficult or impossible situation—set the standard for all tragedy to come. Meanwhile, Aristotle's *Poetics* marked the development of serious critical consideration of drama and theater. The Greeks were leaders in comedy as well: Aristophanes's Old Comedies, which poked fun at contemporary political, social, and cultural events as well as personalities, set the standard for later satire.

Classical Greek theater buildings were huge outdoor spaces built into hillsides which accommodated audiences attending religious festivals in honor of the god Dionysus. Behind the orchestra, which was a circular playing space, the scene building served as the basic scenic unit. The performers, all of whom were males, acted in a style that apparently did not conform to everyday life. The chorus was an integral element of all classical Greek drama and theater.

Major changes took place during the later Hellenistic period. New Comedy, which was concerned with domestic and romantic situations, prepared the way for almost all popular comedy to follow and continues to influence contemporary playwrights. The drama of the Hellenistic period was not as noteworthy as that of the classical era, but the ascendancy of the actor was an important development, prefiguring our contemporary star system. The huge raised stage in theaters, distinctive footwear and large headdress in costuming, and the founding of the Artists of Dionysus, a theater guild for actors, all indicate the focus on the performer. The permanency of the stone theater structure points to the permanent hold theater was to have on western civilization.

While theater continued to flourish in Greece long after 146 B.C., it was no longer pure Greek theater but theatrical art influenced by the omnipresent Roman civilization, and therefore Rome is the place we turn to next in studying the evolution of the dramatic arts.

Chapter Three

THE ROMAN THEATER

As Greece declined in power and importance, another civilization began to emerge in Europe. Located on the Italian peninsula, its center was the city of Rome, from which it took its name.

Where Greece was noted for its creativity and imagination—in art, architecture, and philosophy—Rome came to be known for its mastery of more practical arts: law, engineering, and military conquest. And just as Rome's achievements as a civilization were more down-to-earth than those of Greece, so too was its theater. Instead of stressing high-minded tragedy, it focused on comedy and other popular entertainments, comparable to our movies, television, and rock music concerts. Taking off from Greek New Comedy, the Romans developed a form of domestic farce that

Masks for a comedy by Terence *The two most famous dramatists of the Roman theater were the comic writers Plautus and Terence. In their plays the characters were all stereotypes and the actors playing the parts wore masks to depict their specific characteristics. Shown here is a shelf of masks—from a ninth century manuscript—for characters in* Andria *by Terence. (Photo—Vatican Library.)*

The Roman Theater

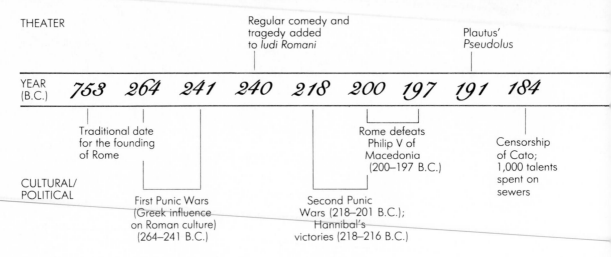

THEATER			Regular comedy and tragedy added to *ludi Romani*				Plautus' *Pseudolus*	
YEAR (B.C.)	*753*	*264*	*241*	*240*	*218*	*200*	*197*	*191*	*184*

Traditional date for the founding of Rome

First Punic Wars (Greek influence on Roman culture) (264–241 B.C.)

Second Punic Wars (218–201 B.C.); Hannibal's victories (218–216 B.C.)

Rome defeats Philip V of Macedonia (200–197 B.C.)

Censorship of Cato; 1,000 talents spent on sewers

CULTURAL/ POLITICAL

has remained the prototype of this kind of entertainment straight through to today's situation comedies on TV.

HISTORICAL BACKGROUND: THE REPUBLIC AND THE EMPIRE

Rome was founded, according to legend, around 750 B.C. and for over 200 years was ruled by a series of kings. Around 500 B.C. the kings were overthrown and a republic, which was to last nearly 500 years, was established. During the early years of the republic, there were three main classes in Rome: the patricians (the rich upper class that ruled the country through the Senate); the plebeians (ordinary citizens who gradually gained an equal voice in government through a people's assembly); and the slaves (who made up roughly half the population). For those who were free, the republic offered a representative form of government.

After the republic was well established and had extended its control over much of Italy, the Romans were challenged by Carthage, a nation based in a seaport in North Africa. During the third century B.C., Rome engaged in a lengthy conflict with Carthage known as the Punic Wars and finally emerged victorious. As a result, Rome controlled large parts of the central and western Mediterranean, including Spain, Sicily, Sardinia, and parts of North Africa. And it was at this time that Rome also came into contact with Greece and saw first-hand Greek art and culture, including theater.

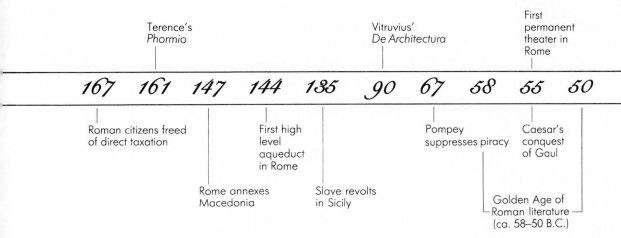

During the first century B.C., the Roman republic began to show signs of serious strain. By this time, Rome had control of far-flung territories, and the problems of governing so vast an area—along with the difficulties of maintaining the checks and balances of its political system—led to upheavals and wars. In the midst of the turmoil, Julius Caesar made himself a dictator but was subsequently assassinated by a group led by Brutus, who in turn was defeated in battle by Mark Antony and Octavian. (These events served as the basis for Shakespeare's famous play about Caesar.)

The republic could not survive these shocks, and in 27 B.C. Rome became an empire with one supreme ruler. This form of government continued for several centuries, during which time most of the civilized Western world was unified under Roman rule. The empire included most of the lands bordering on the Mediterranean Sea and all of Europe through what is now Spain, France, and Britain, and the Balkans.

Throughout their long history, the Romans were always practical. Their laws dealing with property, marriage, and inheritance have continued to influence Western civilization to the present day. The Romans were also great engineers and architects, developing aqueducts and roadways. Today, 2,000 years later, modern highways throughout Europe are built on the foundations of roads laid by the Romans, and a number of their aqueducts, though no longer in use, are still standing.

Religion was also of the utmost importance in Roman history. While the Romans worshipped gods who were counterparts of the Greek deities, they also worshipped large numbers of other divinities: to their own

The Roman Theater

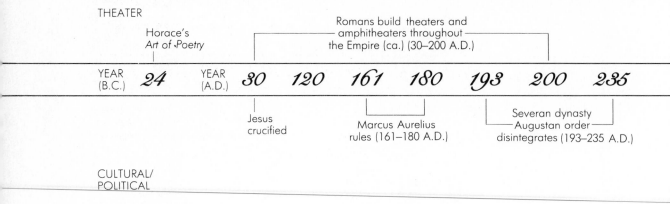

Horace's
Art of ·Poetry

Romans build theaters and
— amphitheaters throughout —
the Empire (ca.) (30–200 A.D.)

YEAR (B.C.)	*24*	YEAR (A.D.)	*30*	*120*	*161*	*180*	*193*	*200*	*235*

Jesus
crucified

Marcus Aurelius
rules (161–180 A.D.)

Severan dynasty
— Augustan order —
disintegrates (193–235 A.D.)

pantheon of gods, they constantly added the gods worshipped by the people they conquered. The Romans also staged religious festivals in which they incorporated theatrical elements.

The birth of Christianity had a profound influence on the Roman world. The Romans persecuted the early Christians, but in the fourth century A.D., Emperor Constantine, who founded Constantinople, the capital of the eastern empire, was converted to the new belief; thus began the eventual conversion of much of the Roman world to Christianity. The Greek and Roman religions condoned theatrical events, but the early Christians considered the theater pagan and therefore evil. The role of the church was a contributing factor to the subsequent decline of theater in the later years of the Roman empire. Before coming to that, however, we should look at the theater that flourished in Rome and note why it is significant for us today.

THE ROMAN THEATER

When the Romans turned to theater, they were strongly influenced by Greek art and culture—as they were in sculpture and architecture—and borrowed freely from the Greeks.

The Romans are thus not known for their innovations in theater nor for fostering it as a high art. Rather, in their adaptation of theatrical practices from the Greeks and use of them for their own purposes, the Romans are significant because of their development of theater as popular entertainment. Their writers took the New Comedy of Greece

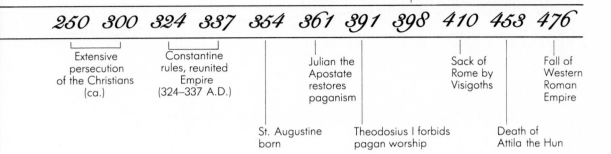

Council of Carthage decrees excommunication for those who attend theater rather than church on holy days, actors forbidden sacraments

| 250 | 300 | 324 | 337 | 354 | 361 | 391 | 398 | 410 | 453 | 476 |

Extensive persecution of the Christians (ca.)

Constantine rules, reunited Empire (324–337 A.D.)

Julian the Apostate restores paganism

Sack of Rome by Visigoths

Fall of Western Roman Empire

St. Augustine born

Theodosius I forbids pagan worship

Death of Attila the Hun

and perfected a form of comedy that was popular with the masses. These Roman comedies are the direct ancestors of all Western situation comedy; they set the pattern that continued through many centuries and was followed by the screwball Hollywood movies of the 1930s, the Broadway comedies of the same period, and the comedies on TV.

The Romans also built many theater buildings to make theater available to large numbers of people. They redesigned the Greek amphitheater and constructed impressive theater buildings throughout the empire. Rome's many conquests led to prosperity for its citizens, who, because of their wealth and slave labor, had an abundance of leisure time. To help fill the leisure time they offered theater, not just at a few festivals, but many times during the year.

The festival called the Ludi Romani, which was dedicated to Jupiter, the Roman equivalent of Zeus, was the first major Roman festival to incorporate theater. The festival, although dating back to the sixth century B.C., did not include drama until 240 B.C., which was just about when the Romans came into contact with Greek culture. Five more official festivals eventually incorporated theater, and in addition, an increasing number of days were set aside for minor festivities and theatrical activities.

Historians estimate that in A.D. 354 theatrical presentations were staged on one hundred days of the year. Despite this extensive theatrical activity, the Romans are not noted for serious drama. Roman theater flourished for nearly seven centuries, but the works of only three Roman playwrights—Plautus, Terence, and Seneca—have survived, and of these, the first two are noted for comedy. They are, however, key figures in the history of comedy.

The Colosseum in Rome *The Romans were engineers and architects, who built roads, aqueducts, temples, and theaters. They were also fond of popular entertainment. These two interests were combined in the construction of colosseums, such as this one in Rome— seating 50,000 spectators—completed in 80 A.D. and still standing today. (Photo—Editorial Photocolor Archives.)*

Roman Comedy: Plautus and Terence

Plautus, in the last part of the third century and the first part of the second century B.C., wrote comedies which used Greek New Comedy as a model. Like New Comedy, his plays neither employ choruses nor deal with contemporary political and social issues; instead, they are comedies detailing the trials and tribulations of romance. Their characters are recognizable, recurring stock types, the most popular of whom was the parasite, a comic personage living off others and motivated purely by sensual desires. The courtesans, lovers, and overbearing parents are other popular characters. Plautus's comedies are farces—broadly comic pieces using exaggerated actions and highly improbable plots—and employ such farcical comic techniques as mistaken identity.

The Menaechmi is a typical comedy by Plautus. A man known as Menaechmus, from Syracuse, is searching for his lost twin brother, also named Menaechmus, who had been kidnapped as a child. As the play begins, the first Menaechmus arrives in Epidamnus and finds himself in front of a house which, unknown to him, belongs to his lost brother. Since the long-separated twins look alike and have identical names, much comic confusion is based on their being mistaken for one another. The wife of one, for instance, mistakes the other for her husband. As the plot becomes more and more complicated, the play grows funnier and funnier. The farcical, slapstick confusion is finally resolved when the twins are reunited.

Many stock Roman characters can be found in *The Menaechmi*. Peniculus is the parasite, Erotium is a comic courtesan, and Messenio is the comic servant of the Menaechmus from Syracuse. The minor characters include a domineering wife, a doddering father-in-law, and a quack doctor.

The Roman comic writer who followed Plautus by a few years was Terence. While Terence's plots are as complicated as Plautus's, Terence's style is different: more literary and less exaggerated. Terence's *Phormio* dramatizes the attempts of two cousins, Antipho and Phaedria, to overcome their fathers' objections to their lovers. Both young men are aided in winning their lovers by Phormio, the tricky parasite, and by dramatic coincidences. While the plot complications and stock characters are similar to those found in Plautus's *The Menaechmi*, *Phormio* is less farcical and slapstick. Much of the humor is verbal, and there is less physical comic action but more sparring with words, which makes Terence's work less theatrical than that of Plautus. It should also be noted that while much of Plautus's dialogue was meant to be sung, as in a modern musical comedy, Terence's dialogue was spoken.

A Funny Thing Happened on the Way to the Forum   This 1962 Broadway musical, starring Zero Mostel, in the center, is testimony to the enduring qualities of Roman farce comedies. Written by Bert Shevelove and Larry Gelbart, with words and music by Stephen Sondheim, the musical is based on several plays by the Roman writer Plautus, particularly Miles Gloriosus, Mostellaria, *and* Pseudolus. *(Photo—Fred Fehl.)*

ℙLAUTUS
(Titus Maccius Plautus)
(ca. 254–184 B.C.)

Plautus was the most popular of all Roman comic writers. According to Cicero, the Roman critic, Plautus was "choice, urbane, talented, and witty." Plautus's plays were written to entertain, and they delighted Romans up to the time of the empire, when mime became the favorite entertainment. Even when his plays were no longer produced, they were read and admired for their farcical situations and mastery of colloquial Latin. In modern times, adaptations of plays by Plautus have continued to be extremely popular.

Born in Umbria, Plautus went to Rome at an early age and became an actor. When he began writing his own plays, Plautus took his familiarity with song, dance, and native Italian farce and combined it with characters and plots from the New Comedy of Hellenistic Greece. By concentrating on domestic situations and romance, he gave new life to the plot formula: boy meets girl, boy loses girl, boy gets girl.

Though he adapted his plays from Greek comedies, Plautus made them thoroughly Roman by using colloquial language, local allusion, and parody, especially parody of the Roman legal and military system. He used comic repetition and digression, humorous monologues, and a variety of character types—especially parasites and slaves—to amuse the audience.

Over one hundred plays were attributed to Plautus, but no more than forty-five are considered authentic. Twenty of his plays and the fragments of a twenty-first survived and have been used as models by playwrights from the Renaissance to the present day, including Shakespeare, Ben Jonson, and Molière. Rodgers and Hart's musical *The Boys from Syracuse* is based on Plautus's *The Menaechmi*, while *A Funny Thing Happened on the Way to the Forum* includes material from his *Miles Gloriosus* and *Pseudolus*. Some of Plautus's other well-known plays are *Amphitryon*, *The Rope*, *Casina*, and *The Pot of Gold*. (The dates of individual plays by Plautus are unknown but they are presumed to have been written between 205 and 184 B.C.)

TERENCE
(Publius Terentius Afer)
(ca. 185–159 B.C.)

After Plautus, the most important Roman comic writer was Terence. Where Plautus's plays were robust and broadly entertaining, Terence stressed characterization, subtlety of expression, and elegant language.

Terence based much of his work on Greek models. To answer charges that he plagiarized materials from Greek comedies, Terence wrote that he did "not deny having done so," and added that he "means to do it again." Since reworking Greek comedies was a common practice of other Roman authors, it is likely that the criticism of Terence was motivated by other reasons, perhaps jealousy of his talent and his rapid rise in social status.

Terence's life itself was dramatic. He was born in Carthage, an enemy of Rome, and brought to Rome as a slave. The Afer in Terence's name probably indicates that he was an African, and therefore he may have been the first major black playwright in the Western theater. His owner, a senator, educated the young playwright, freed him, and possibly introduced him to a literary circle that included a group of prominent writers and philosophers.

Terence's association with the high society of his time is reflected in his comedies. His plays are noted for their subtle humor and cultivated Latin. He often used a double plot, placing two characters in similar love situations and examining their differing reactions. Though his plays were admired by his learned friends, the populace preferred more lively entertainments.

Subsequent periods, such as the Middle Ages and the Renaissance, however, held the plays of Terence in great esteem. His plays, more than those of any Greek or Roman dramatist, were used as literary models in the convents and monasteries of the Middle Ages and the schools of the Renaissance. The simple style of the Latin and the high moral tone of the plays made them popular with teachers and scholars.

Terence wrote six plays, all of which have survived: *Andria* (166 B.C.); *The Mother-in-Law* (165 B.C.); *The Self-Tormentor* (163 B.C.); *The Eunuch* (161 B.C.); *Phormio* (161 B.C.); and *The Brothers* (160 B.C.).

Roman Tragedy: Seneca

The only tragic playwright of note in the Roman period was Seneca. (Debate continues among theater historians over whether Seneca's dramas were staged during his lifetime or whether he wrote them as "closet dramas" not intended for production.) On the surface, Seneca's plays appear to be similar to Greek tragedies. His plots are reworkings of Greek tales and, like the Greeks, he employs the chorus. But his tragedy is quite distinct. His choruses are not integral to the dramatic action, and unlike Greek dramatists, Seneca emphasizes violent spectacle. Those scenes which the Greeks banished from the stage—stabbings, murders, suicides—are often the climactic onstage moments in Seneca's works. In Seneca's *Thyestes*, for example, Thyestes eats the flesh of his children and drinks their blood in full view of the audience; and in his *Oedipus*, Jocasta cuts out her womb and Oedipus blinds himself onstage.

The interest in violent spectacle has, of course, later historical parallels. In our own contemporary cinema, there are numerous examples of suspense films that emphasize brutally realistic moments of violence. Some of these are artistically interesting, such as the films of Alfred Hitchcock (*Psycho* and *The Birds*). The majority, however, exploit sensational violence: hatchet murders, animals and insects that prey on humans, demonic forces let loose.

Seneca does not exploit violence; he relates it to his themes and the tragic circumstances of his characters. Seneca's characters do not suffer from tragic flaws, but instead are obsessed by a single motivation. In *Thyestes*, for instance, Atreus is obsessed with revenge. Because his characters are consumed by a single motivation, Seneca's plays appear to be highly melodramatic. Supernatural beings often appear in the dramatic action, adding to the melodramatic quality. Seneca's dialogue contains long, detailed monologues, and his characters frequently spout moralistic axioms. Seneca employs a five-act structure rather than the distinct episodes of Greek tragedy. While his stage popularity has never matched that of the Greek tragedians, his influence on later periods is noteworthy. Shakespeare, for example, was greatly influenced by Seneca's dramatic style; *Hamlet* is often discussed as a Senecan revenge tragedy which contains much onstage violence and the appearance of a supernatural character, the ghost of Hamlet's father.

Horace and Dramatic Criticism

Like Roman drama, Roman dramatic criticism was also based on the work of others, especially Aristotle. Horace, who is sometimes called the Roman Aristotle, outlines his theory of correct dramatic technique in his *Ars Poetica (The Art of Poetry)*. Horace argues that comedy and tragedy must be distinct genres, or types, of drama, and that there should be no mixture of the two. Tragedy should deal with royalty while comedy should depict common persons. The playwright's task, according to

ＳＥＮＥＣＡ
(Lucius Annaeus Seneca)
(ca. 4 B.C.–A.D. 65)

The chief Roman tragic writer whose plays have survived is Seneca. Though there is no absolute proof of his identity, it is generally believed that he is the Roman writer by that name who served as tutor to the Emperor Nero.

Senaca's life contained a contradiction. As a writer, he espoused *stoicism*, a philosophy of moderation and calm acceptance of whatever happens. In his personal life, though, he was something of a voluptuous epicure, enjoying the pleasures of the flesh which stoics were supposed to forgo. These extremes are a mirror of the contradictory forces present in the Roman life of the times.

Seneca was born in Córdoba, Spain. Sent to Rome at an early age, he explored a number of philosophies, including one based on a vegetarian diet, before beginning his essays on stoicism and his career in politics. By A.D. 32, he was a noted orator, and, in fact, Caligula, the mad Roman emperor, was so jealous of Seneca's oratorical skills that he considered executing him. Instead, the emperor exiled the playwright for two years, hoping he would die. Seneca was exiled again for seven years by Messalina, wife of Emperor Claudius, probably for political reasons, though the charge was adultery with the emperor's niece.

In A.D. 49 Seneca was recalled to Rome by Agrippina, Claudius's new wife, to be tutor to her son, Nero. When Nero became emperor in 54, Seneca became one of his chief advisors, running the government for five years and amassing a fortune. He fell from power in 62, and in 65 the emperor ordered him to commit suicide. Being ordered by a ruler or a court to take one's own life was a common practice in Greece and Rome, and Seneca the stoic obeyed calmly, discussing philosophy to the end.

Seneca's nine plays, *The Trojan Women, Medea, Oedipus, Phaedra, Thyestes, Hercules on Oeta, The Mad Hercules, The Phoenician Women,* and *Agamemnon,* are the only surviving examples of Roman tragedy based on Greek myths. (Individual dates for Seneca's plays are not known.) Seneca's structure—five episodes separated by choral odes—was frequently used as a model by Renaissance playwrights.

All of Seneca's plays show the devastating effect of moral evil on society, illustrated by scenes of violence and horror; his characters are usually driven by a single obsession to their doom. Though most commentators contend that Seneca's plays were "closet drama," meant to be read, not staged, it is possible that they were declaimed—that is, recited at gatherings of his noble admirers—or staged with only a few gestures pantomimed rather than with realistic effects.

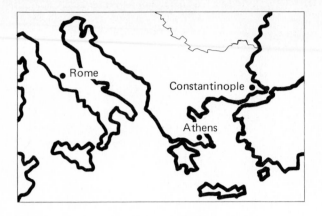

The ancient world *Western theater was born in Athens, Greece. After the emergence of Roman civilization, the center of theater moved to Rome. At the height of its power, the Roman Empire extended far beyond the regions shown here. In 330 A.D., the Roman Empire, which by then had begun to decline, was divided into two parts by the Emperor Constantine: Rome became the capital in the west, and Constantinople in the east.*

Horace, is to create easily recognizable stock characters. One of Horace's most important notions (not found in Aristotle) is that drama should not just entertain audiences, but should also instruct them or teach them a lesson. Horace lists a series of additional dramatic axioms: plays are to be written in five acts, no violence should be presented on stage (Seneca obviously did not heed this Horatian precept), the use of the deus ex machina should be avoided, and the chorus should be an individual character, not a group of people. Horace also supports the three-actor rule.

As should be apparent, many of Horace's principles have their roots in Aristotle's *Poetics*. There are, however, important differences between the two: Horace was far more dogmatic and prescriptive. As was so often true of the Romans, Horace was codifying rules, while Aristotle was simply describing the dramatic technique of the classical Greeks, without providing rigid guidelines.

Popular Entertainment

If the Romans were not creators of great drama, they did develop a variety of popular entertainments, many of them adopted from the Etruscan and Greek cultures. Popular entertainments appeal to all levels of society, and no educational, social, or cultural sophistication is required in order to appreciate them. Some historians argue that twentieth-century American culture—with such highly developed popular entertainments as television, film, rock concerts, and other less sophisticated dramatic arts—is much like Roman culture. Many of the Roman entertainments correspond to modern circus arts. Chariot racing (the modern equivalent of which would be auto and stock car races) was popular from the seventh century B.C. through the sixth century A.D. Equestrian performances, acrobatics, wrestling, and prizefighting were also quite popular. Gladiatorial combats were included in festivals at the close of the second century

HORACE
(Quintus Horatius Flaccus)
(65–8 B.C.)

Just as Aristotle was the chief critic and theoretician of the ancient Greek theater, the best-known writer of dramatic theory and criticism in the Roman period was Horace. His *Ars Poetica (The Art of Poetry)* (24–20 B.C.) is the only Latin treatise on dramatic criticism still in existence.

In his essay, Horace surveys the history and theory of dramatic poetry. Less detailed and profound than Aristotle, Horace stressed rules, such as one that comedy and tragedy must never be combined. Horace felt that writers should provide both pleasure and profit to their audience, an opinion that Renaissance critics made a rule of drama. Son of a freed slave, Horace was a poet who became the friend of Virgil and other leading literary figures of the early Roman Empire. He was famous for his lyric poetry, the *Satires* and the *Epodes*, as well as *The Art of Poetry*.

Horace was born in Venusia, an Italian town that had once been a Greek colony. His father, a government collec-tor of market dues, sent the young writer to study both in Athens and Rome so that he might qualify for a high government post. During the civil war that followed the assassination of Julius Caesar, Horace fought with Brutus's army at Philippi. (These events are covered in Shakespeare's play.) Pardoned by Augustus, the new emperor, Horace went to Rome, obtained a government post, and began writing.

At that time, wealthy Romans, following the lead of the emperor, supported literature and the arts, and Horace's literary patron gave him a farm which freed him from further financial worries so that he could concentrate on his writing. His careful craftmanship, humor, and use of language attracted the attention of the emperor, who commissioned the poet to write a fourth book of odes.

When he died, Horace was the leading lyric poet of his time, and his *Ars Poetica* has influenced critics from the Renaissance onward.

An actor in mime or farce *This small figure, a Greco-Roman bronze from the period 300–100 B.C., represents the type of performer who kept theater alive in the Roman world when there was little formal theatrical activity. A stock character known as Dossenus, he offers evidence of caricature and the grotesque in the mime performances of the period. (Photo—The Metropolitan Museum of Art, Rogers Fund, 1912.)*

B.C. These were not make-believe combats but actual battles to the death between men. The *naumachia* were sea battles staged on lakes, man-made bodies of water, or flooded arenas; the first such sea battle was organized by Julius Caesar in 46 B.C. Wild animals were often employed in popular entertainments; they were also exhibited and used for battles in arenas or for combat with unarmed humans.

Special buildings were constructed to house these spectacles. The Circus Maximus, constructed in 600 B.C. for chariot races and frequently remodeled thereafter, seated over 60,000 spectators. The most renowned amphitheater constructed by the Romans was the Colosseum, built in A.D. 80. The caverns beneath the arena may have housed many Christians waiting to be sacrificed to wild beasts. (The slaughter of early Christians by lions was viewed by the Roman populace as a spectacular diversion.)

The Romans also developed popular entertainments which were more truly theatrical. Roman mime, like Greek mime, included gymnastics, juggling, songs, and dances. Short dramatic and risqué (that is, sexually suggestive) comedic skits were also presented. (The Romans enjoyed sexually provocative dramatic material, and the Emperor Heliogabalus, in the first part of the third century A.D., forced mimes to perform actual sexual acts.) The mimes performed in *found spaces*, that is, available spaces in such places as town squares or open courtyards that could be utilized for performances even though not specifically designed for such purposes. Mimes provided the primary theatrical entertainment at the Roman fertility festival, the Ludi Florales, from about 238 B.C. Even though mime troupes were allowed to entertain at festivals, they, like the Greek mimes, were castigated for being transients and for including women within their ranks.

A unique Roman stage presentation was the pantomime. Requiring a single dancer, a chorus, and musical accompanists, Roman pantomime might be compared to ballet. The major performer danced a mythological, historical, or occasionally comical story, with the chorus chanting the narrative and explaining the action. Pantomime performers were often sponsored by emperors and members of the nobility.

ROMAN THEATER PRODUCTION AND ACTING PRACTICES

Roman production practices differed slightly from those of Greece. Festivals were under the jurisdiction of a local government official who contracted with the *dominus*, or head, of an acting troupe. The dominus, who was usually the leading actor, organized his troupe, made financial arrangements, bought dramas from playwrights, hired musicians, and made arrangements for costumes. Since several companies were hired for each festival, there was an atmosphere of "unofficial" competition, with popular performers vying for rewards from prestigious audience members. Popular entertainments, however, frequently overshadowed the traditional dramatic presentations.

Acting companies hired to stage drama were composed of at least six male members, with the Romans ignoring the three-actor rule adhered to by the Greeks and endorsed by Horace. Roman acting technique emphasized detailed pantomime and broad physical gestures, which were necessitated by the size of the Roman theaters; it also stressed beautiful vocal delivery. Two-thirds of the lines in Plautus's comedies, for example, were sung, much as in contemporary musical comedies.

Actors in the modern theater who play the same kinds of roles over and over again are less esteemed than those who perform a variety of roles. The Romans, however, admired performers who specialized in playing one type of role and refined their stock characterizations. Facial expression was unimportant since full head masks, constructed of linen, were worn. Only mime performers appeared without masks.

The position of actors in Roman society continues to be debated by theater historians. Some believe that actors were usually slaves and that the dominus who organized the troupe was a free man who purchased his company's performers. Other historians note that the "stars" in the Roman theater were highly respected, financially well rewarded, and socially accepted. Roscius and Aesopus were two such stars, and when they died in the first century B.C., the former left an estate estimated to have been worth the equivalent of $1 million, while the latter left approximately $500,000. The majority of actors, however, were probably slaves or unesteemed members of Roman society, barely able to survive financially.

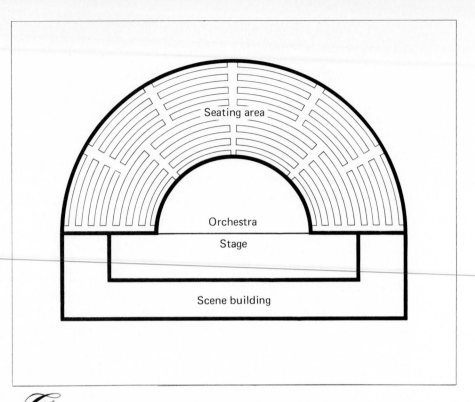

*G*round plan of typical Roman theater   *Roman theater, in contrast to Greek theaters, were free-standing structures—all one building—with the stone stagehouse connected to the seating area. The orchestra was a semicircle instead of a full circle as in Greek theaters. The stage was long and wide, and the stagehouse several stories high with an elaborate façade.*

Theater Buildings and Scenic Elements

Roman theater buildings were also based on Greek models. Ironically, the Romans did not construct a permanent theater structure until 55 B.C.; thus, during the period of Plautus and Terence, there were no permanent spaces for the presentation of the works of the best playwrights Rome ever produced. Instead, temporary wooden structures, probably similar to the later permanent ones, were erected. The Roman theaters contained the same three units found in the Greek buildings: the *cavea* (the Roman version of the theatron, or audience seating area), the *orchestra*, and the *scaena* (the Roman skene, or stage house).

The Roman structures, however, were different from the classical Greek ones. The Romans had developed the arch and other engineering techniques that allowed them flexibility in construction. They put this knowledge to good use in building theaters. Roman theaters were usually not built into hillsides but were free-standing structures with the tiered audience section connected to the stage house. The cavea, or audience seating area, was often larger than the Greek theatron, with the average capacity of a Roman theater being 25,000 spectators. The Roman planners also attempted to make the audience comfortable: to protect the spectators from the intense heat, awnings were set up and fans blew air over cooled water to act as a primitive form of air-conditioning.

The scaena, or stage house, was attached to the seating area to create a single architectural unit, and in between was the orchestra, which was semicircular rather than circular. The orchestra, however, was rarely used for staging, but rather for seating government officials and for the flooding required for sea battles. In front of the scaena was a large raised stage 5 feet high called the *pulpitum*, whose dimensions varied from 100 feet by 20 feet to 300 feet by 40 feet. (The last dimension is the length of a football field.) Few modern-day performers will have the opportunity to act on a stage that huge.

The scaena, or stage house, was the unique feature of the Roman theater structure. Two or three stories high, it was used for storage and dressing space, and a roof extended out from the scene building over the stage to provide the actors with protection from the elements. Two side wings enclosed the pulpitum and connected the scaena to the cavea. The *scaena frons*, or facade of the scaena, was elaborate and ornate, with statuary, columns, niches, and three to five doorways; the central doorway was the largest and had stairs leading up to it. The facade was meant to represent a typical Roman street scene, the basic scenic requirement of Roman comedy, and could also be employed to represent a palace, the customary tragic setting.

The scaena frons could act as the basic scenic element because the Romans, following the Greek tradition, did not require a unique environment for each play. The Romans, however, did try to alter slightly the scaena frons by employing the periaktoi, the three-sided scenic unit described in the previous chapter. Where the periaktoi were located on the high pulpitum or stage house is a matter of conjecture; possibly they were placed in the doorways on each side of the large central portal.

The Romans also employed curtains to aid in altering the scenic environment. There were two types of curtains: the *auleum* and the *siparium*. The auleum was a front curtain which was raised and lowered on telescoping poles from a trench in front of the stage. Given the size of the scaena, the auleum could not mask the entire facade; instead, its function was to mask actors before they were revealed to the audience, much in the way that front curtains in theaters continue to be employed. The siparium, a painted backdrop placed against the scaena frons, slightly altered the appearance of the facade. Because of the size of the scaena frons, the siparium could never completely mask the permanent three-dimensional background.

Much of what we know about Roman theater architecture comes

The Roman theater at Orange *The Romans built theaters throughout their empire that circled the Mediterranean Sea. One of the best preserved is at Orange, France. Built in the first or second century A.D., the building is near the center of the town. Note the semicircular orchestra, and the large stage area. Also the stagehouse at the back with its ornate façade with niches for statues and other adornments. (Photo—Giraudon.)*

from Marcus Vitruvius, who lived in the first century B.C. and whose ten-volume work *De Architectura* reveals how much of Roman architecture was based on Hellenistic models. Vitruvius's massive treatise, which includes a discussion of theater buildings, became particularly influential in the Italian Renaissance when it was rediscovered.

THE DECLINE OF ROMAN THEATER

In the fourth century A.D., it was clear that the Roman empire was beginning to fall apart. In 330 the Emperor Constantine established two capitals for the empire: Rome in the west and Constantinople in the east.

From that point on, the center of gravity moved from the west to the east, toward Constantinople, and the city of Rome became less and less of a factor.

The downfall of Rome, marked in A.D. 476 by the unseating of the western Roman emperor by a barbarian ruler, was caused by the disintegration of the Roman administrative structure and the sacking of Roman cities by the northern barbarians. The fall of the western Roman empire coincided with the downfall of the Roman theater. Yet the fall of Rome was not the only explanation for the deterioration of the theater. The theater itself became less and less of an art and more of an entertainment to the point where it often became difficult to distinguish between theatrical offerings and circuses, between gladiatorial contests and the pantomimes described above.

Another important consideration in understanding the decline of Roman theater is the rise of Christianity. From the outset, the Christian church was opposed to theater. Early Christians pointed to the connection between theater and pagan religions, and the church fathers argued that the evil characters portrayed onstage taught immorality to their viewers. The sexual content of the Roman entertainments offended church leaders, who were equally alarmed by their frequent satirical attacks on Christianity. As a result, the church issued various edicts condemning the theater and its participants. In 398, a church council decreed that anyone who went to the theater rather than to church on holy days would be excommunicated, and performers were not allowed to take part in holy rites. These attacks had far-reaching historical ramifications. As late as the seventeenth century, the French playwright Molière was refused Christian burial because he was an actor-dramatist.

Ironically, the institution that condemned the theater to perdition was to revive the dramatic art five centuries later when the Roman Catholic church became the catalyst in western theater's rebirth. But this was later; the early Christian church opposed the theater, and this was one reason why the theater as an organized institution disappeared for the time being.

The invaders from the north plundered the cities of the Roman empire, and, after a time, no large centers of culture remained. People scattered, and in many places the buildings that had housed government offices, schools, and performing spaces were abandoned. The plays of the Greek and Roman dramatists and the writings of Aristotle and Horace were lost or forgotten. The tradition of theater that had stretched virtually unbroken for nearly a thousand years, from the Greeks in the fifth century B.C. through the early centuries of the Christian era, was at an end.

The dispersal and destruction of educational, political, and cultural institutions led later historians to call the period after the fall of the

Roman empire the "Dark Ages." Many present-day historians believe that this label is too negative and simplistic. The fall of the Roman empire did not occur overnight; the empire had been deteriorating from within for many years. Meanwhile, the medieval system of self-contained, church-centered communities had begun to emerge by the seventh and eighth centuries. It would be some time, though, before the theater was again a full-fledged institution in Europe.

Summary

While the Romans borrowed many Greek conventions, including the introduction of drama and theater into religious and civic festivals, they modified them so that they became uniquely Roman. The Romans did not produce great plays, but the New Comedies of Plautus and Terence, as well as the tragedies of Seneca, are noteworthy because of their influence on later playwrights. Horace's *Ars Poetica* was an attempt to establish dramatic rules for Roman dramatists. Instead of significant drama, Roman civilization developed sophisticated forms of popular entertainment.

The Roman theaters were usually huge outdoor buildings. Unlike the Greek theaters, all the elements in the Roman playhouses were connected, and the most significant elements were the ornate facade of the stage house and the huge raised stage. For scenic variety, the Romans were the first to employ curtains. The male actors who performed in these playhouses, in contrast to the Greeks, were professionals.

Ironically, the Roman Catholic church, which attacked the theater during the first centuries of the Roman empire, became involved in the art's rebirth during the Middle Ages. We turn to this rebirth in the next chapter.

Chapter Four

When we begin examining the Middle Ages, it is important to remember that historical divisions of history are artificial and used primarily to make it easier to discuss historical developments. In western culture the period from A.D. 500 through 1400 is referred to as the Middle Ages or the medieval period, and the years between 1400 and 1650 are known as the Renaissance (the era when the classics of Greece and Rome were rediscovered). But these dates are arbitrary: in some cases the Middle Ages are extended to 1450 or 1500, and in other cases the Renaissance is said to have begun by 1350. It is often a question of which country or which art form one is studying, because developments vary from one country to the next and from one branch of art to another. Thus, the Renaissance came to Italy before it came to France and England, and

Minstrels and jugglers *During the Dark Ages—the period between the fall of the Roman Empire and the start of the Middle Ages—musicians, acrobats, mimes, and other performers kept theater alive. This picture from an eleventh century French book (Tropaire de Saint Martial) shows one man playing a flute and another juggling. Such performers continued to perform throughout the medieval era. (Photo—Bibliotheque Nationale, Paris.)*

The Medieval Theater

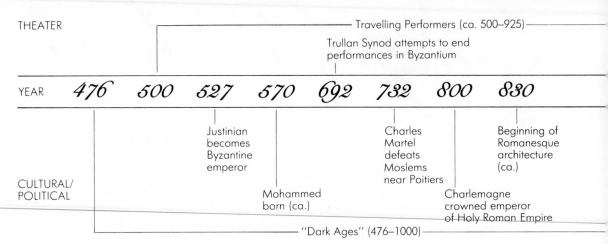

Renaissance painting had emerged while the theater was still in its medieval phase. For example, the greatest medieval drama was created between 1350 and 1550, a period when Renaissance painting and sculpture were already established. When discussing medieval theater, therefore, we will be examining a period extending through 1550, the latter part well past the time when most cultural historians would argue that the Renaissance had begun.

This overlap between the medieval and Renaissance periods points up the fact that theatrical developments often seem to lag behind other cultural developments. To suggest that theater lags behind, however, is not to demean the art form. As we noted in Chapter 1, theater is a reflection of society and is particularly concerned with people and their relationships to each other and the rest of society. It takes time for shifts in these relationships to be absorbed, and therefore it is not surprising that theater artists need time to digest and mirror societal transformations.

BYZANTINE THEATER

Before examining the changes in western society during the Middle Ages, we should turn our attention briefly eastward because of events that were occurring there. When Rome fell in A.D. 476, only the *western* Roman empire collapsed. The eastern Roman empire, centralized in A.D. 330 by Constantine in Constantinople (today Istanbul, Turkey), continued to function until 1453. Withstanding expansion by the Islamic peoples,

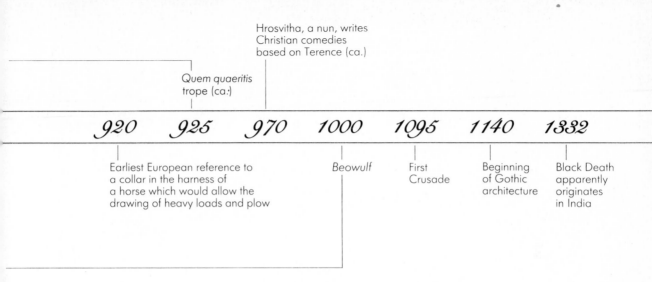

Hrosvitha, a nun, writes
Christian comedies
based on Terence (ca.)

Quem quaeritis
trope (ca.)

920   925   970   1000   1095   1140   1332

Earliest European reference to
a collar in the harness of
a horse which would allow the
drawing of heavy loads and plow

Beowulf

First
Crusade

Beginning
of Gothic
architecture

Black Death
apparently
originates
in India

Byzantium, as the eastern empire was known, synthesized three important influences: ancient Greece, Rome, and Christianity. The western world came into contact with Byzantium during the Crusades, the religious wars that were undertaken to prevent Islamic expansion. The people of the western world, however, looked on the eastern empire as an inferior civilization, and a sharp split between east and west occurred in 1054, when eastern Christianity broke from western Christianity, refusing to acknowledge the supremacy of the papacy.

The theatrical practices of Byzantium were reminiscent of those during the Roman empire. The large arena known as the Hippodrome in Constantinople was the Byzantine equivalent of the Circus Maximus and Colosseum, and the popular entertainments of Rome flourished in the east. These Roman-style popular presentations, however, are not what makes the Byzantine empire important to theater history. Rather, it is that the Byzantine empire was the preserver of the manuscripts of Classical Greek drama: the plays of Aeschylus, Sophocles, and Euripides and the criticisms of Aristotle. When the eastern empire fell in 1453, these manuscripts were transferred to the western world and became part of the Renaissance's rediscoveries of the past.

THE MIDDLE AGES IN WESTERN EUROPE

Most discussions of medieval society are concerned with western developments through the Dark Ages (from A.D. 500 to 1000), and the High Middle Ages (from about 1000 to 1400). The Dark Ages are so called

The Medieval Theater

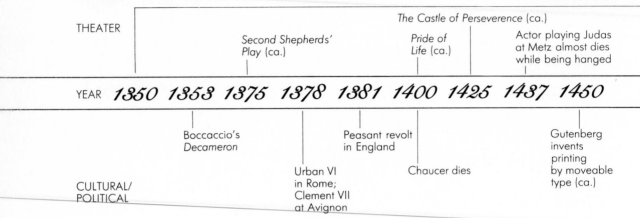

THEATER		Second Shepherds' Play (ca.)	Pride of Life (ca.)	The Castle of Perseverence (ca.) Actor playing Judas at Metz almost dies while being hanged
YEAR	*1350 1353 1375*	*1378 1381*	*1400 1425*	*1437 1450*
CULTURAL/ POLITICAL	Boccaccio's Decameron	Urban VI in Rome; Clement VII at Avignon	Peasant revolt in England Chaucer dies	Gutenberg invents printing by moveable type (ca.)

because historians originally viewed the period as one in which few cultural and historical advances were made. Most historians now argue that the Dark Ages set the groundwork for the advances made during the High Middle Ages.

During the Dark Ages, the vestiges of the Roman empire were overrun by barbarians, primarily from the north, and institutions established by the Romans were toppled; Roman towns and roadways fell into disuse. The institution that stepped in to provide a semblance of order to the chaotic society was the Roman Catholic church. As noted before, the Roman empire had been Christianized prior to its fall, and when the pagan barbarians invaded, they were converted to the new belief. The church's power was centralized in Rome under the pope; when Charlemagne became the most powerful secular ruler in Europe, during the ninth century, he was crowned emperor of the Holy Roman Empire. Secular rulers were always subject to the church's influence.

By about 1000, medieval society began establishing its own patterns of organization, and between the years 1000 and 1400 major advances were made in most areas of human endeavor. During this period, the powerful church, though frequently questioned and threatened, was ever present.

Medieval society was primarily agrarian and people everywhere were close to the land, rarely straying far from the immediate area where they were born and brought up. During the Middle Ages, the development of mechanical inventions—heavier plows, better harnesses, and windmills —made agricultural work easier. The three-field system, dividing agricultural land holdings into three parts, so that crops could be rotated and each plot could remain unplanted once every three years, prevented soil depletion and increased production.

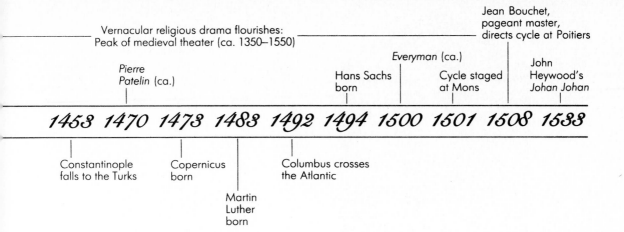

Vernacular religious drama flourishes:
Peak of medieval theater (ca. 1350–1550)

Jean Bouchet,
pageant master,
directs cycle at Poitiers

Everyman (ca.)

Pierre
Patelin (ca.)

Hans Sachs
born

Cycle staged
at Mons

John
Heywood's
Johan Johan

1453 1470 1473 1483 1492 1494 1500 1501 1508 1533

Constantinople
falls to the Turks

Copernicus
born

Columbus crosses
the Atlantic

Martin
Luther
born

Medieval society developed *feudalism* as a means of political organization. Under this system, lords, or counts, who controlled large areas of land, protected less wealthy landholders. In return for his protection, the lord's subjects, or vassals, agreed to provide military service, consult with the lord, and pay occasional fees. Under the vassals were the peasants, or serfs, who were attached to their lord's land and required to work the land. For this they received protection and a minimal return. Medieval society was the first western culture not to employ slavery on a large scale. Serfs, though bound to the land, had a better status than slaves; serfs had recognized privileges and at times could move to other areas.

Feudalism helped establish a hierarchical system of power: the counts were below the dukes, the vassals were below the counts, and the serfs were below the vassals. In France, the great lords chose a monarch. Some historians argue that the growth of national monarchies at the close of the Middle Ages developed directly out of feudalism.

During the High Middle Ages, there was a rebirth of towns due to the expansion of commerce and trade. The towns, which were self-governing units, were independent of the feudal system, and this led to a liberalizing of feudalism and possibly to the eradication of serfdom in the fifteenth century. Within the towns, merchants and craftsmen, such as butchers, weavers, and goldsmiths, organized themselves into guilds to protect their interests and privileges. (A rough parallel might be drawn to our contemporary trade associations.) Under the guilds, vocational training was organized: in order to become a master craftsman, for instance, one would have to serve first as an apprentice and then as a journeyman. The guilds controlled the number of individuals entering the professions.

Intellectual life also progressed during the Middle Ages. In the Dark Ages, monks recopied influential manuscripts, and as a result the

The Madonna Enthroned   Painted by the Italian artist Giotto in the early fourteenth century, this depiction of the Madonna and Christ child shows the strong religious preoccupation of the medieval period. It was also the era when great cathedrals were built in Europe. As in art and architecture, so, too, in drama, the focus was on religion, especially plays based on Bible stories. (Photo—Editorial Photocolor Archives, Inc.)

monasteries were the centers of learning. (In the late tenth century, a nun in a convent in Germany, Hrosvitha of Gandersheim, wrote religious plays—probably unproduced in her lifetime—patterned on those of the Roman dramatist Terence.) During the High Middle Ages, knowledge spread, and by 1500 there were over 100 universities in Europe. In the twelfth century, Western Europeans, such as the scholarly monks in monasteries, rediscovered the writings of Aristotle. Still, the "queen of the sciences" remained theology, or the study of religion, which had been the main intellectual pursuit of the early Middle Ages. A battle between secular and religious studies was developing slowly in the High Middle Ages, leading to an explosion that would occur in the Renaissance. A reflection of this struggle is found in the theater of the Middle Ages, with the nonreligious, or secular, theater forming one part, and the religious theater forming the other.

SECULAR THEATRICAL ACTIVITY OF THE MIDDLE AGES

Throughout the Dark Ages and into the High Middle Ages, the professional theatrical tradition was kept alive by wandering minstrels, mimes, and jugglers. These performers, who were attacked by the church as being pagan and sacrilegious, continued the tradition of the touring player that can be traced back to ancient Greece. Other secular entertainments inspired by festival activities, such as May Day games, were enjoyed by the conquering barbarians. The church was unable to coerce the pagans into renouncing these activities even after they were converted to Christianity.

These minor forms—indicative of the desire to keep the theatrical impulse alive—came to fruition in the High Middle Ages. Out of the festival celebrations came two forms of secular drama: folk plays, dramatizing the heroic exploits of folk heroes, and farce, which comically depicts universal human weaknesses. Secular farce seems to have also been influenced by such church-related events as the Feast of Fools and the festival of the Boy Bishop. During the Feast of Fools, young clergymen chose a bishop or pope of fools who was allowed to misuse his religious power; they also sang and danced indecently, burlesqued sermons and services, and staged plays satirizing the church. The Festival of the Boy Bishop was a similar but tamer event.

Such popular festivities, which were criticized by the church's hierarchy, contained the seeds of farce. There was something earthy and basic about these comic pieces; as a result, they had an appeal that continued for many years to come and eventually found their way into the plays of Shakespeare and other writers of his time. While most medieval folk plays have not survived on their own, several farces have, including the French play *Pierre Patelin* (ca. 1470) and the works of the German Hans Sachs (1494–1576). A popular variation of French farce was the *sottie*, which often poked fun at contemporary figures as well as social and religious concerns.

At about the same time, vagabond players began organizing into troupes and finding wealthy patrons among monarchs, lords, and merchants. The type of entertainment often presented to these patrons was the *interlude*, a short dramatic piece staged between the courses of a banquet. Rather than a theater space, a large banquet hall was employed, but European professional players, who usually toured a great deal, were accustomed to performing in such temporary improvised spaces.

With the rise of the monarchy in various parts of Europe, nonreligious court entertainments became more popular. An intriguing medieval dramatic form staged for European royalty was the *street pageant*. By the fifteenth century, allegorical, biblical, and mythological dramatizations, honoring visiting monarchs, were staged along the town route. These were pantomimed tableaux with occasional narration.

THE DEVELOPMENT OF LITURGICAL DRAMA

Given the omnipresent church, the most noteworthy theatrical activity of the medieval period was religious. We might ask how the church, which attacked the theater so vehemently in the late Roman empire and the Dark Ages, became the instrument of the theater's rebirth. We have noted that religious rites invariably contain theatrical elements, and the religious rituals of Roman Catholicism are no exception. They had many elements that contained the seeds of the rebirth. The celebration of the mass, the clergy's garb, the church space, the musical accompaniment, and the annual symbolic events—the burial of the cross on Good Friday and its resurrection on Easter Sunday—are all inherently theatrical.

Church drama seems to have developed along with changes in liturgical music. By the ninth century, extended musical passages, known as *tropes*, had been added to services; later, lyrics were appended to these passages. The mass was the most rigid of the numerous daily services and, for that reason, liturgical drama was most often interpolated into other services, such as the hours, which varied from day to day.

Medieval records tell us that one trope, often called the *Quem quaeritis* trope, was added to the introductory section of the Easter Sunday mass in the year 925. The Latin words *Quem quaeritis*, meaning "Whom do you seek?", are the first words spoken in the trope. They are the question asked by an angel when the three Marys visit the tomb of Christ. When the women reply that they are seeking Christ, the angel announces that Christ is not in the tomb but has risen. We do not know whether the trope of 925 was acted out by performers playing the three Marys and the angel, but between 965 and 975 it definitely became a tiny play. We know this because these are the dates for the *Regularis Concordia*, a book by Ethelwold, bishop of Winchester, England, describing the way the *Quem quaeritis* trope was to be performed.

It is a reasonable assumption that prior to 965—and certainly soon after—many tropes on different parts of the Bible had begun to be staged. For example, over 400 plays dealing with the visit of the Marys to the tomb have been found in various parts of Europe. By the year 1000, then, liturgical dramas, consisting of many short plays on various parts of the Bible, had been incorporated into church services. Once again, as in ancient Greece and in several countries of the orient, theater had emerged as that distinctive art form in which people impersonate characters and act out a story in front of an audience.

The Staging of Liturgical Drama

Liturgical dramas were written in Latin and presented by members of the clergy with the assistance of choirboys. At first, the presentations were staged in monasteries, but as the popularity of these liturgical plays grew in the years between 1000 and 1200, they were transferred to churches. The transfer was also made possible by the development of Gothic church architecture, which provided appropriate settings and playing areas for the dramatic presentations.

There were two basic elements employed when staging the liturgical dramas within the church spaces: the *mansion* and the *platea*. The mansion was a scenic structure depicting a locale needed for the biblical tale. The scenic units could be elaborately and specially constructed, or they could be existing areas within the church, such as the altar or the crypt. Mansions were set up around the larger playing area, known as the platea. Since the mansions were much too small to perform in, they were employed to indicate locale; once this was accomplished, the entire platea became the acting area.

The medieval convention of multiple, simultaneous settings is difficult for modern audiences to conceive of. We are most accustomed to having one locale presented at a time; if various locales are set up on a modern stage, lighting helps the audience to focus on a particular area of the stage. In the medieval church, however, the various mansions were visible at all times, with the audience having to "blackout" in their minds those not in use.

Interestingly enough, some twentieth-century avant-garde theater troupes have designed theater spaces where several playing areas have been used simultaneously. In the contemporary theater, however, this technique has most often been employed to shatter the theatrical illusion of realistic drama and force the audience to become aware of the fact that they are watching a play. The medieval theater, which was highly conventional, did not use, or need, the simultaneous settings to point up theatrical illusion. In the early English liturgical dramas, for example, males performed all roles and church vestments served as costuming. The acceptance of multiple settings was in keeping with these conventions; it was also part of the medieval world-view that all times and places were tied together in God's scheme of things.

The religious drama we have been discussing was written and performed in Latin, the language of scholarship and the church. When people attended church there were many Latin words they understood— phrases from the mass, for example, such as *In nomine Patris, et Filii, et Spiritus Sancti*, which means "In the name of the Father, the Son, and the Holy Spirit." But since Latin was not the language spoken every day, the dialogue in the plays was usually not understood by members of the audience. In order for the plays to be more meaningful and immediate, they began to be written and presented in the languages used by ordinary people: Italian, French, Spanish, English, and so forth. The term for such everyday speech is *vernacular*, and so a new form of drama emerged: religious vernacular drama.

THE DEVELOPMENT OF RELIGIOUS VERNACULAR DRAMA

In addition to the change of language from Latin to the vernacular, another important development occurred with the move of the productions of religious dramas from inside the church buildings to stages erected outside.

Historians continue to debate over how church drama performed in Latin metamorphosed, or was transformed, into outdoor vernacular drama, which began to be presented outside the churches in the thirteenth century. Though many scholars argue that the later vernacular drama developed independently, some historical connection between Latin and vernacular drama seems likely.

Among the reasons suggested for the move outside are the following: the elaborate productions were difficult to house in the churches; the cost was becoming burdensome; church officials were opposed to the employment of holy spaces for theater. Whatever the reasons, between 1350 and 1550, vernacular religious drama presented outside the churches flourished in several European countries, especially England, France, and Spain.

Two types of religious vernacular dramas were popular: (1) *mystery* or *cycle plays*, and (2) *miracle plays*. The mystery plays dramatized a series of biblical events, spanning the period from the creation to the last judgment. These dramas were distinct from the liturgical plays mentioned earlier. First, they were not staged individually but as a series presented on one occasion. (When a number of plays were presented in a sequence, they constituted a "cycle" of plays, which is how the term originated.) Corpus Christi, a spring festival meant to remind laypersons of the church's belief that the wine and bread taken in communion become the blood and body of Christ—a belief given papal sanction in 1311—was frequently the occasion for these presentations. Cycle plays were also staged during other spring celebrations.

Mystery or Cycle Plays

Since the mystery plays were written in the vernacular and staged outdoors, they were meant to appeal to large audiences and to popular tastes. Thus, they were filled with anachronisms, which means that characters and events were often presented outside the proper historical sequence. The mysteries are set in biblical times, but the characters are medieval in nature. Abraham and Isaac, for example, are not dramatized as Old Testament Jews but as medieval Christian serfs. Old Testament characters in the cycle plays speak of saints who have not been born yet. The anachronisms made the biblical characters more identifiable to audiences and also drew parallels between biblical and medieval times. Abraham and Isaac, Noah, Joseph, and the Virgin Mary were depicted as ordinary men and women just like the friends and neighbors of medieval audience members. The charm and directness of these characterizations is still evident when we read the plays today.

To further popularize their biblical adaptations, medieval dramatists highlighted the spectacular. (Modern audiences are still mesmerized by the spectacle of the Bible, as evidenced by the popularity of epic biblical films.) Comedy was also introduced as a means of making the mystery plays more appealing; Noah's wife, for example, was caricatured as a shrew. The fact that so many of the cycle plays contain farcical characters

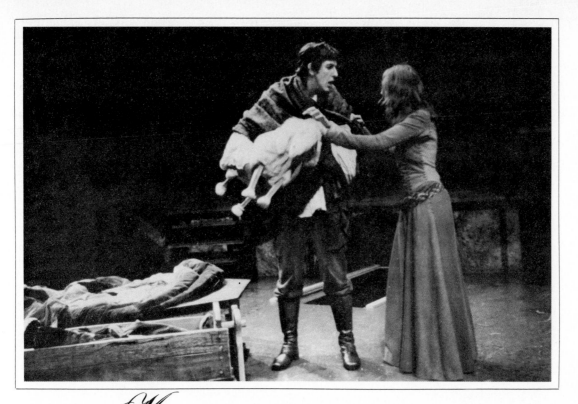

$\mathscr{M}$edieval cycle plays *The religious drama of the Middle Ages was usually arranged in a cycle of short plays based on events in the Old and New Testaments of the Bible. Seen here is a scene from a modern production of* The Second Shepherds' Play, *showing Mak and his wife. Mak stole a sheep from the shepherds who were on their way to visit the Christ Child at the manger. (Photo—Milwaukee Repertory Theater.)*

and scenes as well as anachronistic contemporary references is an indication of the secular drama's impact on the religious plays. Much of what is popular in the medieval mysteries is reminiscent of folk plays and farces.

The most renowned mystery play is *The Second Shepherds' Play* (ca. 1375) from England's Wakefield cycle. The first section of the drama comically depicts the stealing of a sheep from three shepherds by the rogue Mak. When the three shepherds search for the missing sheep in Mak's home, Gil, his wife, pretends it is her newborn child. The shepherds return a second time to offer gifts to Mak's "child" and discover that the infant is the stolen sheep. Though thievery was a capital offense in medieval law, the lenient shepherds merely throw Mak around in a blanket. The humble and just shepherds are then called by an angel to visit the newly born Christ child, to whom they bring gifts in the second section of the play. The farcical "birth" of the first section, therefore, sets the stage for the holy nativity. In addition, other parallels are drawn between the plots. The first "child" is a sheep, just as Christ is the lamb of God, and in both sections there are scenes of adoration and gift-giving.

The Second Shepherds' Play employs most of the standard dramatic techniques of the medieval cycle play. Written in the vernacular and in verse, the play is filled with anachronisms. The shepherds are characters out of the Middle Ages, not the Bible; they complain about their lords and feudal conditions, and even though Christ is not born until the close of the play, they pray to him and to various saints throughout the initial section. Though the play dramatizes the birth of the Christian savior, this event is preceded by an extended comic section exhibiting the influence of secular farce on the medieval religious drama.

Miracle plays, another popular form of religious drama, were similar to the mystery plays in dramatic technique. Instead of biblical tales, though, miracle plays were based upon the lives of saints. Though one deals with biblical tales and the other does not, mystery and miracle plays are so similar that some literary critics do not distinguish between the forms. For that matter, the term "miracle" was first used to describe all medieval drama; only in the 1700s did it come to denote a play staged on the feast-day of a saint and honoring his or her legendary feats. The most popular subjects of the miracle plays were the Virgin Mary and St. Nicholas. In England, the legends of St. George were also frequently dramatized.

A NEW FORM OF DRAMATIC STRUCTURE: THE EPISODIC

In previous chapters, we studied the first important dramatic form to emerge in the western theater, the *crisis* drama developed in Greece and Rome. The second major dramatic form to develop in the western tradition is the *episodic* form found in medieval religious drama. The dynamics of episodic drama stand in marked contrast to those of crisis drama.

The structure of Greek drama was formal and somewhat rigid. In a typical Greek play, the plot begins near the climax of the story, there are very few major characters, the locale of the action is limited, often to one place, and comedy and tragedy are not mixed in the same play. In the religious drama that began to emerge in the Middle Ages, the dynamics were quite different. In *The Second Shepherds' Play*, the action shifts abruptly from a field to Mak's hut to Christ's manger some distance away, and comic and serious elements are freely intermingled. Obviously a play about the birth of Christ should have a serious element, but the taste for earthy farce was irrepressible in English religious drama and so became a part of the dramatic mixture.

Also, in *The Second Shepherds' Play* there is not a single plot, as in crisis drama, but two separate stories that are related: Mak and the theft of the sheep, and the visit to the Christ child. Following two stories at once suggests the way these plays achieved a kind of unity and advanced a theme. The method could be called *metaphoric.* (A metaphor is a poetic device in which one thing is called something else, as in the phrase "the Lord is my shepherd"; God is not actually a shepherd, but a worshipper who feels that God is *like* a shepherd says that God *is* one.)

In medieval drama there are parallel plots and related images that work metaphorically, so that the whole becomes greater than the separate parts. Mak steals a lamb and Christ is often called the lamb of God. As we move from the story of Mak to the story of Christ's birth, we are aware of two babies and two lambs, and the echo or reverberation between these two ideas brings the parts of the drama together to create a forceful dramatic image.

Frequent changes in time and place, such as occur in *The Second Shepherds' Play,* did not bother medieval audiences, who were not concerned with a realistic or literal rendition of a story. In a series of cycle plays, the story unfolded from beginning to end and often involved a great many characters. In this form of theater, instead of the economy and compression of Greek drama, we find an expansiveness and a juxtaposition of elements. We switch from one element to another: from one group of characters to a different group; from one historical period to another; from one story line to another; from comedy to serious drama. The tension and excitement, as well as the meaning, often come from this shifting back and forth. In addition, there is the poetic unity achieved in the manner described above.

The episodic structure of the cycle plays was logical given the medieval world-view that all time was part of God's continuum. The biblical past was considered part of the medieval present; because of this, anachronisms were not seen as incongruous, nor were sudden changes in time and place. Parallels can be drawn to some of the era's triptych paintings, many of which were designed as church altar pieces, wherein three separate religious scenes were illustrated side by side in the same work of art.

This form of drama was in its infancy in the medieval period, but it became the foundation for highly complex plays in later years, such as those of English playwrights like Shakespeare and Spanish dramatists like Lope de Vega. In this way, the episodic approach to dramaturgy entered the mainstream of western drama, along with the Greek crisis form, as one of the two predominant forms from the sixteenth to the twentieth century.

PRODUCING THE CYCLE PLAYS

Earlier in this chapter we discussed the production of liturgical dramas within the church building. When we turn to the presentation of cycle plays outside the church—both mystery and miracle plays—we find that production techniques varied throughout Europe. In the continental countries, confraternities (religious guilds or clubs) were most often the producers; in northern England this function was fulfilled by the trade guilds. Frequently town councils assisted in the financing and scheduling, although the church continued to oversee the outdoor religious theatrical events. In England plays were often assigned to the trade guild that seemed "appropriate." *The Last Supper*, for example, might have been presented by the bakers (because of the bread served by Christ), the *Noah* play by the shipbuilders, and *The Gift of the Magi* by the goldsmiths. Because of the guilds' participation, the presentations were often civic and commercial events, with the cycle plays providing the trades and craftsmen with opportunities to show off their abilities.

Actors, both on the continent and in England, were amateurs. As the productions became more complex, professionals may have supplemented the amateur casts. Customs regarding the use of women as performers varied: women performed in France but were excluded in England. Due to the extensive scope of the cycle plays, doubling, with performers playing two or more different parts, was not unusual. Rehearsal time was minimal, with fewer than five rehearsals for an individual cycle play being common. Amateur actors agreed under oath to perform and were fined for missing or disrupting rehearsals. Since nonprofessionals were employed, they were usually type-cast and requested to repeat roles when the cycles were restaged. (Type-casting means that people who have certain qualities in real life are picked to play characters with similar qualities. A tough-looking man with a strong voice, for instance, would be cast as Cain, who kills his brother Abel, and an innocent-looking young woman would play the Virgin Mary.)

Cycles were usually undertaken once every two to ten years, and many of them were extremely elaborate. A passion play presented at Valenciennes, France, in 1547 lasted twenty-five days, and *The Acts of the Apostles*, given in 1536 at Bourges, France, lasted for forty days, using a cast of 300 performers.

The financial burden to the individual performer could be great, but the task was undertaken as a religious duty. If an actor, for example, was unable to attend work due to production obligations, he was forced to hire a replacement at his job. Actors also provided their own costumes, though usually this was not a burden since most characters were costumed in medieval garb. Performers were assisted in obtaining unusual costumes; for example, God was costumed as the pope, his earthly representative, while angels wore church vestments with attached wings.

Due to the complexity of these productions, a pageant master was hired to oversee all the production elements. During the Middle Ages, then, we have the first instance of a theater practitioner hired solely to supervise, much like a modern-day director.

Processional Staging

Two traditions for staging the cycle developed: (1) *processional* and (2) *stationary*. The English, Spanish, and Dutch seem to have primarily presented their mystery plays in a processional fashion while the rest of Europe chiefly presented stationary productions. Recent research suggests, however, that both forms of staging were probably used in most countries.

In processional staging, audience groups assembled in various places and the cycle play was set up on a wagon which moved from locale to locale, so that the play could be presented separately at each audience area along its route. Numerous questions, however, remain unanswered regarding processional staging in England. For example, what did the pageant wagons look like? One theory suggests that the wagon was a two-storied structure on four to six wheels, with the bottom level serving as a curtained dressing area, and the second level containing scenery and acting space. This hypothesis has been challenged, though, because such wagons would have been too large and unwieldy to move through the narrow streets of the medieval English towns and would not have provided enough area for acting.

A second theory suggests that one-story wagons carrying the scenic requirements were used in conjunction with bare scaffold carts for acting, with changes taking place in the curtained-off back area of the scenery cart. This hypothesis is based on the Spanish practice of pulling scenery wagons up to a platform for performances. However, the Spaniards employed two to four scenic carts per play.

The most radical theory argues that true processional staging was too complicated: those towns that set aside only one day for the religious theatrical event could not have staged a complete cycle at a series of locales, and since the plays were not uniform in length, it would have been difficult to coordinate a processional production. Because of these problems, some scholars argue that the pageant wagons, containing scenery and possibly actors in a mute tableau, were paraded through the town much like floats in a modern parade. The wagons were then all pulled up to a stationary stage for performance.

There may be debate about the precise form processional staging took, but there is no question that it was a major type of theater presentation in the Middle Ages, particularly, as noted before, in England, Spain, and Holland.

Stationary Staging

The second major form of production for cycle plays was stationary staging. In this form—the predominant one throughout Europe—a series of small scenic mansions stood side by side. Usually a huge platform stage was erected in an open courtyard of a town or in the town square.

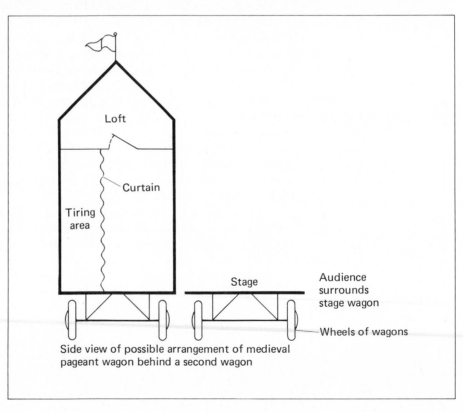

Loft

Curtain

Tiring area

Stage

Audience surrounds stage wagon

Wheels of wagons

Side view of possible arrangement of medieval pageant wagon behind a second wagon

Pageant wagons   One form of staging medieval religious plays was the pageant wagon, which could be rolled into a town or a field nearby. The wagon—or wagons—would be set up to serve as a stage, with a backstage area for costume changes. We do not know exactly how these worked, but shown here are two suggestions or speculations. At the top is a model of a pageant wagon in a town square. The wagon has a platform with a cloth covering the bottom part (from which devils could emerge). The bottom drawing shows two wagons side by side; one serves as a stage platform while the other is a place for changing costumes and hiding special effects. (Photo—the Cleveland State Univ., Theatre Arts Area; drawing based on one from Wyckham's Early English Stages.*)*

On occasion the pulpitum, or stage area, of an abandoned Roman amphitheater was employed. While the platforms were usually outdoors, smaller indoor stages were sometimes used. Scenic units—the mansions that were mentioned above—were placed side by side on the stage or, in some instances, directly on the ground. At times, the cycles were divided into sections by intermissions, some of them as long as twenty-four hours, during which the mansions could be changed and/or rearranged.

The relationship between the audience and the stage varied; occasionally the spectators viewed the action from all sides, in what was almost a theater-in-the-round, but sometimes they viewed the action from three sides or from only one. Audience accommodations were temporary: those persons closest to the stage stood, and farther back scaffolding and box seats were erected where people sat. Rooms in nearby houses and adjoining rooftops provided additional accommodations.

The most popular and spectacular mansions, representing Heaven and Hell, were placed on opposite ends of the platform, with Heaven being elevated and frequently containing flying machinery—that is, equipment to lift performers aloft. The entrance to Hell was most often depicted as the head of a monster which spewed forth fire and smoke. In between Heaven and Hell were less intricate mansions illustrating various earthly locales.

Special effects, referred to as *secrets*, were enormously popular and ingeniously worked out. Their popularity and proliferation necessitated the hiring of a secrets master to oversee the stage effects. In France, the flood for the *Noah* play (referred to in Chapter 1) was staged by storing barrels of water on the rooftop above the platform stage and releasing the water at the proper time. On stationary stages, actors impersonating heavenly beings could be "flown in" from the roofs of adjoining buildings. On movable stages, characters could be flown in from the tops of the wagons while trapdoors allowed actors to be raised and lowered. Shiny surfaces were employed to reflect light and create "halo effects," the halo being quite common in medieval religious painting and also popular in the religious theater. Between 1350 and 1550, religious drama sparked many innovations in staging.

*O*utdoor stages at Valenciennes *A popular form of medieval staging, especially on the European continent, was a series of stage areas set alongside each other. In the one at Valenciennes, France, shown here in a model, the action would move from one area to the next. At the far left is heaven or paradise, at the right Hell, and in between are other "mansions" representing various Bible scenes. (Photo—The Cleveland State University, Theatre Arts Area.)*

THE NEUTRAL PLATFORM STAGE

One aspect of medieval staging that was to have important ramifications for the theaters of England and Spain in the years to come was the concept of a neutral, nonlocalized platform stage. A pageant wagon might have a specific scenic background, and stationary settings might have mansions for individual scenes, but in both cases the most important playing area was a stage platform in front of these settings. (It will be recalled that dramas presented inside the church employed a platea—a generalized area where most of the performance took place.)

We know from the texts of many cycle plays that the action often moved from one locale to another instantaneously. In *The Second Shepherds' Play*, for instance, the shepherds are in a field one moment, at Mak's house the next, and at Christ's manger a few minutes later. In *Abraham and Isaac*, the characters are in one place preparing to go to a mountaintop, and after a few steps across the stage, have arrived there. To accomplish such abrupt, sudden transitions, the audience had to regard the platform itself as a neutral area, not a specific locale. In the audience's imagination the stage could become whatever the play indicated it was: a field, a room in a house, or a mountaintop.

As was the case with dramatic structure, this concept of stage space differs from Greek and Roman practice. Instead of a specific locale, such as the palace of Oedipus or Agamemnon, the stage was like a writing slate that can be erased: a place could be designated and then "wiped clean" so that another locale could be assigned to it. Shifts of locale could be carried in the imagination of the spectators rather than by changes of scenery, such as we sometimes have in the modern theater.

MORALITY PLAYS

Thus far in this chapter we have focused mainly on the religious cycle plays, but another important form of medieval drama was the *morality play*. The morality play attempts to teach a moral lesson through the use of allegorical characters. In allegory, people represent ideas: one character stands for charity, another for integrity, another for greed, and so forth. In these plays, characters often undertake a journey through which they learn their moral lesson. Some critics describe the morality plays as "station" dramas because the protagonist, during the journey, is confronted by a series of crises. (The connection to Christ journeying through the "stations of the cross" is obvious.)

Scholars debate whether to categorize the morality plays as religious or secular, partly because the main characters are ordinary men and

Everyman   The best known morality play from the Middle Ages, shown here in a recent production, is the story of Everyman, called to die by the figure of death. In the play, whose main object is to teach a lesson, abstract ideas become characters. Everyman tries to forestall his death and to get others to come with him, but all refuse except Good Deeds. (Photo—The New York Public Library at Lincoln Center, Astor, Lenox and Tilden Foundations.)

women rather than the saints or biblical figures of the miracle and cycle plays. Regardless of how they are categorized, the important thing to remember is that the plays dealt with moral issues and were deeply rooted in Christianity.

Everyman remains the most popular example of the morality play. The character of Everyman, obviously representing all of humanity, is told by Death, a messenger of God, that his earthly life is over. Unprepared for death and afraid to journey alone to the next world, he seeks a companion. He speaks to a number of characters, each representing an abstract idea (for example, Worldly Goods, Kin, and Beauty), but none of them will accompany him except Good Deeds. The lesson that Everyman—and the audience—learns is that only Good Deeds are of any assistance when one is summoned by Death.

One important aspect of the morality play shows up later in plays of the Renaissance, particularly in England. Frequently the basis of these dramas was a struggle between two forces, one good and the other evil, for the soul of the main character. This could be between God and the devil or between a good angel and a bad angel; the crucial factor was the battle waged between the two sides for a person's soul. In the English Renaissance, we will see this idea refined by the playwright Christopher Marlowe and developed still further by Shakespeare in several of his plays.

Returning to the medieval morality plays, though their subject is religious, by the early sixteenth century, they, unlike the mystery and miracle plays, were probably staged by professional performers. The introduction of professional actors was in keeping with the transition from the religious to secular theater which is mirrored in the morality plays of the late Middle Ages. The text of *Everyman*, however, suggests that staging techniques for moralities were similar to those for the cycle plays and used the same concept of the neutral platform stage.

THE DECLINE OF THE RELIGIOUS THEATER

The weakening of the church in the sixteenth century, culminating in the widespread Protestant Reformation, was one of the reasons for the demise of religious theater. Roman Catholicism, blaming the religious theater for weakening the church, withdrew its support, a good example being the outlawing of religious drama in Paris in 1548. On the other hand, Protestantism viewed religious drama as a tool of Catholicism and hence Queen Elizabeth I, as head of the Anglican church, banned religious drama in England in 1559. Another reason for the decline of the religious drama was that its secular qualities finally overwhelmed the religious material. The farce of *The Second Shepherds' Play* and the focus on the human struggle in the morality play *Everyman* were steps in the development of the great secular drama of the English Renaissance.

Still, the medieval religious stage—in the form of drama it developed, and in its staging practices—was to be a major influence on the theater and drama of later ages, particularly of Elizabethan England and the Spanish Golden Age. Furthermore, there continues to be a thriving religious theater in many parts of the world today. A significant example is the controversial community-staged *Oberammergau Passion Play*, which is produced annually in Germany. (Debate rages over whether the play's portrayal of Jewish characters is anti-Semitic. In the medieval cycle plays dealing with the life of Christ, Jews were often presented negatively.) While works like this one remain important spiritual experiences for their audiences, religion was no longer the central concern of most theater following the Middle Ages.

Summary

During the Dark Ages, touring minstrels kept the theatrical tradition alive. Later, the theater of the Middle Ages was reborn in the Roman Catholic church. Musical and dramatic interpolations added to the religious services grew into liturgical dramas; these plays, written in Latin and dramatizing biblical events, were staged in the churches by the clergy. In the fourteenth century, plays in the language the people spoke, known as vernacular drama, developed. Mystery or cycle plays, which depicted a series of biblical tales, were staged and acted outdoors by guilds in northern England and by confraternities on the continent.

In England, Spain, and Holland, the mysteries were usually presented on pageant wagons which probably traveled through the medieval towns. On other parts of the continent, a large open playing space, with a series of scenic mansions set side by side, was common. Miracle plays, another form of vernacular drama, presented the legends of the saints. A medieval dramatic form difficult to categorize is the morality play, which presents allegorical characters and moral lessons and was staged by professional performers.

Medieval plays employed simple, direct dramatic techniques that called on the imaginations of the spectators. There was frequent use of symbols and great freedom in shifts in time and space.

Secular theater also flourished in the Middle Ages. During the High Middle Ages folk drama and farce developed, and at the courts of the emerging monarchs, professional performers were employed. The influence of the secular theater can be seen in the farcical and folk elements of the cycle plays.

Part Two

THE THEATER OF THE RENAISSANCE

The Renaissance was an age of humanism, discovery, and exceptional art. Renaissance is a French word that means "rebirth." During the historical period known as the Renaissance—roughly from 1400 to 1650—European culture is said to have been reborn. The rebirth consisted of a rediscovery of past cultures, but equally important was a new view of human possibilities. Rather than look on human beings as tiny figures on the lower rungs of the universe, with the deity and divine beings at the top of the hierarchy, people began to regard the individual as important and having enormous potential.

A significant part of the Renaissance was the rediscovery of the Greek and Roman civilizations. For the first time in several centuries, the heritage of these civilizations—their art, literature, and philosophy—became available, largely through the rediscovery of ancient manuscripts. The achievements and ideas of Greece and Rome struck a sympathetic chord with the men and women living in Italy and France in the fourteenth century, and they hoped to create a new classical civilization to match the old.

But other things were happening aside from the rediscovery of the past. The major distinction between the Middle Ages and the Renaissance was the secularization of society, that is, the move away from religion. The dominance of the Roman Catholic church was eroded as Renaissance society became more concerned with "this world" than the "next world" (the latter being the afterlife in heaven).

There was a great sense of experimentation and discovery during the Renaissance, and the parallels to our own times are striking. The exploration of the new world during this period created the same kind of excitement as our opening up the frontiers of space. Columbus sailing across the Atlantic and claiming the Americas was like the astronauts landing on the moon, or the space shuttle leaving and returning to earth. The discovery of gunpower transformed military strategy, as the invention of the atomic bomb has done in our own day. Gutenberg's printing press opened up the world to the masses as do radio, film, and television today. There is another parallel in economics: at the end of the Renaissance, seventeenth-century society suffered from terrific inflation just as we have. The questions about God, rulers, and humanity's place in the universe which shook the Renaissance world continue to reverberate in our own time.

The Renaissance also witnessed a burst of theatrical activity throughout Europe. Such Italian innovations as the proscenium-arch theater, painted perspective scenery, the neoclassical rules for playwriting, the birth of opera, and the commedia dell'arte affected the art for the next 200 years. ("Neo" means a new, or different, form of something from the past, and thus "neoclassical" refers to the revival or adaptation in the Renaissance period of the classical practices of Greece and Rome.) The French neoclassical drama and theater of the late seventeenth century were greatly influenced by these Italian developments. While the theaters of the English Renaissance and Spanish Golden Age were distinctly different from those of Italy and France, they were no less active and innovative.

The impact of the Renaissance on the theater art is still apparent today. When we sit in a proscenium-arch theater or enjoy a Shakespearean play produced at a summer festival, we are taking part in the rich theatrical heritage of the Renaissance.

Chapter Five

THE THEATER OF THE
ITALIAN RENAISSANCE

During the Renaissance, European culture advanced dramatically, and the center of activity was Italy, which, like classical Greece, was not a unified nation but a group of independent city-states. European politics changed markedly during the Renaissance as the autocratic rule of kings and princes superseded the decentralized feudal system and the dominance of the church throughout Europe. Politics was looked on as a science by Machiavelli, an Italian author, statesman, and political philosopher, who argues in his book *The Prince* (1513) that a ruler must do whatever is necessary and practical—even if it borders on the unethical—in order to protect his subjects.

The entrepreneur, or enterprising merchant, became the key economic figure. Particularly in Italy, the merchant class grew in strength

Characters from commedia dell'arte   *The most important development in acting in the Italian Renaissance was the emergence of the commedia dell'arte, a style of presentation in which dialogue was improvised by actors around a fixed scenario, and stock characters were employed. The two seen here are Pantalone, always a lecherous miserly old Venetian, on the right, and Pulcinella, a Neapolitan servant, on the left. (Photo—Bibliotheque Nationale, Paris.)*

The Theater of the Italian Renaissance

THEATER

12 of Plautus' lost
plays rediscovered

YEAR	*1321*	*1396*	*1429*	*1434*	*1440*	*1450*	*1452*	*1469*	*1475*	*1484*

Death of
Dante

Cosmo
de Medicis
rules
Florence

Gutenberg
moveable
type (ca.)

Lorenzo
de Medicis
rules
Florence

"Birth of
Venus" by
Boticelli

CULTURAL/
POLITICAL

Founding of Platonic
Academy in Florence

Da Vinci
born

Michaelangelo born

Manuel Chrysoloras opens Greek classes
in Florence; beginning of revival of
Greek literature in Italy

and power, and as the merchants' wealth increased, they had leisure time to fill; they were also anxious to display their fortunes. As a result, a patronage system developed, in which wealthy merchant-princes, such as the Medici family in Florence, financially supported artists.

DEVELOPMENTS DURING THE RENAISSANCE

Renaissance art is quite different from the art of the Middle Ages, as can be seen when paintings of such artists as Michelangelo and Leonardo da Vinci are compared with medieval art. During the Middle Ages, paintings —such as Giotto's *Madonna Enthroned* (ca. 1310)—were concerned with religion. Although many Renaissance artists also took their inspiration from religion—good examples are Michelangelo's *David, Moses,* and the ceiling in the Sistine Chapel, and Da Vinci's *The Last Supper*—these artists treat their religious subject matter secularly. No longer are the religious personages ethereal; instead, they are human beings with whom we can identify.

Art techniques also changed drastically during the Renaissance. Paintings became more realistic through the use of new materials and techniques. The introduction of oil paints made portraits more natural, and *perspective* was introduced and refined. Perspective means that the painting reflects the way a scene looks to the human eye: objects in the distance are smaller than those in the foreground, and parallel lines—

Vitruvius'
De Architectura
published

Plays by Aristophanes
published by Aldine Press
in Venice

Machiavelli's
comic play
Mandragola (ca.)

Ariosto's
I Suppositi

Bibbiena's
La Calandria

1486 1492 1494 1498 1500 1503 1504 1509 1512 1513

Columbus
discovers
America;
DaVinci draws
a flying
machine

DaVinci's
"Mona Lisa"

Sistine
Chapel
(ca.)

Michelangelo's
"David" (ca.)

Machiavelli's
The Prince

Italian wars spread
Italy's cultural influence;
weaken her politically

such as those looking down a long alleyway—converge in the distance. With the eye of the beholder being attracted to the painting's vanishing point, perspective gives the illusion of depth; the human subjects in Renaissance art were thus placed within realistic backgrounds.

In literature, the major Renaissance movement was humanism. The humanists focused on human beings rather than the gods and were preoccupied with describing humanity and human powers. They studied and imitated the Greeks and Romans. Further, the printing press, invented in the mid-fifteenth century by the German Johannes Gutenberg, made literature available to great numbers of people, and this aided the spread of literature rediscovered from the past.

The Renaissance was also a period of invention and exploration. In a move away from the otherworldly concerns of the Middle Ages, people in the Renaissance were anxious to explore and conquer the world around them. Their sailing expeditions, which discovered many parts of North and South America and circled the globe, brought new wealth to the old world. Although the Renaissance began in Italy, other European countries initiated the exploration and exploitation of the new world. Columbus, who reached America in 1492, was sponsored by the monarchy of Spain, and Portugal led in the circumnavigation of Africa and the development of a sea route to India. The English, Dutch, and French were also successful explorers.

Scientific advances revolutionized western civilization's perception of humanity's position in the universe. The Polish scientist Copernicus,

The Theater of the Italian Renaissance

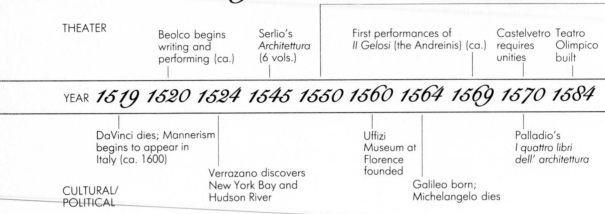

THEATER									
	Beolco begins writing and performing (ca.)	Serlio's *Architettura* (6 vols.)			First performances of *Il Gelosi* (the Andreinis) (ca.)		Castelvetro requires unities	Teatro Olimpico built	
YEAR	*1519* *1520*	*1524*	*1545*	*1550*	*1560*	*1564*	*1569*	*1570*	*1584*
	DaVinci dies; Mannerism begins to appear in Italy (ca. 1600)		Verrazano discovers New York Bay and Hudson River		Uffizi Museum at Florence founded	Galileo born; Michelangelo dies		Palladio's *I quattro libri dell' architettura*	
CULTURAL/ POLITICAL									

the German mathematician Kepler, and the Italian astronomer Galileo proved that the sun, not the earth, was the center of the universe. These men demystified the cosmos and provided mathematical formulas for understanding astronomical phenomenon. (The invention of the telescope, of course, aided in these scientific breakthroughs.) Though Galileo was condemned by many philosophers and theologians because his theories questioned long-held beliefs—and was forced by the church to recant his discoveries—his ideas eventually won out.

As a part of this general cultural and social revolution, the theater in Italy was transformed radically between 1550 and 1650. The Italian Renaissance witnessed major innovations in four areas of the theater arts: (1) acting, (2) dramatic criticism, (3) theater architecture, and (4) scene design.

ITALIAN DRAMA

As was pointed out earlier, different aspects of theater are in the forefront in different historical periods. Neither the Roman theater nor the medieval theater, for example, is noted for great playwriting, and the same is true of the Italian Renaissance. Much of the drama written during the Italian Renaissance was presented at academies (formal places of learning) or for wealthy patrons, and almost none of it left a lasting mark.

The Italians wrote comedies and tragedies based on those of antiquity—going so far as writing their early dramas in Latin—but their staid and dry adaptations never equaled the Greek and Roman originals. The Italians also imitated the Greek satyr plays—the comic, ribald short

Peak of Commedia dell'arte (1550–1650)

| Sabbionetta Theater built | Peri's Dafne | Il Gelosi troupe disbands upon the death of Isabella Andreini | Aleotti uses flat wing (ca.) | Teatro Farnese built | Sabbattini's *Manual for Constructing Theatrical Scenes and Machines* | Torelli's pole and chariot (ca.) |

1588   1589   1597   1604   1606   1618   1638   1642   1645   1650

Catherine de Medicis, Queen Mother of France, dies

Galileo dies

pieces presented as a follow-up to Greek tragedies—in a form they called *pastorals*. The subject matter of these Renaissance dramas is romance, and the characters are usually shepherds and mythological creatures who inhabit the forests and countryside, but unlike the Greek satyr plays, the Italian pastorals are not bawdy or obscene. The most famous example of these pastoral plays is Torquato Tasso's *Aminta* (1573).

The Italians also developed the *intermezzi*—short pieces depicting mythological tales—presented between the acts of full-length plays. The intermezzi, which required spectacular scenic effects, were usually thematically related to the full-length works they accompanied. Although popular in the sixteenth century, this form disappeared in the 1600s.

The Development of Opera

Opera, the only theatrical form of the Italian Renaissance that did survive, was developed at a Florentine academy at the close of the sixteenth century. The inventors of opera, in keeping with the Renaissance desire to revive classical forms, believed that they were recreating the Greek tragic style, which had fused music with drama. Though opera is quite dramatic, and for that reason can be considered part of drama, it is usually studied as a part of music. This is because the libretto, which is the text of an opera, is often secondary to the musical composition. Since most operas are completely sung, the dramatic action, the mood of the piece, and the characters are created through the songs and music. The two basic operatic elements are the aria and the recitative. An aria is a solo song accompanied by the orchestra; duets, trios, and quartets are sung by two, three, and four persons respectively. The recitative is sung

*M*oses by Michelangelo *Though Moses is a religious figure, the emphasis has shifted in this sculpture from the deeply spiritual concerns of medieval art—with heavenly figures surrounded by halos—to the forceful depiction of men and women. The painters and sculptors of the Renaissance gloried in the human figure, just as the Greeks and Romans had. Drama, too, focused on human concerns. (Photo—The Bettmann Archive, Inc.)*

dialogue. Understandably, great opera stars must be both actors and singers.

The earliest operas written by the Italians were composed for ceremonial occasions at court, such as weddings and birthdays, and were based on Greek mythology and ancient history. Jacopo Peri's *Euridice* (1600) and Claudio Monteverdi's *Orfeo* (1605), for example, dealt with the Greek myth of Orpheus, who went into the underworld, Hades, to try to bring back his wife, Eurydice.

By the mid-seventeenth century, several public opera houses had been constructed in Venice, indicating the widespread popularity of the new form.

When we turn to the modern period in opera, we might note that in addition to such works as Alban Berg's *Wozzeck* (1921) and *Lulu* (1934), the contemporary American and British musical theaters have produced shows that might be categorized as modern operas. George Gershwin's *Porgy and Bess* (1935), Stephen Sondheim and Hugh Wheeler's *Sweeney Todd* (1978), and Andrew Lloyd Weber and Tim Rice's *Jesus Christ Superstar* (1971) and *Evita* (1978) are operatic, using recitative, instead of dialogue, to move the dramatic action along. Hit songs in operatic-style musical comedies are the modern-day equivalents of arias. Because they employ popular music, these shows are more accessible to contemporary audiences than the grand operas of earlier centuries.

COMMEDIA DELL'ARTE

When we move from opera to *commedia dell'arte*—a form equally as popular as opera in Renaissance Italy—we move to pure theater. Commedia dell'arte is Italian for "comedy of professional artists." Commedia thrived in Italy from 1550 to 1750. It was not a written, literary form. Rather, commedia presentations were improvised, meaning that the performers had no set text but invented the words and actions as they went along. Scenarios—short scripts without dialogue—were written by company members, and these scripts provided outlines of the plot. Using these outlines actors created the dialogue and were expected to move the action of the comedy along through improvisation. Commedia compa-

The versatility of commedia performers   Coming out of the long tradition stretching back to Roman times and coming through the Middle Ages, commedia dell'arte performers were musicians, acrobats, and mimes as well as actors. In this drawing by Jacques Callot, we see on the left, an actress in the part of a young female lover who plays the tambourine, and the masked actor on the right dancing. (Photo—Victoria and Albert Museum, London.)

Modern commedia costumes *The strong influence of commedia dell'arte continues to the present—in comic business, in stereotype characters, and in costuming. In Pippin, the 1972 Broadway musical, costume designer Patricia Zipprodt based many of her costumes—including the half-masks shown on performers here—on the outfits and masks of commedia characters. (Photo—Martha Swope.)*

nies, usually consisting of ten performers, seven men and three women, were traveling troupes that possibly were the successors of the Greek and Roman mimes. Commedia performers usually staged comedies although there were instances when they presented tragedies and pastorals.

The conventions of the commedia dell'arte made the actors' task simpler than the requirement of improvisation would suggest. Commedia actors played the same stock characters throughout most of their careers. Among the popular comic personages were the lecherous, miserly old Venetian, *Pantalone*; the foolish pedant who was always involved in his neighbor's affairs, *Dottore:* the cowardly, braggart soldier, *Capitano;* and the sometimes foolish, sometimes sly servants known as the *zanni. Arlecchino,* or *Harlequin,* was the most popular of the comical servants. The commedia scenarios also contained serious young lovers whose romantic involvements were often blocked by Pantalone and Dottore.

Since the performers fused their personalities with those of their characters, improvisation became easier. Also, since the performers worked together, playing the same characters for extended periods of time, they were adept at creating comic interaction on the spur of the moment. All commedia characters employed standard *lazzi*, which were repeated bits of comic business. The Capitano, for example, would become so entangled in his sword that it would appear to be a ludicrous phallic symbol. (Film and television comics of the twentieth century have their own personal lazzi.) The commedia actors also employed conventional entrance and exit speeches as well as prepared musical duets.

The commedia characters wore traditional costumes, such as Harlequin's patchwork jacket and the Dottore's academic robes, so that the audiences could recognize them immediately. Another significant addition to Harlequin's costume was the *slapstick,* a wooden sword used in the comic fight scenes in the commedia scenarios. Today we use the term slapstick for comedies emphasizing physical horseplay. Masks, covering either the whole face or part of the face were also an essential element of the commedia costumes. Pantalone's mask, for example, always had a huge hooked nose. The young lovers did not wear masks.

Commedia dell'arte was enormously popular with audiences. The most successful companies were often organized by families and chose names which were meant to characterize them, for example, I Gelosi (the Zealous), I Fideli (the Faithful), I Confidenti (the Confident), and I Accesi (the Inspired). Most companies employed a profit-sharing plan, and members shared in the profits as well as the expenses and losses of the company. The commedia performers were flexible: they could perform in town squares, in unused theater spaces, in the homes of wealthy merchants, or at court. The success of the commedia dell'arte is indicated by its popularity outside of Italy, particularly in France.

The commedia's historical significance is reflected in the influence it has exerted on later theater practitioners. Commedia's stock characters, who seem to have evolved from personages found in ancient mime as well as in the plays of Plautus and Terence, were further refined by later playwrights. The miserly merchant Pantalone, for instance, is the ancestor of the avaricious Harpagon in the late-seventeenth-century French play *The Miser* by Molière, and the comic servant Pulcinello evolved into Punch in the English Punch and Judy puppet shows. The improvisatory nature of the commedia has influenced many avant-garde twentieth-century theater companies, including the politically oriented San Francisco Mime Troupe popular in America in the 1960s and 1970s.

Comparisons can also be drawn between many of the classic film comics—including Charlie Chaplin, Laurel and Hardy, the Marx Brothers, Abbott and Costello, and the Three Stooges—and the Renaissance commedia dell'arte performers. The zany films of the Marx Brothers, for example, employed many techniques reminiscent of commedia. The stars Groucho, Harpo, and Chico portrayed the same kinds of characters, with slight deviations, in all of their movies. They created stock characters, with Groucho as the unsuccessful pedantic gigolo, Harpo as the lecherous, musically inclined mute, and Chico as the conniving immi-

The Marx Brothers—modern commedia characters *These stars of stage and screen each had a distinctive outfit, walk, and other characteristics—the modern equivalent of commedia dell'arte characters. They were so well established that they are imitated by other actors: Donald Corren, Charles Janesz, Stephen Mellor, and J. Fred Shiffman, imitate Chico, Harpo, Groucho, and Zeppo. (Photo—Joan Marcus, Arena Stage, Washington.)*

grant. Much of the action and dialogue, to the chagrin of their screenwriters, was improvised. At the same time, the Marx Brothers employed standard lazzi and stock costumes. Groucho walked with a stoop and toyed with a cigar, and Harpo always wore the long trenchcoat, carried a horn, and mimed messages. Audiences enjoyed seeing the repetition of the wildly comic business of these characters as they became involved in different complicated situations.

DRAMATIC RULES—THE NEOCLASSICAL IDEALS

As we have suggested, the written drama of Renaissance Italy was not historically significant. Nevertheless, the dramatic rules formulated by Italian critics, known as the *neoclassical ideals*, were important because they dominated dramatic theory for nearly 200 years.

Francesco Andreini

Isabella Andreini

I GELOSI
(ca. 1569–1604)

The theatrical company I Gelosi (The Zealous) became the most acclaimed commedia dell'arte acting troupe in Europe through the talents of two performers, Francesco and Isabella Andreini. I Gelosi was formed about 1569 from the remnants of another noted company; after 1578, when Francesco Andreini became one of the group's leaders and married Isabella, it reached its greatest renown.

Francesco Andreini (1548–1624) acted with the troupe for several seasons before his marriage. Originally, he had played the character of the innamorato, or male lover, but then he switched to his most famous role, as the military figure Captain Spavento. As a young man he had been a professional soldier, and it is likely that this experience helped to shape his performance. Francesco was also a poet, musician, linguist.

At the age of sixteen Isabella Canali (1562–1604) married Francesco Andreini and began her stage career as the innamorata, or female lover, of the company. The leading poets of Italy and France wrote verses praising Isabella's beauty and charm, but she was as renowned for her wit, intelligence, and virtue as she was for her beauty. A Latin scholar, she also wrote sonnets, songs, and pastorals.

Friends of the Andreinis included Italian and French nobles and princes—the prince of Mantua was godfather to one of their seven children. In 1600, Henry IV of France invited the troupe to Paris for his wedding to Marie de Médicis. They stayed in Paris for four years, winning the esteem of both Henry and his queen. On the journey back to Italy, Isabella had a miscarriage, and she died at Lyons, France, where the entire city turned out for her funeral.

After Isabella's death, Francesco disbanded the troupe and retired from the stage. One of their sons, Giambattista, became a renowned commedia actor and an author.

The neoclassicists argued that they were formulating rules that would force dramatists to emulate the Greeks and Romans. They suggested that their ideals were derived from an examination of Greek and Roman models and from their interpretations of Aristotle and Horace. It is important to remember, though, that the neoclassicists were far more rigid than Aristotle and had many more rules, which they applied with greater strictness. Aristotle, in fact, did not actually prescribe rules so much as analyze what Greek dramatists had done. The neoclassicists, however, wanted to set down mandates for future playwrights. Three of the major neoclassical critics were Julius Caesar Scaliger (1484–1558), Lodovico Castelvetro (1505–1571), and Antonio Minturno (d. 1574).

An overriding concern of the neoclassicists was for verisimilitude, by which they meant drama that was "true to life." This verisimilitude, however, was not the kind of "realism" we find in modern drama, in which the characters and the situations are individualized: a real family shown in a real living room or kitchen, for example. The neoclassicists wanted stock dramatic situations and stock characters, but they insisted that these be recognizable and verifiable from real life.

The Unities of Time, Place, and Action

The most famous mandate growing out of the desire for verisimilitude was the insistence on the observance of the unities of time, place, and action.

The *unity of time* required that the dramatic action in a play should not exceed twenty-four hours. A few radical neoclassicists argued that the unity of time should be limited to twelve hours, while the most radical wanted the time of the dramatic action to match the amount of time provided for the presentation. If the play lasted two hours, the action should cover the same time period.

The *unity of place* restricted the action of a play to one locale. There were again varying interpretations of this rule; liberal neoclassicists argued that one locale permitted a dramatist to present scenes within the same general location; for example, dramatizing various scenes within the same city was allowable.

The *unity of action* (the only unity suggested by Aristotle) insisted that there be only one central story, involving a relatively small group of characters. This meant there could be no subplots, such as the one we find in Shakespeare's *King Lear*, where the story of the Duke of Gloucester and his two sons is a subplot to the story of Lear and his three daughters.

The neoclassicists also defined *genre*—a French word meaning "type" or "category"—in a very narrow fashion. Tragedy dealt with royalty, comedy with common people; tragedy must be resolved calamitously, comedy must be resolved happily. The two genres must never be

𝒞urope in the Renaissance The theatrical activities of the Renaissance spread through much of western Europe. Beginning in Italy, where important playhouses were built and rules of drama developed, it moved to France, England, and Spain. In the latter three countries—especially in cities like Paris, Rome, and Madrid—playwrights produced significant dramas, theater spaces were constructed, and acting companies formed.

mixed, and the function of all drama was to teach moral lessons. In short, all drama must be didactic.

There were numerous minor rules. Characters must act in a decorous fashion and their actions must be morally acceptable to the audience. Onstage violence was forbidden. Since the neoclassicists were obsessed with verisimilitude, they condemned several Greek and Roman dramatic conventions for not being true to life. For instance, the neoclassicists banished the chorus and the deus ex machina, and for the same reason they opposed using the soliloquy, which is a monologue through which a character reveals inner thoughts by speaking those thoughts aloud. Those authors who ignored these precepts were vigorously attacked by the neoclassicists.

As noted earlier, the Renaissance was an era in which there was a widespread desire to analyze and explain the world. Just as the great advances in science and exploration grew out of the desire to map out the universe, so, too, the neoclassical ideals came from a need to map out the workings of great classical drama. The neoclassicists believed that they were the proper authorities to discern the rules and regulations for the theater through their analysis of the rediscovered drama. It should be noted, though, that the neoclassicists were exceedingly literal-minded in applying their ideas to drama.

Despite the extreme rigidity of the neoclassical ideals, they were closely adhered to in many European countries. In France, for example, Cardinal Richelieu—the most powerful man in the government of Louis XIII—established the French Academy in 1636. The Academy strictly upheld neoclassic principles, censuring those playwrights who deviated from them. The French dramatist Corneille, for instance, was attacked by the Academy because his play *The Cid* (1636–37) seemed to ignore the neoclassical rules.

There were, of course, countries in which the neoclassicists were largely ignored—Elizabethan England and Spain in its Golden Age—but the ideals were an important influence during the Renaissance. Beyond that, they established dramaturgic rules that would be sharply debated for several centuries to come.

SIGNIFICANT QUESTIONS OF CRITICISM

Thus far we have looked at several important figures in theatrical theory and criticism: Aristotle, Horace, and now the Italian critics of the Renaissance. When we study the history of western theater, three key issues emerge which divide theoreticians. By the time of the Renaissance, all three issues had surfaced in the works of the critics mentioned above, and this is an opportune time to pause and look at these issues which continue to influence western criticism.

The first is that some criticism is *descriptive*, or analytical, while other criticism is *prescriptive*. Descriptive criticism analyzes what has gone before. Thus, Aristotle in the fourth century B.C. wrote about the Greek drama of the previous century. Modern critics who examine the works of a dramatist like Eugene O'Neill or a period like the American theater of the 1920s and 1930s are usually writing descriptive criticism. They attempt to tell us what type of drama was written, how it was put together, what it means, and so forth.

In prescriptive criticism, the writer argues for a certain point of view, sets down rules, and prescribes formulas. This approach is often referred to as *didactic*, that is, intended for instruction. Most neoclassic critics of the Italian Renaissance were doing just that: telling playwrights what they could and could not write. So, too, were the writers and theoreticians of the French Academy in the seventeenth century. In the nineteenth century, Emile Zola (1849–1902), another Frenchman, set forth a program for naturalism in the theater. Zola argued that drama must adhere closely to the laws of nature as they were understood at that time. In the twentieth century, the German playwright Bertolt Brecht argued for a theater that instructed its audience, especially in political matters. All of these are prescriptive critics.

Both kinds of critics—the descriptive, or analytical, and the prescriptive—make important contributions.

A second issue that has divided critics through the centuries moves from the nature of criticism to the nature of the art work being criticized. This is the question of whether or not drama should be didactic. The issue here is not whether critics should instruct their readers but whether the play itself should teach a lesson and be morally uplifting. Many critics feel that art need not—indeed, should not—be didactic; that art is its own excuse for being. These critics would argue that in distilling life and presenting its essence, art provides a unique mirror in which we see ourselves. If we *learn* from that—which we might very well do—so much the better, but it is not incumbent on art to teach a lesson, which is the job of teachers and clergymen. People taking this position would argue that in some cases making art didactic might distort it beyond recognition. How, for example, do you make a simple landscape painting or an abstract design morally instructive?

On the other side are critics who insist that all art must be didactic. The Roman writer Horace first raised this issue. He did not insist on instruction in drama, but he did say that entertainment joined with instruction was the best kind of drama. In certain periods—in seventeenth-century England and France—attacks were made on the theater for being immoral. Writers like Molière in France and Ben Jonson in England defended the theater on the basis that it *did* teach a lesson.

This controversy continued into the twentieth century. We have already mentioned Bertolt Brecht, and in the 1950s there was a famous debate between absurdist playwright Eugène Ionesco and critic Kenneth Tynan (1927–1980) on this question. Ionesco took the view that didacticism is not a primary function of art, and Tynan argued that it was.

A third issue that engaged critics for several centuries concerns dramatic structure. The debate was set in motion by the Italian neoclassical critics and carried forward by the French Academy. It concerns the strict rules of structure set forth by the neoclassical critics: insistence on verisimilitude and the unities of time, place, and action.

As we will see in later chapters, the plays of the Spanish playwright Lope de Vega and of Shakespeare and his fellow Elizabethan playwrights followed a different structure—the episodic. Lope de Vega wrote a spirited defense of his approach to structure, and in the eighteenth century, the German critic Gotthold Lessing questioned the neoclassical rules and praised the dramaturgy of Shakespeare.

The question of neoclassic structure raged for several hundred years, but unlike the debate over didacticism, it had subsided by the nineteenth century.

*S*tage of the Teatro Olimpico   *Completed in 1584, this 3000-seat theater in Vicenza, Italy is the oldest surviving theater from the Renaissance. The stage attempted to duplicate the façade of the Roman scene house and had five alleyways leading off the stage. The model here shows the three alleyways in the back wall; there is also one in each side wall. (Photo—The Cleveland State University, Theatre Arts Area.)*

The debates we have looked at stemmed largely from the dramaturgic rules set down by Italian critics in the Renaissance, but rules of criticism were not the only theatrical concern of the period. Theater architecture was very much on people's minds as well.

THEATER ARCHITECTURE

The architects of the Italian Renaissance revolutionized theater construction. Since much of the drama written during the Renaissance was staged at the academies, the changes made in theater architecture frequently occurred within these institutions. Three specific buildings exhibit the gradual development of Italian theater architecture, and fortunately all three buildings are still standing. The oldest surviving theater constructed during the Italian Renaissance, the Teatro Olimpico in Vicenza, Italy, was initially designed by the architect Andrea Palladio (1518–1580) for the Olympic Academy in that city. When Palladio died, Vincenzo

Scamozzi (1552–1616) completed the building in 1584. The premiere production in the Olimpico was Sophocles's *King Oedipus* in 1585.

The Olimpico was designed as a miniature, indoor Roman theater. Its auditorium, accommodating 3,000 spectators, consisted of elliptical benches connected to the scaena, or stage house; this arrangement created a semicircular orchestra. There was a raised stage, about 70 feet by 18 feet, in front of the scaena. The ornate facade of the scene house, patterned after the Roman scaena frons, was designed to appear like a street. There were five doors in the facade—three in the back wall and one on each side—and street scenes, painted in perspective, were placed behind the back openings.

In 1588 Scamozzi constructed a tiny 250-seat theater in Sabbioneta, Italy. The theater, paid for by the duke of Mantua, was erected for the Academia dei Confidenti and had only one vista, which extended from one side of the stage to the other. The vista was the perspective scenic view painted on the sides and back of the stage area. Some historians believe that the Sabbioneta single-vista design influenced the architect Giovan Battista Aleotti (1546–1636), who was responsible for the Italian Renaissance's most famous theater building, the Teatro Farnese, completed in 1618 in Parma. The Farnese had a typical court- and academic-theater auditorium, with raised horseshoe seating, accommodating 3500 spectators, and a semicircular orchestra in front of the stage. The orchestra was employed for additional seating or for flooding with water. (This spectacular practice was adopted from the Romans.)

The theater at Sabbionetta, Italy Built in 1588 by Scamozzi, this small indoor theater—which still stands—was based on Roman models. Here, looking from the stage toward the rear of the theater, we see the small semicircular orchestra, the curved, bleacher-type seating, and above that, a row of columns topped by statues. The theater at Sabbionetta is a transition between the older Roman theaters and the proscenium theaters of the Rennaissance. (Photo—Federico Arborio Mella, Milan.)

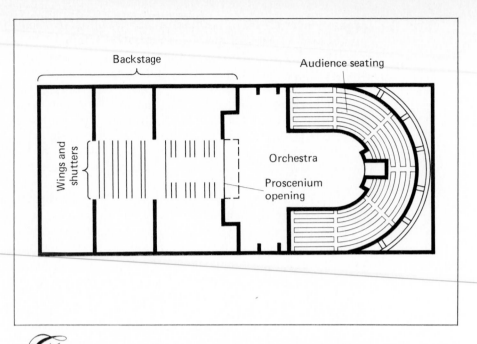

Backstage

Audience seating

Wings and shutters

Orchestra

Proscenium opening

round plan of Teatro Farnese *Completed in 1618, the Teatro Farnese was the first theater to employ the proscenium arch—the opening behind which scenery and stage machinery are concealed. (Note the large backstage area.) The horseshoe-shaped auditorium held 3500 spectators, and a semicircular orchestra was placed between audience and stage. (Based on a drawing in Theater Design, George C. Izenour.)*

What was revolutionary in the Teatro Farnese was its *proscenium-arch stage*. The proscenium-arch stage—also known as the picture-frame, peephole, or conventional stage—is still the most commonly used type of theater space. The audience, facing in one direction, views the action through the arch, which frames the stage picture. (In many modern theaters, the "arch" is not rounded but rectangular.) The proscenium hides the stage mechanisms for scene changes and special effects from the audience, thus increasing theatrical illusion. The proscenium arch, along with Renaissance scene-design innovations, was the impetus for the development of greater realism in the theater.

Why did the Italians develop the proscenium arch? Its roots have been traced to several sources: (1) the thyromata (large openings in the stage house) of the Greek Hellenistic theaters, (2) the large central portals of the Roman theaters, (3) the triumphal arches employed for medieval pageantry, and (4) the frames employed for perspective paintings during the Italian Renaissance. While its origins are debatable, the development of the proscenium arch is of supreme importance in western theater.

Along with developments in the stage arrangement, there were also changes in the auditorium where the spectators sat. The Italian revolution in auditorium design occurred in the Venice public opera houses, four of which had been constructed by 1641. Since these proscenium-arch houses were commercial ventures, and needed as many paying customers as possible, they required larger audience areas than the academy theaters. The opera houses were designed with "pit, boxes, and galleries," an auditorium style previously employed in England and Spain. However, combining the "pit, box, and gallery" auditorium with the proscenium-arch stage made the Venice opera houses innovative.

The *pit*, in which audience members stood, was the open area on the house floor extending to the side and back walls. Built into the walls were tiers of seating. The lower tiers were usually the most expensive since they were divided into separate private *boxes*. The upper tiers, called the *galleries*, contained open bench seating. The pit, a raucous area where audience members ate, talked, and moved around, and the galleries were the least expensive accommodations. The expensive boxes were frequented by the upper classes. The proscenium-arch theater with the pit, box, and gallery seating became the standard theater space throughout the world for over 200 years.

Scene Design

Advances made in scene design during the Italian Renaissance were no less impressive. Perspective drawing, which had become such an important part of Renaissance painting, was introduced into the theater. (Perspective, it will be remembered, is creating on a flat surface the sense that a scene is three-dimensional and disappears into the distance. In

Serlio's tragic setting The Italian architect and designer, Sebastiano Serlio, introduced the notion of perspective—with its sense of three-dimensionality—to scene design. In a book on architecture he set forth three basic types of settings: tragic, comic, and pastoral. This model shows his tragic setting with the scene disappearing into the distance. (Photo—The Cleveland State University, Theatre Arts Area.)

$\mathcal{S}$EBASTIANO SERLIO
(1475–1554)

An Italian architect, painter, and designer, Sebastiano Serlio is an important figure in the history of scene design. In the second book of his work on architecture, published in 1545, Serlio devoted only a small portion to the theater, but that section was to influence European theater for the next 100 years.

Serlio helped introduce the notion of perspective—with its sense of visual realism—into scene design. He also established stock settings for the three main types of drama: tragedy, comedy, and pastoral.

Before writing his treatise on architecture, Serlio had studied extensively and had worked as both a painter and an architect. The son of an Italian ornament painter, Serlio went to Rome to work with Baldassare Peruzzi, the first designer to apply the principles of perspective to the stage. In Rome he also studied the many examples of classical architecture in the city. He eventually settled in Venice.

In 1537, the year of Peruzzi's death, Serlio published the first section, Book IV, of his proposed seven-volume work on architecture. Serlio used ideas from Vitruvius, the Roman architect who was the source for classical architectural theory, and from the unpublished notes and designs of Peruzzi, but he combined these sources in a new way. He took architectural theory and fused it with detailed, practical instructions on building.

His method can be seen in the section on theater, where he tells how to construct a theater building and also how to light the stage, color the lights, make moving heavenly bodies, and produce thunder and lightning.

Serlio became a court architect, and his knowledge of his duties came from practical experience; he served many princes, most notably Francis I of France at the palace of Fontainebleau. His books were translated and circulated throughout Europe, where they became the basic texts for architecture and for stage design.

other words, it creates the illusion of depth.) Sebastiano Serlio, in *Architettura* (1545), described the earliest methods for creating perspective settings. Serlio believed that there were three basic settings for all dramas: (1) the tragic setting, showing a street of stately houses; (2) the comic setting, showing a common street scene; and (3) the set for the pastoral, depicting trees, hills, and cottages.

To create these settings Serlio recommended that a series of *angled wings*—that is, flats hinged in a fixed position and painted in perspective —be placed behind one another on both sides of the stage. Each angled wing gave the appearance of a house and included three-dimensional ornamentation. The set was enclosed in the back by either a painted *backdrop* or two painted *shutters.* To assist the illusion of perspective, the tops of the painted houses were constructed so that they slanted downward. The back area of the stage, according to Serlio, was to be *raked*—that is, slightly inclined or slanted—so that the bottoms of the wings slanted upward, thereby also aiding the illusion of the perspective. Later on in the Italian Renaissance, permanent theaters were designed with raked stages. Today, when we describe areas onstage, we refer to the area farthest from the audience as "upstage." In Renaissance theaters this area was literally "up," or higher, while the front of the stage was "down." In our modern theaters, stages are usually not raked; the seating for the audience is.

The angled-wing settings were difficult to change. Another designer, Nicola Sabbattini, in his *Manual for Constructing Theatrical Scenes and Machines* (1638), described primitive methods for scene changing, including the use of the Greek periaktoi, the three-sided scenic device mentioned earlier. By the early 1600s, however, angled wings were replaced by *flat wings.* A series of individual wings on each side of the stage, parallel to the audience, were placed in a progression to the back of the stage and enclosed at the very back by two shutters that met in the middle. The final element in these perspective settings was provided by the overhead borders—strips across the top of the stage—to complete the picture.

The method of scene shifting utilized with settings of this kind is often referred to as the *groove system.* The wings and shutters were placed in grooves on and above the stage floor. Because of the grooves, they could slide off stage easily and quickly, and a new series of wings and shutters, in place behind the initial ones, would be revealed to the audience immediately when the first set was removed. In this fashion, a number of sets were positioned one behind the other, allowing for rapid scene changes. The major problem with this system was coordinating the removal of the flat wings by scene shifters at each groove position. (Renaissance theaters had curtains, but since they were employed only at the beginning and conclusion of a presentation, scene changes were not hidden.)

One final innovation facilitated scene changing. Giacomo Torelli between 1641 and 1645 developed the *pole-and-chariot* system. Poles

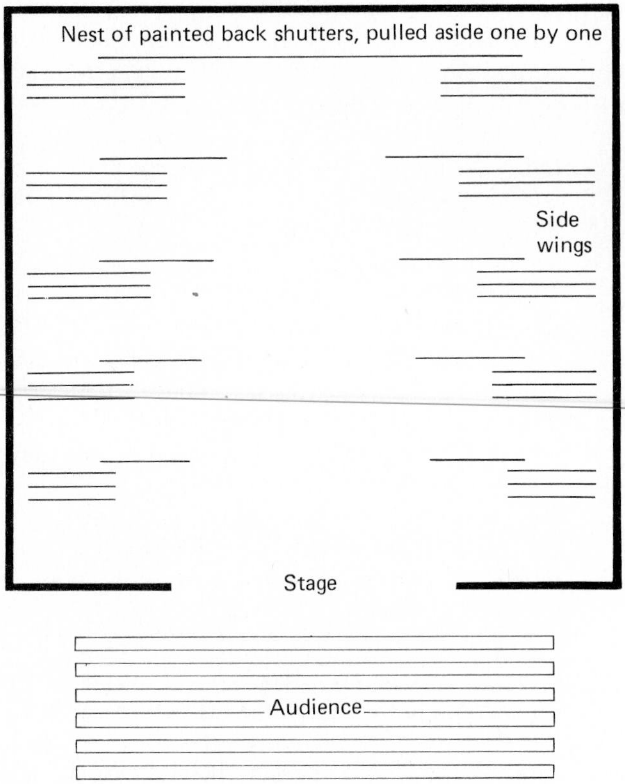

Nest of painted back shutters, pulled aside one by one

Side wings

Stage

Audience

Renaissance stage with side wings and back shutters

The groove system of scene changes During the Italian Renaissance the groove method of shifting scenery was perfected. Along the sides of the stage, in parallel lines, scenery was set in sections. At the back, two shutters met in the middle. Together, these pieces formed a complete stage picture. When one set of side wings and back shutters was pulled aside, a different stage picture was revealed.

were attached to the flats; these poles continued below the stage floor, where they were connected to wheels ("chariots") and placed in tracks. In this way, the flats could move offstage smoothly; by connecting a series of ropes and pulleys, the entire set could be removed by turning a single winch. Except in England, Holland, and later in the United States, the pole-and-chariot system was adopted widely throughout the world.

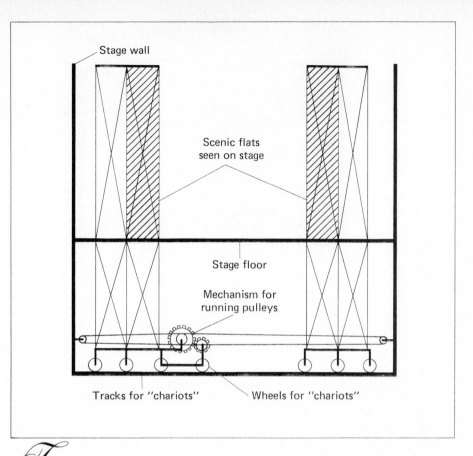

Stage wall

Scenic flats
seen on stage

Stage floor

Mechanism for
running pulleys

Tracks for "chariots"   Wheels for "chariots"

*T*he pole and chariot system   *This method of changing wings and back shutters was developed by Torelli. When a series of wheels and pulleys below the level of the stage—attached on frameworks to the scenery above—were shifted, the scene changed automatically. Because the mechanisms were interconnected, scene shifts could be smooth and simultaneous. (Based on a drawing in the Rees Cyclopedia XX, 1803.)*

$\mathcal{G}$IACOMO TORELLI (1608–1678)

For his many spectacular stage settings and scene changes Giacomo Torelli was nicknamed "the great wizard." His elaborate stage machinery and designs were influential in both Italy and France, and his method of shifting scenery became the standard throughout continental Europe.

Torelli came to the stage from an unlikely background. Born to a noble family of Fano, Italy, he was given an education befitting his rank. Though we do not know for certain, it is possible that he studied design in Pesaro and Ferrara, two theatrical centers near his home. At some point Torelli must have offended his family because he was disinherited in his father's will. By 1640, he was designing in Venice, a city that was developing into an opera center.

It was at the Teatro Novissimo in Venice that Torelli developed the staging methods that were to make him famous. Here he perfected the pole-and-chariot method of scene shifting, which allowed an entire set of flat wings to be changed by turning one winch. Audiences were astounded by the many variations of scene changes he explored with the new system. Another innovation was the occasional use of cutout flats that produced the effect of three-dimensional trees and shrubs.

In 1645 the internationally renowned designer was invited to Paris to stage an opera sponsored by the royal family. After his arrival he found that he was expected to work on the opéra with an Italian commedia dell'arte troupe. He considered this an indignity and protested to the queen, but with no success. Ironically, the opera, *La Finta Pazzo*, was a great success at court and hastened the adoption of Torelli's scenic inventions in Paris.

Though he married a French noblewoman, and staged many successful productions for the court, notably Corneille's *Andromède*, Torelli was disliked for his Italian background and for his association with Cardinal Mazarin, the king's Italian minister. When Mazarin died in 1661, Torelli was ordered to leave France. Most of his French designs were destroyed by Gaspare Vigarani, a rival Italian designer at court. Torelli returned to Fano, his birthplace, where he staged his last production in 1677 at the theater he had designed there.

Summary

The innovations of the Italian Renaissance in the areas of theater architecture and scene design have been unparalleled in the history of the theater. For the next 200 years, anyone attending a theater anywhere in Europe would be in a proscenium-arch playhouse watching the stage action from either the pit, a box, or a gallery. The scenery would consist of painted-flat wings and shutters which could be shifted either by Torelli's mechanized pole-and-chariot system or, as in England, Holland, and the United States, by stagehands who pulled them off in grooves.

The Italian Renaissance also saw the development of the neoclassical rules of dramatic structure, and of opera and the commedia dell'arte. Although the period left us few significant plays, the rigid neoclassical structural rules shaped much of the world's drama through the eighteenth century. The improvisatory actors' theater known as the commedia dell'arte remained popular into the 1700s and has influenced many contemporary theatrical experimenters.

The Italian Renaissance was more than the rebirth of the theatrical art form; in many respects, it was a period that witnessed the restructuring of the theater.

Chapter Six

THE THEATER OF THE ENGLISH RENAISSANCE

The English Renaissance, though it began later than the Renaissance in Italy, was equally explosive and led to major developments in English society, culture, and especially, theater.

THE ENGLISH RENAISSANCE

The English Renaissance is frequently referred to as the Elizabethan period, so-called because the major political figure during this time was Queen Elizabeth I, who reigned for forty-five years, from 1558 to 1603. The English Renaissance actually began during the reign of Henry VII, who became king in 1485, and ended with the Puritan takeover of

Shakespeare's comic creations *The English Renaissance saw remarkable achievements in theater. The high point in drama were the plays of Shakespeare: both comedies and tragedies. Here we see two of Shakespeare's unforgettable comic characters from* Twelfth Night: *the self-important Sir Toby Belch on the left, and his sidekick, Sir Andrew Aguecheek on the right. (Photo—Susan Cook/Martha Swope Associates, The Acting Company.)*

The Theater of the English Renaissance

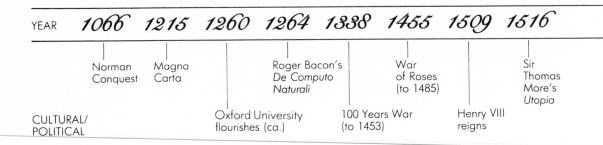

YEAR	*1066*	*1215*	*1260*	*1264*	*1338*	*1455*	*1509*	*1516*
	Norman Conquest	Magna Carta		Roger Bacon's *De Computo Naturali*		War of Roses (to 1485)		Sir Thomas More's *Utopia*
CULTURAL/ POLITICAL			Oxford University flourishes (ca.)		100 Years War (to 1453)		Henry VIII reigns	

England and the subsequent removal of Charles I in 1649; during this 165-year period English society rose to unequaled heights.

The secularization of English society, which had begun at the end of the Middle Ages, was reinforced by Henry VIII's break with the Roman Catholic church. Henry wanted to have his marriage to Catherine of Aragon annulled so that he could marry Anne Boleyn. In 1534, when the pope refused, Henry declared that the papacy no longer had any authority in his kingdom, establishing the Church of England (also known as the Anglican church) as an independent religious entity with himself as its head. The establishment of Anglicanism was part of the Protestant Reformation sweeping through Europe and cutting away at the power of Roman Catholicism.

The English Renaissance peaked during the reign of Elizabeth, Henry VIII's daughter by Anne Boleyn, and one reason was Elizabeth's ability to unite the English people. After Henry VIII's death and the brief reign of his only son Edward VI, Mary I became queen and attempted to reinstate Catholicism in England. (Because of the numerous executions during her reign, which lasted five years, she was nicknamed Bloody Mary.) Elizabeth, however, who became queen after Mary's death, strengthened the Anglican church; with the execution of another Mary, her cousin Mary Stuart (known as Mary, Queen of Scots), Elizabeth ended the Catholic claim to the English throne.

Another step in England's break with Catholicism came a year later in 1588 with the defeat of the Spanish Armada; with this victory England proved that she was not to be ruled by the Spanish Catholics. The defeat of the Armada also proved that England controlled the seas, and her naval

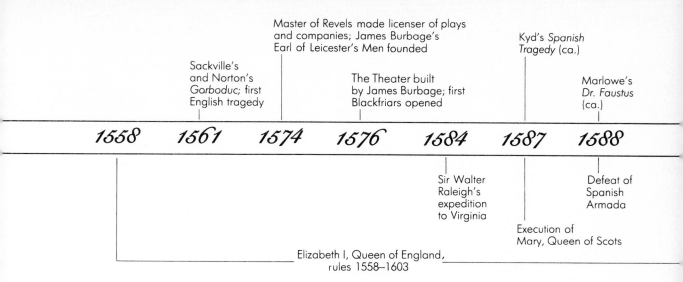

Master of Revels made licenser of plays
and companies; James Burbage's
Earl of Leicester's Men founded

Kyd's *Spanish Tragedy* (ca.)

Sackville's
and Norton's
Gorboduc; first
English tragedy

The Theater built
by James Burbage; first
Blackfriars opened

Marlowe's
Dr. Faustus
(ca.)

1558   1561   1574   1576   1584   1587   1588

Sir Walter
Raleigh's
expedition
to Virginia

Defeat of
Spanish
Armada

Execution of
Mary, Queen of Scots

Elizabeth I, Queen of England,
rules 1558–1603

superiority allowed her to take full advantage of the Age of Discovery—
the period of intense exploration of new lands—especially in the Americas.

Throughout the English Renaissance, language and literature flourished. The Renaissance in English literature was inaugurated in 1516 with the publication of Thomas More's *Utopia*, a political romance describing an ideal country. The English were intrigued by language, and Queen Elizabeth herself was an amateur linguist. But at the heart of the English Renaissance in literature and arts was the theater.

THE EARLY DRAMA OF THE ENGLISH RENAISSANCE

The development of the drama during the English Renaissance can be divided into several periods. Under Henry VII and Henry VIII, *interludes* —brief dramatic entertainments written and staged by professionals— were presented at court and in the homes of nobles. From the early 1500s through about 1580, English *school drama* flourished. These plays, written at the universities, usually exhibited Greek and Roman influence, but many medieval dramaturgical techniques were also employed. Two of the best-known school dramas were *Ralph Roister Doister*, written in the late 1530s, and *Gammer Gurton's Needle* written in the late 1550s. Both plays were rollicking comedies based on Roman models but were written in English and incorporated medieval elements.

The popularity of drama in the schools is frequently cited as a reason for the later development of boys' acting companies. These companies, composed of child actors, were first established by Elizabeth for court

The Theater of the English Renaissance

THEATER

Alleyn's Lord Admiral's Men and Burbage's Lord Chamberlain's Men the major companies in London

Second Blackfriars built by James Burbage

The Globe Theater built

Shakespeare's *Hamlet* (ca.)

Lord Chamberlain's Men become the King's Men

Jonson's *Volpone*

YEAR 1594   1596   1599   1600   1603   1606   1607

James I begins reign

Jamestown, Virginia, founded

CULTURAL/ POLITICAL

——— Continued reign of Queen Elizabeth I ———

entertainments. One of the boys' masters, Richard Farrant, convinced the queen in 1575 to allow his boys' company to give plays to the public. For these public presentations, the boys' companies used the Blackfriars Hall, a private theater space, and many major playwrights provided them with dramas.

Among the playwrights who provided the boys' companies with scripts were members of a group of dramatists known as the *University Wits*. The Wits, almost all of whom were university graduates and professional dramatists, wrote plays based on Roman models and introduced medieval elements into them as well. These crude full-length dramas paved the way for Shakespeare and his contemporaries.

THE ELEMENTS COME TOGETHER IN ELIZABETHAN DRAMA

Earlier we said that there are times in history when a number of elements come together to make important achievements possible. The fifth century B.C., in Greece was such a period, and so was Elizabethan England, when many elements—politics, exploration, literature, and learning—came together. In the same way that events combined to produce a favorable climate for the country, so they did the same for the playwrights of the period, who included not only William Shakespeare, but Christopher Marlowe, Ben Jonson, and a number of others.

Many influences contributed to the art of Shakespeare and his contemporaries. We can see, for example, important Roman influences on

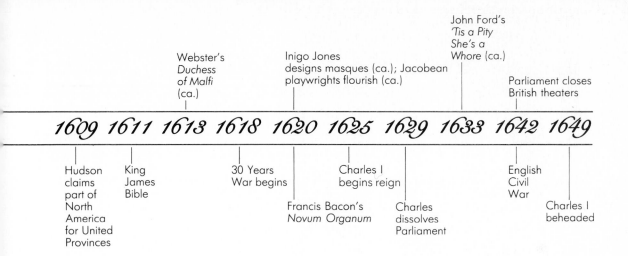

Webster's
*Duchess
of Malfi*
(ca.)

Inigo Jones
designs masques (ca.); Jacobean
playwrights flourish (ca.)

John Ford's
*'Tis a Pity
She's a
Whore* (ca.)

Parliament closes
British theaters

1609   1611   1613   1618   1620   1625   1629   1633   1642   1649

Hudson
claims
part of
North
America
for United
Provinces

King
James
Bible

30 Years
War begins

Charles I
begins reign

English
Civil
War

Francis Bacon's
Novum Organum

Charles
dissolves
Parliament

Charles I
beheaded

the Elizabethan drama. The following elements from Seneca's plays—revenge-obsessed characters, the presentation of onstage violence, and supernatural beings—were used freely by playwrights of the period. The comic plots and techniques of Terence and Plautus were also adapted by the English; as an example, Shakespeare's *Comedy of Errors* was an adaptation of Plautus's *The Menaechmi.* The Elizabethan dramatists, in some instances, employed stories from Roman and English history and also borrowed plot lines from Italian Renaissance literature. (Shakespeare, for instance, reworked stories from Italian novellas in several of his plays.)

In discussing the medieval theater we spoke of the plays in which the episodic structure began to emerge. (Episodic structure involves a number of characters and a series of scenes ranging through time and shifting from place to place.) Following this pattern, the dramatic structure of the English Renaissance was almost totally counter to the Italian neoclassical ideals. While the Italians attempted to resurrect the crisis drama of the Greeks, the Elizabethans pursued the episodic structure of medieval drama.

The English rarely observed the unities of time, place, and action, and rather than tell one story, they often employed parallel plots or subplots which related to the main dramatic action. The Elizabethans presented violence onstage and filled their plays with supernatural characters. The soliloquy, attacked by the Italians, was a popular English dramatic convention. Like the Italians, the Elizabethans featured heroes and heroines of royalty or nobility in tragedies and lower-class characters in comedies, but the English were not as rigid as the Italians about such

*P*ortrait of Queen Elizabeth   *The personality who dominated the English Renaissance was Queen Elizabeth, who reigned from 1558 to 1603. During this period, religious strife was lessened, England's naval superiority was proven, colonization of the New World was begun, and language and literature flourished. The theater, in particular, reflected the achievements of the Elizabethan Age. (Photo—Editorial Photocolor Archives, Inc.)*

distinctions. They often mixed the two social groups, and had comic scenes in serious plays. A good example of this is Thomas Preston's *Cambises*, written about 1561: in the subtitle the play was referred to as "A Lementable Tragedy Mixed Full of Pleasant Mirth."

The physical stage that had been developing in England was well-suited to the episodic plays of the Elizabethan dramatists. In the chapter on medieval theater, we spoke of the neutral space of the platform stage used for mystery plays: the stage that could become any place the dramatist designated. In the English Renaissance, this stage had evolved to the point where it was ideal for staging plays in which scenes moved freely from one place to another, and from one time to another. Thomas Kyd's *The Spanish Tragedy*, written around 1587, is a case in point. In Acts I and II, we move from the court of Spain to the court of Portugal, back to the court of Spain, then to the palace of a nobleman, a garden, and so forth.

The Spanish Tragedy was an important forerunner of later plays in more ways than one; it skillfully incorporated a number of devices that had come to the forefront during the sixteenth century, such as episodic structure, ghosts, soliloquys, and the revenge theme. The stories chosen by Kyd and his contemporaries established the material that would be used shortly thereafter by Shakespeare and his colleagues.

Marlowe and the "Mighty Line"

The most famous of the University Wits mentioned above was Christopher Marlowe, who advanced the art of dramatic structure and contributed a gallery of interesting characters to English drama. He also perfected another element that was to prove central to later Elizabethan plays,

arlowe's Dr. Faustus *The most important Elizabethan playwright prior to Shakespeare was Christopher Marlowe. Marlowe's best known play is* Dr. Faustus, *about a man who sells his soul to the devil. The Federal Theater production shown here starred Orson Welles (center) in the title role. (Photo—New York Public Library at Lincoln Center, Astor, Lenox and Tilden Foundations.)*

CHRISTOPHER MARLOWE
(1564–1593)

Christopher Marlowe was the first significant dramatist to emerge in the Elizabethan period. In his plays, including *Tamburlaine, Parts I and II* (ca. 1587), *The Tragical History of Dr. Faustus* (ca. 1588), *The Jew of Malta* (ca. 1588), *The Massacre at Paris*, (ca. 1592), and *Edward II* (ca. 1592), he established blank verse as the medium of dramatic expression and perfected the chronicle play, a historical play that emphasizes important public issues.

Marlowe's verse and subject matter, as well as some of his dramatic techniques, influenced the work of Shakespeare. *The Massacre at Paris* and *The Jew of Malta* show Marlowe's interest in exploring the Machiavellian character. *Edward II* is an exploration of the personal tragedy of a king, while *Faustus* explored the tragedy of the damnation of a human soul. All of the plays are noted for the beauty of their dramatic verse.

The son of a Canterbury shoemaker, Marlowe attended Corpus Christi College, Cambridge, on a scholarship, receiving his B.A. in 1584. He continued his studies for his M.A., though he had become a secret government agent. A letter from the queen's privy council, submitted to explain his frequent absences, thanked him for his service to the country and requested that he be granted his degree, which he received in 1587.

Marlowe's writing career began at Cambridge, and when he moved to London, he became one of the University Wits, a circle of young writers who had studied at Oxford or Cambridge. With Thomas Nash, one of the group, he is listed as coauthor of *Dido, Queen of Carthage*. His first solo drama, *Tamburlaine the Great, Part I*, was performed in 1587, and the second part of *Tamburlaine* was produced the following year. He continued as a government agent and, in 1589, spent two weeks in Newgate Prison for killing a man in a street fight.

Little is known about Marlowe's personal life, but it was said that he held unorthodox religious views and had difficulties with the law. In May of 1593, the queen's privy council ordered his arrest on a charge of atheism. Before he could be apprehended, Marlowe was stabbed to death in a tavern brawl by a man named Ingram Friser, with two government agents as accessories to the killing. Friser was acquitted for acting in self-defense. It is possible that Marlowe's death was a planned assassination because of his government activities. In any case, his death cut short the life of one of Elizabethan England's most talented playwrights.

namely, dramatic poetry. Critics speak of "Marlowe's Mighty Line," by which they mean the power of the dramatic verse Marlowe developed. As an example, the title character from Marlowe's *Dr. Faustus* makes a pact with the devil to give up his life if the devil will grant him a number of wishes. One of these is to be with the beauteous Helen of Troy, and when Faustus meets Helen, Marlowe gives him these lines to speak:

Was this the face that launched a thousand ships,
And burnt the topless towers of Ilium?
Sweet Helen, make me immortal with a kiss.

This verse is *iambic pentameter*, meaning that there are five beats to a line, with two syllables to each beat and the accent on the second beat. In Marlowe's hands, dramatic verse in iambic pentameter developed strength, subtlety, and suppleness, as well as great lyric beauty.

Another element which Marlowe developed originated in medieval morality plays. It will be recalled that in *Everyman* good and bad forces vie for the soul of the main character. This notion had become an accepted theme in English drama, and Marlowe used it in his *Dr. Faustus*. In that play, a good angel and a bad angel attempt to influence Faustus; the abstract notion from the morality plays had been incorporated into an Elizabethan full-length drama. Shakespeare built on this element from Marlowe and frequently had opposing forces fighting for the soul of the heroes. In *Macbeth*, for example, the witches and Lady Macbeth are an evil force and Banquo and Macduff's children are a positive one. In *Hamlet* the forces—the Ghost of Hamlet's father on one side and King Claudius on the other—contend within Hamlet's mind.

When Shakespeare appeared on the scene around 1590, the stage for great drama was set. He took the elements that had been established—the Senecan devices, the episodic plot structure, the platform stage, the stories from English history, Roman history, Roman drama, and Italian literature, the powerful dramatic verse—and fused them into one of the most impressive bodies of plays ever created.

Shakespeare excelled in many aspects of theater. An actor and member of a dramatic company, he understood well the technical elements of theater. His plots in the episodic form are exemplary; his verse, especially in the power of his metaphors and the music of the language, is extraordinary; his characters often seem like living people, so well-rounded and carefully detailed are they. It will help to understand Shakespeare's accomplishments if we look closely at one of his plays.

Shakespeare's *Hamlet*

Perhaps the most famous and most often produced drama of the English Renaissance is Shakespeare's *Hamlet*, written about 1600 or 1601. Just before the events in the play begin, Hamlet's father, the king of Denmark, dies. He is succeeded on the throne by his brother Claudius, who marries Gertrude, his widow and Hamlet's mother. Hamlet thinks his father died of natural causes, but as the play opens his father's ghost reveals to him that he was murdered by Claudius and Gertrude and urges Hamlet to avenge his death.

During the course of the play, conspiracies and intrigues swirl about the Danish court. In order to confound his enemies, Hamlet feigns madness. His fiancée, Ophelia, is part of a plan to unmask him: her father sets up a supposedly accidental meeting between Hamlet and Ophelia, convinced that Hamlet's behavior when he thinks he is alone with Ophelia will prove that his unhappiness comes only from loving her. Ophelia's father and King Claudius watch from behind a screen, but when Hamlet comes in, he pretends to be insane, and Ophelia is so confused by his rejection of her that she later goes mad and commits suicide.

Not certain whether Claudius really killed his father, Hamlet stages a play that proves his guilt, but when Hamlet goes to kill Claudius he finds him at prayer and does not go through with the deed. He then meets with Gertrude and accidentally kills Ophelia's father, mistakenly thinking he is Claudius. Meanwhile, Claudius has arranged with two supposed friends of Hamlet, Rosencrantz and Guildenstern, to take Hamlet to England and kill him, but Hamlet turns the tables on them and returns to Denmark. In the final scene, Hamlet duels with Ophelia's brother, Laertes; the Queen takes poison intended for Hamlet; and Hamlet finally kills Claudius just before dying himself.

Hamlet illustrates how the influences of earlier drama came together during the English Renaissance and how complex they were. Shakespeare's tragedy is reminiscent of Seneca's plays, particularly in the use of the revenge theme (Hamlet, Laertes, and Fortinbras quest after vengeance), onstage violence, supernatural apparition (the ghost of Hamlet's father), feigned and real madness, and the soliloquies in which Hamlet reveals his inner thoughts. Because Elizabethan playwrights were expected to turn out dramas quickly for the popular theater, they often adopted other dramas, literary pieces, and history. Many scholars believe that Shakespeare's tragedy is a reworking of an earlier *Hamlet,* perhaps written by Thomas Kyd; this initial version was based on a thirteenth-century Danish history and its 1576 French adaptation.

Following the tradition that had developed in Elizabethan drama, Shakespeare made no attempt to follow the structural rules set down by Italian neoclassical critics. The episodic technique derives from medieval practice. Rather than observing the unities, the action frequently shifts from one locale to another, and much time passes as Hamlet plots against Claudius. Comic relief is provided by the gravediggers; while preparing Ophelia's burial place, they joke about corpses and skulls and are generally irreverent.

But Shakespeare, like other Elizabethan dramatists, was not neces-

*H*amlet in Central Park's Delacorte Theater *The continuing popularity of Shakespeare is illustrated in the many productions of his plays staged at festivals every summer. This New York Shakespeare Festival production of* Hamlet *had an all-star cast: Stacey Keach as the enigmatic hero, James Earl Jones as King Claudius, Colleen Dewhurst as Queen Gertrude, and Raul Julia as Laertes. (Photo—George E. Joseph.)*

sarily reacting against neoclassic rules. Rather, he and his fellow dramatists were forging a new and powerful dramatic form that followed different rules. In the episodic structure of *Hamlet*, Shakespeare develops a forceful, imaginative play that has its own dynamics.

As the scene shifts from one locale to another, we move from private scenes to public ones: from scenes with Hamlet alone giving a soliloquy or in conference with a friend to scenes of pageantry in the throne room at court. Shakespeare skillfully alternates these scenes so that each section illuminates or forms a counterpoint to the one just before and just after. Also, there is a subplot in which Fortinbras, the prince of Norway, attempts to avenge his father's death by fighting the Danes, who he felt had wronged his father.

In creating the rich tapestry of his play, Shakespeare shows tremendous skill in pulling the many diverse elements together to form a unified

$\mathcal{W}$ILLIAM SHAKESPEARE
(1564–1616)

Considered by many the greatest playwright who ever lived, William Shakespeare is unquestionably the supreme dramatist in the English language.

Shakespeare was born in Stratford-on-Avon, and though he spent many years in London as a member of a theatrical company, he never neglected his ties to his hometown. Most of his land investments were in or around his birthplace, including New Place, one of the largest houses in the town, which he bought in 1597. He also used his money to pay his father's debts and restore his family to prosperity and honor.

When William Shakespeare was born, in 1564, his father, John Shakespeare, was a prosperous glover and town alderman whose wife, Mary Arden, was the daughter of a yeoman farmer and landowner. As the son of a burgess, or town official, young William was entitled to a free education at the King's New School in Stratford, an institution that prepared students for university entrance. When the young Shakespeare was thirteen, however, his father suffered business losses, so he was probably withdrawn from school and apprenticed to a trade. Town records mention William Shakespeare in November 1582, when he married Anne Hathaway, who was several years older. Their daughter Susanna was born in March of 1583, and twins, Hamnet and Judith, were born in 1585.

Shakespeare's actions and whereabouts between 1585 and 1590 are not recorded, but by the latter date he had left Stratford and was in London working as an actor and playwright.

For the next twenty-three years, except for 1593–94, when the theaters were closed because of a plague and he wrote his narrative poems, Shakespeare was a working member of a London theatrical company. From 1595 until his retirement, he was associated with the Lord Chamberlain's Company, London's leading troupe. As an actor, he favored small but significant roles like the Ghost in *Hamlet*. His duties as a company playwright probably took most of his time, for besides writing plays, he was also expected to help stage them. As a shareholder in the company and a part-owner of the theater, he was also involved with the management of the troupe.

The following are some of Shakespeare's best-known plays, together with the approximate dates when they were first presented. Tragedies: *Romeo and Juliet* (1595), *Julius Caesar* (1599), *Hamlet* (1601), *Othello* (1604), *Macbeth* (1605–6), *King Lear* (1605–6). Comedies: *Comedy of Errors* (1592), *A Midsummer Night's Dream* (1595), *Much Ado About Nothing* (1598), *As You Like It* (1599), *Twelfth Night* (1601). Histories: *Henry IV, Parts 1 and 2* (1597–98), *Henry V* (1599).

After the Globe Theater, where his plays were produced at the time, burned in 1613, Shakespeare retired to his home in Stratford and became one of the town's leading citizens. He died three years later.

picture. One way is through theme; the idea of a web of corruption and conspiracy permeates the play, and the subplot of Fortinbras seeking revenge for his father parallels Hamlet's efforts to avenge his father.

Another accomplishment is the creation of a fascinating group of characters. Probably no person in literature has been analyzed or written about more than Hamlet, and actors and audiences continue to debate interpretations of his character. Why does he behave the way he does—because he is unable to act, too melancholic, too calculating, suffering from an Oedipal complex, or some combination of these? So subtle and complex is Shakespeare's creation that the play offers no clear answer.

Still another feature of *Hamlet* is the consummate dramatic poetry. Hamlet's speeches, such as "To be, or not to be," and "O, what a rogue and peasant slave am I," are frequently quoted even today, and many phrases from the play have become part of our everyday language. Hamlet's words describing human beings at their best provide an excellent example of Shakespeare's language:

What a piece of work is a man! how noble in reason!
how infinite in faculties! in form, and moving, how
express and admirable! in action how like an angel!
in apprehension how like a god! the beauty of the
world, the paragon of animals.

Shakespeare has been rightly praised, not only for the individual parts of the play—plot, characters, language, and so forth—but for the way he put the parts together; as has been proved time and time again, the play works well on the stage.

How were plays like *Hamlet* staged in Shakespeare's day? This brings us to the subject of staging procedures and acting in the English Renaissance.

THE THEATERS: PUBLIC AND PRIVATE

If the English drama was distinctly different in structure from that of the Italian Renaissance, the Elizabethan playhouse and staging practices also developed counter to Italian practices. In the theaters that the English masses attended, the proscenium arch and painted-perspective scenery were never introduced. There were two types of theaters open to Elizabethan audiences: public and private.

The public theaters were the primary playing spaces for the professional adult companies until 1610. Between 1576 and 1642, at least nine open-air public theaters were built just outside of London. The first theater, constructed by James Burbage in 1576, was called simply The Theater. The most famous, though, was the Globe, constructed by Richard and Cuthbart Burbage, James's sons, for the Lord Chamberlain's Men in 1599. Because of the scanty amount of primary source material (original documentation), we can only hypothesize about the nature of the outdoor public theaters.

Estimates of the audience capacity of the public theaters range from 1500 to 3000. The exact shape of the building varied; some buildings are said to have been circular, others octagonal, and at least one, the Fortune, we know was square. Audiences were accommodated in the pit, boxes, and galleries, usually with three tiers of seating around the sides of the theater. One tier was divided into boxes, which were known as the lords' rooms because they were frequented by the wealthy; according to the Puritans, who attacked the theater, and who are, therefore, not totally reliable, prostitutes, on occasion, rented these spaces, thus giving the theater a notorious reputation.

During the reigns of James I (1603–1625) and Charles I (1625–1642), known respectively as the Jacobean and Caroline periods in English history, wealthy audience members sat on the stage. The undivided tiers, or galleries, were equipped with bench seating. On the house floor, in front of and on the sides of the stage, was the standing area known as the yard, and the lower-class audience members who stood there were known as "groundlings." All strata of society, then, attended productions at the public theaters.

The stage, a raised platform surrounded by the audience on three sides, was closer to a contemporary thrust stage than a proscenium arch. (There are some historians who have hypothesized that the public theaters were arena spaces, with the audience encircling the stage, but most scholars do not subscribe to this theory.) Spectators were never very far from the stage, with those in the back wall galleries approximately 27½ feet away. Trapdoors, leading below the platform, were available; the gravediggers' scene in *Hamlet*, for instance, was staged with a trap in the Globe Theater.

Behind the raised platform was the stage house, known as the *tiring house*, which functioned much like a Greek skene. The three-story building served as a place for changing costumes as well as storing properties and set pieces. The tiring house was the basic scenic piece in the Elizabethan public theaters. Exits into and entrances from the tiring house indicated scene changes.

There is a great deal of controversy regarding the appearance of the tiring house. The first level had two doorways, one on each side. Historians have maintained, even though there is little pictorial evidence, that Elizabethan drama requires a "discovery space" on the first level; this space, it is argued, is necessitated by the spectacular Elizabethan "reveal" scenes wherein, for example, a dead body is revealed to the audience. The most famous example of such a scene occurs in Shakespeare's *Hamlet*. Polonius, Ophelia's father, hides behind a curtain in Queen Gertrude's bedroom so that he can eavesdrop on her conversation with Hamlet. Believing Polonius to be Claudius, Hamlet stabs him

An Elizabethan public playhouse   *This drawing, based on a sketch from the period, indicates the kind of open air theater in which the plays of Shakespeare and his contemporaries were first staged. A platform stage juts into an open yard while three levels of enclosed seats—divided into boxes and galleries—rise above the yard. (Drawing from C. Walter Hodges,* The Globe Restored, *courtesy of W. W. Norton & Co., Inc.)*

through the curtain. When the curtain is drawn the body is revealed to the audience. Where did the actor playing Polonius hide?

Three major theories have been formulated. The least complicated suggests that Polonius stood behind one of the doors. The problem with this theory is that a highly climactic scene would be obscured for many of the spectators in the public theater. A second hypothesis proposes that there was a curtained area between the two doors leading into the tiring house. This "inner" area would serve as the hiding space. The final theory argues that an "inner" space would require a climactic scene to be staged upstage from the audience and this would have been highly unpopular, since the Elizabethans expected intimate contact with the dramatic action in their theaters. Instead, supporters of the third hypothesis argue that a "pavilionlike" structure, extending out from the tiring house, was erected between the two doors; the pavilion's curtained lower level made the staging of the reveal possible.

An upper playing area—that is, a sort of second-story platform at the back of the stage—is also required in many Elizabethan dramas. Again,

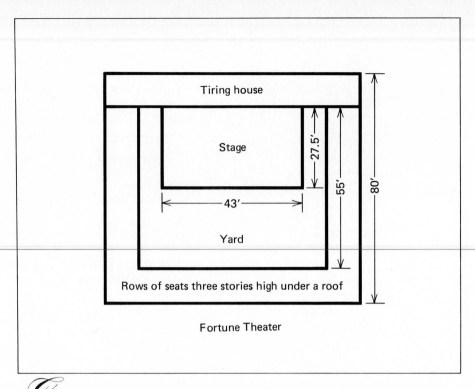

Tiring house

Stage

27.5'

43'

55'

80'

Yard

Rows of seats three stories high under a roof

Fortune Theater

*G*round plan of the Fortune Theater   *The only English Renaissance theater for which we have a number of specific dimensions is the Fortune. From the builder's contract we know the size of: the stage, the standing pit, the audience seating area, and the theater building itself. The building was square, the backstage area ran along one side, the stage was rectangular and the audience—both standing and sitting—was on three sides.*

this has led to much controversy regarding the tiring house's appearance. The best-known example of a scene requiring an upper playing area is the balcony scene in Shakespeare's *Romeo and Juliet*. Some suggest that windows above the doors were employed. Those scholars who support the "inner below" theory for reveal scenes argue for a similar "inner above" space between the two windows in the tiring house. Those who subscribe to the pavilion theory for the reveal space further argue that the roof of the tentlike edifice provided an upper playing space.

The third level of the tiring house, referred to as the musicians' gallery, probably housed the musicians providing musical accompaniment for the plays. A roof, extending out from the tiring house, protected the stage. This roof, called the Heavens or the Shadows, was supported by pillars in some theaters and was suspended from the back in others. A flag was flown from the top of the tiring house to advertise that a performance was taking place.

When we attempt to pinpoint the influences that led to the construction of the outdoor public theaters, we again see how numerous elements came together in the English Renaissance. As noted earlier, the neutral platform stage was copied from medieval practice by the Elizabethans for their episodic plays. However, the influence of the Roman theater building can also be detected in the facade of the tiring house. Furthermore, the Elizabethans were following the tradition of earlier sixteenth-century English performers, who presented plays on a platform stage with a scenic structure erected as a background at one end of an innyard. In such a temporary public theater, there was standing room in the open courtyard and galleries in the walls of the building surrounding it. Another influence may have been the bear-baiting arenas; such spaces were used for the popular English entertainment in which chained bears were attacked by trained dogs. A temporary stage and tiring house could turn the arena into a public theater.

The private theaters were indoor spaces, lit by candles and high windows. The designation "private" often causes confusion because the word implies exclusion of certain classes. In England at this time the so-called private theaters were open to the general public. They were usually smaller, however, seating about 500 spectators, and for this reason more expensive than the public theaters. The pit of the private theaters, which faced the stage in only one direction, contained backless benches. The platform stage extended to the side walls with the galleries and boxes facing the stage on three sides. Other than these differences, historians believe that the private theaters were similar to the public spaces. (There are, again, many controversies surrounding the configuration of the Elizabethan private spaces.)

SOURCES FOR THEATER HISTORY

At this point we should pause in our examination of the English Renaissance theater to discuss the reasons for the confusion surrounding the appearance of the era's playhouses. To do so requires that we become familiar with some of the problems in theater research.

In order to reconstruct past theatrical production techniques and events, historians consult primary sources, that is, materials that survive from the period under study. Imagine, for example, the kind of materials that might help scholars of the twenty-first century reconstruct the theater of the 1980s. These could include surviving playhouses, scripts, sketches of costumes, models of sets, reviews, promptbooks, contracts, autobiographies, and photographs. Of course, all sources need to be carefully examined and interpreted; future historians will have to ask, for example, whether the reviewers describing a 1980s Broadway opening had particular biases that colored their opinions, and whether to take at face value the autobiography of an actor who represents himself as having been of crucial importance in certain productions. Making such determinations about the reliability of sources is an essential aspect of the theater historian's job. History is not simply accumulating information but analyzing its validity and significance.

Few sources have survived to help us in reconstructing the theatrical arts of the periods we have already examined. Still, many can be cited. Vase drawings are visual sources for illustrating the classical Greek dramatic arts. Ruins like those at Epidauros and Delphi are essential to our reconstructions of the Hellenistic theater, and the theater at Orange in France is a well-preserved Roman playhouse. Bishop Ethelwold of Winchester left a description of the staging of the sixteenth-century *Quem quaeritis* trope, while medieval town documents reveal some of the arrangements made for producing cycle plays. Drawings by Serlio illustrate the developments in early Italian Renaissance scene design.

Of course, the conclusions about theatrical practices drawn from these materials are open to various interpretations: the sources do not tell us everything. For example, in the Hellenistic playhouses the skenes have not survived. Furthermore, in many eras, care was not taken to preserve theatrical artifacts, because the art was viewed as popular and not lasting. The ephemeral nature of the live theater, which implies that once the event is completed it disappears, means that the art work itself does not survive to be studied.

The problem of recreating the Elizabethan public playhouse is an example of the difficulties surrounding theater research. Few documents survive and controversy surrounds most of them. The principal visual source is a copy of a drawing of one of the London theaters, the Swan, done in 1596 by a visiting Dutchman, Johannes de Witt. Since what we have is not the original, and because the sketch was done by someone not completely familiar with English stage practices, there are questions surrounding its validity and accuracy. There are also interpretive battles regarding the sketch. For example, historians debate over what is depicted in the drawing as going on in the playhouse. If you believe a performance is in progress, then the conclusions you draw will be quite different from those you will draw if you think a rehearsal is being held. Another unanswered question is: Are the people in the second level of the tiring house audience members or actors?

Aside from the de Witt drawing, the contracts for the construction of two theaters, the Fortune in 1600 and the Hope in 1613, also survive. These give dimensions and other facts about the theaters. Yet they, too, can be frustrating pieces of evidence for the researcher. The Fortune contract, for example, takes for granted a familiarity with the appearance of other Elizabethan public playhouses. Often the contract calls for features of the 1599 Globe Theater to be copied, but unfortunately we do not know exactly what the Globe looked like. The Hope Theater, on the other hand, is not a representative example; since it doubled as an arena

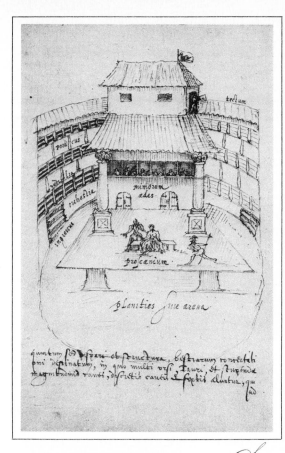

*S*ources of Theater History   *Presented here are three illustrations often used for conjectural reconstructions of the Elizabethan public playhouse. All three also illustrate the problems faced by the theater historian. The drawing (upper left) of the Swan Theater, an Elizabethan playhouse, is a copy of the sketch made by a Dutch visitor in 1596. While the sketch illustrates the platform stage, tiring house, yard, and galleries, controversy remains. Is the sketch complete? If so, where is the reveal space? Who are the people in the "gallery"? Is this a rehearsal or a performance? The illustration (lower left) from William Alabaster's* Roxana *(1630) seems to show a performance staged in the late Renaissance. The curtained space could be an "inner-below" for reveal scenes. But again, who are the people in the gallery above the stage? Also, is this actually a public playhouse, or a converted court hall? The third drawing (upper right) is from Francis Kirkman's* The Wits; or Sport upon Sport *(1972). Obviously the sketch was drawn after the English Renaissance and is therefore a questionable source. Is this a real playhouse, an imaginary one, or perhaps one from the Commonwealth period? Given the controversy surrounding sources, it is understandable that there is no definitive reconstruction of the English Renaissance public theater. (Photos—University Library, Utrecht; The Folger Shakespeare Library, Washington, D.C.)*

for bear-baiting, its platform stage and tiring house could be removed so that the yard could be cleared.

Turning to scenery, debate over the amount and complexity of its use in the public theaters often revolves around interpretations of Philip Henslowe's diary. Henslowe, along with his son-in-law, the actor Edward Alleyn, managed the theater company called the Lord Admiral's Men, and his diary contains lists of scenic pieces and props. Many of them, however, are not fully or clearly described.

Given the paucity of primary sources and their frequent lack of clarity, it is no wonder that so many debates rage over Elizabethan staging practices. This should be kept in mind as we turn our attention back to scenery and costumes.

SCENIC AND COSTUME PRACTICES IN THE PUBLIC AND PRIVATE THEATERS

Elizabethan scenic practices were quite distinct from those of the Italian Renaissance. The Elizabethans did not use painted-perspective scenery in their public and private theaters, and the stage space did not represent a specific locale. Instead, the episodic nature of the English drama required the ability to suggest rapid scene changes. This was accomplished in various ways. Spoken decor was employed; characters in the plays would describe the setting of the action, indicating that they were in a castle, a forest, or a bedroom. This is a practical reason for the lengthy poetic descriptions of locales in Shakespeare's dramas. The departure from the stage of all onstage characters, and the entrance of a new group would signal a scene change, and actors would also bring out minimal properties to suggest each locale. For example, a throne could indicate the interior of a palace in *Hamlet*. The facade of the tiring house provided a constant scenic background.

Costuming followed the conventions and traditions of the medieval English theater. While the dramas of the era exhibit a great deal of historical and geographical variety, the Elizabethans were not overly concerned with accuracy; most costuming was in the contemporary Elizabethan fashion. Even though *Hamlet* takes place in medieval Denmark, clothing in the original production would have been Elizabethan. There were, however, certain traditional costumes employed for antiquity, folk heroes, supernatural creatures, and racial groups. (Some historians believe, for example, that ancient Greek and Roman characters wore a toga over Elizabethan clothing.)

ACTORS AND ACTING COMPANIES

Throughout the English Renaissance, the monarchy exerted substantial legal control over the theater. The number of acting companies allowed to perform was restricted by law, and according to a 1572 ordinance, all troupes had to be sponsored by a nobleman whose rank was no lower than baron. All plays and companies, by decree of Queen Elizabeth in 1574, had to be licensed by the Master of Revels, a royal official. Later, under James I, only members of the royal family were allowed to sponsor companies. In return for performing for their patrons, the companies received small financial subsidies, occasional allowances for costumes (and sometimes even clothing from their patrons' wardrobes), and legal protection. The companies were named after their patrons: the company, for instance, of which Shakespeare was a member was known as the Lord Chamberlain's Men.

Elizabethan acting companies—each of which had approximately twenty-five members—were organized on the sharing plan. Under this system there were three categories of personnel in a company: shareholders, hirelings, and apprentices. Shareholders, the elite members of the company, received a percentage of the troupe's profits as payment for their services. Their fortunes, however, would fluctuate with those of the company. Hirelings were actors contracted for a specific period of time and for a specific salary, and they usually played minor roles. Apprentices —young performers training for the profession—were assigned to shareholders. Apprentices were provided with room, board, and experience, and had hopes of later becoming shareholders. Since the theaters in which many of these troupes performed were owned by the organizers of the companies, star members, known as householders, were given part-ownership in the theaters as an added inducement to remain with their organizations.

The style of acting employed by the Elizabethans continues to be debated. Some historians point to Hamlet's advice to the players as proof that the English were concerned with realistic acting. (For example, Hamlet says to the actors, "Nor not saw the air too much with your hand, thus, but use all gently.") Others suggest that the speech indicates the lack of realism in Elizabethan acting and that Shakespeare, speaking through Hamlet, is protesting its absence. Most of the Elizabethan acting conventions seem to argue against realism. There were no actresses, and young boys played women's roles. (Today it may be difficult for us to imagine that the sensuous Cleopatra and the romantic Juliet were first performed by young males.) Since the plays required huge casts, doubling of roles was not uncommon.

The rigorous performance schedule also seems to argue against realistic performances. English companies rarely produced the same play on two consecutive days, and they had to be able to revive instantaneously plays in their repertoire. Thus, their primary concern was not for a carefully realized production but for the delivery of their lines. Actors were provided with *sides,* which contained the lines and cues of their parts rather than full scripts. Improvisation must have been employed frequently. Hamlet's speech to the players suggests that comic actors

THE LORD CHAMBERLAIN'S MEN
(ca. 1594–1642)

"Hee adds grace to the Poet's labours: . . . He entertaines us in the best leasure of our life," wrote one Elizabethan in praise of actors. Elizabethan dramatists were matched by excellent actors and acting companies. The most famous company—both for its actors and its dramatist—was the Lord Chamberlain's Men, in which Shakespeare acted and for which he wrote most of his plays.

In 1594, after the closing of the theaters because of the plague, several actors who had been with other companies formed a new troupe under the protection of Henry Carey, Lord Hunsdon, who was the lord chamberlain. The group included Richard and Cuthbert Burbage, the clown Will Kempe, and the actor-playwright William Shakespeare. At first the new troupe played at the Rose, but it soon moved to a playhouse called The Theater, which was owned by the Burbages' father. It also performed at court and for special groups, like the lawyers of Grey's Inn.

When the government closed the London theaters in 1597 because of an offensive satire, it is likely that the company toured the provinces until the theaters reopened. When on tour, the company had to secure a license in each town, and this placed the troupe at the mercy of the local magistrates. In spite of the problems, the group probably toured the towns outside of London for part of each season.

In 1599, when the lease on the land for The Theater expired, some members of the company built the Globe Theater as a permanent home for an ensemble that had become the best in London. Richard Burbage, who had first come into prominence in the role of Richard III, was acclaimed the finest tragic actor in London, playing Hamlet, King Lear, and Othello. The company's repertory included plays by Shakespeare, Jonson, Dekker, Beaumont and Fletcher, and Tourneur. Their only serious rival was the Lord Admiral's Men, under Edward Alleyn, also a fine tragic actor.

In 1603, the troupe was taken under the protection of the new king, James I, and became the King's Men. Kempe left the company to dance across the Alps, and he was replaced by Robert Armin, a noted clown. Though the Blackfriars Theater became its winter home in 1608, the company still played at the Globe during the summers until it burned in 1613. The theater was rebuilt and was used by the company until 1642, when the theaters were closed and the group disbanded.

often deviated from the scripts. *Plots*, outlines of the dramatic action of the various plays, were posted backstage so that performers could refresh their memories during performances. Since rehearsal time was minimal —with rehearsals being run by playwrights or leading actors—the prompter, or bookholder, became an integral figure during the presentations.

Richard Burbage, the leading actor in the Lord Chamberlain's Men, performed the chief role in many of Shakespeare's plays and was probably the most famous Elizabethan performer. Shakespeare, as we have said, was also an acting member of the company. Edward Alleyn was Burbage's counterpart in the Lord Admiral's Men. (These two companies were the most popular in Elizabethan England.) Will Kempe, also of the Lord Chamberlain's Men, was a leading comic actor, and Shakespeare's attack on comic improvisation, found in the advice Hamlet gives to the strolling players as they prepare to perform for the royal family, was probably directed against Kempe. The Prince of Denmark warns the performers to "speak no more than is set down for them. For there be of them that will themselves laugh, to set on some quantity of barren spectators to laugh too, though in the mean time some necessary question of the play be then to be considered. That's villainous and shows a most pitiful ambition in the fool that uses it."

CHANGES IN JACOBEAN AND CAROLINE DRAMA

Queen Elizabeth died in 1603, but the great Elizabethan dramatists, including Shakespeare and Ben Jonson, continued to write plays. Ben Jonson's comic masterpiece *Volpone*, for example, was staged in 1606. In Jonson's comedy, the conniving Volpone dupes old men out of their riches by pretending to be old and dying. Volpone's servant, Mosca, promises each of them that when his master dies, they will inherit his fortune. Volpone's desire for the wife of one of the old men and Mosca's greed eventually lead to their undoing.

During the reigns of James I and Charles I, drama began to change in England. (The reign of Jamea I, 1603–1625, is known as the Jacobean period and the reign of Charles I, 1625–1649, as the Caroline.) Plays became more sensational, violent, melodramatic, and contrived than the great Elizabethan dramas. John Webster's *The Duchess of Malfi*, is probably the most renowned Jacobean tragedy. In Webster's melodramatic play, the widowed Duchess of Malfi secretly marries her servant Antonio. When her villainous brothers discover that she has married and had children by Antonio, they separate the lovers. Later, they have the Duchess, her servant, and two of her children murdered. When Antonio, who does not know of his wife's death, returns, he is accidentally killed. The couple, however, is avenged by the brothers' guilt-ridden henchman.

Another development in English drama in the early 1600s was the mixing of serious and comic elements. Such plays generally had many of

*B*EN JONSON
(1572–1637)

As a playwright, literary critic, and poet, Ben Jonson was one of the first writers in England to champion the neoclassical principles, and in his work he sought to prove that one could please the public by using these rules. Known for his sharp wit and imperious manner, he became an arbiter of literary taste, presiding over a group of younger poets which regularly met at the Mermaid Tavern in London.

In such plays as *Everyman in His Humour* (1598), *The Alchemist* (1610), and particularly *Volpone* (1606), Jonson developed a "comedy of humours" whose principal characters had an excess of one trait, or "humour." Unlike many of his contemporaries, who did not consider drama literature, he considered his plays to be important works, and he personally supervised their printing in 1616. He was also unlike other English writers of his period in championing the neoclassical structure of drama though his own plays did not always adhere strictly to the rules. His other writings include volumes of poetry, an English grammar, and, despite his preference for the neoclassical, a laudatory introduction to the collected plays of his friend, William Shakespeare.

Jonson's learning and social stature were acquired through his own efforts. Raised in a poor section of London, he was a scholarship student at Westminster School, and though he wanted to attend college, his stepfather, a bricklayer, apprenticed him to a bricklayer. To escape that trade he joined the army and served in the Netherlands, where he killed a man in single combat. He married after his return to London in 1582, but he and his wife were incompatible and lived apart from each other after 1603.

In the 1580s, Jonson continued his studies on his own and worked as a strolling player; at this time he also began writing for Henslowe's theater. In collaboration with Thomas Nashe, he wrote *The Isle of Dogs*, a satire that proved so offensive that the authorities closed the London theaters and imprisoned those involved with the production, including Jonson. He was imprisoned again in the following year for killing an actor in a duel.

When he was released, he became involved in the "War of the Theaters," using his satiric comedies to ridicule his rivals. Jonson had made many friends among the nobility, and when James I inherited the throne in 1603, the playwright became prominent at court. His collaboration on the satire *Eastward Ho!* landed him in prison again, but he was again restored to royal favor and became court poet. From 1605 to 1625, he composed the court masques, expanding the form to include an "anti-masque," a burlesque of the main theme. Jonson often quarreled with the designer Inigo Jones over the use of spectacular settings, which the dramatist felt detracted from his poetic allegories. Eventually Jonson retired, though he wrote several plays for the public theaters before his death in 1637.

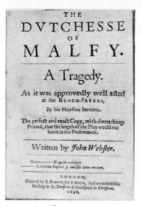

THE
DVTCHESSE
OF
MALFY.

A Tragedy.

As it was approvedly well acted
at the BLACK-FRIERS,
By his Majesties Servants.

The perfect and exact Copy, with divers things
Printed, that the length of the Play would not
beare in the Presentment.

Written by *John Webster.*

LONDON;
Printed by I. Okeswith, for I. Benson, And are to be sold at
his shop in St. Dunstans Churchyard in Fleetstreet.
1640.

JOHN WEBSTER
(ca. 1580–1630)

The most important tragic writer of the Jacobean period (1603–1625) was John Webster. In his preface to *The White Devil*, Webster shows a thorough knowledge of Latin and an understanding of drama. He also reviles most playgoers for being "ignorant asses," makes frequent use of Latin proverbs and quotations, relates an anecdote about Euripides, and praises his fellow playwrights.

Aside from the fact that he was a man of wit and learning, little is known about John Webster's life. An actor of the same name toured with an English company in Germany in 1596, and a man named John Webster was admitted to the Middle Temple to study law in 1598, and it is possible that one or both of these was the playwright. Webster's early plays, written in collaboration with Thomas Dekker, included two popular comedies, *Westward Ho!* (1604) and *Northward Ho!* (1605). *The White Devil* (1612) and *The Duchess of Malfi* (1613–14), two tragedies, are considered his masterpieces. Webster also wrote a tragicomedy, *The Devil's Law Case* (1623), and collaborated with several playwrights on other works. Thomas Heywood, the playwright, refers to him in the past tense in 1634, so it is assumed he was dead by then.

Though his life is shrouded in uncertainty, and though his dramatic output was small in comparison with other Jacobean playwrights', Webster is considered a major playwright because of his two tragedies. Regarded as the finest tragedies of that time next to Shakespeare's, both plays are passionate studies of love and political intrigue in Renaissance Italy. The dramas contain violence and horror, grotesque comedy and satire, as well as lyrical poetry. Throughout the plays there is a brooding, ominous sense of evil and corruption in the world. Because of their spectacular elements and melodrama, Webster's plays are ranked below Shakespeare's.

Webster's pessimism, similar to the mood of certain present-day dramas—black comedies and the like—is a reason for the frequent revival of his tragedies in modern times.

the qualities of tragedy but with a happy ending. Francis Beaumont and John Fletcher, two playwrights who often worked in collaboration with each other, excelled at this form.

Court Entertainments

A form of theater not found in either the public or the private theaters was the *masque,* an elaborate type of entertainment featured at court. The masque flourished during the reign of James I, Queen Elizabeth's successor to the throne. Masques were elaborate and professionally staged mythological allegories intended to praise the monarch. They were embellished by music and dance, and also frequently used amateur performers from the court. Ben Jonson was the major playwright of this form but stopped writing masques in 1631 because he believed that his literary contributions were overshadowed by the elaborate scenic trappings. While many other dramatists continued to provide scripts for the masques, the major creative artist, as Jonson correctly pointed out, was the designer.

In the first decade of the seventeenth century, Inigo Jones, a designer who had studied in Italy, began to introduce Italianate architectural and design innovations into the court masques. Temporary proscenium arches, wing-and-shutter settings, painted-perspective designs, and the groove system were, by the 1630s, employed at court. These were the only instances of these Italian scenic developments in England prior to

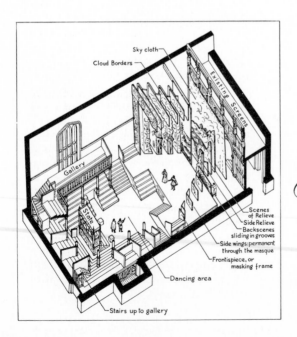

*I*nigo Jones' design for the masque *Florimene* (1635) *This conjectural reconstruction shows the Banqueting Hall in the Whitehall Palace arranged for the presentation of a court masque. Italianate scenic devices were introduced into these spectacles. Painted wings and shutters shifted in grooves were employed to complete the illusion of perspective. (Photo—Richard Leacroft,* The Development of the English Playhouse.)

*F*RANCIS BEAUMONT
(ca. 1584–1616)

*J*OHN FLETCHER
(1579–1625)

During the English Renaissance there were many well-known writing teams, but the most famous collaborators were Francis Beaumont and John Fletcher. At one time fifty-two plays were attributed to the joint authorship of Beaumont and Fletcher, but subsequent scholarship has shown that the two collaborated on no more than nine plays. The other plays were written by each man individually or with another playwright, but they are so similar in style and subject that the names of the two playwrights are invariably linked to them.

In their collaboration on plays like *Philaster* (ca. 1610) and *A King and No King* (ca. 1611), Beaumont and Fletcher accelerated the development of tragicomedy, a genre that focused on serious themes but called for a happy ending. Jacobean theater audiences were becoming increasingly aristocratic and demanded romance and witty satire. The two men wrote plays in the ornate, superficial, and somewhat artificial style that was popular and later influential, especially during the Restoration.

The two playwrights came from similar upper-class family backgrounds. Beaumont was the son of a justice of common pleas while Fletcher's father was president of a college at Cambridge and later bishop of Bristol and of London. Both playwrights attended college, but neither completed his degree. Beaumont also entered the Inner Temple in 1600 to study law. The names of the two men are first linked in 1607 in the introductory remarks to Jonson's *Volpone*. During their partnership they supposedly roomed together in Bankside, where they shared everything, including clothes and women.

Beaumont's marriage in 1613 ended the partnership. His most famous solo play is *The Knight of the Burning Pestle*, a comedy and literary burlesque. He died in 1616. Fletcher, after the breaking of the partnership, collaborated with several other playwrights, chiefly Philip Massinger. Shakespeare and Fletcher worked together on *Two Noble Kinsmen* (1613) and *Henry VIII* (1613). Upon Shakespeare's retirement, Fletcher became chief dramatist for the King's Men until his death in 1625.

$\mathcal{I}$NIGO JONES
(1573–1652)

The English theater that flourished in the Elizabethan and Jacobean periods followed scenic practices that had evolved from the medieval theater. It was Inigo Jones, court architect and designer for both James I and Charles I, who brought the Italian innovations in scene design to England. These included temporary proscenium (picture-frame) arches, systems for changing scenery, and painted-perspective stage sets. In his settings for the court masques Jones introduced the methods of staging that were to become standard after the Restoration.

Jones's designs were influenced by the works of Parigi and Palladio, which he had studied on his visits to Italy. Though he was the son of a London cloth worker and therefore not wealthy, he had traveled to Italy by 1603 to learn painting and design. He became a portrait painter for Christian IV of Denmark before a commission from the king's sister, Queen Anne of England, brought him to the court of James I. His first stage designs were the scenery and costumes for *The Masque of Blackness* (1605), which also began his long and stormy collaboration with the court poet Ben Jonson.

By 1610, Jones had become surveyor of works to Henry, prince of Wales, but Henry died in 1612, and the designer lost his job. He returned to Italy to study in 1613–14 and on his return was appointed surveyor of works to the king, a position that involved the building, rebuilding, and improvement of royal houses. In 1619–22 Jones built the Banqueting House at Whitehall as a home for the court masques, but it was not used for this purpose because King Charles did not want his ceiling ruined by torch smoke. Jones's restoration of St. Paul's Cathedral influenced the architect Sir Christopher Wren and laid the foundation for the English classical school of architecture.

Jones was vain and dictatorial, though an able administrator. His famous quarrel with Jonson resulted in the poet's loss of favor at court, and scenic splendors became the chief purpose of the masque, culminating in the wonders of *Salmacida Spolia* in 1640.

Political troubles caused the suspension of the masques after that date, and Jones then served the king as a designer of field arms and armor during the civil war. Captured in 1645, Jones was stripped of his estate and imprisoned, but he was released later and his property was restored. He died in 1652. Four hundred and fifty of Jones's drawings for the masques remain, and they have been published, most recently, in a two-volume work.

1642. The pole-and-chariot scene-shifting system, however, was not introduced.

The English Renaissance Ends

Though Charles I was not deposed—and beheaded—until 1649, the English Renaissance ended in 1642, for by then the civil war between supporters of Charles I and the Puritan-backed Parliament had begun. From 1649 through 1660, England was ruled not by a monarch but by Oliver Cromwell and his Puritan followers. When Cromwell died in 1658, his son took control of the English government.

The Puritans were violently opposed to the theater; they believed that playgoing was an inappropriate way to spend one's leisure time and that the theater, as a den of iniquity, taught immorality. Not surprisingly then, in 1642 the Puritans outlawed all theatrical activities. While surreptitious entertainments were staged between 1642 and 1660, the vital theater of the English Renaissance came to an end. Not until the restoration of the monarchy was the English theater to flourish again.

Summary

The English Renaissance was as theatrically rich as the Italian Renaissance. The greatness of this era was based on the development of brilliant drama: some critics believe that the plays of Christopher Marlowe, William Shakespeare, and Ben Jonson have been unequaled in the history of the theater. The English plays did not follow neoclassical principles but refined the episodic structure which had originated in the Middle Ages.

The imaginative staging techniques of the English Renaissance drama were also a refinement of medieval conventions. The Elizabethan theater, with its open platform stage and tiring house, allowed for rapid scenic transformations through the use of language and properties, as well as entrances and exits. There were two types of playhouses: the larger, outdoor public theaters, and the more expensive, indoor private theaters. Many of the performers, all of whom were male, were greatly renowned; they included Edward Alleyn, of the Lord Admiral's Men, and Richard Burbage, of the Lord Chamberlain's Men.

English theaters open to the public did not employ Italian staging practices such as the proscenium arch and painted-perspective wing-and-shutter scenery. These scenic innovations were introduced into the court entertainments designed by Inigo Jones for James I and Charles I.

Chapter Seven

THE THEATERS OF THE SPANISH GOLDEN AGE AND NEOCLASSICAL FRANCE

During the sixteenth and seventeenth centuries, Italy and England offered contrasting styles of production and playwriting. The Italian theater featured painted scenery and plays influenced by the classical tradition, stressing the unities of time, place, and action. England, however, featured the neutral platform stage and an episodic play structure derived from medieval theater conventions.

These same contrasting styles show up as well in France and Spain. The Renaissance in Spain, dating from about 1550 to 1650, is usually referred to as the Spanish Golden Age. The theater and drama of the Golden Age, like that of Elizabethan England, refined medieval practices, and while historians cannot point to a direct influence, the drama and theater of the Spanish Golden Age and of the English Renaissance are

The Miser by Molière *The most famous comic playwright of the French Renaissance—and one of the best comic playwrights of all time—was Molière. He was particularly masterful at creating characters who carried an idea or an obsession to excess. Here is a good example: the miser clutching his money box to his breast. The actor in this Lincoln Center Repertory production is Robert Symonds. (Photo—Martha Swope.)*

The Theater of the Spanish Golden Age

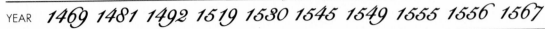

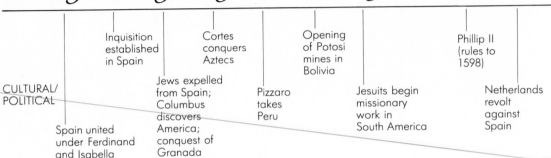

THEATER					Lope de Rueda, Spain's first popular playwright (ca.)		City Councils assume responsibilities for the staging of autos (ca.)		

YEAR *1469 1481 1492 1519 1530 1545 1549 1555 1556 1567*

CULTURAL/ POLITICAL	Inquisition established in Spain	Cortes conquers Aztecs	Opening of Potosi mines in Bolivia			Phillip II (rules to 1598)		
	Jews expelled from Spain; Columbus discovers America; conquest of Granada	Pizzaro takes Peru		Jesuits begin missionary work in South America		Netherlands revolt against Spain		
Spain united under Ferdinand and Isabella								

remarkably similar. On the other hand, the French neoclassical drama and theater, dating from approximately 1600 to 1700, were influenced directly by Italian neoclassical practices.

SPAIN IN THE GOLDEN AGE

As in other European countries, the societies of both Spain and France underwent major transformations during this period. In the late fifteenth century, King Ferdinand and Queen Isabella unified Spain and provided political stability, thereby setting the stage for the Spanish Renaissance. During the Spanish Golden Age, Spain became a leading world power, primarily due to her exploration and conquest of the new world. Spain was a naval power to be reckoned with. (Because Spain was so powerful, England's defeat of the Spanish Armada in 1558 was regarded as a major shift in the balance of power, and thereafter England's naval might was dominant.) Spain also remained a devoutly Catholic nation in the face of ths Protestant Reformation, which had swept much of the rest of Europe. In order to keep Spain Catholic, the church instituted the Inquisition, a type of court that investigated and punished any seeming heresy and any religious lapses among converts to Catholicism and their descendants.

In 1492, the same year that Columbus discovered America, Isabella and Ferdinand ordered the expulsion of the Jews of Spain and several years later of the Moors. The Moors, who were Moslems, were the descendants

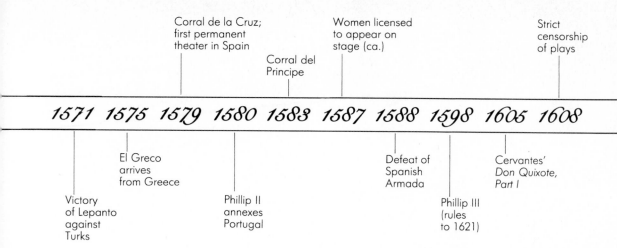

1571 1575 1579 1580 1583 1587 1588 1598 1605 1608

Above the timeline:

Corral de la Cruz; first permanent theater in Spain

Corral del Principe

Women licensed to appear on stage (ca.)

Strict censorship of plays

Below the timeline:

El Greco arrives from Greece

Victory of Lepanto against Turks

Phillip II annexes Portugal

Defeat of Spanish Armada

Phillip III (rules to 1621)

Cervantes' *Don Quixote, Part I*

of the North African tribes that had conquered much of Spain in the eighth century. After the Catholic reconquest it was felt that they were still potential enemies. The Jews were culturally and ethnically no different from Christian Spaniards, but since they were not Catholics, they were detracting from the country's goal of total religious unanimity. The expulsion of the Moors and Jews resulted in Spain's losing some of her most notable doctors, philosophers, merchants, and scholars.

SPANISH THEATER

Most theater historians compare the drama and theater of the Spanish Golden Age to that of Elizabethan England. Unlike the English, however, the Spaniards not only adopted the techniques of the medieval religious dramas but continued to produce these dramas throughout the Golden Age and beyond: until 1765, in fact. (In the town of Elche in Spain, a mystery play telling the story of the death and assumption of the Virgin Mary is still performed in the basilica by the townspeople during a festival each August. This mystery has been performed by the people of Elche continuously from the fifteenth century.)

From about 1550 the Spanish religious dramas were written and produced by professionals and funded by local municipalities, and as time went by, the line between religious and secular professional theater became less and less pronounced.

The Theater of the Spanish Golden Age

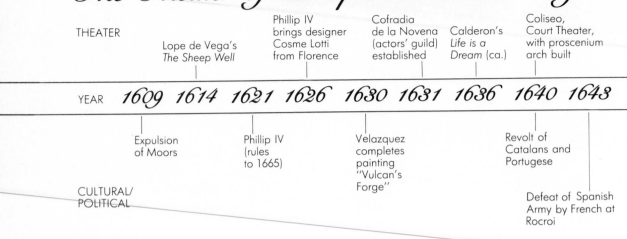

THEATER		Lope de Vega's *The Sheep Well*		Phillip IV brings designer Cosme Lotti from Florence		Cofradia de la Novena (actors' guild) established	Calderon's *Life is a Dream* (ca.)		Coliseo, Court Theater, with proscenium arch built	
YEAR	*1609*	*1614*	*1621*	*1626*	*1630*	*1631*	*1636*	*1640*	*1643*
CULTURAL/ POLITICAL		Expulsion of Moors		Phillip IV (rules to 1665)		Velazquez completes painting "Vulcan's Forge"		Revolt of Catalans and Portugese / Defeat of Spanish Army by French at Rocroi	

Spanish Religious Drama

The Spanish religious dramas, referred to as *autos sacramentales*, combined the elements of morality and mystery plays with popular secular farce. The staging of the Spanish religious dramas was similar to English medieval staging: the Spaniards employed *carros*, or pageant wagons, in a processional fashion, moving the presentation through the various parts of the town in which it was performed. (See Chapter 4.) At first two carros and a portable platform were used for each auto. Later four carros were used, and stationary platforms were set up in each of the town's playing areas.

Spanish Comedias

Secular drama developed side by side with the religious drama. Created by the same artists, secular drama flourished in Spain between 1550 and 1700. The full-length plays, known as *comedias*, usually dealt with themes of love and honor, and the leading characters were often minor noblemen. Comedias could be serious or comic—or a mixture of the two—and like the English plays were episodic in form rather than adhering to the neoclassical rules. The unities were ignored, the supernatural was often employed, and rather than a five-act structure, comedias were written in three.

Besides full-length plays, the Spaniards developed many popular, short, farcical forms which were presented on the same program with comedias. The amount of dramatic activity during the Spanish Golden

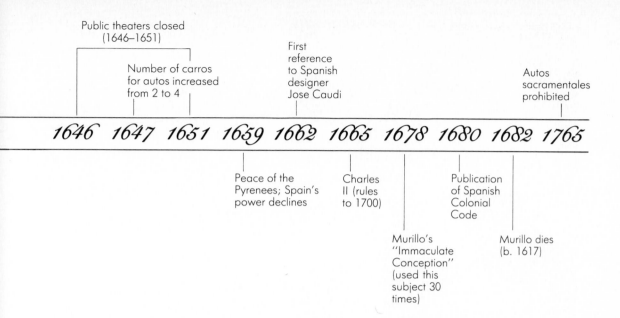

Public theaters closed
(1646–1651)

Number of carros
for autos increased
from 2 to 4

First
reference
to Spanish
designer
Jose Caudi

Autos
sacramentales
prohibited

1646 1647 1651 1659 1662 1665 1678 1680 1682 1765

Peace of the
Pyrenees; Spain's
power declines

Charles
II (rules
to 1700)

Publication
of Spanish
Colonial
Code

Murillo's
"Immaculate
Conception"
(used this
subject 30
times)

Murillo dies
(b. 1617)

Age was remarkable; even Cervantes, the author of *Don Quixote*, wrote for the theater.

The major playwrights of this period were Lope de Vega and Calderón de la Barca, and a good example of the episodic structure of Golden Age Spanish drama can be found in Lope's *The King, the Greatest Alcalde*. (ca. 1620–23). It is the story of a farmer who promises that his daughter Elvira can marry the peasant Sancho. When Sancho seeks approval for the marriage from his lord, Don Tello, the latter agrees, but when Don Tello sees Elvira he wants her for himself. He postpones the wedding and later kidnaps Elvira. The peasant Sancho appeals to the king, who after several complications comes to the town in disguise. When the king discovers that Don Tello has already forcibly seduced Elvira, he orders Don Tello to marry Elvira and then has him executed so that Elvira will be widowed honorably and can marry Sancho.

As can be seen from this brief sketch, there is a piling-up of scenes. In typical episodic fashion, the play takes place over an extended period of time and includes thirteen scenes. It also has a large cast of fifteen speaking roles as well as a number of nonspeaking parts. In their dramatic form Spanish plays of the Golden Age are very close to Elizabethan drama. As for their subject matter, however, they seem closer to the swashbuckling films of the 1940s, romantic novels, and TV soap operas.

The Public Theaters: The Corrales

The nonreligious plays of writers like Lope de Vega and Calderón were staged in public theaters known as *corrales*. The corrales were construct-

*M*urillo's *Immaculate Conception*
(1678) *The Spanish painter Murillo used
this subject some thirty times. The painting
illustrates the concern in the Spanish
Golden Age with religion, which was also
present in much of the era's drama. Spain
continued the medieval tradition of
producing religious plays long after other
countries had turned to secular material.
(Owner, Pardo Museum, Madrid/Photo,
European Art Color, Peter Adelberg.)*

*T*he Mystery of Elche *In the town of
Elche in Southern Spain, this medieval
religious play has been produced
continuously since the fifteenth century.
The play is put on by the townspeople, who
play all the parts, handing them down from
one generation to the next. In this recent
production, the young boy on the right
takes the part of the Virgin Mary while
others look on. (Photo—The Folger
Shakespeare Library, Washington, D.C.)*

LOPE FÉLIX DE VEGA CARPIO
(1562–1635)

Lope de Vega was one of the two most famous playwrights of Renaissance Spain. He was also one of the most prolific playwrights of all time and is reputed to have been the author of an amazing 2000 plays, of which 470 still survive. Lope established a distinctive episodic structure for Spanish drama in his works, and it is one of history's most fascinating coincidences that he lived at exactly the same time as Shakespeare and wrote in a similar form. Like Shakespeare's, Lope's plays contain many scenes and large casts of characters, and range over both time and space. Besides his plays, Lope wrote twenty-one volumes of prose and poetry.

As a dramatist, Lope had one aim: to please the audience. He made this point clear in his treatise *The New Art of Playwriting* (ca. 1609) in which he defended his episodic style. He wrote plays in every genre, covering almost every possible topic and using characters from all parts of Spanish society. Several of his plays, including *The Sheep Well* (ca. 1614), deal with the attempts of the peasants to secure justice, while others, like *The Dog in the Manger* (ca. 1615), are "cape and sword" plays revolving around the intrigues of the minor nobility. Though Lope preferred to have happy endings for his plays, he wrote several tragedies, including *The Knight from Olmedo* (ca. 1620–25), one of his finest plays. Translations of his works were circulated throughout Europe and were influential in the development of the French theater.

It is difficult to imagine when Lope had time for writing, for he led a most active life. Born in 1562 in a working-class family, he attended several Jesuit universities and at one point studied for the priesthood. Abandoning school, he joined the navy, took part in an expedition to the Azores, and became embroiled in the first of his many love affairs. Banished from Madrid for eight years because of one of his intrigues, he immediately broke the ban to kidnap and marry a young noblewoman. He then sailed with the Spanish Armada and on his return to Spain served several noblemen. His affair with the actress Micaela de Luján provided further stimulus to his writing career.

A growing interest in religion led Lope de Vega to join a lay confraternity, and in 1614, when he was widowed for the second time, he became a priest. Neither his playwriting nor his womanizing was affected by his new religious occupation. Philip III appointed Lope to be director of the court theater, a post he held until his death in 1635.

$\mathscr{P}$EDRO CALDERÓN DE LA BARCA
(1600–1681)

After Lope de Vega died, Pedro Calderón de la Barca became Spain's most popular playwright. Calderón wrote plays in a variety of styles, but they all reflect the authoritarian religious atmosphere of Spain. Many revolve around the favorite Spanish concerns of love and honor, and some examine violent family situations, a reflection of Calderón's own authoritarian father and of the country's social patterns. In *Life Is a Dream* (ca. 1636), he develops the idea that a man is responsible for his own actions and must choose a path from a maze of possibilities.

For court entertainments, Calderón wrote and produced poetic musical dramas like *Love, the Great Enchanter* (1637). His religious plays *(autos sacramentales)*, like *Baltassar's Feast* (1634) and *The Great World Theater* (1649), combine image-filled poetry with philosophy. Many of his plays, translated first into French and then into English, influenced the playwrights of neoclassical France and Restoration England.

A year before his death, Calderón drew up a list of the plays he had written. It contained 111 secular plays and 70 autos sacramentales, a remarkable total for a man who mixed playwriting with several other careers.

As a young man, Calderón's first career choice was the priesthood. The son of a wealthy government official, he entered the Jesuit University of Alcalá in 1614, the year he wrote his first play. After a few years of study he left school in 1620 to enter government service. In 1623, he began to write plays for the court, becoming a leader among the court poets. His plays were also successful in the public theaters, and when Lope de Vega died in 1635, Calderón, as Spain's most popular dramatist, became director of the court theater. Philip IV knighted him for his services the following year.

Calderón changed careers again in 1640, joining the army to help suppress the Catalan rebellion. He proved to be a good soldier, but was discharged two years later for medical reasons. With both the court and public theaters closed, he was forced to find other work, so he became secretary to the duke of Alba. After the death of his brothers and his mistress, Calderón returned to religion and was ordained a priest in 1651. Though he ceased to write for the public stage, he continued to write religious autos for the Corpus Christi celebration. He was reappointed to his court post as director of theater in 1663 and held that position until his death in 1681. Calderón's death is said to mark the end of the Spanish Golden Age.

The Sheep Well by Lope de Vega   *This Spanish playwright was one of the most prolific of all time. He wrote religious plays, history plays, swashbuckling adventure plays. One of the best known works is* The Sheep Well, *which is about an entire village. A scene from the play is shown here in a production in Minsk, Russia, by the White Russian Jewish Theater. (Photo—New York Public Library at Lincoln Center, Astor, Lenox and Tilden Foundations.)*

ed in the courtyards of inns, and most, like the Elizabethan public theaters, were open-air spaces. (Some, however, were roofed over with a canvas cover.) The typical Spanish inn of the period was a three-story structure built around a rectangular central courtyard. The Spaniards ingeniously converted the existing architectural layout of the courtyard into a theater space.

The stage in the corral was a platform erected opposite the entrance to the yard; access into the yard was usually through a tavern. The yard floor, or *patio*, was primarily an area for standing, like the pit of the Elizabethan public theater. However, in the front of the patio, near the stage, semicircular benches called *luñetas*—literally "small moons"— were erected. In the back wall opposite the stage, above the tavern, was a gallery known as the *cazuela*, or "hen's roost," which was the only area in which unaccompanied women could be seated. In many corrales, there

$\mathcal{T}$he Corral del Principe *This nineteenth century drawing is a speculative rendition of an open-air theater in Madrid during the Golden Age. It is incorrect in some details, but gives a strong sense of what such a theater was like. It is accurate, for example, in depicting the following: the seating in the first third of the pit, the windows on the adjoining buildings used as boxes, and the platform stage.*

were two galleries above the cazuela for local governmental officials and religious leaders. Along the side walls of the yard were elevated benches, known as the *gradas*. The boxes *(aposentos)* were nothing more than balcony windows of the buildings around the courtyard from which the stage could be viewed. The makeup of the corrales, therefore, was quite distinct from the developing proscenium-arch theaters in Italy and much closer to the Elizabethan public theater. The inn courtyard theaters were temporary at first but later became permanent theater spaces.

Scenery in the Corrales

The scenic conventions in Spain were also similar to those in England. The Spaniards erected a two-story facade behind the platform stage as the basic scenic construction; a curtain, props, and/or flats might be employed in conjunction with the facade. There were three openings for entrances, exits, and discoveries as well as an upper playing area. The facade, therefore, served the same function as the Elizabethan tiring house. Spoken decor—that is, dialogue which indicated locale—was also used.

During the Spanish Renaissance, the proscenium arch and perspective scenery were introduced only at court; again, this parallels English theater developments. The first proscenium-arch theater in Spain, the Coliseo, was a court theater completed in 1640 at the king's palace in Madrid which was designed by Italian architects.

Spanish Acting Companies

In Spain during the Golden Age, acting troupes consisted of sixteen to twenty performers and, unlike the Elizabethan companies, also included women. In many places on the European continent—in contrast to England—women had been allowed to act in medieval religious drama. The practice of including actresses in Spanish companies during the Renaissance was an outgrowth of this custom. The church, though, was not supportive of the use of actresses; as a result, the Spanish government was forced to impose stringent restrictions on women working in the theater; only women who were married or related to an actor in a troupe could be employed. Most Spanish acting troupes during the Golden Age were *compañias de partes*—sharing companies like those of Elizabethan England. Some companies, however, were organized by a manager who contracted performers for a specific period of time.

The Close of the Spanish Golden Age

Between 1650 and 1700, with Spain's military, political, economic, and cultural decline, the Spanish Golden Age came to an end. While no significant drama was written following the death of Calderón de la Barca in 1681, the theater of the Spanish Golden Age had been as vital as that of Elizabethan England. The theaters and scenic practices in Spain were almost identical to those in England, and the numerous popular dramas by Lope de Vega and Cálderon are structurally similar to those of William Shakespeare.

FRANCE IN THE NEOCLASSICAL ERA

The contrast between theatrical practice in Spain and the neoclassical theater of France is striking. The French adhered very closely to the conventions of the Italian Renaissance. Also, the Renaissance theater did not reach its zenith in France until a later period, partly due to the religious civil wars taking place there between Catholics and Protestants

The Theater of Neoclassical France

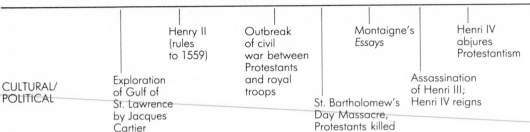

THEATER	Confrerie de la Passion (founded 1402) given monopoly on Paris theater	Religious plays prohibited; Hôtel de Bourgogne opens; perspective scenery used for first time at Lyon for performance celebrating marriage of Henri II and Catherine de Medicis	Alexandre Hardy, first professional playwright, flourishes

YEAR	*1518 1534–5 1547 1548 1562 1572 1580 1589 1593 1597*

CULTURAL/ POLITICAL	Exploration of Gulf of St. Lawrence by Jacques Cartier	Henry II (rules to 1559)	Outbreak of civil war between Protestants and royal troops	St. Bartholomew's Day Massacre, Protestants killed	Montaigne's *Essays*	Assassination of Henri III; Henri IV reigns	Henri IV abjures Protestantism

(Huguenots). The religious civil war was brought to an end in 1594 when Henry IV, a Protestant who ascended to the throne in 1589, converted to Catholicism. Although Henry renounced his Protestant beliefs, he resolved France's religious strife by formulating the Edict of Nantes. This revolutionary proclamation offered non-Catholics, and especially the Huguenots, equality and tolerance under French law.

Thus in the seventeenth century a stable French society was able to flourish, particularly under Louis XIV, who reigned from 1643 to 1715. Like England, Holland, Spain, and Portugal, France profited from exploration of the new world. Among the important areas the French explored and colonized were Canada and the Louisiana Territory.

The Italianization of France

While the theater and drama of the Spanish Golden Age and the Elizabethans were similar in many respects, the dramatic arts of the French neoclassical era were direct descendants of the Italian Renaissance. Many reasons can be cited for the Italianization of French society and theater between 1600 and 1700. For one, members of the Medici family, the renowned merchant-princes and patrons of the arts who ruled the prosperous Italian city of Florence during the Renaissance, married into the French royal family. Henry II, who ruled from 1547 to 1559, was wed to Catherine de Medicis. When Louis XIII inherited the throne of France in 1610, he was only nine; his mother, Marie de Medicis, controlled the French government.

The other major political force during Louis XIII's reign was Cardinal

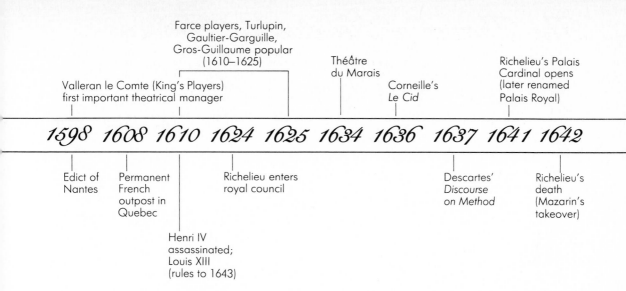

Farce players, Turlupin,
Gaultier-Garguille,
Gros-Guillaume popular
(1610–1625)

Valleran le Comte (King's Players)
first important theatrical manager

Théâtre
du Marais

Corneille's
Le Cid

Richelieu's Palais
Cardinal opens
(later renamed
Palais Royal)

1598 1608 1610 1624 1625 1634 1636 1637 1641 1642

Edict of
Nantes

Permanent
French
outpost in
Quebec

Richelieu enters
royal council

Descartes'
*Discourse
on Method*

Richelieu's
death
(Mazarin's
takeover)

Henri IV
assassinated;
Louis XIII
(rules to 1643)

Richelieu, who also advanced Italian culture in France. In 1643, the year after Richelieu's death, Louis XIII died. Because his son, Louis XIV, was only five when he became king, the Italian-born Cardinal Mazarin, who had replaced Richelieu, wielded the real power. In other words, French government, and in turn French culture, was heavily influenced by the Italians.

FRENCH THEATER

The Italian influence on the French theater can be seen most clearly in the drama of the period. The most noted seventeenth-century French dramatists were Pierre Corneille, Molière, and Jean Racine. Corneille and Racine are remembered for their neoclassical tragedies, Molière for his comedies.

French Neoclassical Drama

The controversy over Pierre Corneille's *The Cid* illustrated the strict adherence to the Italian neoclassical rules by the French. In Corneille's drama, a medieval Spanish hero, the Cid, kills the father of Chimène (the woman he loves) in a duel of honor and goes on to conquer the Moors, win another duel, and convince Chimène to marry him: all in twenty-four hours. Corneille's hero is an invincible medieval superman who fights to uphold justice, morality, personal honor, and national honor. The play was virulently attacked by the French Academy, a literary

The Theater of Neo-classical France

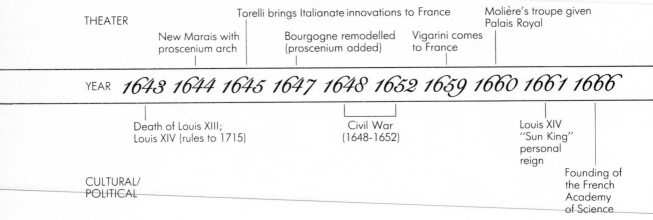

THEATER

New Marais with proscenium arch | Torelli brings Italianate innovations to France | Bourgogne remodelled (proscenium added) | Vigarini comes to France | Molière's troupe given Palais Royal

YEAR *1643 1644 1645 1647 1648 1652 1659 1660 1661 1666*

Death of Louis XIII; Louis XIV (rules to 1715) | Civil War (1648-1652) | Louis XIV "Sun King" personal reign | Founding of the French Academy of Science

CULTURAL/ POLITICAL

society founded by Cardinal Richelieu, because the members felt that it violated the neoclassical rules.

It was argued, for example, that *The Cid*, though observing the unity of time, stretches credibility by cramming so much action into twenty-four hours. Along with this Corneille appears to mix dramatic genres, because his serious play has a happy ending. In addition, the agreement of Chimène, the heroine, to marry her father's murderer was attacked as being inappropriate behavior for a character of her stature. Corneille vigorously defended the dramaturgy of the *The Cid*. Nevertheless, all of his dramas other than *The Cid*, rigidly adhere to the neoclassical precepts.

The same is true of Jean Racine's tragedies. Racine's *Phaedra*, for instance, based on the Greek play *Hippolytus* by Euripides, is a perfect example of neoclassicism. In *Phaedra*, the heroine, who is the second wife of King Theseus, falls in love with her stepson, Hippolytus. Racine's play is so arranged that all the events occur in one place—outside of a room in Theseus's palace—and cover only a few hours. The action is also unified, being confined to Phaedra's love for Hippolytus. Having heard that Theseus is dead, Phaedra confesses her love for Hippolytus, first to her maid and then to Hippolytus himself. Hippolytus reacts with disgust to her declaration, and shortly thereafter Phaedra discovers that Theseus is alive and will soon be returning to the palace.

To avoid shame at having openly declared her love for her stepson, Phaedra allows her maid to spread the false word that it was Hippolytus who made advances, not she. Theseus, believing the false report, invokes

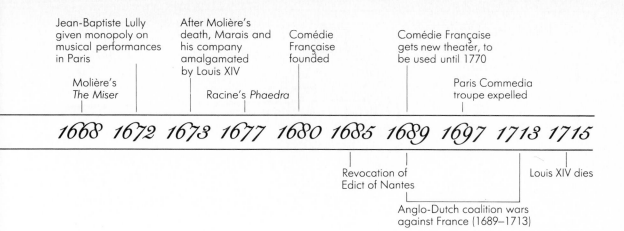

Jean-Baptiste Lully given monopoly on musical performances in Paris

Molière's
The Miser

After Molière's death, Marais and his company amalgamated by Louis XIV

Racine's Phaedra

Comédie Française founded

Comédie Française gets new theater, to be used until 1770

Paris Commedia troupe expelled

1668 1672 1673 1677 1680 1685 1689 1697 1713 1715

Revocation of Edict of Nantes

Louis XIV dies

Anglo-Dutch coalition wars against France (1689–1713)

a god to punish Hippolytus, and the young man is slain. Phaedra is grief-stricken and confesses her guilt to Theseus before taking poison herself.

Because the play begins near the final crisis and occurs in a short space of time, information from the past—that is, background material required by the audience to understand the play—must be reported in exposition. Racine manages this element well, and also masterfully articulates Phaedra's inner emotional conflicts. Racine's handling of language, including his beautifully balanced phrases (in a line of poetry known as the alexandrine), established a model that was to be followed in France for the next three centuries. To this day, French playwrights put a premium on the verbal skills and intellectual arguments of their characters.

Among all the French neoclassical playwrights, however, the one who still exerts the most influence on the modern theater is Molière. A leading actor-manager and playwright, Molière is noted for such famous "comedies of character" as *The Misanthrope* (1666), *The Miser* (1668), *Tartuffe*, and *The Would-Be Gentleman*. In these plays Molière creates exaggerated character types and makes fun of their eccentricities. The misers, misanthropes, and hypochondriacs found in his plays are still recognizable to twentieth-century audiences.

Many critics note the influence of the commedia dell'arte on Molière, particularly because the character types found in his plays resemble the stock types in commedia. In *The Miser*, for example, Harpagon is an avaricious old man reminiscent of Pantalone. He courts the young woman whom his son, Cléante, loves and betroths his

𝒫IERRE CORNEILLE
(1606–1684)

Pierre Corneille, along with Racine, was one of the two major French tragic dramatists of the seventeenth century.

A native of Rouen, Corneille was the son of a wealthy lawyer. Following his father's career, he obtained an appointment in the department of waterways and forests. He wrote a comedy, *Mélite,* on the side, and after an acting troupe played it successfully in Paris in 1629, he began to spend much of his leisure time writing plays. His early comedies attracted the attention of Cardinal Richelieu, who induced him to join the "Society of the Five Authors" commissioned to write plays for the cardinal's entertainment. Corneille found it difficult to write to order and incurred the cardinal's wrath for altering a part of the plot assigned to him.

Corneille's most famous play, *The Cid* (1636–1637), about the conflict between love and honor, was written after he joined the society. Though *The Cid* was immensely popular with audiences —as it has continued to be to the present day—strict neoclassicists severely criticized its violation of decorum and probability. Furthermore, these critics at-

tacked the stretching of the rules calling for unity of time, place, and action. The great debate that the play precipitated over the neoclassical rules led to the ascendency of the French Academy, which upheld their supremacy.

Corneille's famous tragedies *Horace* (1640), *Cinna* (1641), *Polyeucte* (1643), and *Rodogune* (1645) are models of adherence to neoclassical theory and established him as the most renowned playwright in France. He was elected to the French Academy in 1647 and continued to write until 1652, when a poorly received tragedy and uncertain political conditions caused his early retirement from playwriting. The minister of finance was able to persuade Corneille to return to playwriting in 1659, and he continued to write for the rest of his life.

As a dramatist, Corneille viewed theater as a spectacular art. He wrote plays with heroic characters in suspenseful and surprising situations which force them to act. Long before his death in 1684, Corneille was known as "the great Corneille," and *The Cid* had been translated and produced all over Europe, assuring his lasting fame.

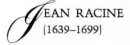

JEAN RACINE
(1639–1699)

Along with Corneille, the chief French tragic playwright of the seventeenth century was Jean Racine. French neoclassical tragedy, with its rigid dramatic structure, was a difficult form to write, and many of the plays were stilted and lifeless. Racine, however, was able to take that restricted form and produce tragedies noted for their range, passion, and poetry.

In his tragedies—especially *Phaedra* (1677), *Bérénice* (1670), and *Andromache* (1667)—Racine showed his ability to create dramatic tension through concentration and characterization. By compressing the dramatic action Racine increased the pressure on the chief character of the play, one who was usually trying to reconcile a driving passion with honor and devotion to duty. The tension builds rapidly, the pressure becomes too much, and the character, tragically, begins to come apart.

The strictness of the neoclassical form matches the strictness of Racine's own upbringing. Orphaned at the age of four, he was raised first by his grandparents and then by his aunt, who was in a convent at Port-Royal. She enrolled the boy in the convent school, where he received an excellent but strict and austere education. In 1658 he went to Paris to continue his studies and became a lawyer, but he spent much of his time with literary groups. With the publication of an ode on the marriage of Louis XIV in 1660, he left school to concentrate on a literary career.

Racine was determined to succeed in his new career as a playwright and was a constant plotter and intriguer; consequently he made many enemies. Though Molière had given the first performances of the tragedian's works and had given him advice and encouragement, Racine transferred one of his plays from Molière's troupe to a rival company. He also persuaded Mme. du Parc, his mistress, to leave Molière and join the rival group, an act for which he was severely criticized. Racine, however, had the support of several prominent writers, the court, and the king's mistress, and he did not hesitate to use their influence to thwart those who opposed him. In his rise to prominence Racine had made enemies, and in 1677 these enemies caused the failure of his play *Phaedra* by having another play open on the same night as the premiere of Racine's play. After this, Racine forsook the theater, married, and obtained an appointment as royal historiographer.

When Racine retired from playwriting he returned to the strict religious beliefs of his youth. He remained in King Louis's favor for many years, and, at the request of the king's second wife, wrote two pageants for her girls' school. Finally he lost the king's favor because of his rigid religious ideas. He returned to Port-Royal and died in 1699 after a long illness. It is ironic that *Phaedra*, which was a failure when it opened, has become one of the most famous French tragedies of all time.

*T*heatrical entertainment at Versailles   *The palace at Versailles, about eleven miles from Paris, was designed for Louis XIV and built between 1669 and 1685. The geometric order and ornateness of the buildings reflect the artistic spirit of neoclassical France. The theatrical presentation shown here in front of the palace is a further indication of the opulence of the age. (Photo—The Metropolitan Museum of Art, New York.)*

daughter to an old man who does not require a dowry, even though she loves the younger Valère. His exaggerated miserliness is the basic obstacle to his children's happiness.

Molière's contrived plots, which adhere to the neoclassical rules, are frequently resolved by a deus ex machina. In *The Miser*, for example, Anselme, the old man to whom Harpagon's daughter is promised, coincidentally turns out to be the lost father of both Valère and the girl Cléante loves. Anselme allows his rediscovered son and daughter to marry Harpagon's children so that everyone can live happily ever after. Molière's plots, characters, and slapstick elements make his comedies popular with modern audiences.

French Theater Buildings and Scene Design

Though the growth of the French theater prior to 1600 was inhibited due

MOLIÈRE
(Jean-Baptiste Poquelin)
(1622–1673)

"If it be the aim of comedy to correct man's vices, then I do not see for what reason there should be a privileged class," wrote Molière in defense of his play *Tartuffe* (1664), which had scandalized French audiences for its portrayal of religious hypocrisy. Several of his other comedies also shocked audiences, not because of their subject matter, but because he insisted on truthfully depicting people's vices and follies. His plays nevertheless earned the respect and patronage of enlightened theatergoers.

Writing in the same restrictive neoclassic form as Corneille and Racine—the dialogue in many of his plays consisted of rhyming couplets—Molière remains one of the most popular dramatists of all time. In plays such as *The School for Wives* (1662), *The Doctor in Spite of Himself* (1666), and *The Would-be Gentleman* (1670), he combined the farcical humor of the Italian commedia dell'arte with a gift for witty dialogue and a keen eye for human foibles.

Had he wanted financial stability, Jean-Baptiste Poquelin, as Molière was christened, could have had two other careers. As the son of an upholsterer in the service of the king, he could have followed his father's profession. He also had the ability to become a lawyer, but in 1643 he left school, changed his name to Molière, and founded the Illustre Théâtre with the Béjart family of actors. The theater went bankrupt in 1645 and Molière was imprisoned for debt. Forced out of Paris by poor economic conditions, the troupe played in the provinces until 1658.

During this time, Molière became an accomplished comic actor, noted for the subtlety of his performances. As a leader in the company, along with his mistress, Madeleine Béjart, Molière was able to coach the company in his method, developing a disciplined ensemble.

In 1558 an influential patron secured a royal audience for the troupe. King Louis XIV was much impressed by Molière's work, and the group was allowed to share a theater in Paris with an Italian commedia troupe, a situation that left them constantly struggling for funds. Besides being the company manager and an actor, Molière wrote about one-third of the troupe's plays. Although many of his plays were successes with the public and at court, others, like *Tartuffe*, were banned.

The king made Molière's troupe "The King's Men" in 1665 and the dramatist wrote many court pageants and plays. By 1672, however, Louis's favor had gone to the composer Jean-Baptiste Lully, and Molière had to work harder for financial stability. Molière's home life was also unhappy. His wife, Armande Béjart, who was much younger than the playwright, became noted for her flirtations. Exhausted and suffering from a lung ailment, Molière collapsed during a performance of *The Imaginary Invalid* (1673) and died that night. Because he was an actor and France at that time had laws preventing actors from receiving Christian burial, his funeral was held at night.

to religious civil war, the French, nonetheless, were the first Europeans after the Romans to construct a permanent theater building. The Hôtel de Bourgogne, constructed by the Confraternity of the Passion—a religious order that had been granted a monopoly for the presentation of religious drama in Paris—was completed in 1548. Unfortunately for the Confraternity of the Passion, French religious drama was also outlawed in 1548 and forced to rent its space to touring companies. The Hôtel de Bourgogne was the sole permanent indoor theater building in Paris for nearly a century.

The Bourgogne, constructed seventy years before the Teatro Farnese in Italy, was not a proscenium-arch theater; instead, the building was a long and narrow structure with a platform stage at one end. In front of the stage was the standing pit *(parterre)*, and around the side and back walls were boxes and undivided galleries. Up to the seventeenth century, the scenic practices employed in this space were basically medieval.

When the Théâtre du Marais opened in 1634, the Hôtel de Bourgogne had competition. The Marais was a converted indoor tennis court, tennis being a popular Parisian diversion at the time. Prior to the opening of the Marais, if the Bourgogne was already leased to a theatrical company, additional companies could perform in Paris in temporarily converted tennis courts. Since the indoor tennis courts were long, narrow buildings like the Bourgogne and contained galleries for viewing the sport, they were easily transformed into theaters. By erecting a platform stage at one end of the building and installing temporary galleries, a theater space nearly identical to the Hôtel de Bourgogne was available. Not surprisingly, then, the second major Parisian theater building was a permanently converted tennis court.

The Italianate influence on French theater architecture became evident in 1641 when Cardinal Richelieu erected the Palais-Cardinal, renamed the Palais-Royal following his death. The Palais-Cardinal was the first proscenium-arch theater in France and also contained Italianate scene-shifting machinery. In 1645 the Italian scenic wizard Giacomo Torelli was employed by Cardinal Mazarin to design in this theater.

Following the construction of Richelieu's theater, the Italian influence dominated French theater architecture and scene design. The Théâtre du Marais and the Hôtel de Bourgogne were remodeled into proscenium-arch theaters in the 1640s. Painted-perspective, wing-and-shutter scenery—shifted by the pole-and-chariot system—was also employed in the two remodeled theaters. The French obsession with spectacular scenic presentations resulted in the construction of the Hall of Machines in 1660; this theater was designed by Gaspare Vigarini, the Italian artist who replaced Torelli at the court of Louis XIV. The stage in the Hall of Machines, while only 52 feet wide, was 140 feet deep to allow for elaborate scenic equipment.

French proscenium-arch theater buildings deviated slightly from those of the Italian Renaissance. In the back wall opposite the stage was the *paradis*, or "heavens," an area located above the boxes in the rear that

A French tennis court—suitable theater space *An early seventeenth-century illustration of a French tennis court of the kind that was converted to use as a theater. A platform stage would be set up at one end and seating would be added on the floor. The Theatre du Marais in Paris is a good example of a playing space that was made from a converted tennis court. (Bibliotheque Nationale, Paris)*

contained inexpensive bleacherlike seating. At the close of the seventeenth century, members of the French upper class were frequently seated on the stage.

The Comédie Française

Another major theater building of the French neoclassical period was the Comédie Française. This space housed the French national theater founded by Louis XIV in 1680. In 1673, there were five government-supported companies in Paris: the Opera, an Italian commedia dell'arte troupe, the Hôtel de Bourgogne company, the Théâtre du Marais company, and a troupe led by Molière. After Molière's death, Louis ordered the playwright's troupe to merge with the Marais company, which thereafter performed as the Molière-Marais troupe.

In 1680, Louis XIV organized the French national theater by consolidating the Bourgogne troupe with the Molière-Marais company; for nine years the combined company, known as the Comédie Française, used the Théâtre de Guénégaud. In 1689, the national theater company moved into its own building, which was a converted tennis court; the sight lines

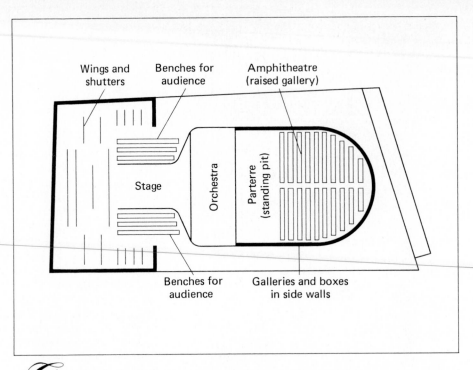

Ground plan of the Comédie Française   *The French national theater performed in this playhouse for eighty one years, beginning in 1689. It contained a proscenium-arch stage with machinery for scene shifts, and a horseshoe-shaped auditorium for improved sight lines. The parterre was where audience members stood while the amphitheater contained bleacherlike seating. (Adapted from Adolphe Jullien,* Les Spectateurs sur le Theatre, *1875.)*

of the new theater were significantly better than in other contemporary French spaces because of the interior horseshoe-shape construction.

Acting Companies

The acting companies housed in these neoclassical theaters were organized under the sharing plan, with *societaires,* as shareholders, and *pensionnaires,* who were contracted to perform minor roles. Women were members of the neoclassical companies and could become societaires. Troupes spent little time on rehearsals, which were supervised by the playwright and/or the leading actor of the company. Once a play was performed, the troupe was expected to be able to revive it at a moment's notice, and the bill at theaters was changed daily.

Giraudon

THE COMÉDIE FRANÇAISE
(founded 1680)

In 1680 there were two acting companies in Paris. (The Molière and Marais troupes had combined to form one of them.) That year Louis XIV ordered the two troupes to form a united company. Louis gave the new company a monopoly on the performance of all spoken drama in French, thereby taking it under the wing of the state and making it the first national theater in the world. To distinguish it from the Comédie Italienne, which was also based in Paris, it was called the Comédie Française. (The term *national theater* indicates a theater that is supposed to represent the entire nation. Britain, for example, has a National Theater in London.)

The new company had a number of distinguished players: Marie Champmeslé, a renowned tragic actress; Michel Baron, considered to be the finest serious actor of the seventeenth century; and Armande Béjart, Molière's widow and a versatile commedienne. Excellence in acting became a hallmark of the company and its members have included many of France's leading actors: Adrienne Lecouvreur, La Clairon (Claire Leyris de la Tudi), Henri Louis Lekain, François Joseph Talma, Élisa Félix Rachel, Benoît Constant Coquelin, Sarah Bernhardt, and Jean-Louis Barrault.

To keep order among so many talents, the company was organized under the sharing plan of Molière's troupe; with some modifications, the troupe still follows the plan today. Shares in the company were granted to the *societaires*, or leading members, of the company, according to each actor's status, with some getting less than a full share. The societaires were responsible for all policy, including the selection of plays. Vacancies caused by retirement, resignation, or death were filled from the *pensionnaires*, actors hired by the troupe on a fixed salary. To become a pensionnaire, one had to successfully audition in both comedy and tragedy. The *doyen*, or head of the company, was the actor with the longest service in the troupe.

The Comédie Française survived both the French Revolution and the problems created by the company's organization. An appointment as a societaire sometimes encouraged an actor to be complacent and arrogant because of his secure position. The lack of outlets for plays had a stifling effect on French drama, accelerated by the fact that the societaires preferred plays that were imitative rather than innovative. In the nineteenth century, with the popularity of melodrama and the boulevard theaters, the Comédie suffered financially. Throughout its long history, however, it has preserved the best of French classical drama—Corneille, Racine, and Molière—as well as a distinguished tradition of classical acting.

Summary

Though different in approach, the Spanish Golden Age and the French neoclassical era were both theatrically rich. The Spaniards developed dramatic and theatrical practices quite similar to those of the Elizabethan English: the structure of their comedias was episodic; the Spanish corrales were reminiscent of the English public theaters, and staging practices in both types of playhouses were almost identical. But Spanish drama had features that were characteristically its own. The plays dealt with Spanish heroes and heroines: both common people and the nobility. Also, the Spaniards continued to produce religious drama during the Golden Age and they employed women as performers.

Meanwhile, the French theater expanded on and refined Italian Renaissance practices. Most of the drama, including the tragedies of Corneille and Racine and the comedies of Molière, followed the neoclassical rules. The plays of seventeenth-century France, however, achieved a quality and distinction far exceeding those produced in the Italian Renaissance. As for the theater buildings in which plays were performed, by the mid-seventeenth century, French theaters were proscenium-arch spaces which contained painted-perspective, wing-and-shutter scenery. The establishment of the Comédie Française, the government-supported French national theater, in 1680, was a milestone in theater history.

Part Three

Part Three

Between 1660 and 1875, people in Europe and America undertook to change the world—politically, industrially, and educationally. The English monarchy was restored in 1660, but in the years to come the power of kings and queens would be diminished and in many cases abolished. The end of the eighteenth century saw both the American and French revolutions. The French returned to authoritarian rule in the early nineteenth century with Napoleon, but kingship was never to be the same again. Socially, during this period, there was a significant increase in the size and importance of the middle class.

The eighteenth century was known as the Age of Enlightenment. People thought that the mind was all-powerful, and that all problems could be solved by applying the intellect to them. The next century, the nineteenth, was termed the Century of Progress. It was the era of the industrial revolution, with the development of machines for manufacturing and transportation.

Just as ideas were supposed to solve problems in the eighteenth century, industrialization was supposed to solve them in the nineteenth. Workers in factories would get wages that would allow them to buy goods, and the factories themselves would supply goods for everyone. It did not work out exactly as planned, but this approach indicates the optimism of the time.

The changes that occurred socially and politically were mirrored in the arts. Music moved from the baroque world of Bach and Handel to the classicism of Mozart and Beethoven, and finally to the romanticism of Schubert, Chopin, and Liszt. Similarly, the theater during this era was one of transition. The roots of our modern theater can be found in many of the transformations which took place in the theaters of the English Restoration and the eighteenth and early nineteenth centuries.

The era's many theatrical innovations are too numerous to list. The modern version of the proscenium-arch theater—the kind we still have on Broadway and across the country—was born. Technology was introduced into scene design, with more realistic stage effects becoming popular. Primitive candle lighting gave way to more controllable gas lighting. (In 1881, electricity was to be introduced.) Historically accurate costumes became more commonplace, and costumes were designed to reflect characterization.

The business of theater as we know it today, including the rise of the theatrical entrepreneur, the demise of the repertory company, the establishment of the long run, and the star system, all evolved during these years. The art of acting slowly became more concerned with portraying everyday life, and the director became the controlling artist in the theater.

The dramatic forms of these two centuries, including the comedy of manners, romanticism, melodrama, and the well-made play, are copied by contemporary writers, with melodramatic films and TV shows being the direct descendants of nineteenth-century popular drama. The American dramatist Arthur Miller has employed the well-made play, and British playwright Alan Ayckbourn's *The Norman Conquests* and *Bedroom Farce* are comedies of manners. Looking closely at contemporary theater, we see how indebted we are to the dramatic arts of these years of change.

Chapter Eight

THE THEATER OF THE
ENGLISH RESTORATION

As was noted at the close of Chapter 6, Charles I of England was removed from the throne by Oliver Cromwell and the Puritans after a bitter civil war lasting from 1642 to 1649. In 1649 Charles was beheaded. For the next eleven years England was governed without a monarch; instead, Cromwell, along with a Parliament that had been purged of any opponents to his policies, controlled the nation. This is known as the period of the commonwealth. But when Cromwell died in 1658, his son was unable to keep control of the English government, and in 1660 Charles II, who had been living in France, was invited by a newly elected Parliament to come out of exile to rule England. The monarchy, in other words, was restored, and this gave the name "Restoration" to the period that followed.

Restoration comedy   *An emphasis on style, gossip, intrigue, and plot complications are the hallmarks of English Restoration comedy. A good example is* The Way of the World *by William Congreve. In the scene shown here, Lady Wishfort in the center is reading a letter intended to dupe her; looking on are the maid Foible and a servant Waitwell who, as part of the scheme, is disguised as a nobleman. (Photo—Martha Swope.)*

The Theater of the English Restoration

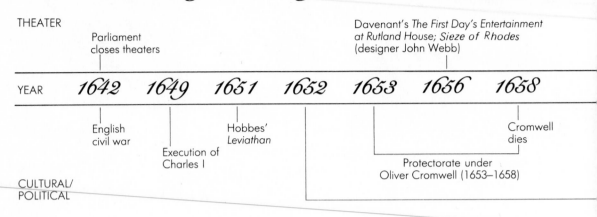

THEATER

Parliament
closes theaters

Davenant's *The First Day's Entertainment
at Rutland House; Sieze of Rhodes*
(designer John Webb)

| YEAR | 1642 | 1649 | 1651 | 1652 | 1653 | 1656 | 1658 |

English
civil war

Execution of
Charles I

Hobbes'
Leviathan

Cromwell
dies

Protectorate under
Oliver Cromwell (1653–1658)

CULTURAL/
POLITICAL

THE RETURN OF THE MONARCHY

The reinstatement of the monarchy also meant the restoration of other institutions: Parliament, the legislative body that made laws; the Anglican church (known in the United States as the Episcopal church), the official church formed by Henry VIII when he broke with the Roman Catholic church; the cavalier gentry who were the nobles—the lords, dukes, earls, etc.—who had titles and owned land. The gentry were next in rank to the royal family.

Though Parliament was restored, Charles II opposed giving it power and, in the final years of his reign, ruled without Parliament. When Charles died in 1685, he was succeeded by his brother, James II. James II's reign was turbulent because of his conversion to Catholicism; when James II's wife gave birth to a son, a Catholic line of succession threatened Protestant England. For this reason, Parliament, in 1688, invited James II's daughter Mary, who was a Protestant, and Mary's Dutch husband, William of Orange, to rule England. William and Mary deposed James II in the bloodless Glorious Revolution in 1688.

Many historians consider that England entered a new phase with the accession of William and Mary in 1688 and therefore that this date marks the end of the Restoration period. In the theater, though, the developments of the Restoration begun in 1660 continued until the turn of the century, and so Restoration drama continued from 1688 to 1700. When William died in 1702 and Mary's sister, Anne, was crowned queen, both the theatrical restoration had come to an end.

Political thought in England was transformed during this era by the philosophers Thomas Hobbes (1588–1679) and John Locke (1632–1704),

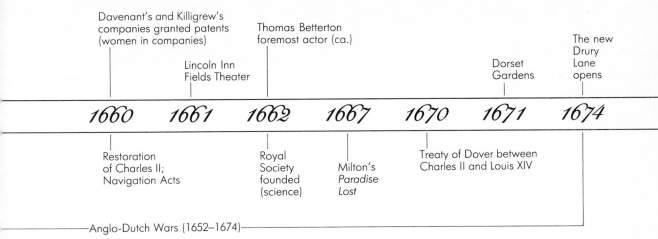

Davenant's and Killigrew's
companies granted patents
(women in companies)

Thomas Betterton
foremost actor (ca.)

The new
Drury
Lane
opens

Lincoln Inn
Fields Theater

Dorset
Gardens

1660   *1661*   *1662*   *1667*   *1670*   *1671*   *1674*

Restoration
of Charles II;
Navigation Acts

Royal
Society
founded
(science)

Milton's
*Paradise
Lost*

Treaty of Dover between
Charles II and Louis XIV

Anglo-Dutch Wars (1652–1674)

both of whom were proponents of the concept of natural law. According to Hobbes and Locke, there are laws in this world which are naturally right and should not be violated by any ruler, and those who violate them should be removed from power. Since human beings are rational creatures, Hobbes and Locke believed that these natural rights could be discerned by reason.

Hobbes and Locke, however, believed in different forms of government as a means of protecting natural law. Hobbes theorized, in *Leviathan*, that people give up their freedom of action to absolute rulers in order to secure civil order and peace. (Hobbes compared the structure of government to the Leviathan, a biblical monster.) Absolutism is meant to ensure individual welfare and uphold natural rights; for this reason, Hobbes's ideal absolute ruler is the antithesis of such twentieth-century totalitarian dictators as Adolf Hitler and Josef Stalin.

Locke, on the other hand, preferred a representative government with a constitution, arguing that rulers are responsible to their people and serve as their representatives. Governments are created to protect life, liberty, and property. Rebellion against governments which violate these rights is more acceptable than allowing such violations.

The views of Hobbes and Locke became highly influential in the following century. Enlightened despots, monarchs who believed that they ruled for the good of their people, modeled themselves after the ideal absolutist described by Hobbes. The leaders of the American and French revolutions were clearly influenced by the writings of Locke.

In England, there were more than political and religious transformations during the reigns of Charles II, James II, and William and Mary. Immediately following the Restoration, England expanded rapidly into

The Theater of the English Restoration

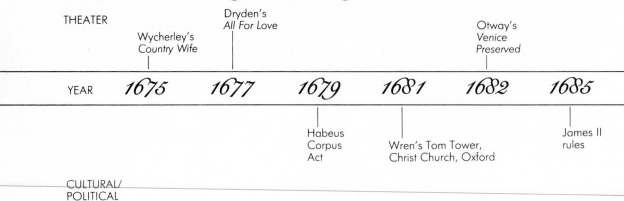

THEATER		Wycherley's Country Wife		Dryden's All For Love					Otway's Venice Preserved		
YEAR	*1675*		*1677*		*1679*		*1681*		*1682*		*1685*
CULTURAL/ POLITICAL					Habeus Corpus Act		Wren's Tom Tower, Christ Church, Oxford				James II rules

the new world, with her colonies spreading from New England to the Carolinas. The East India Company established trading posts in Surat, Madras, Calcutta, and Bombay. Cultural and scientific advances were also made. In 1662 the Royal Society of London for Improving Natural Knowledge was established; Sir Isaac Newton, renowned for his experiments with gravity, was an original member. During the Restoration the great architect Christopher Wren rebuilt St. Paul's Cathedral, which had been destroyed by the Great Fire of London in 1666. In other words, following the restoration of the monarchy there was also a restoration of trade, science, and culture.

THE COMMONWEALTH THEATER

With the restoration of the monarchy the English theater came to life again. The Puritans had closed the theaters in 1642, and until 1660 theatrical activity was severely curtailed. During this time Elizabethan playhouses were dismantled and actors persecuted. Nevertheless, the antitheater laws were not completely effective and entertainments were surreptitiously organized. *Drolls*, shortened versions of full-length plays, usually comedies, were the dramas most often staged. An important theatrical producer during the commonwealth period was William Davenant, who had been a playwright prior to the closing of the theaters by the Puritans. In 1656, Davenant presented *The First Day's Entertainment at Rutland House* and *The Siege of Rhodes*. Davenant was able to circumvent the antitheater ordinances by claiming that his presentations were musical entertainments and by staging them, at first, at his private

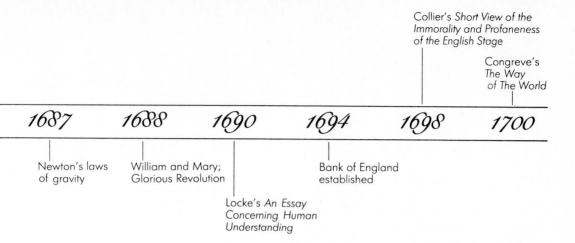

Collier's *Short View of the Immorality and Profaneness of the English Stage*

Congreve's *The Way of The World*

| 1687 | 1688 | 1690 | 1694 | 1698 | 1700 |

Newton's laws of gravity

William and Mary; Glorious Revolution

Locke's *An Essay Concerning Human Understanding*

Bank of England established

residence. By the mid-1650s, however, subterfuge was not all that necessary, since opposition to the Puritans was increasing.

Davenant's *The Siege of Rhodes* was particularly significant because of its employment of the proscenium arch and wing-and-shutter setting, a type of stage arrangement that represented a clear departure from the platform stage of Shakespeare's day. The design of Davenant's theater was by John Webb (1611–1672), the son-in-law of Inigo Jones. Webb's employment of Italianate devices was not surprising, because his father-in-law had introduced such devices in court entertainments prior to the abolition of the monarchy by Cromwell.

RESTORATION THEATER: ENGLISH AND ITALIAN TRADITIONS MEET

Stage practices during the English Renaissance did not follow those of the Italian Renaissance, but during the Restoration, Italian practices—which had been introduced in the Jacobean and Caroline court entertainments, as well as in Davenant's commonwealth presentations—truly took hold. The Italian influence was reinforced by England's contact with neoclassical France in the late seventeenth century. French culture was influential in Restoration society because Charles II had spent his exile in France and because of James II's ties with Catholic Europe. The magical, illusionistic devices of the proscenium-arch theater, in which painted-perspective wing-and-shutter sets could be changed before the audience's eyes, became part of the English stage. Still, much of the Elizabethan theatrical tradition remained prevalent. The fusion of Elizabethan stage conven-

$\mathscr{S}$t. Paul's Cathedral *When an earlier St. Paul's Cathedral in London was destroyed in the Great Fire of 1666, the famous architect Christopher Wren (1632-1723) was commissioned to rebuild it. His baroque design for the building reveals a heavy French and Italian influence. Similar influences were felt in the theater of the time when Continental practices transformed both English playhouses and dramatic form. (Photo—Editorial Photocolor Archives, Inc.)*

tions with those of the Italian and French theaters resulted in the unique flavor of Restoration drama, theater buildings, and set designs.

Restoration Drama

The serious drama of the Restoration is rarely read or produced today. Its heroic tragedies, popular between 1660 and 1675, dealt with extraordinary heroes undertaking extraordinary deeds. These contrived plays, which deal with the themes of love and honor, are reminiscent of the dramas of the Spanish Golden Age and the French neoclassical era. Another type of serious drama, usually referred to as Restoration tragedy, became popular during the last quarter of the seventeenth century. The Italianate influence is immediately apparent in Restoration tragedies because of their adherence to the neoclassical rules. John Dryden (1631–1700), the most noted author of Restoration tragedy, in his *All for Love* (1677), transformed Shakespeare's *Antony and Cleopatra* into a neoclassical tragedy. It was not unusual for Restoration playwrights to rework Shakespeare into the neoclassical mold. *Romeo and Juliet,* for example, was provided with a happy ending. Nahum Tate (1652–1715), who altered the ending of *King Lear,* was among the best known of the Shakespearean adapters.

The great plays of the English Restoration, however, were the comedies. Two renowned playwrights of Restoration comedy were William Wycherley and William Congreve. Restoration comedies, many influenced by the French dramatist Molière, are *comedies of manners.* They poke fun at the social conventions and norms of the time and

$\mathscr{S}$IR WILLIAM DAVENANT
(1606–1668)

$\mathscr{T}$HOMAS KILLIGREW
(1612–1683)

The revival of the English theater in the last part of the seventeenth century—after its suppression by the Puritans—came about through the efforts of Sir William Davenant and Thomas Killigrew. Both men were familiar with the English theatrical tradition, for they had been active in the precommonwealth theater, but their leadership was to take the English stage in a new direction.

Davenant's theatrical ties went back to Shakespeare, who supposedly was a frequent visitor to his father's Oxford inn and also Davenant's godfather. After briefly attending Lincoln College, Oxford, Davenant began writing plays and collaborated with Inigo Jones on several court masques. In 1638, he succeeded Ben Jonson as poet laureate. Knighted in 1643 for his service to the Royalist cause, he was imprisoned by the Parliamentary forces for a year.

Killigrew, also a supporter of the Royalist cause, had stayed with the royal family throughout its exile in France. Before the closing of the theaters he had written a number of tragicomedies. According to the diarist Samuel Pepys, Killigrew was a "merry droll" and a favorite of Charles I.

Davenant's *The Siege of Rhodes* is considered to be the first English opera. It was also the first production in which actresses appeared on the English stage and the first to use changeable scenery in a public performance. In 1660, Davenant went to France to persuade Charles II to grant him a license for a theater. That year Charles II gave both Davenant and Killigrew a patent that gave them a monopoly on theatrical productions in London.

After they had suppressed several unlicensed troupes, the two managers divided their company. Killigrew formed the King's Company with the older, more experienced actors, while Davenant's Duke's Company had several promising young actors, including Thomas Betterton, the best actor of the Restoration. Davenant's company, even after his death in 1668, proved to be the stronger and better managed of the two. Killigrew, who had been made Master of the Revels in 1673, with authority over all theater in England, was often in financial difficulty. In 1682, a year before Killigrew's death, the two companies were united to prevent his troupe from going bankrupt.

satirize the preoccupation of the Restoration's upper class with reputation, even though most of their upper-class characters are disreputable.

The universe of these plays is one in which marital infidelity abounds yet goes unpunished. No wonder, then, that the Puritans attacked the Restoration theater. In 1698 Jeremy Collier, a minister, authored *A Short View of the Immorality and Profaneness of the English Stage*. Some historians suggest that Collier's treatise marks the end of the theatrical Restoration; following his attack, sexual content was toned down, and in eighteenth-century English comedy, morality was stressed.

The dramatic structure of Restoration plays combines features of the Elizabethan theater with those of the neoclassical theater of Italy and France. In *The Country Wife*, for instance, Wycherley employs elements of both the crisis and episodic forms. The action is far more unified than in a Shakespearean play, with fewer scene shifts. At the same time, unlike the plays of Racine and Molière, it moves from place to place and employs more characters and even a subplot. The characters in Restoration comedy are stock types, with their names usually describing their distinctive personality traits. A common character type is the fop who believes himself to be witty and fashionable when in reality he is not. Also, comic language devices, such as the double entendre and witty repartee, abound.

William Wycherley's *The Country Wife*

Written in 1675 and influenced by Molière's *The School for Wives* (1662), William Wycherley's *The Country Wife* is an intriguing example of Restoration comedy. The main character, Horner, spreads the rumor that he is impotent because of a venereal disease he contracted while abroad. His doctor, Quack, substantiates the rumor, and Horner uses this "cover story" to gain access to his acquaintances' wives. The one he most desires is Margery Pinchwife, a naive woman whose husband keeps her locked away in the country and who tries to disguise her as a boy when they are in town.

Coming on Pinchwife and the disguised Margery in the street, Horner realizes that she is a woman in a man's clothing and takes advantage of the situation to make amorous advances, hugging and kissing her in front of her husband, who can do nothing. At the conclusion, Horner's overall plan proves successful, and by the end he has made love not only to Margery but to the other wives as well. Still, he goes unpunished. Also, during the course of the dramatic action, Horner's compatriot, Harcourt, in a subplot, steals away Pinchwife's sister, Alithea, from her intended husband, Sparkish.

The play exhibits all of the characteristics of Restoration comedy. The characters' names, for example, are indicative of their desires and personalities: Horner wishes to cuckold his acquaintances, and his name comes from the seventeenth-century image of a husband with an adulterous wife being depicted as a man wearing horns. Quack obviously is a

WILLIAM WYCHERLEY
(1640–1716)

In his plays William Wycherley satirized the elegant, dissolute society of Restoration England. In his life, however, he was a member of that society, participating fully in all the vices and follies that he ridiculed in his plays.

Like many Restoration dramatists Wycherley wrote few plays; playwriting for him was a way of proving cleverness and wit rather than a serious profession. Unlike his contemporaries, he showed the faults of all members of the glittering society rather than just making fun of the usual comic butts. A well-read man, he borrowed characters and situations from several sources, mainly Molière and Terence. He was also a master of the sexual humor of his time (such as using words with double meanings), provoking shock among the more prudish audiences of later centuries. Congreve, his fellow playwright, wrote that Wycherley's purpose was "to lash this crying age" with his satire.

As the son of a landowner, Wycherley had the correct family background for entrance into society. He was educated first in France and then, briefly, at Oxford. He began studying law at the Inner Temple in London but was soon practicing pleasure instead of law. His first comedy, *Love in a Wood*, produced in 1671, attracted the attention of the duchess of Cleveland, the king's mistress, who did not hesitate to share her favors.

Wycherley soon became one of London's leading wits and was sponsored at court by the duke of Buckingham, one of Charles II's favorites. Three more of the dramatist's comedies were successfully produced: *The Gentleman Dancing-Master* in 1672, *The Country Wife* in 1675, and *The Plain-Dealer* in 1676. After the last play, Wycherley went to sea and fought in the Dutch wars. When he fell ill, the king gave him money to recuperate in France and promised to make the playwright tutor to one of his sons.

Instead, Wycherley married a wealthy, jealous countess in 1681, and lost the king's favor. When the dramatist's wife died the following year, he became involved in litigation over the estate and, losing, spent seven years in debtors' prison before James II paid his bills and gave him a small pension. Wycherley married a young woman eleven days before his death in 1716, supposedly to aggravate his nephew.

The Country Wife One of the best known Restoration comedies of manners is this play by William Wycherley, filled with wit, repartee, intrigue, and sexual innuendo. The title character is Margery Pinchwife, seen in this scene on the right. Her husband, on the left, disguises her as a boy so that other men will not steal her from him, but Horner, the hero of the play, seduces her anyway. (Photo—Martha Swope.)

disreputable doctor, and Harcourt courts Alithea diligently. Fidget and Squeamish are nervous about their reputations, while Pinchwife does not want his wife pinched by other men. Sparkish, the fop, thinks he is a great wit—a social "spark"—when in reality he is dimwitted.

Wycherley also makes effective use of the double entendre. In the "china closet scene," Horner and Lady Fidget are in another room supposedly examining Horner's china. The audience realizes, however, that Horner is making love to Lady Fidget offstage while her husband is onstage. When Mrs. Squeamish arrives, she, too, asks to see his china. When Horner tells Mrs. Squeamish he has no more, the audience knows that china has become a code word for sex and that Horner is unable at that moment to make love.

The Country Wife satirizes upper-class Restoration society: Wycherley pokes fun at those persons who are more concerned with their reputations than with their actions. Today, the sexual content of Wycherley's comedy seems as up-to-date as any of the popular sex farces of our contemporary theater and film.

Congreve's *The Way of the World* (1700) is often cited as a bridge between Restoration comedy and eighteenth-century English sentimental comedy, which stresses traditional morality: the sinful are punished and the virtuous are rewarded. Like Restoration comedy, *The Way of the World* contains a number of characters involved in adulterous affairs as well as the traditional stock characters, but as in sentimental comedy, its two young lovers, Mirabell and Millamant, are united, while the wicked characters, Fainall and Marwood, are punished.

Restoration Audiences

Many of the Restoration comedies, including *The Country Wife*, indicate that audiences of that era, unlike modern-day spectators, were quite spirited during theatrical presentations. The fop Sparkish in *The Country Wife* describes how audience members purchased fruit from the "orange wenches" (many of whom were prostitutes), spoke back to the actors, arranged assignations with members of the opposite sex, and attended the theater to be seen rather than to see the play. These extratheatrical activities provoked attacks by religious leaders opposed to the art. Restoration audiences consisted primarily of members of the upper class, the group whom the playwrights of Restoration comedy were satirizing in their plays.

Those who have attended the theater in different periods and in various countries have varied significantly. In some periods, theater audiences have encompassed all types of people in a society, the poor as well as the rich; at other times, audiences have included people from only one social class. In ancient Greece, for instance, in the medieval theater, and in Elizabethan public theaters, the audiences included virtually all strata of society. By contrast, productions at European courts—such as masques—were seen only by nobility and royalty. Similarly, in the English Restoration theater only a small portion of society—the upper class—attended the theater.

When theater is aimed at a narrow group such as this, it generally means that playwrights tailor their plays specifically for the audience they know will be watching. Because of the special nature of the material, the plays are not likely to have the universality of plays written for a wider audience. Even so, the subjects of social pretentiousness and sex dealt with in Restoration comedy are familiar to sophisticated society in any age.

Actors and Their Companies

The most obvious change from the English Renaissance to the Restoration theater was the appearance of actresses on the English stage for the

*W*ILLIAM CONGREVE
(1670–1729)

Commenting on the fate of dramatists, William Congreve, in the prologue to his play *The Way of the World*, wrote:

Of those few fools who with ill stars are cursed,
Sure scribbling fools called poets, fare the worst.

His words proved to be prophetic, for that comedy ended his brief playwriting career. With his four comedies, however, Congreve established his reputation as one of the Restoration's finest dramatists.

Congreve, the son of an English army officer, had been raised and educated in Dublin, where the writer Jonathan Swift was one of his schoolmates. Returning to England to study law at the Middle Temple, he instead became involved in the literary and social life of Restoration London. His first literary venture was an undistinguished novel; Congreve turned next to playwriting with *The Old Bachelor*, produced in 1693 to great acclaim.

With Congreve's first success as a playwright came financial stability. This, in turn, led to a series of government appointments secured for him through influential friends. Always careful with his money, he acquired a reputation for miserliness in later life. His second comedy, *The Double Dealer* (1694), was less successful, but *Love for Love*, produced in the following year by the actor Thomas Betterton, was Congreve's greatest stage triumph. A tragedy, *The Mourning Bride* (1697), was also well received, but *The Way of the World* —later considered to be the best Restoration comedy—was a failure when it was first produced in 1700, and Congreve quit writing for the stage.

One of the reasons for the failure of *The Way of the World* was the changed moral climate in England, precipitated by Jeremy Collier's pamphlet, *A Short View of the Immorality and Profaneness of the English Stage* (see p. 190). Congreve attempted to answer the charges, but Collier made the stronger argument, leaving the playwright looking weak and foolish. By 1700, English society was changing, and the witty, elegant, superficial characters who people Congreve's plays were no longer representative.

Through his four comedies, Congreve assured himself of a place in the best literary and social circles of London —as a friend of Pope, Swift, Steele, and Gray—for the rest of his life. Congreve died in 1729, and was buried in Westminster Abbey.

first time. The presence of women was exploited in those Restoration comedies in which actresses were forced by plot complications to disguise themselves as men. In *The Country Wife*, as pointed out above, Margery Pinchwife's husband forces her to dress as a male in order to prevent acquaintances from flirting with her when he takes her out. While dressing actresses in tight breeches might not seem sexually provocative to modern audiences, eighteenth-century religious leaders found this stage practice highly licentious.

There were other, less outwardly visible transformations in the Restoration acting companies, especially in regard to the organizational structure. The sharing plan of companies like the Lord Chamberlain's Men almost disappeared in London during the course of the Restoration. Rather than sharing in the profits and losses of their companies, London actors were hired for a specific period of time at a set salary. The move from the sharing plan to the *contract system*, as the practice was called, marked the decline of the actors' control over the theatrical art in London.

At the same time, the Restoration witnessed the rise of theatrical entrepreneurs who were often partial owners of theater buildings and companies. The most notorious and successful theatrical businessman of the late Restoration and early eighteenth century was the lawyer Christopher Rich, who at the turn of the century controlled the patents Charles II had issued to both Davenant and Killigrew. Rich's insufferable financial practices, such as withholding some of his performers' pay and not providing reasonable salaries, led some actors in his group to rebel and establish their own company.

The rise of the entrepreneur as a powerful theatrical force was, of course, a step in the development of modern theater business. A good example in today's commercial theater is the American producer David Merrick, who was responsible for such musicals as *Hello, Dolly* and *42nd Street*. Outside of London, however, provincial companies, including those established in the thirteen colonies of North America, continued to employ the sharing play, with the actors still the controlling force.

In order to increase their set wages, actors were provided with yearly "benefits." Each major performer was provided with a "benefit performance" from which he or she kept all of the profits. Frequently ticket prices for these benefit performances were increased so that the performer's earnings would be greater. A few minor performers might share the profits from one benefit performance. The benefit system was employed in the English theater from the Restoration through the nineteenth century.

Restoration acting companies were larger than those of the English Renaissance. However, playwrights were rarely members of English Restoration troupes. Instead, they were paid by a variation of the benefit system, receiving the profits of the third night of their play's premiere run. By the turn of the century, they might also receive the profits of the sixth consecutive night of the initial run. It should be remembered, however, that the Restoration was not like the modern theater, in which long runs are more common. Many plays never succeeded in running three nights in a row.

Most historians agree that the acting style of the English Restoration, particularly for tragedy, was bombastic and, therefore, emphasized over-blown oratorical delivery. Thomas Betterton, the leading actor of the Restoration and the leader of the revolt against businessman Christopher Rich, was noted for his vocal prowess. Some historians have argued that comic acting may have been more realistic.

Actors learned their craft through apprenticeships and usually played a specific range of roles, that is, one man played serious heroes, another low-comedy types, and so forth. As in the Elizabethan theater, long runs were unusual, so companies changed their bills frequently, and actors had to develop the skills of quick study and retention. Rehearsals for new plays rarely extended past two weeks; a revival merited little more than a run-through on the day of the presentation. If the play was new, the playwright assisted in the initial rehearsals. However, much of the rehearsal process was the responsibility of the company's actor-manager, who was often a lead actor in the troupe.

Given the rehearsal procedures, the Restoration actor-manager was never able to assume the functions of the modern director, telling the performers where to move onstage and how to interpret their roles. For that matter, most rehearsals simply ascertained whether or not the performers knew their lines; we know from first-hand accounts that frequently, on opening night, they did not. Out of necessity, actors fell back on conventional stage-movement patterns; for example, much of the dialogue was presented at the front of the stage directly to the audience.

Governmental Regulation of the Theater

Government regulations played an important role in Restoration theater production. When the theater was restored in 1660, the rules established during the reign of Elizabeth to oversee the theaters were reinstituted. The Master of Revels took control of the theater and issued licenses to three theatrical entrepreneurs. Charles II, however, as noted earlier, issued patents to William Davenant and Thomas Killigrew that superseded those issued by the Master of Revels; this resulted in Davenant and Killigrew's monopolizing the London theater.

By the early eighteenth century, the monopoly seemed unenforceable; the monarchs following Charles II had made exceptions to the patents, and other companies operated in defiance of the monopoly. In 1737, Parliament, questioning Charles II's right to issue the patents without its approval, passed the Licensing Act, which was a new attempt to regulate the London theater. Under this act, two theaters, Drury Lane

ℰLEANOR NELL GWYNN
(1650–1687)

Nell Gwynn's remarkable career—taking her from the slums of London to the king's palace—can be attributed to her beauty and high spirits, and to the unique conditions of Restoration society. After over twenty years of Puritan rule, English society's main preoccupation after 1660 was pursuing pleasure. Theater was one of the fasionable entertainments, and one of the attractions of the theater was the introduction of actresses to the English stage.

The daughter of the keeper of a bawdy house and an unknown father, Nell Gwynn grew up in the London slums. She allegedly began her theatrical career as a girl selling oranges at the Theatre Royal, Drury Lane. At the theater she attracted the attention of Charles Hart, the leading actor, and became his mistress and acting protégé, making her stage debut in December 1664. As an actress, she relied on her natural wit and charm; she excelled in singing and dancing but was a total failure in tragedy. "Breeches roles," requiring her to wear male attire, and the delivery of prologues and epilogues were her specialties.

While Nell Gwynn was not typical of all Restoration actresses, in some ways she was representative. Actresses were still a novelty, and many were assiduously pursued by Restoration gallants. It was no disgrace to be someone's mistress, and because the theater was prestigious, actresses were favored as mistresses. There were probably as many affairs within the acting companies as there were with outsiders. Some actresses, however, like Anne Bracegirdle, were as celebrated for their virtue as Nell Gwynn was for her impropriety.

With her delivery of the epilogue to John Dryden's *Tyrannick Love* in 1669, Nell Gwynn attracted the attention of King Charles II. She became his mistress and left the stage, settling in a house in Pall Mall. In 1670 she returned to the theater to play in Dryden's *Conquest of Granada*. She had two sons by the king; the older one became the duke of St. Albans while the younger died in childhood.

It seems that Nell Gwynn's rise in social status did little to change her, except to make her more extravagant. She never denied her origins or claimed to be more than the king's mistress, and unlike his other favorites, she never meddled in politics. Her chief concerns were the king's amusement, her children, and entertaining his friends. Recognizing her faithfulness, Charles, on his deathbed, told his brother, "Let not poor Nelly starve." James II rescued her from her creditors and gave her a pension that enabled her to live comfortably until her death in 1687.

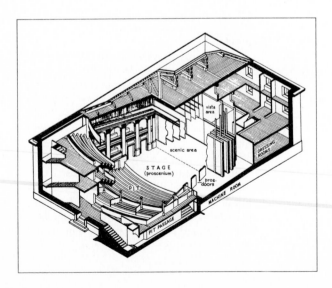

*D*rury Lane Theater *This English theater began during the Restoration and has continued to the present. The drawing above is from a later period, but the reconstruction at the left is of the Restoration period. Note the horseshoe-shaped pit for the audience and the two doors on each side of the stage. (Photo—Stone Collection, Victoria and Albert Museum, London; drawing from Richard Leacroft, in The Theatre, Roy Publisher, page 34.)*

𝒟RURY LANE THEATER

The origins of the Drury Lane Theater, a London playhouse still in existence, go back to the patent that Charles II granted to Thomas Killigrew in 1662. Killigrew built the first Drury Lane, known as the Theater Royal, in Bridges Street in 1663. It was supposed to be handsome and well-equipped, but the writer Samuel Pepys complained of catching cold from the draft and from the rain leaking from the glazed cupola over the pit.

In June of 1672, the building was partly destroyed by fire, and Killigrew took his company to a deserted theater while Christopher Wren built a new one. The new theater opened in March 1674, with the king and queen in attendance. Killigrew's death and his son's mismanagement so weakened the company that the theater was closed in 1676. Thomas Betterton united the two London acting troupes and reopened Drury Lane in 1682. The patent passed to Christopher Rich, who was interested only in making money. Under his mismanagement the theater went bankrupt in 1709 and closed again.

Drury Lane reopened later that same year under new management and ran successfully until Charles Fleetwood got control of the patent. Under Fleetwood's regime there were riots in 1737 over the abolition of free admission for footmen in the gallery and in 1741 at the first performance of Charles Macklin's more realistic reinterpretation of Shylock. (After 1737, the Drury Lane was one of only two legitimate theaters in London allowed under the Licensing Act.)

When Fleetwood faced bankruptcy, David Garrick, the company's leading actor, became manager in 1747. Until this time a few patrons had still been permitted to sit on the stage, but Garrick's reforms included the ending of this practice. Under his careful management, the theater became both prosperous and respected. Garrick was succeeded in 1776 by the playwright Richard Brinsley Sheridan and Sheridan's father-in-law. They enlarged the building between 1791 and 1794, supposedly making it fireproof. When actor John Kemble and his sister, the actress Sarah Siddons, left the company, the managers turned to melodrama and spectacle to prevent bankruptcy. Drury Lane burned to the ground in 1809, and there was no money to rebuild it.

Samuel Whitbread, a brewer and a shareholder in the patent, finally raised the money, and the theater was rebuilt in 1812. Drury Lane's history in the nineteenth century included a procession of managers, some successful at other houses, going into bankruptcy at the theater, until August Harris took over in the 1880s with a policy of spectacular shows and pantomimes. This formula for success has worked until the present time, and Drury Lane has become the home of musicals. The theater supposedly has a ghost: an eighteenth-century gentleman in cloak and riding boots who appears in the upper circle only at matinees when the house is full.

and Covent Garden, were the only ones authorized to present drama for "gain, hire, or reward," and the lord chamberlain became responsible for the licensing of plays. Thus the tradition of governmental regulation established by Queen Elizabeth continued into the Restoration and, beyond that, into the eighteenth century.

Theater Architecture in the Restoration

During the English Restoration, there were three theaters of note in London: Drury Lane, Lincoln Inn Fields (1661), which was a converted tennis court, and Dorset Garden (1671). Though each theater was distinct, all three interiors exhibited a unique fusion of Italianate and Elizabethan features.

By this time, the open-air public theater tradition of Elizabethan England had disappeared, and all Restoration theaters were indoor, proscenium-arch buildings. The area for the audience was divided into pit, boxes, and galleries, with the pit in the Restoration theaters—unlike the pit in French neoclassical buildings—containing backless benches to accommodate spectators. Also, the pit in the English houses was *raked*, or slanted, for better sight lines. The total seating capacity was about 650. In size, as well as in many other respects, the Restoration theaters were similar to the Elizabethan private theaters.

The Restoration stage, which was 34 feet deep, was highly unusual in that it was divided into two equal halves by the proscenium arch. The *apron*—the forestage in front of the proscenium—was 17 feet deep, and the backstage was of equal depth. In contrast, the aprons in twentieth-century proscenium-arch theaters are usually small and inconsequential. In the seventeenth century, only the English had theater buildings with extended aprons; most historians believe that the extended apron was a vestige of the platform stage of the English Renaissance. The apron was the major area for performance in Restoration theaters, and the upstage area housed the scenery. The entire stage was raked to improve sight lines.

The other unique elements of the Restoration stage were the proscenium doors with balconies above them. Most Restoration theaters had two proscenium doors on each side of the stage—a total of four doors—that led onto the forestage. These doors were employed for exits and entrances, and for the concealment scenes—with one character listening out of sight—popular in Restoration comedy. The balconies above the doorways could be employed for balcony and window scenes.

When we take a long look at theater history, we often see threads that run through several eras. The drama of Racine and Molière, for example, is a direct outgrowth of the neoclassical theater of the Italian Renaissance. The plays of these two men, in turn, influenced French theater for the next 300 years. The medieval theater of Spain evolved into the secular dramas of Lope de Vega, just as traces of the English medieval theater

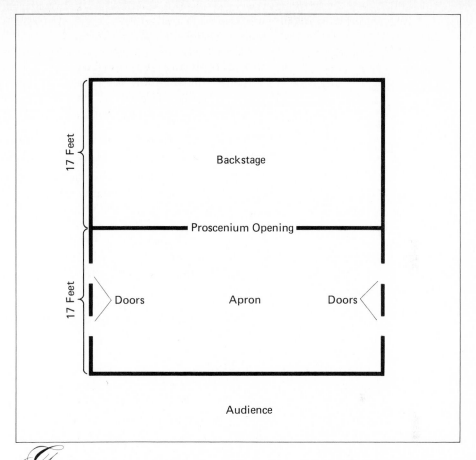

*G*round plan of a Restoration stage   *This stage was an unusual combination of English and Italian Renaissance stages. The Restoration saw the introduction of the Italianate proscenium arch into the public playhouses in England. However, the extended apron, equal in depth to the backstage area, and the two proscenium doors on each side of the stage were vestiges of the Elizabethan platform stage and tiring house.*

show up in the plays of Shakespeare. When we come to the architecture of the Restoration stage, we find the same process at work: the physical arrangement changes and develops, but elements of the earlier Elizabethan stage remain.

We have already suggested that the extended apron of the Restoration theaters was a vestige of the Elizabethan platform stage, but there are other similarities. The doors and balconies of the Restoration stage, for instance, are remnants of the doorways and upper playing areas of the Elizabethan stage. The English were slow to give up familiar features of the Elizabethan stage, and even after the Restoration, English and American proscenium-arch theaters in the eighteenth century contained some of these features.

The stage apron shrank in the 1700s, and the number of doors decreased from two on each side to one. The continued influence of Elizabethan theater architecture kept the English playhouses from becoming exact duplicates of those on the European continent, helping them to retain a distinctly English quality.

Scenery, Lighting, and Costumes

The visual elements—scenery, lighting, costumes—of the Restoration also illustrate the Italianization of the English stage. As noted in Chapter 6, Inigo Jones designed and painted wing-and-shutter settings for court entertainments. His son-in-law, John Webb, employed these scenic devices in his design for *The Siege of Rhodes* at the close of the commonwealth. Not surprisingly, then, during the Restoration, the basic scenic components were wings, shutters—sometimes replaced by rolled backdrops—and borders for masking. The sets, of course, were painted in perspective.

What made the scenic practices of Restoration England distinct from those of Italy and France was that the English rarely employed Torelli's pole-and-chariot system for scene changes. Instead, flats, placed in grooves above the proscenium and on the backstage floor, were pulled off into the wings, revealing new scenery directly behind the old. Because employment of the groove system required that each piece of scenery be removed separately by individual stagehands, scene changes in the English theater could not be synchronized, with all of the scenery moving simultaneously. As a result, audiences were made aware of an impending scene shift by a whistle blown by the prompter to signal the change to the stagehands at each groove position.

Because the curtain was never closed during the course of a presentation, scene changes were carried out in full view of the audience. Even musical entertainments—which were staged between the acts of full-length plays during the Restoration—were presented in front of the scenery already in view. As a result, the audience was always aware of the mechanical aspects of theatrical productions. All through the nineteenth century, the English, except in opera houses, used the primitive groove system for changing scenery.

Throughout the Restoration, companies kept collections of perspective settings that were reused frequently. Stock settings were the norm, primarily because of the expense entailed in having scenery painted. For this reason, most Restoration comedies have similar scenic requirements: the drawing room and the park.

Restoration costuming followed the traditions of the English Renaissance and the French neoclassical era, with contemporary costuming the standard practice. Contemporary garments were appropriate for Restoration comedy, but not for dramas set in past historical eras. While traditional costumes and accessories were occasionally employed as indications for historical figures or eras, there were no real attempts at historical accuracy. For example, the costume worn by an actor playing Shakespeare's Roman character Coriolanus would have consisted of a kind of ballet skirt, breeches, laced boots reaching halfway to the knees, an embroidered jacket, a full wig, and a helmet with plumes. This costume, which was employed well into the eighteenth century, was unrelated to the historical setting of Shakespeare's play. Due to their lack of appropriateness and verisimilitude, the conventions of Restoration costuming, like the scenic practices, would be jarring to modern theater-goers.

Because the Restoration theaters were indoors, lighting was a major concern. Theater performances during the late seventeenth-century normally were given in the afternoon so that windows could provide some natural lighting. Inside, candles were the predominant source of lighting, and chandeliers containing candles were visible above the stage and the audience. Candles were also placed in brackets attached to the front of the boxes. The stage and the audience area were always lit, and footlights —lights on the floor running along the front of the stage—were also employed. In today's theater footlights are rarely used because of the unnatural shadows they create on performers' faces. During the Restoration, however, theatrical artists could not be selective about the quality of the lighting; illumination was the primary concern.

Summary

The Restoration marks a strong Italian influence on English stage practices. The proscenium arch, perspective painting, and wing and shutter (or backdrop) became indispensable elements of the English stage. The French influence was also present, with the neoclassical ideals being introduced into serious English drama. Nonetheless, the English theater maintained its uniqueness. Proscenium-arch doors and balconies, along with the extended apron, were important vestiges of the Elizabethan stage. The comedy of manners, though borrowing from the French neoclassical playwright Molière, was a unique reflection of English Restoration society. Ultimately, the Italian and French influences were fused with English theatrical traditions to form the Restoration theater.

Chapter Nine

THE THEATER OF THE EIGHTEENTH CENTURY

In the textile industry in Berlin, Germany, between 1750 and 1780, the number of looms for making cotton increased from 80 to over 1000, and the number of silk looms jumped from under 300 to more than 2000. These changes are typical of what was happening, not only in Germany, but throughout Europe in the eighteenth century. It was a time of transition. In textiles there was a move away from wool, which had been the main fabric since the Middle Ages; at the same time, manufacturing was still done on handlooms, with the machinery of the industrial revolution yet to come. The transition that marked manufacturing also marked other aspects of life, including the theater. These political, philosophical, economic, and cultural changes paved the way for revolutionary developments in the nineteenth and twentieth centuries.

David Garrick in *Venice Preserved*   *The eighteenth century was an era of great stars. Unlike their predecessors, many of these performers paid close attention to the details of performances and costumes to achieve a greater sense of reality. David Garrick, seen here in a tragedy by Thomas Otway at the Drury Lane in 1762, was probably the finest English actor of his day. (Photo—Victoria and Albert Museum, London.)*

The Theater of the Eighteenth Century

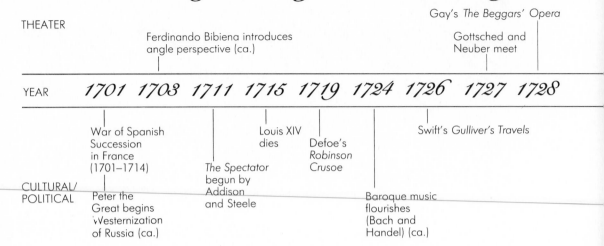

THEATER								Gay's *The Beggars' Opera*
		Ferdinando Bibiena introduces angle perspective (ca.)					Gottsched and Neuber meet	

YEAR	*1701*	*1703*	*1711*	*1715*	*1719*	*1724*	*1726*	*1727*	*1728*

War of Spanish Succession in France (1701–1714)

Louis XIV dies

Defoe's *Robinson Crusoe*

Swift's *Gulliver's Travels*

The Spectator begun by Addison and Steele

CULTURAL/ POLITICAL

Peter the Great begins Westernization of Russia (ca.)

Baroque music flourishes (Bach and Handel) (ca.)

EIGHTEENTH–CENTURY BACKGROUND

Beginning with the eighteenth century, the study of history, and of theater history in particular, becomes more complex. Homogeneous, self-contained societies began to disappear as the world was slowly transformed into a global community. The increase in mercantilism, that is, manufacturing and trade—particularly international trade—affected worldwide populations. The two major eighteenth-century mercantile powers were England and France, and decisions made in these nations directly affected people in such places as North America, India, and Africa. The effect on Africa, for example, was the marked increase in the slave trade.

Prior to the eighteenth century, wars had usually been fought for religious reasons; now they became territorial and economic battles. There were many wars in the eighteenth century, including the War of the Spanish Succession (1701–1714), the War of the Austrian Succession (1740–1748), and the Seven Years' War (1756–1763). The latter, known in America as the French and Indian War, is an excellent example of a battle for mercantile dominance. England and France, the leading mid-eighteenth-century powers in North America, were opponents in the Seven Years' War. As a result of France's defeat, England gained control of Canada and all French territory in North America east of the Mississippi. Spain, which had sided with France, had to cede Florida to England, and in compensation was given the French lands west of the Mississippi (the Louisiana Territory).

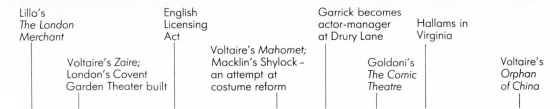

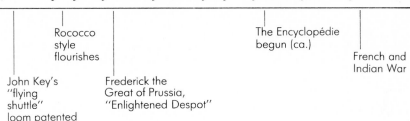

Western Europe prospered more than ever before because of the growth in trade; ingenious and daring investors of capital became extremely wealthy. The profits from the colonial trade filtered down to the emerging middle class. The latter included merchants and others involved in commercial enterprises, and in the eighteenth century they became a social as well as a political force. The lives of those at the bottom rung of the economic ladder, such as the Eastern European serfs, the French peasants, and the dispossessed English farmers, were not, however, improved by the expansion of trade. Some historians suggest that the disparity in wealth between the middle and lower classes became greater during this period.

The eighteenth century, because of the many new developments in learning and philosophy, is referred to as the Age of Enlightenment. France was the center of the Enlightenment, but the movement had international reverberations. The search for knowledge and enlightenment was supported by the educated middle class. Dictionaries and encyclopedias mere in great demand, with possibly the most famous being the multivolumed *Encyclopédie* edited by the French philosopher Denis Diderot between 1751 and 1772.

Besides Diderot, France produced many renowned philosophers in the eighteenth century, including Montesquieu (1689–1755), Voltaire (1694–1778), and Jean-Jacques Rousseau (1712–1778). Montesquieu, in his *The Spirit of the Laws* (1748), called for a separation and balance of powers in government as a means of ending monarchical absolutism. Voltaire argued for religious tolerance. Among those who supported

The Theater of the Eighteenth Century

THEATER

Spectators banished from French stage (ca.)

Boulevard theaters begin to develop in France (ca.)

Piranesi continues to paint his "prison drawings" employing *chiaroscuro*

Gozzi's *Turandot*

Drottningholm completed; Southwark Theater in Philadelphia

John Street Theater in New York

YEAR *1756   1759   1760   1761   1762   1766   1767*

Seven Years' War begins

Voltaire's *Candide*

Rousseau's *Social Contract;* Catherine the Great of Russia begins reign

CULTURAL/ POLITICAL

Voltaire was the German playwright Gotthold Ephraim Lessing (1729–1781), whose *Nathan the Wise* (1779) dramatized the ideal of religious brotherhood. In *The Social Contract* (1762), Rousseau claimed that government existed because of an agreement between the people governed, not between the ruler and those governed. Therefore, governmental officials were representatives and responsible to their constituents. In earlier writings, Rousseau attacked organized society, arguing that humanity was better off in a "state of nature."

The political philosophies of Montesquieu, Voltaire, and Rousseau had noticeable effects on eighteenth-century Europe and America. While many rulers were absolutists, believing that their powers were God-given and, therefore, could not be questioned, some monarchs, known as enlightened despots, rejected this concept of "divine right." They favored religious tolerance and wished to reform their societies for the good of their people. Two major political and social upheavals, the American Revolution (1775–1783) and the French Revolution (1789–1799), were based on the ideals of the Enlightenment. Thomas Jefferson's political philosophy, as expressed in the Declaration of Independence, was rooted in Enlightenment thought; the American Constitution was a version of Rousseau's social contract. The French revolutionaries' cry for liberty, equality, and fraternity originated in the philosophies of Montesquieu, Voltaire, and Rousseau. Unfortunately, the ideals of the French Revolution were compromised by the Reign of Terror; instead of liberty, equality, and fraternity, the French wound up with Napoleon in 1799.

The new knowledge characteristic of the era also had practical applications. Late eighteenth-century inventions facilitated the industrial revolution in the nineteenth century; the flying shuttle, the spinning

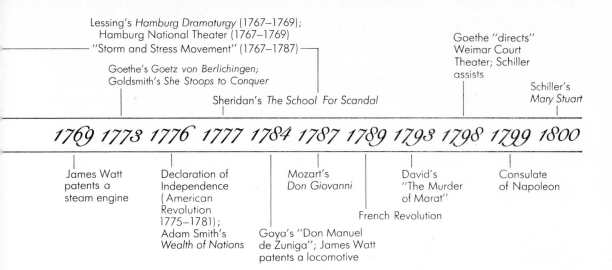

Lessing's *Hamburg Dramaturgy* (1767–1769);
Hamburg National Theater (1767–1769)
"Storm and Stress Movement" (1767–1787)

Goethe's *Goetz von Berlichingen*;
Goldsmith's *She Stoops to Conquer*

Sheridan's *The School For Scandal*

Goethe "directs"
Weimar Court
Theater; Schiller
assists

Schiller's
Mary Stuart

1769 1773 1776 1777 1784 1787 1789 1793 1798 1799 1800

James Watt
patents a
steam engine

Declaration of
Independence
(American
Revolution
1775–1781);
Adam Smith's
Wealth of Nations

Mozart's
Don Giovanni

Goya's "Don Manuel
de Zuniga"; James Watt
patents a locomotive

David's
"The Murder
of Marat"

French Revolution

Consulate
of Napoleon

jenny, and the cotton gin revolutionized the textile industry. James Watt's improved steam engine revolutionized manufacturing and transportation.

In the arts during the late seventeenth and early eighteenth centuries, *baroque* was the predominant style. Baroque painters, such as Peter Paul Rubens and Rembrandt, emphasized detail, color, and ornamentation in order to create more of a total visual illusion. Members of the emerging middle class frequently commissioned realistic baroque landscapes and portraits. The most renowned baroque composers, George Frederick Handel and Johann Sebastian Bach, achieved unity of mood and a continuity of line in their musical compositions, but like baroque paintings, their works were filled with movement and action.

In the late eighteenth century another style of art emerged. Called *rococo*, it was typified by the paintings of Jean Antoine Watteau. Though less ornate and grandiose than the baroque, it was still characterized by careful attention to detail.

In the midst of these social, political, philosophical, artistic, and industrial transformations, the theater also changed. There were some major and many minor revolutions in the eighteenth-century theater. While few of the theatrical experiments of the 1700s became generally accepted practices, they served as the foundation for the modern theater.

EIGHTEENTH–CENTURY THEATER

Though some first-rate plays were written during the eighteenth century, this was not a time of outstanding drama in the way that certain previous

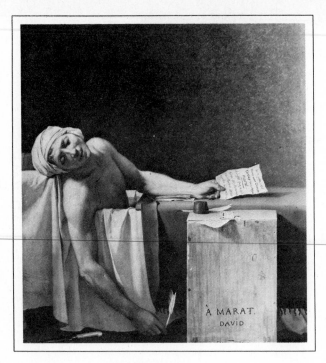

The Death of Marat (1793) by Jacque Louis David *This painting, which depicts the death of a leader of the French Revolution, reflects the artist's concern with the violent political world of his time; it also shows a desire to present a grotesque subject realistically. These same concerns inspired many of the theater artists of the late eighteenth century. (Photo—Editorial Photocolor Archives, Inc.)*

periods had been. Instead, it was an age that glorified star actors and saw the emergence of the director. As for the plays that were written, they were marked by the new dramatic forms that began to appear and serve as evidence of the transitional nature of eighteenth century drama.

The Move Away from Neoclassicism

Much of the early-eighteenth-century drama in Europe adhered to neoclassicism, but as the century progressed there were numerous attempts to deviate from the Renaissance rules. New forms, which defied the neoclassical definitions of genre, were introduced. There were also experiments with the episodic structure employed by William Shakespeare and his fellow Elizabethans.

Many eighteenth-century dramatic forms deviated from the traditional definitions of tragedy and comedy. Denis Diderot championed the *drame*, a new form which was defined as any serious play that did not fit the neoclassical definition of tragedy. *Bourgeois* (middle-class) *tragedy* and *domestic tragedy* were eighteenth-century examples of the *drame*. These forms of tragedy, ignoring the neoclassical requirement of royal protagonists, depicted tragic heroes and heroines who were members of the emerging middle class. These tragedies often were dramatizations of eighteenth-century middle-class morality, with the virtuous being re-

ＤＥＮＩＳ DIDEROT
(1713–1784)

"We are slaves of custom," wrote Denis Diderot in an essay on drama. Through his writings he hoped to bring about changes: he advocated the use of a rationalist philosophy, based on nature and reason, to make things as they should be.

Diderot came from a conservative, middle-class, provincial family in Langres, France. He was sent to Paris for his education and received a master of arts degree from the University of Paris in 1732. For a while he studied law, but he was much more interested in mathematics and languages. In 1734, after a quarrel with his family over the middle-class values, he began to lead a bohemian existence in Paris, living on the Left Bank and earning money as a hack writer. It was during this period that he met the philosopher Jean-Jacques Rousseau, who was to influence his theories. He was reconciled to his family in 1744 after his marriage.

As the reputation of his writings grew, Diderot was approached by a publisher to plan an encyclopedia. Originally it was to have been a translation of an English work, but Diderot saw it as an opportunity to expand knowledge and to expose the reactionary forces in church and state. Work on the book began in 1750 and was not completed until 1772.

One of the subjects that Diderot explored in his writings was the drama. He advocated the formation of a new genre, the *drame bourgeois*, which would seriously examine the problems of ordinary people and provide moral and philosophical conclusions. To accomplish this goal he favored greater realism on the stage, both in the scenic elements and in acting. While the two plays he wrote to illustrate his theories were failures, his ideas were influential, particularly in Germany and France, where a new realistic drama was to develop in the next century.

After the completion of the *Encyclopédie* Diderot no longer had a regular salary. This meant that severe financial problems were added to the harassment he faced for his antigovernment and anticlerical beliefs. To help him, the Empress Catherine I of Russia bought his library, hired him as librarian, and gave him the use of the books for his life. For her, the philosopher drew up a plan on how to govern Russia. His books and manuscripts were sent to Russia after his death in 1784.

warded and the wicked punished. Thus, they were frequently sentimental and melodramatic; that is, they openly appealed to the emotions as they pitted good characters against evil ones. Domestic tragedies focused on bourgeois familial concerns.

The emergence of the middle-class tragic hero mirrored the rise of the bourgeois as an eighteenth-century political and social force. The new middle-class audiences expected dramas to reflect their problems and points of view. *The London Merchant* (1731) by English playwright George Lillo is often cited as initiating the vogue for middle-class tragedies. In this play an apprentice is seduced by an older woman and ends up robbing his kind employer and murdering his uncle. He and the woman are apprehended and sentenced to death.

Later in the century, Diderot in France and Lessing in Germany wrote middle-class and domestic tragedies. While today most bourgeois tragedies seem trite and melodramatic—with unbelievable last-minute reformations of drunken or evil characters—they demonstrated that middle-class characters were fit subjects for serious drama. Many present-day critics believe that modern realistic tragedy, such as Arthur Miller's *Death of a Salesman*, with its emphasis on common family and social concerns, grew out of this form.

The English, along with the French, originated additional dramatic forms. The *ballad opera*, a parody of the Italian opera, was popularized in the 1730s by the success of John Gay's *The Beggar's Opera* (1728). In the ballad opera there was no sung dialogue, known in regular opera as *recitative*; instead, spoken dialogue alternated with songs set to popular, contemporary melodies. Characters in the ballad opera were drawn from the lower classes. Frequently the ballad operas were social and political satires poking fun at contemporary issues.

In France a similar form, known as the *comic opera*, developed. As in the ballad opera, there was no recitative and popular music was used for the songs. Comic opera satirized current events as well as serious dramas. At first, the characters in this minor form were drawn from the commedia dell'arte. By the mid-century, however, comic opera became less satirical and more sentimental and employed recognizable French characters.

The sentimental comedies of eighteenth-century England continue to be produced today. *Sentimental comedy* is like Restoration comedy except that it reaffirms middle-class morality: the virtuous are rewarded and the wicked punished. Sentimental comedies, which are comedies of manners, satirize social conventions and norms, and they also contain many of the character types found in the Restoration comedies.

In the early and middle parts of the century, particularly in France, sentimental comedy featured saccharine, overwrought emotions. The French had a name for this type of drama, *comédie larmoyante*, which means "tearful comedy." Later, though, a balance was restored between

The School for Scandal *Richard Brinsley Sheridan's play of 1777 has the wit, repartee, and concern with social pretentions of Restoration comedy, but more sense of moral justice. In the play, Joseph Surface, on the left, is exposed as the hypocrite he is, and Lady Teazle, on the right, is tempted to leave her husband but remains with him. (Photo—Diane Gorodnitzki, The Acting Company.)*

upholding middle-class virtues and making fun of social pretensions. The major examples of this later form are Richard Brinsley Sheridan's *The Rivals* and *The School for Scandal*. In the emerging American theater, Royall Tyler's *The Contrast* (1787) was patterned after Sheridan's sentimental comedies.

RICHARD BRINSLEY SHERIDAN
(1751–1816)

Richard Brinsley Sheridan is the best-known writer of the sentimental comedies so popular in the late eighteenth century. He was also the author of a noted literary burlesque called *The Critic* and was a successful theatrical manager. Though he is best remembered as a playwright, Sheridan would have preferred to be known as a politician. During his lifetime he combined all three careers, though they sometimes conflicted.

As the son of an actor and a novelist-playwright, Sheridan was familiar with the stage from childhood. Though born in Ireland he was raised in London, where his father's acting career had taken the family. His family hoped that he would study law, but he eloped at 21 with the daughter of a prominent singer and composer. Turning to the stage for a living, he wrote *The Rivals*, which was produced at Covent Garden early in 1775. Though the play failed at its first performance, Sheridan's revisions made it a success. He followed the play with *The Duenna*, a ballad opera, which had an unusually long run of seventy-five consecutive performances.

With these two works, and a short farce, Sheridan became the most promising new dramatist in London. Garrick, who was planning to retire from the management of Drury Lane, was impressed by Sheridan's talent and persuaded the playwright and his father-in-law to become part-owners of the theater. Sheridan wrote several plays for Drury Lane, including *The School for Scandal* (1777), considered the best comedy of manners since the Restoration, and *The Critic* (1779), one of the most famous literary burlesques.

There is an important difference between plays like Sheridan's *The Rivals* and *The School for Scandal* and Wycherley's *The Country Wife*, written 100 years earlier. Though both are comedies of manners, Wycherley's work is far more amoral, perhaps even immoral, in dealing with infidelity and other sexual matters.

As manager of Drury Lane, Sheridan exploited the public taste for spectacle and pantomine and attempted to enforce his monopoly by restricting the unlicensed theaters. Politics, however, had become his chief interest after his election to Parliament in 1780. He held several cabinet posts and was an adviser to the prince of Wales, who later became George III. Sheridan was also one of the best political orators of the day.

After 1808, the year Drury Lane burned, Sheridan's career took a downswing: he lost his Parliament seat, drank heavily, and was constantly in debt until his death in 1816. His comedies, with their witty ridicule of the follies of society, make Sheridan the link between the Restoration and the later comedy of Wilde and Shaw.

The emphasis on sentimentality and morality in the serious and comic drama of the eighteenth century is understandable in light of the era's philosophical outlook. The Enlightenment thinkers, influenced by the late seventeenth-century English theorists Locke and Hobbes, believed that human beings were rational and perfectible and that society could learn from history. The bourgeois tragedies and sentimental comedies underlined the moral optimism of the age.

Still, there were opponents to sentimental comedy, the most well known being the English dramatist Oliver Goldsmith (ca. 1730–1774), who wrote two plays: *The Good Natur'd Man* (1768) and *She Stoops to Conquer* (1773). In his "Essay on the Theatre," which appeared just before the premiere of *She Stoops to Conquer,* Goldsmith attacked sentimental comedy, calling, instead, for a "laughing comedy" which forces audiences to laugh at their own eccentricities and absurdities.

Many late-eighteenth-century German playwrights revolted against the neoclassical ideals and questioned the clear-cut morality found in sentimental comedy and bourgeois tragedy. Lessing, in his critical treatise *The Hamburg Dramaturgy* (1767–69), questioned the neoclassicist interpretation of Aristotle. Furthermore, Lessing expressed admiration for Shakespeare's dramaturgy. German admiration for Shakespeare and the Elizabethans culminated in the Storm and Stress *(Sturm und Drang)* movement. The Storm and Stress dramatists, though not uniform in playwriting technique, rejected dramatic rules. Many of them patterned their works after Shakespeare, copying the episodic structure, the mixture of genres, and the presentation of onstage violence. The Storm and Stress movement—which included such plays as Johann Wolfgang von Goethe's *Goetz von Berlichingen* (1773) and Friedrich Schiller's *The Robbers* (1782)—was the forerunner of nineteenth-century romanticism.

In Italy, during the middle of the eighteenth century, there was a struggle between the playwrights Carlo Goldoni and Carlo Gozzi over which direction Italian commedia dell'arte should take, with Goldoni wanting to make it less artificial than it had been and Gozzi wanting to make it even more fantastic. Their stylistic battle foreshadows the split in the next century between the realists and the antirealists.

GOVERNMENT REGULATION OF THEATERS

In theater production, the eighteenth century was noted in certain countries—England, France, and the independent German states—for governmental attempts to regulate theatrical practices. In many cases, however, ingenious theatrical entrepreneurs found the means to outwit the restrictions.

As noted previously, the English tradition of governmental interven-

CARLO GOLDONI
(1707–1793)

CARLO GOZZI
(1720–1806)

For fifteen years, from 1748 to 1762, the Italian playwrights Carlo Goldoni and Carlo Gozzi carried on a fierce controversy over the future direction of the commedia dell'arte.

As a former lawyer and the son of a doctor, Goldoni belonged to the rising middle class of Venice, and many of his 212 plays reflect the life of that city. Goldoni wanted theater to be more realistic and less fanciful. In his reform of commedia, he discouraged the use of masks and improvisational playing in order to make the characters more lifelike. Tired of the endless quarrel with Gozzi—which was carried out in correspondence and various published articles —Goldoni, in 1762, accepted an invitation from the king of France to write for the Comédie Italienne in Paris. He remained there until his death in 1793.

Gozzi, by contrast, came from a noble but impoverished Venetian family. He began his literary career as a young man and spent much of his life defending Italian culture against corrupting influences. Gozzi felt Goldoni's approach to commedia lowered it to the level of banal, meaningless reality. Instead he proposed a theater of the fabulous, where the commedia would be transformed through the mixture of prose and poetry, and through improvised and planned actions. His ten plays, performed between 1761 and 1765, are fantasies based on popular and oriental myths.

It is hard to judge who won the argument. Goldoni left Venice, but his position at the French court was more prestigious. Gozzi's plays were popular in Italy for a while, but were more appreciated in Germany and in France. As one of the first realistic playwrights, Goldoni heralded the movement that was to dominate the modern period. Many of his plays, including *The Fan* (ca. 1763), *Mirandolina* (ca. 1753), and *The Servant of Two Masters* (ca. 1743), are still performed. Gozzi was an inspiration to the romantics of the early nineteenth century and to the nonrealistic theater of the twentieth century. His *Turandot* (1762), was made into an opera by Puccini, while Prokofiev used his *The Love of Three Oranges* (1761) as the basis for a ballet. *The King Stag* (1762), Gozzi's finest play, is occasionally revived.

Commedia dell'arte continues
Playwright Carlo Goldoni carried forward
Italian commedia but made important
modifications. He dispensed with masks
and insisted on rehearsed dialogue instead
of improvisation. This is Harlequin in a
recent production of Goldoni's The Servant
of Two Masters. *He was a clever, but*
sometimes stupid servant, who always wore
diamond-shaped patch pants.
(Photo—North Carolina School of the Arts.)

tion in the theater could be traced back to Elizabeth, who had issued proclamations limiting dramatic subject matter and had also designated the Master of Revels as the licensor of theatrical companies and plays. When Charles II was restored to the throne in 1660, he issued the first of several "patents" (licenses) to Davenant and Killigrew which resulted in their monopolizing the London theater. When the validity of these patents was questioned, Parliament, in 1737, issued the Licensing Act, which restricted the presentation of drama to the Drury Lane and Covent Garden Theaters and made the lord chamberlain responsible for the licensing of plays. In 1766 the Haymarket Theater was licensed as a summer house.

Numerous theatrical personalities tried to circumvent the Licensing Act. Some managers opened nonlicensed houses hoping that the ordinance would not be vigorously enforced. Since the law applied to persons performing "tragedy, comedy, opera, play, farce, or other entertainment of the stage, for gain, hire or reward," some entrepreneurs argued that they were not profiting from their dramatic presentations. The manager of one unlicensed theater claimed that his audiences were charged admission to hear a concert and that his plays were presented as a free extra. (Musical entertainments were always part of the extended English theatrical bill of the eighteenth century.) Another manager supposedly sold dishes of chocolate, accompanied by theatrical presentations at no additional cost. Another means of circumventing the law was to argue that the type of entertainment presented was not covered by the Licensing Act. Many highly theatrical popular entertainments were not regulated by the statute. One such form was the *burletta*, which, at the turn of the century, was defined as any play with five or more songs per act. Sly theater managers converted nonmusical dramas, such as Shakespeare's plays, into burlettas.

In eighteenth-century France, government restrictions governed the types of plays theaters could produce. The Opera, the Comédie Française (the home of nonmusical drama), and the Comédie Italienne (the home of the commedia dell'arte and, later, of comic opera) were the three major Parisian theaters subsidized by the government. For most of the eighteenth century, *boulevard theaters*, so named because they were located on the Boulevard du Temple, catered to popular tastes by inventing many types of musical entertainments. The boulevard theaters had developed out of the companies performing at the Parisian fairs. The boulevard forms, such as the *comic opera*, were so popular that the government-supported houses incorporated them into their repertoires. In 1791, the leaders of the French Revolution abolished the artificial theatrical restrictions.

German government intervention in the theater was of a more positive nature. Eighteenth-century Germany was not unified and consisted of several independent states. The German theater, which struggled to become established in the early eighteenth century, became an important artistic force during the last quarter of the century. During that period, state-subsidized national theaters were organized in various Germanic states. While subsidization provided stability for the German theater artists, it meant that the government could wield control over the theatrical presentations.

THEATER ARCHITECTURE

Eighteenth-century English playhouses were significantly different from those of the Restoration. The apron, or forestage, in eighteenth-century English theaters shrank, extending out approximately 12 feet from the proscenium arch, while the backstage area became much deeper. There was one proscenium door on each side of the stage leading out onto the apron; above each door was a proscenium box. In contrast to the English theaters, the basic configuration of the eighteenth-century continental theaters followed the Italian Renaissance tradition. A typical theater contained a proscenium-arch stage—without doors or extended apron—as well as pit, boxes, and galleries, and employed pole-and-chariot

*O*pulence in eighteenth century theaters   *New, large-scale playhouses such as this one, were erected throughout Europe in this era. These lavish theaters traditionally contained a proscenium-arch stage with audiences in the pit, boxes, and galleries. This playhouse, which was designed for but never used by the Paris Opera, housed the Comédie Française in the 1800s. (Photo—Bibliotheque Nationale, Paris.)*

scene-shifting machinery.

Theater buildings proliferated throughout Europe in the eighteenth century in such countries as Germany, Russia, and Sweden. Possibly the most significant theater building constructed in this period was Drottningholm in Sweden. Erected in 1766 as part of the royal summer palace outside of Stockholm, it was boarded up in the 1790s and remained closed until the early twentieth century. Today tourists can take the ferry from Stockholm to the palace grounds at Drottningholm in order to explore a perfect working example of an eighteenth-century Italianate proscenium-arch, pole-and-chariot theater. Even the wings and shutters, painted in perspective, remain intact.

Permanent theaters were also constructed in the new world. In the

*he Theater at Drottningholm,
Sweden This theater still has the same
sets and stage machinery that were used
when it was built as a court playhouse in
the eighteenth century. It is an excellent
example of an Italianate proscenium
theater with pole and chariot scene
changing. Each summer, period productions,
such as the one shown here, are presented.
(Photo—Swedish National Tourist Office.)*

colonial era the two most notable were the Southwark Theater (1766) in
Philadelphia and the John Street Theater (1767) in New York City. Later,
two major theaters constructed in the newly established United States
were the Chestnut Street Theater (1794) in Philadelphia and the Park
Theater (1798) in New York. These two American theaters were patterned after eighteenth-century English structures like Covent Garden.

Still, there were important transformations in both types of
eighteenth-century theaters. In order to accommodate the new middle-
class audiences, the houses became larger; for example, in London's
Drury Lane, the seating capacity grew from about 650 in 1700 to about
3000 in 1800. The interiors were ovoid (egg-shaped) so as to improve sight
lines. By the end of the century, even the French pits contained backless
benches. Spectators were removed from the stage in England and France
by the middle of the century: their removal was in keeping with Denis
Diderot's "fourth-wall convention." According to the French philosopher's theory, the audience should not disturb the performance nor

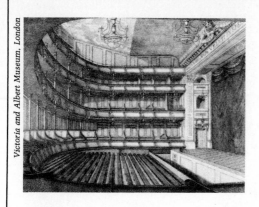

COVENT GARDEN
(Opened 1732)

When John Rich, holder of one of the patents for London theaters, ended the season of 1731, he began a subscription to raise funds for building a new theater in Box Street, Covent Garden. Unlike his father, Christopher Rich, a lawyer who had bought the patent as a business investment and was a poor manager, John Rich was an able manager and an accomplished performer.

The Covent Garden Theater, a London playhouse that still exists today, opened on December 7, 1732, with a revival of *The Way of the World.* Under Rich the bill featured extravagant pantomimes with animals, tumblers, and contortionists, as well as revivals of old plays. From 1737 to 1843 Covent Garden and Drury Lane were the only two theaters in London sanctioned by the Licensing Act to produce legitimate drama. The survival and management of both theaters are important, therefore, for providing a showcase for British drama over a sustained period of time.

When Rich died in 1761, his son-in-law managed the theater and concentrated on opera. From 1767, when the family sold the patent, until 1803, Covent Garden had a series of managers. To meet rising costs, the theater was enlarged twice, in 1787 and in 1792, so that it held about 3000 spectators.

John Philip Kemble, an actor, bought a share of the patent in 1803. He and his sister, Sarah Siddons, performed there until their retirements. Covent Garden's sensation for 1804 was Master Betty, a child actor so popular that Parliament adjourned to see him. The theater burned down in 1808, and Kemble tried to recoup his losses by raising prices when it reopened in 1809. This resulted in the Old Price Riots, which began on opening night and lasted for sixty-one days until Kemble backed down.

Charles Kemble, who had succeeded his brother in 1817, presented *King John* in 1824 with the first complete set of historically accurate scenery and costumes. When he found himself in financial difficulties, he was rescued by his daughter, Fanny Kemble, whose stage success helped him to pay his debts.

Others attempted to manage Covent Garden in the nineteenth century with little success. William Charles Macready, the actor, had a fine company that performed in quality plays, but he refused to keep successes running. Madame Vestris staged several carefully researched Shakespearean revivals, but she also failed. A fire destroyed the theater in 1856 and it was rebuilt in 1858. The theater was then turned over to opera, and, except for occasional dramatic performances, has continued to be the home of opera and ballet ever since.

A Bibiena set design *During the eighteenth century, one family dominated scene design in Europe: the Bibiena family in which the second, third and fourth generations carried on the tradition begun by Giovanni Bibiena. This 1720 stage setting is a typical Bibiena design with its vast scale, its ornateness and elegance, and its perspective disappearing in several directions. (Photo—Victoria and Albert Museum, London.)*

should the actors acknowledge the spectators. In short, it should be as if there were an invisible glass wall between the audience and the actors. While the "fourth-wall convention" did not become an accepted theatrical practice until the nineteenth century, the removal of audience members from the stage was a step in this direction.

Scene Design Innovations

The Italian influence on scene design in the eighteenth century was pervasive. Most continental theaters employed Italianate wing-and-shutter settings, painted in perspective, and shifted by Torelli's pole-and-chariot mechanism. (American theaters, as well as the English and Dutch, employed the groove system for scene shifting.) Additional elements occasionally incorporated into the painted designs included : (1)

Detail from a Bibiena design.

THE BIBIENA FAMILY
(from 1690 to 1787)

For nearly 100 years, from 1690 to 1787, the name Bibiena was synonymous with scenic design throughout Europe. Seven members from three generations of the family were designers. The Bibienas are noted for the following innovations: (1) the use of baroque art in their designs, (2) the vastness of the scale of their settings and the elaborate ornamentation they contained, and (3) their use of angle perspective. Angle perspective means that a design has several vanishing points rather than the single vanishing point employed since the Renaissance. (See the biography of Sebastiano Serlio in Chapter 5.) Angle perspective gives a scene more complexity and depth than single-point perspective.

The family originally came from a town near Florence, Italy, where Giovanni Maria Gialli (1625–1665), an artist and the founder of the family, was born. His two sons, Ferdinando (1657–1743) and Francesco (1659–1739), studied painting in Bologna, Italy, and then studied scene design under Rivani, who had worked for Louis XIV at Versailles in France. Francesco became ducal architect at Mantua, Italy, and built theaters in Vienna, Rome, Verona, and Nancy. He also assisted his brother Ferdinando with the spectacles at the court of Charles VI in Vienna. Before Ferdinando came to Vienna he had worked in Parma and Barcelona and had published several books.

Ferdinando's sons also became designers. Allesandro (1687–1769) was court painter and architect to the elector of the Palatinate in Germany. Antonio (1700–1774) worked with his father in Vienna and also in Bologna and Mantua, while Giovanni Maria (ca. 1704–1769) built a theater near Lisbon. Giuseppe (1696–1757) was the most noted of the brothers. He succeeded his father as court designer in Vienna and also worked in Munich, Prague, Dresden, and Bayreuth. Before his death in Berlin, Giuseppe published his designs in three series of engravings.

Giuseppe's son Carlo (1728–1787) was the last to follow the family profession. He also traveled the widest, working in Germany, France, the Netherlands, London, Naples, Stockholm, and St. Petersburg. The sets that he designed for the court theater at Drottningholm, Sweden, are still in use today. Some of his designs were also published.

Together, the Bibienas established a style of scene design—on a grandiose scale—that dominated the stage throughout the eighteenth century.

borders at the top to mask the fly space; (2) ground rows, which were silhouette cutouts along the stage floor; (3) large scenic cutouts, such as painted trees, which could be shifted by the pole-and-chariot system; (4) rolled backdrops which replaced the shutters; and (5) act drops, which were the curtains at the front of the stage.

Italy was the birthplace of many scenic innovations in the eighteenth century, just as it had been in the Renaissance. The most influential Italian designers and theater architects of the period belonged to the Bibiena family. Members of this family, through several generations, worked as scene designers. Typically, Bibiena designs were grandiose, lavish, and ornate, in keeping with the baroque style. The family worked throughout Europe and frequently at royal courts. The most noted members were the brothers Ferdinando and Francesco, who worked during the early 1700s and introduced angular or multipoint perspective. The painted sets of the Italian Renaissance had pulled the eye to a central vanishing point, but in the Bibienas' designs, the eye was attracted to various vanishing points, thus breaking the standard visual pattern. The Bibienas' sets also seemed to extend beyond the proscenium arch, while the Renaissance designs seemed totally framed and enclosed by the arch.

The other major changes in scene design during this century included a concern with the creation of mood, attempts at depicting recognizable locales, attempts at historical accuracy, and more frequent employment of three-dimensional properties. The Italian Giambattista Piranesi (1720–1778) heightened the atmospheric quality of designs by emphasizing the contrast between light and shadow in painting, a technique known as *chiaroscuro*. Philippe Jacques de Loutherbourg (1740–1812) was among the designers who introduced local color into their settings. Loutherbourg, hired by the English actor-manager David Garrick for the Drury Lane Theater in 1771, worked at this theater for a decade. Local color refers to the inclusion in designs of places audience members recognize in their own community; in eighteenth-century London this would have meant such landmarks as the Tower of London and London Bridge. The interest in recreating recognizable locales in scene design was in keeping with the popularity of eighteenth-century landscape painting. The introduction of local color was a move away from the neoclassical stock-set tradition. Still, eighteenth-century theater companies could not afford to construct unique settings for each production—such as theaters have today—because of the prohibitive cost.

The developing interest in ancient history in the middle of the century also led some designers to experiment—albeit usually unsuccessfully—with historical accuracy in settings. The real explosion in historically accurate designs occurred, as we shall see, in the nineteenth century.

During the 1700s, more three-dimensional, practicable elements were introduced into the painted stage settings. The climactic scene, for example, in Richard Brinsley Sheridan's sentimental comedy *The School for Scandal* required a screen for concealment.

These developments would lead eventually to the realism of the *box set*, an arrangement in which flats are cleated together at angles, rather than set up parallel to the audience, in order to form the three-dimensional walls of a room. Recent research suggests that the Italian designer Paolo Landriani (1770–1838) employed the box set in the last decade of the eighteenth century at Milan's La Scala Opera House. There are other scholars, however, who argue that the box set may have been used, on occasion, even as early as the Italian Renaissance. Regardless of when it was first employed, the box set revolutionized scene design in the nineteenth century and became an integral element in realistic staging. Even if the box set was not actually introduced in the eighteenth century, the increased employment of practicable elements began to transform the painted wing-and-shutter settings and paved the way for it.

There were also experiments with stage lighting in the late 1700s, with attempts to mask lighting sources, to employ silk screens for coloring, and to introduce oil lamps and other replacements for candles. These primitive lighting sources were not easily controlled, however, and the auditorium as well as the stage had to remain lit.

Attempts at Historical Accuracy in Costuming

Theatrical costuming remained a primitive art throughout most of the eighteenth century. Actors and actresses, who often provided their own wardrobes, believed that the chief criterion for a costume was that it show the performers off to the best advantage. Traditional, conventional costumes for specific characters and eras were common. On the English stage, for example, the Italian Jew Shylock, in adaptations of Shakespeare's *The Merchant of Venice*, was always costumed with red hair and a large nose. Production costumes were not unified, nor was there much concern for the appropriateness of costumes for characters or time period. Eighteenth-century costuming experiments did not make an immediate impact on these stage practices; rather, they were the seeds that flowered into a theatrical revolution in the next century.

Daring theater artists throughout Europe experimented with historically acurate costuming. These attempts often were not the exact historical reconstructions we are accustomed to today, but the artists were not totally to blame; accurate historical information was limited and audiences expected the traditional stage costumes. Those artists who veered from the accepted conventions were ridiculed by the audience. Nevertheless, in 1741, the English actor Charles Macklin (ca. 1700–1797) attempted to present a truly Jewish Shylock, while in 1772 he performed Macbeth in Scottish garb. In France, three performers, Marie-Justine

*C*harles Macklin as Shylock *Macklin was one of several oustanding eighteenth century actors who strove for greater reality and authenticity in their roles. Macklin caused a sensation with his portrayal of Shylock from* The Merchant of Venice. *The part had been played as a caricature before, but in his dress and manner Macklin created a convincing and moving character. (Photo—The Folger Shakespeare Library, Washington, D.C.)*

Favart (1727–1772), La Clairon (1723–1803), and Henri-Louis Lekain (1729–1778), experimented with costuming supposedly appropriate for their characters' social positions, nationalities, and historical eras. The German actor-manager Friedrich Ludwig Schroeder (1744–1816) apparently employed historically appropriate garments in a 1774 production of Goethe's *Goetz von Berlichingen*. The first steps were important in setting the stage for greater historical accuracy in later periods.

ACTING: GREATER SOCIAL ACCEPTANCE AND AN EMPHASIS ON THE "NATURAL"

The eighteenth century was an era of well-known and enormously popular performers. All across Europe popular and successful actors and actresses developed dedicated followings. Some of these performers worked to improve their colleagues' social status, but by and large actors remained suspect members of society. Others strove to create more natural, individualized characterizations, but these innovators were not in the mainstream.

The predominant approach to acting in the eighteenth century was "bombastic," emphasizing the performers' oratorical skills. Standardized patterns of stage movement were necessary because of the limited rehearsal time and the frequency of changes in the bills. Actors, more often than not, addressed their lines to the audience, not to the person to

CAROLINA NEUBER
(1697–1760)

German theater in 1720 consisted of traveling troupes which played farces and improvised comedies at fairgrounds. The literary critic Johann Gottsched wanted to elevate the quality of German theater by improving the repertoire with plays based on French models and refining the acting style. Until he saw the company headed by Carolina Neuber, he could not find a troupe to carry out his reforms. Neuber, whose name before her marriage was Carolina Weissenborn, was responsible for a number of important reforms in German theatrical practice. She attempted (1) to upgrade performances by banning a popular clown character from the stage, (2) to improve the social standing of her actors and actresses, and (3) to get better plays for her company.

Born in 1697, Carolina eloped with Johann Neuber, a young clerk, in 1718, to escape from her tyrannical father. After serving as apprentices in several companies, the Neubers formed their own troupe about 1725 and secured a license to perform at the Leipzig Easter Fair. In the company, Carolina insisted on the memorization of lines and careful rehearsals instead of improvisation. She shared Johann Gottsched's desire to improve German theater, so she was quite willing to perform his model repertoire. They began their collaboration in 1727. She was strong-willed and popular enough to impose her views on her company and her public.

The collaboration between Neuber and Gottsched lasted twelve years, but in 1739 the friction between the independent actress and the dictatorial critic caused a break. In 1740 the Neubers took their troupe to Russia, introducing modern theater to that country. When they returned to Germany the following year, Gottsched had allied himself with another troupe. The final break came when Carolina Neuber replaced the togas the critic had specified for one of his plays with flesh-colored tights. After the break, Gottsched attacked the actress in his reviews; she in turn called him a "bat-eared" critic in one of her prologues.

After Carolina's company broke with Gottsched, it began to decline. The Neubers continued to struggle until the outbreak of the Seven Years' War in 1756 impoverished them. Carolina died in 1760, a year after her husband. Her alliance with Gottsched, the first between the literary and the performance areas of theater in Germany, laid the foundation for the German theater, which developed into the most vital in the western world by 1800.

whom they were supposed to be speaking, and fell back on improvisation. In Europe and America, actors were often employed by "lines of business," that is, according to type. Normally, actors "possessed their parts"; once they performed a role, it remained theirs until retirement or death. In the midst of these conventional practices, there were some innovators.

In the 1730s, the German actress Carolina Neuber attempted to improve the social status of the performers by policing the morality of the members of her company. Furthermore, there were attempts to treat the acting craft and profession seriously. For example, Denis Diderot wrote *The Paradox of Acting*, a theoretical treatise on acting. In it he suggested that the more emotion the performer actually feels, the less the audience feels—a view that runs counter to most contemporary realistic-acting theories. Attempts to establish acting schools in England and France were further indications of the new serious attitude toward the art in the eighteenth century.

The list of eighteenth-century actors and actresses who rejected the bombastic, conventionalized style for a more natural approach includes the English actors Charles Macklin and David Garrick, the French performers Michel Baron (1653–1729), Adrienne Lecouvreur (1692–1730), La Clairon, and Henri-Louis Lekain, and the German performer Friedrich Schroeder. All of these performers rejected the emphasis on declamation (a formal way of speaking), the use of stereotypical patterns of blocking (set movements on stage), and the singsong delivery of verse. All supported individualized characterizations and more careful rehearsal procedures. Because these performers worked in traditional eighteenth-century companies, they were restricted by traditional stage practices and did not attempt to create everyday life on stage. Nevertheless, they were the ancestors of our modern realistic performers.

The Emergence of the Director

In terms of the future, possibly the key development in the eighteenth century was the emergence of the modern director. Prior to this century, as we have noted, playwrights and/or leading actors normally doubled as the directors of stage business. (The medieval pageant master was a distinct exception.) Since these individuals had more pressing primary concerns, actual directing was minimal; furthermore, little time was spent on preparing a production in rehearsal. What was missing in the theater, then, was someone to oversee and unify the stage productions, to assist performers, and to ensure the appropriateness of a production's visual elements. Two eighteenth-century figures are often cited as being the "fathers" of modern stage direction because they assumed all of these responsibilities: the English actor David Garrick and the German playwright, poet, and novelist Johann Wolfgang von Goethe.

DAVID GARRICK
(1717–1779)

David Garrick, with his reforms in staging, revitalized the eighteenth-century English stage and won for it the respect of all of Europe. Because he oversaw the entire production process, Garrick is often said to have been an early director.

Garrick's first stage success came at the age of 11 in a school play. His father, an army officer, provided Garrick with a good education, including a term at Dr. Samuel Johnson's academy. A financial legacy enabled the future actor and his older brother to enter the wine trade. While working at the London branch of the company, he became acquainted with prominent actors and producers, including Charles Macklin, with whom he discussed theories of realistic acting.

Resolved to try the stage as a career, Garrick played several roles at Goodman's Fields, a small theater outside of London. On October 18, 1741, he appeared there as Richard III and swept London with his acting. Though he was slender and of medium height, he had expressive features and dark, piercing eyes. He often based his characters on life, visiting the markets and the law courts to study people. His repertoire included over ninety roles, and he was equally good in comedy and tragedy.

In 1747 Garrick became one of the patent holders at the Drury Lane Theater. He took an active part in the management of the theater, where he assembled a distinguished acting company. As a manager he also wrote prologues and epilogues for revivals, adapted old plays, and occasionally wrote new works. The reforms he instituted, such as longer rehearsal periods and banning spectators from the stage, made Drury Lane the dominant London theater until his retirement in 1776.

Though his rivals considered him vain and snobbish, Garrick was a cultured gentleman who enjoyed the company of literary and society figures. When he died in 1779, he was buried in the Poets' Corner of Westminster Abbey. His friend Dr. Johnson wrote, "I am disappointed by that stroke of death that has eclipsed the gaiety of nations, and impoverished the public stock of harmless pleasure."

JOHANN WOLFGANG VON GOETHE (1749–1832)

Johann Wolfgang von Goethe was responsible for a number of important innovations in the German theater, comparable to those of David Garrick in England. Both Goethe and Garrick pointed the way toward the modern conception of the stage director.

A man of many talents, Goethe, in addition to being a theatrical producer, was a playwright, critic, and philosopher. He was also a minister of the court of Weimar, Germany, running everything from mining activities to court theatricals with efficiency.

As the son of a wealthy Frankfurt merchant, Goethe enjoyed an excellent education. He studied at the University of Leipzig, the cultural capital of Germany, and in his enthusiasm wanted to learn everything. But the mental strain and a whirlwind love affair brought on a physical collapse that forced him to leave school. At home, he became interested in religious mysticism, alchemy, astrology, and occult philosophy. It was at Strasbourg, where he finished his studies, that he became involved with the Storm and Stress movement in German literature and wrote his first play, *Goetz von Berlichingen* (1773), in Shakespearean style. The Storm and Stress movement, which emphasized the wide-ranging adventures of independent-minded heroes, was the forerunner of the romanticism of the nineteenth century.

Goethe continued to write plays, poetry, and a novel during his brief law practice, but in 1775 he accepted a post at the court of Weimar as director of theater. The post soon expanded to the running of almost the entire duchy. Tired of the constant demands on his time, and seeking spiritual renewal, he went to Italy in 1786 and stayed two years.

In Italy, Goethe discovered the beauty of the Greek and Roman ruins, which precipitated a shift to classical themes and forms in his writing. When he returned to Weimar, he shed most of his court duties and devoted himself to writing and scientific research. A friendship with the dramatist Friedrich Schiller led Goethe to take a renewed interest in the court theater, which he had neglected for several years.

Sharing a common belief that drama should transform ordinary experience and reveal ideal truths, the two writers transformed the Weimar theater, Schiller with his plays and Goethe with his stagings. A severe taskmaster, Goethe laid down strict rules for the actors, beating time with a baton to get proper rhythm in speech. He created one of the most perfect acting ensembles ever seen to that time. After Schiller's death in 1805, Goethe gradually lost interest in the theater and became an increasingly remote figure until his death in 1832. Goethe's own playwriting efforts culminated in his long dramatic poem *Faust* (Part I, 1808; Part II, 1831).

Between 1747 and 1776 David Garrick was a partner in the management of the Drury Lane Theater and, therefore, responsible for artistic decisions. As the company's leading performer, he championed the more natural style of acting. Garrick argued for careful development of characters' individual traits as well as for meticulous preparation and research. His directorial policies were in keeping with his acting theories. Garrick's rehearsals, which could last for weeks, were quite extended in comparison to the usual eighteenth-century practice. Garrick was also a strict disciplinarian: he required his actors to be on time, to know their lines, and to act, not simply recite, during rehearsals. Penalties for infractions of these rules were established. As part of his reformation of eighteenth-century English stage practices, Garrick banished spectators from the stage.

Garrick was also concerned with the appropriateness of his productions' visual elements. Following the lead of Charles Macklin, Garrick experimented with historically accurate and appropriate costuming, and he is often credited with attempts to "mask," or hide, stage lighting. Garrick was also responsible for the hiring of de Loutherbourg as Drury Lane's innovative scene designer. Finally, he also wrote many plays and adaptations for his company. Thus, Garrick was a complete theater artist, undertaking many of the responsibilities assigned today to the director. Still, he was confined by tradition and the commercial practices of the eighteenth-century English theater.

Unlike Garrick, Goethe was not restricted by commercialism nor was he an actor in the company he directed. In 1775 the noted author was invited to oversee the court theater at Weimar, Germany. Initially Goethe did not take his theater duties seriously, but by the 1790s he had become a dictatorial director, or *regisseur*, and had established the reputation of the Weimar court theater. (Unlike Garrick's Drury Lane, Goethe's theater was state-subsidized.)

Goethe rehearsed for lengthy periods of time and expected his actors to work as a unified ensemble company, and like Garrick, he penalized those who broke his rehearsal rules. Goethe, however, was not an advocate of the more natural style of acting; instead, he believed actors should address themselves to the audience and not to each other. While he followed routine blocking patterns, he did emphasize careful stage composition, that is, the pictorial arrangement of performers on stage. Goethe's conventional approach to acting was reflected in his "Rules for Actors," which contains many seemingly ludicrous regulations. For example, he wrote that "the actor should show no pocket handkerchief on stage; even less should he blow his nose, still less should he spit. It is frightful to be reminded of these natural occasions. One may have with him a small handkerchief, as indeed is now the fashion, as a help in case of need."

Nonetheless, Goethe's regulations forced his actors to take the craft and profession of acting seriously. He included rules for stage movement, vocal technique, and deportment, or behavior, in daily life and also worked on establishing a uniform stage German so that his performers did not speak in a variety of dialects. He carefully oversaw the settings and costumes and was a proponent of historical accuracy. Goethe even trained his audiences by establishing rules for spectator conduct; the only appropriate audience reactions, he insisted, were applause and the withholding of applause. Our modern tradition of audience decorum was established by Goethe. In short, the working methods Goethe employed at the Weimar court theater between 1794 and 1817 influenced many of the nineteenth-century directors who are considered to be the founders of the modern theater.

Summary

The eighteenth century was an era of theatrical experimentation. In drama, many new forms were developed, including ballad opera, comic opera, middle-class tragedy, and sentimental comedy. Innovative playwrights moved away from the neoclassical rules; the German Storm and Stress movement, which included such authors as Goethe and Friedrich Schiller, argued against strict dramatic rules. Many plays were Shakespearean in structure.

In scene design, the Bibienas introduced multipoint perspective and Piranesi employed chiaroscuro. Also, local color and three-dimensional properties became more common in settings. Charles Macklin, Marie-Justine Favart, and Friedrich Schroeder were among those who experimented with historical accuracy in costuming. While acting, for much of the century, was bombastic, such performers as Macklin and David Garrick attempted to make performing styles more natural. In the last half of the century, Garrick and Johann Wolfgang von Goethe established the practices of modern directing.

While the experimenters of the eighteenth century did not transform the theater overnight, they helped set the stage for the modern theater.

Chapter Ten

THE THEATER FROM 1800 to 1875

Theater in the nineteenth century built on the innovations of the preceding century and paved the way for the modern theater, which began in the years immediately following 1875. Major social changes took place in the period from 1800 to 1875: the industrial revolution, technological advances, and the rise of nationalism.

(Although this chapter covers the period between 1800 and 1875, most historical demarcations, as we have noted earlier, are arbitrary. Johann Wolfgang von Goethe, for example, discussed in the last chapter as a playwright and director, continued to work in the early 1800s. Also, some of the personalities we will discuss had careers that began prior to 1875 but continued long after, and we will make occasional references to events which occurred after 1875 but were closely related to preceding events.)

A nineteenth century specialty—the well-made play *The nineteenth century saw a number of craftsmen at work in the theater including playwrights, who perfected the well-made play—a tightly constructed drama in which all parts fit neatly together. One of the best such writers was the Frenchman Sardou; a scene between a husband and wife from his play* Lets Get a Divorce *is shown here. (Photo—Gary W. Sweetman, Asolo Theater, Florida.)*

The Theater between 1800 and 1875

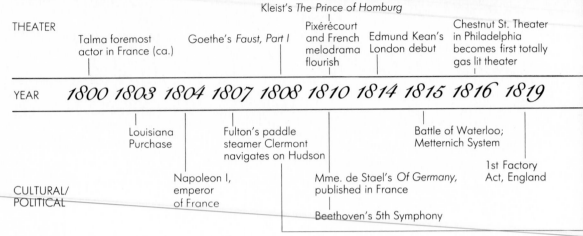

THEATER							Kleist's *The Prince of Homburg*					
	Talma foremost actor in France (ca.)		Goethe's *Faust, Part I*			Pixérécourt and French melodrama flourish		Edmund Kean's London debut		Chestnut St. Theater in Philadelphia becomes first totally gas lit theater		

YEAR	1800	1803	1804	1807	1808	1810	1814	1815	1816	1819

| CULTURAL/ POLITICAL | | Louisiana Purchase | | Fulton's paddle steamer Clermont navigates on Hudson | | | | Battle of Waterloo; Metternich System | | |

Napoleon I, emperor of France

Mme. de Stael's *Of Germany*, published in France

1st Factory Act, England

Beethoven's 5th Symphony

SOCIETAL TRANSFORMATIONS IN THE NINETEENTH CENTURY

Possibly the most important societal transformation of the early nineteenth century was the industrial revolution, which entailed the replacement of hand tools and human power by machinery as well as the development of factories and the factory system. Many inventions—including the improved steam engine, which transformed textile manufacturing, the leading industry of the time—were developed during this period. The foremost textile-manufacturing nation, and therefore the leader of the industrial revolution, was Great Britain.

The industrial revolution, which required centralized labor forces for the factory system, spurred urbanization and eroded traditional European agrarianism. The populations of European and American cities grew, but the way of life created by industrialization was far from pleasant for the working classes. City environments were polluted by coal, and housing was poorly constructed, cramped, and in short supply. Since the factory system required large numbers of unskilled laborers, whole families, including women and children (at first children as young as 6 years old), were employed at minimal wages; work days lasted fourteen hours.

The industrial revolution, however, was a boon to the middle class, which was further strengthened financially. In acknowledgment of its new power, legislatures passed reform acts beneficial to the middle class throughout the nineteenth century. Among other things, these liberalized the qualifications for voting and for holding elected office. By 1884, three-quarters of all adult males in Britain could vote, as opposed to only

sented white performers made up as caricatured blacks. (For a complete discussion of minstrelsy, see Chapter 16.) The most popular minstrel company was the Christy Minstrels, which staged over 2700 performances between 1846 and 1856. Burlesques were usually takeoffs on serious plays; for example, burlesque often satirized Shakespearean works and popular melodramas. (A modern-day equivalent is provided by the takeoffs on popular films and television shows.) Later in the nineteenth century, the burlesques began to include female dancers; it was not, however, until the twentieth century that the form became a combination of comedians and strippers.

Throughout the nineteenth century, concert halls, saloons, and playhouses presented collections of entertainments—including songs, dances, acrobatics, and animal acts—on one bill; these developed into the popular variety and vaudeville presentations of the late nineteenth and early twentieth centuries. Today, television is the home of variety entertainment. The *Ed Sullivan Show* in the 1950s and 1960s was the electronic descendant of this theatrical form.

The renowned popularizer of the circus was P. T. Barnum (1810–1891), who developed the art of spectacular advertising in order to attract mass audiences to his entertainments. Barnum's earliest successes were at the American Museum in New York City from the 1840s through the 1860s. There he exhibited human curiosities and presented variety acts and plays. Among the curiosities Barnum discovered were Joyce Heth, who he claimed was the 140-year-old nurse of George Washington; the Fiji Mermaid, which was the head of a monkey sewn onto the body of a fish; and the midget Tom Thumb. Between 1841 and 1865 Barnum sold 37,500,000 admissions to his American Museum. In the 1850s, Barnum became involved with the circus, which was in many ways a spectacular touring version of his museum; he advertised the circus as "the greatest show on earth."

The increase in the number of spectators and types of entertainments resulted in the construction of more and larger playhouses throughout the western world. With the advent of better rail transportation, the dramatic arts were also brought to new areas and audiences; the transcontinental railroad, for example, made theater more accessible to people in places like California. The passion that audiences felt for the theater accounted for the immense popularity of the era's star performers. It also helps to explain several infamous theater riots which mirrored the intense emotional involvement of audiences with the art, and also the social upheavals prevalent at the time.

Popularity of Theater Leads to Riots

When London's Covent Garden Theater was remodeled in 1809 and prices for admission were raised, the actor-manager John Philip Kemble (1757–1823) was confronted by the Old Price Riots. The lower-class audiences were also upset that the third-tier gallery had been turned into expensive private boxes rented for the season. For sixty-seven nights noisy audiences disrupted performances by chanting, sounding noisemakers, and throwing objects. Eventually the management of Covent Garden gave in; the old prices for the pit were restored and the number of boxes reduced.

Another theater riot took place in Paris in 1830, when *Hernani* by Victor Hugo (1802–1885) premiered at the Comédie Française, the home of French neoclassical drama. As we shall see, Hugo was a staunch romantic and, therefore, opposed to neoclassicism. For fifty-five nights rioting and fighting broke out in the theater between supporters of neoclassicism and advocates of romanticism.

The most violent of the nineteenth-century riots occurred outside of New York's Astor Place Theater and grew out of the rivalry between the English star William Charles Macready and the American star Edwin Forrest. Forrest, who was noted for his portrayal of melodramatic heroes, blamed Macready, known for his more subtle realistic style of performance, for his earlier unsuccessful English tour. When Macready appeared at the Astor Place Theater on May 8, 1849, he was prevented from performing by Forrest's working-class fans. The English star was convinced by his aristocratic admirers to perform again on May 10. A mob of 15,000 assembled outside of the playhouse and began to attack the building. The infantry was called out to disperse the mob, and when the riot finally ended, twenty-two people had been killed and many more wounded.

While these events illustrate the passionate involvement of nineteenth-century audiences, they also mirror the social changes of the era. The Old Price and Astor Place riots reflected the battle between the working and upper classes in the 1800s; the militancy of the lower classes in the theaters foreshadowed later social revolutions. Furthermore, the Astor Place Riot mirrored the century's growing nationalistic fervor; the battle between Forrest's and Macready's fans was partially a result of anti-British sentiments in America. For that matter, many of the popular dramas of the century touched on nationalistic concerns. For example, Anna Cora Mowatt (1819–1870), one of America's first significant female playwrights, in her comedy of manners *Fashion* (1845), dramatized how the values of hard-working America were more honest than the social pretensions of Europe. The character Adam Trueman in *Fashion* was a descendant of an earlier popular stock figure in American melodramas and comedies known as the stage Yankee, a representative of the values of hard-working, unpretentious, rural America.

The passion for the theater was also mirrored in the intense desire of some of the century's most renowned literary figures to write dramas. Such authors as Lord Byron, John Keats, Percy Bysshe Shelley, Charles

*A*stor Place Riot   *This riot, in New York City in 1849, was the result of nationalistic fervor and the passionate involvement of theater audiences. The riot occurred when working-class fans of the American star Edwin Forrest attacked the theater in which English actor William Charles Macready, who had supposedly insulted Forrest, was performing. (Photo—Metropolitan Museum of Art, Bequest of Edward W. C. Arnold, 1954.)*

Dickens, and Henry James noted the ability of drama to reach and affect mass audiences and attempted to write plays, though their efforts were unsuccessful.

The popularity of the theater between 1800 and 1875 has not been equaled in modern times. Today, the theater no longer holds the same kind of central position. Parallels could be drawn to the movies and television, with the presentation of similar kinds of entertainment, the attraction of mass audiences, and the popularity of the media's stars. Still, the intense passion of nineteenth-century audiences, which erupted during the riots mentioned above, has rarely been witnessed in other entertainments. In our own times, the only possible parallel might be the emotional intensity of rock concert audiences.

Turning to the types of plays being produced, three major forms of drama came to the fore between 1800 and 1875: romanticism, melodrama, and the well-made play.

Romanticism

Romanticism, influenced by the German Storm and Stress movement, was a revolutionary literary trend of the first half of the nineteenth century. The most noted romantic dramas of the period were Goethe's *Faust* (Part I, 1808; Part II, 1831) and Victor Hugo's *Hernani* (1830). Hugo, in the introduction to his play *Cromwell* (1827) outlined the characteristics of the romantic drama. The romantics rejected the neoclassical rules; in fact, they rejected all artistic rules, suggesting that geniuses created their own rules. Since many of the romantics copied the structural techniques of Shakespeare, their plays were episodic and epic in scope, but unlike Shakespeare, they were often more interested in creating dramatic mood and atmosphere than in developing believable plots or depth of character. The romantics argued against the purity of genre and believed that all subject matter—the grotesque as well as the ideal—was appropriate for the stage; often they employed the supernatural in their plays. The romantic hero was frequently a societal outcast, for example, a bandit, who quested for justice, knowledge, and truth. One of the most common themes was the gulf between human beings' spiritual aspirations and their physical limitations.

Romantic dramatists were often imbued with the independent spirit of the times. Both the American and French revolutions had occurred at the end of the eighteenth century, and ideas of freedom and liberty were in the air. These playwrights put in their plays heroes who fiercely defended notions of individuality and independence. This is another excellent example of drama serving as the mirror of an age.

Melodrama

The term *melodrama* means "song drama" or "music drama." Though the word originally comes from the Greek, it usually refers to a theatrical form made popular by the French at the end of the eighteenth century, and the beginning of the nineteenth. The "music" in the term refers to the background music that accompanied these plays, similar to that played with silent movies and now found as a background in films. In these melodramas a premium was put on surface effects, especially those creating suspense, fear, nostalgia, and other strong emotions in the audience. The plays were written in such a way that these feelings were easily aroused.

The heroes and heroines of melodrama were clearly delineated and stood in sharp contrast to the villains; the audience sympathized with the good characters and despised the bad ones. In addition to the heroes and villains, melodrama had other easily recognized stock characters: the threatened female, the sidekick (a comic foil to the hero), and the promiscuous fallen woman who, even after repenting, is punished for her wicked past. This underscores the highly moral tone of traditional melodrama; the conflict between good and evil was clearly and firmly established, and virtue was always victorious.

In order to keep the audience's interest, melodrama, both in the past and the present, features suspenseful plots with a climatic moment at the end of each act. The modern equivalents are TV adventure stories—private detective and cop shows—that have a climax, such as a car crash, a sudden confrontation, or the discovery of important evidence, just before the break for a commercial.

An example of a climactic act ending in a nineteenth-century melodrama is the close of Act I of *The String of Pearls*, written in 1847 by George Dibdin Pitt (1799–1855). This is a play about Sweeney Todd, the demon barber of Fleet Street in London, and is the story on which the 1979 Broadway musical *Sweeney Todd* was based. In the 1847 play, Sweeney has been killing customers in his barber shop and turning the bodies over to Mrs. Lovett to bake into meat pies. At the end of Act I, Sweeney decides to get rid of those around him, including Mrs. Lovett, but she overhears his plans. In a few short lines the action accelerates. She demands half the profits; he insists that he will deduct her share of money she owes him. She draws a knife and is about to attack him when he pulls out a pistol and shoots her. He then throws her body into a fiery furnace as the curtain of the first act falls.

Since melodrama is primarily an escapist form, visual spectacle and special effects are stressed. Contemporary disaster films, such as *The Towering Inferno* and *The Poseidon Adventure,* are highly visual melodramas. Car chases, omnipresent in contemporary detective melodramas, grow out of the tradition of melodramatic spectacle. The nineteenth-century melodramatic playwright Dion Boucicault (1822–1890) employed many similar, though not as elaborately created, special effects; in his *The Streets of New York* (1857), a tenement burned onstage.

Most types of nineteenth-century melodramas have modern-day equivalents. The domestic melodrama grew into the soap opera. The frontier melodrama has become the western. The crime melodrama is now the popular mystery or detective show. The nautical melodrama, which dealt with sailors and pirates, was the forerunner of the swashbuckler film. The equestrian melodrama, which featured horses performing spectacular tricks, was the ancestor of various TV and film melodramas starring animals, including Lassie and Rin Tin Tin.

There has been, however, a major thematic change in modern

$\mathcal{M}$usical version of a melodrama *The story of Sweeney Todd, a barber who cut the throats of his victims and gave them to his colleague Mrs. Lovett to make into meat pies, was dramatized several times in the nineteenth century as a stage melodrama in London. A 1979 Broadway musical,* Sweeney Todd, *was based on the same story. It starred Len Cariou as Sweeney and Angela Lansbury as Mrs. Lovett. (Photo—Martha Swope.)*

melodramas; a change that is most discernible in the films of the 1960s and 1970s. During the nineteenth century, audiences did not question societal, religious, or moral norms; in the last two decades, partly because of the Vietnam war and political scandals, audiences have questioned traditional values and no longer believe that good and evil are so easily delineated. In films like *The Wild Bunch, Bonnie and Clyde,* and *The Godfather,* characters who in the past would have been regarded as villainous were presented heroically, while the forces of law were shown to be evil. Likewise, traditional stereotypes, including racist portrayals of blacks and sexist presentations of helpless women, have been rejected. The transformations in melodrama from the nineteenth to the late twentieth century strongly mirror our society's changing beliefs and values.

The Well-Made Play

Many of the popular melodramas of the nineteenth century employed the well-made-play structure. The term *well-made* is meant to describe a play that mechanically builds to its climactic moments. The basic goal of the playwright is to arouse the audience's interest in the plot's numerous and contrived climaxes. In the nineteenth-century form, there was little emphasis on truthful emotions or characterizations, and when critics today describe a play as "well-made," they are usually being condescending. Still, the form was used more creatively by later dramatists, and therefore its characteristics should be more fully outlined.

The well-made play emphasizes careful cause-and-effect development and is usually a tightly constructed crisis drama. The action often revolves around a secret known to the audience but not to the characters. The opening of the play carefully spells out the needed background information, or exposition. Throughout the play the dramatic action is clearly foreshadowed, and each act builds to a climactic moment. The major scene in a well-made play is the "obligatory scene," wherein the characters in conflict meet in a showdown confrontation. The plots of all well-made plays are carefully resolved so that there are no loose ends.

An example of well-made-play construction is found in *Let's Get a Divorce* by the French playwright Victorien Sardou (1831–1908). The exposition presents a picture of a bored young housewife and also makes mention of a liberal new divorce law that has been proposed in France. In her restlessness the wife flirts with her husband's young cousin. The cousin, hoping to make the woman his mistress, fakes a report that the divorce law has actually been passed and argues that she should become his lover because under the new law she can soon become his wife. Meanwhile, the husband encourages the scheme, knowing that if it goes through, he will reverse positions with the young cousin and become in his wife's eyes an exotic, out-of-reach lover instead of a familiar husband. The "obligatory" showdown scene comes in a restaurant, where everything is sorted out and the wife returns to her husband.

Throughout the well-made play, devices of various kinds, such as letters and lost documents seem to motivate the dramatic action. For example, the plots of two of the most famous nineteenth-century well-made plays revolve around specific dramatic devices: *A Scrap of Paper* by Sardou and *A Glass of Water* by Eugéne Scribe (1791–1861). These two Frenchmen were the most renowned practitioners of the well-made play. As we will see in the next chapter, the logical, causal structuring of the well-made play was to influence the "father of modern dramatic realism," Henrik Ibsen.

THE ACTING PROFESSION

In acting, the nineteenth century was a period of great stars; many performers throughout the world were idolized by the audiences who flocked to see them. Some of these performers amassed—and frequently lost—fortunes. Many of these actors were not simply national stars but became international figures. The major changes in the business and art of acting were, in part, caused by the rise of the star performer. During the nineteenth century, the traditional repertory company, a troupe of actors performing together for a set period of time in a number of plays, slowly disappeared. Early in the century, touring stars had performed with local repertory companies, though as transportation improved, not only stars but full productions—known as combination companies—began to tour, destroying the local repertory troupes.

At about the same time, the long run became more common, and popular plays ran for more than 100 consecutive performances. Edwin Booth's *Hamlet*, for example, ran for 100 straight nights in 1864 in New York City. The long run made hiring a repertory company impractical; instead, by the close of the century—as in today's commercial Broadway theater—a company was hired to perform a single play for the length of its run.

The movement away from the repertory company was a significant change for actors. Today, performers in the commercial theater are usually freelance artists; they are hired for an individual show. If the production is unsuccessful, they must audition for new presentations. Many critics suggest that the demise of the repertory company made the lives of actors and actresses more unstable because they were no longer hired for a set period of time. Furthermore, the repertory company allowed young performers to be trained by actually performing; beginners were hired to play various minor roles in the troupe's repertory. Contemporary performers have more difficulty in finding opportunities to learn through actual stage experience.

The shortening of the evening's bill in a typical production also diminished the need for repertory companies. By 1900 the bill—which previously had included a full-length play, a curtain raiser or afterpiece, and entr'acte entertainments—consisted only of the full-length drama. (An afterpiece was a short play following the full-length drama; a curtain raiser preceded the main play; entr'acte entertainments were variety acts, such as songs, dances, and acrobatics, presented during the breaks in the full-length plays.) By 1875 the repertory company was disappearing. Not all repertory troupes disbanded, but in the commercial theater they became the exception, not the rule.

Acting Styles

Most historians agree that performers in the classical, romantic, and melodramatic styles dominated the stage in the nineteenth century. The early-nineteenth-century English stars John Philip Kemble and his sister Sarah Siddon (1755–1831)—noted for their dignified, carefully planned,

EDWIN BOOTH
(1833–1893)

The reputation of Edwin Booth as America's finest actor has survived for over 100 years, and his name will always be linked with Hamlet, his greatest role. In his innovations in staging, which are not as well known, he anticipated scenic developments of the next thirty years.

Though Booth's father was a famous actor, Junius Brutus Booth, Edwin was not encouraged in his stage career. His family felt that his younger brother, John Wilkes Booth, had inherited their father's fiery acting ability. Young Edwin, having proved adept at calming his father's mad moods and restraining his drinking, began accompanying his father on tours at the age of 13. He made his dramatic debut in 1849 in a bit role to relieve an overworked prompter, and continued to play small parts in his father's company. When the two toured the west, Edwin decided to remain there and played several seasons in repertory.

Edwin Booth's New York debut in 1857 established him as the most promising young actor in America. Physically, he was short and slight, with piercing eyes and a rich melodious voice. His acting, particularly his Hamlet, was noted for its depth of character, grace, and freedom from mannerisms. His re-cord of playing Hamlet for 100 nights in New York was not surpassed until 1923.

Booth believed that art, including the theater, should inspire and ennoble. In 1869, to carry out his ideas, he built his own theater in New York, where for five years he produced a series of magnificent Shakespearean productions. Abandoning the wing-and-groove method of scene shifting, he used heavy set pieces and free-standing scenery to create historically accurate settings. He also returned to the practice of using the uncorrupted texts of Shakespeare's plays many years before it was followed by others in England. Poor financial management forced Booth's theater into bankruptcy in 1874, and for the rest of his life he was a touring star.

Booth's touring took him to England, where he alternated the roles of Iago and Othello with Henry Irving, and to Germany, making him the first American actor to achieve international fame. In his private life, Booth was a quiet, almost melancholy man surrounded by personal tragedies. His beloved first wife died after two and one-half years of marriage; his brother assassinated Abraham Lincoln; and his second wife went mad after the loss of their infant son.

Edwin Booth had the respect and friendship of the leading literary and cultural figures of the day. Because he felt that acting was an honorable profession, he endowed the Players' Club in 1888 as a place where actors and other gentlemen could meet. Booth presented the club with his house on Gramercy Park, New York City, where he lived until his death in 1893.

𝒮ARAH BERNHARDT
(1845–1923)

ℰLEONORA DUSE
(1859–1924)

Though there were many excellent performers at the end of the nineteenth century, two women, Sarah Bernhardt and Eleanora Duse, dominated the international stage. They played many of the same roles, yet each had a distinctive acting style.

"Madame Sarah" was the more flamboyant of the two, and her eccentricities and temperment are legendary. In 1862, she made her debut at the Comédie Française, and she continued an intermittent, stormy relationship with that company until 1880. Slim, with large, dark eyes, Bernhardt was a master of stage technique, but her chief asset was her voice, which was often compared to a golden bell. Twice she managed theaters in Paris, and she was also a sculptor and a writer of poetry and plays. She toured the United States many times and became legendary for demanding her salary in gold and for supposedly sleeping in a coffin.

While Bernhardt looked backward to the "grand style" of the nineteenth century, Duse foreshadowed the sincere realism of the twentieth century.

Eleanor Duse was as quiet and reclusive as Bernhardt was flamboyant. A child of actors, she made her stage debut at 4; at 14 she was playing Juliet. After her parents died, she struggled for several years until she appeared in Naples in 1879 as Thérèse Raquin in Emile Zola's play of the same name, astonishing the critics with the anguish in her performance. After touring as leading lady to the popular actor Cesare Rossi, she formed her own company.

Duse's repertoire included the poetic dramas of Gabriele d'Annunzio, her lover, the melodramas of Dumas and Sardou, and the realistic plays of Ibsen. Slender and attractive, she wore no makeup but used her expressive face, eyes, and gestures to convey the thoughts of the character. She was apparently the epitome of a natural, totally believable actress who projected sincerity and an inner fire rather than outward flamboyance. She retired in 1909 because of ill health, but financial reverses forced her to return to the stage after World War I, and she died while on tour, in Pittsburgh in 1923.

Talma in Hamlet François-Joseph Talma was the greatest actor in the French theater of the late eighteenth and early nineteenth centuries, and the leading member of the Comédie Française. Noted for his emotional, romantic presentations, Talma strove for consistency in costuming and carefully developed characterizations. Here, as Hamlet, he confronts Gertrude, played by Mlle. Duchenois. (Photo—Harvard Theater Collection.)

and detailed performances—were the most renowned classical actors. On the other hand, the great romantic stars were noted for their emotional outbursts, punctuating dramatic moments with strong physical gestures, making vocal points (that is, emphasizing specific speeches and lines), and relying upon inspiration. Among the great British romantic actors were Edmund Kean (1787–1833) and George Frederick Cooke (1756–1812), who became an early touring star in America. America's first native-born star, Edwin Forrest (1806–1872), whose performances stressed his physical prowess, is often characterized as a romantic performer. The major French stars of the century, François Joseph Talma (1763–1826), Sarah Bernhardt, and Benoît Constant Coquelin (1841–1909) belonged to this movement. The melodramatic performers were known for their portrayals of specific character types and for their emphasis on emotional display.

Many actors, however, continued to prepare the way for modern realistic performing. They were dedicated to acting in a true-to-life style, which meant that their stage movements, vocal patterns, and characterizations reflected those observed in everyday life. Performers of this type included the English actors William Charles Macready, Marie Wilton

$\mathcal{W}$ILLIAM CHARLES MACREADY
(1793–1873)

William Charles Macready was an important figure in the English theater of the nineteenth century, both as an actor and as a director. In many of his innovations he built on the foundation laid by David Garrick a century before.

As the son of an actor and provincial manager, Macready grew up with the theater, but he entered Rugby School to prepare for a law career. In 1810, following his father's death, he went on the stage—temporarily he thought—to support the family. After six years in the provinces, he made his London debut at Covent Garden as Orestes in *The Disturbed Mother*, a bad tragedy. He next played villains in a series of melodramas, winning acceptance as an actor but developing a growing loathing for the profession. He was finally allowed to play Richard III in 1819 and began to excel in tragic roles.

Macready was a dignified, studious actor who thoroughly researched and rehearsed each role. In his performances he introduced the "Macready pause," in which he stopped momentarily during the delivery of his lines in order to give the impression that he was thinking. He was a pioneer in stage realism.

Hoping to apply his principles to the acting of others, Macready directed companies at Covent Garden and Drury Lane from 1837 to 1843. One of the first directors to impose blocking—planned stage movements—on his actors, he also made them act during rehearsals rather than lifelessly go through the motions. The scenic elements of his productions were united by an image or theme from the play and were carefully researched and elaborately staged.

Besides his improvements in staging, Macready sought to improve the repertoire. He convinced the leading literary figures to write for the stage and produced plays by Browning and Byron. Charles Dickens, his friend and a supporter of his efforts, tried several times to write a stageworthy comedy. Macready was also one of the first to begin restoring Shakespearean texts to something closer to the original versions.

Macready's management at both Covent Garden and Drury Lane was not a financial success, partially due to his policy of playing no drama more than four times a week. After he left management, he toured England and played America twice. His rivalry with the American actor Edwin Forrest, sharpened by quick tempers on both sides and anti-British sentiment, led to the Astor Place Riot of 1849 in New York, where several people were killed.

In 1851 Macready retired from the stage, devoting the rest of his life to his family and his literary friends. His work in the theater paved the way for the realistic acting and staging of the late nineteenth century.

Bancroft (1839–1921), and her husband, Squire Bancroft (1841–1926); the American Edwin Booth; the Russian Mikhail Shchepkin (1788–1863); and the Italian actress Eleanora Duse.

The fact that much of the acting between 1800 and 1875 was based on stereotypical physical gestures and vocal patterns can be seen in the work of Françoise Delsarte (1811–1871), the era's major acting theorist and teacher. Delsarte believed that actors could convey emotions and inner thoughts by imitating specific gestures and body movements. The French theorist's system is rejected by modern realists because it proposes that all human beings react in the same physical fashion and does not allow for individual characterization. Delsarte's method, however, did require that actors' physicalizations be based on observations of everyday life, a practice later realistic systems also stressed as a means of obtaining artistic inspiration.

Further Developments in Directing

The art of directing, as established by David Garrick and Johann Wolfgang von Goethe in the eighteenth century, was further refined and developed in the nineteenth. The goal of the innovators was to create a unified stage picture, particularly through greater amounts of rehearsal time and more careful attention to production details. Many experimented with historical accuracy in scenery and costuming. Some expected a more realistic style of performance from their companies.

In England and America one can point to numerous actor-managers who took greater interest and care in creating their stage productions. In almost all instances, these individuals oversaw their productions' visual elements, required careful rehearsals, experimented with blocking patterns, and are often credited with moving the theatrical art toward greater realism. The people in this group include Macready, who managed Covent Garden from 1837 to 1838 and Drury Lane from 1841 to 1843; Madame Vestris, who managed the Olympic Theater from 1831 to 1838 and Covent Garden from 1839 to 1842 (all of these theaters were in London); Edwin Booth, who managed a number of theaters in New York, including his own, from 1869 to 1874; and Henry Irving, who managed the Lyceum Theater in London from 1878 to 1898.

On the European continent, a number of individuals significantly developed the art of directing, including two Germans, Richard Wagner and Georg II, the duke of Saxe-Meiningen. Since these two artists were not actors within their companies, they were closer to our modern conception of the director. Richard Wagner's theory of the *Gesamtkunstwerk* (the unified operatic work of art) has been a major influence on modern directing theory. According to the German composer, an opera, which consists of various musical and theatrical elements, needs to have a controlling figure to unify the production. Wagner insisted that this individual must have dictatorial control; at the Bay-

ℋENRY IRVING
(1838–1905)

Henry Irving was the most acclaimed actor on the English stage during the last part of the nineteenth century. He was also one of the last great actor-managers in the English theater, responsible for innovations in staging and lighting. Irving was one of the first modern directors in that he insisted on a totality of effect in his productions. He employed the best stage designers of the day, rehearsed his large corps of stagehands so that scene changes would be smooth and precise, and experimented with the control of stage lighting. In 1895 Irving became the first English actor to be knighted, a recognition of his work and of his high professional standards.

Born John Henry Brodribb, Irving spent four years as a clerk in London before changing his name and becoming an actor. By 1871, when he had his first London success as Mathias in Leopold Lewis's *The Bells*, Irving had spent fifteen years on the stage, playing over 500 roles with provincial and London companies. He followed his success as Mathias with other lead roles in melodrama, and in 1874 played Hamlet for a record-breaking 200 nights.

Though he was faulted for such physical flaws as an unmelodious voice and a shambling gait, as well as for his unusual characterizations, Irving was a master of gesture and pantomime by which he communicated the character's feelings and thoughts. Not a romantic leading man, he excelled in melodrama and in roles like Iago, which allowed him to portray scorn, malignancy, horror, and fear.

Irving became manager of the Lyceum Theater in 1878 and for twenty-one years staged productions that were known for their totality of effect and scenic splendor. His leading lady, Ellen Terry, brought beauty, freshness, and vitality to all her roles. Together, they became one of the most renowned stage duos of the century. Irving gave up the management of the Lyceum in 1898, after several unprofitable seasons. His farewell London performance was at Drury Lane in 1905. Irving died while on tour and was buried in Westminster Abbey. Describing him, the actress Ellen Terry wrote, "He was quiet, patient, tolerant, impersonal, gentle, close, crafty, incapable of caring for anything outside of his work."

reuth Festspielhaus, Wagner put his theory into practice, becoming the theater's *regisseur*, the French term for director.

Most important were the staging innovations made by Wagner, as director of the Festspielhaus, in order to increase stage illusion. Musicians were forbidden to tune their instruments while in the orchestra pit, and audience members could not applaud during the course of the presentation. Wagner is also often credited with being the first director to extinguish the house lights in order to focus the audience's attention on the stage.

The duke of Saxe-Meiningen, a small state in northwestern Germany, took control of his court theater in 1866, and between 1874 and 1890 made the Meiningen Players the most renowned company in the world. A major reason for the duke's ability to organize such a successful theatrical venture was his unlimited financial resources. He was assisted in his notable artistic ventures by his third wife, Ellen Franz, who, as the company's *dramaturg*, or literary manager, selected and adapted scripts, and by Ludwig Chronegk, who, as the company's director, carried out the duke's ideas for staging. The duke, as the director of many Shakespearean and romantic dramas, revolutionized stage production. He rehearsed for extensive periods of time, refusing to open a show until he believed it was ready, and was most noted for his intricately planned crowd scenes, which employed company actors rather than amateur supernumeraries (nonspeaking performers). As an opponent of the star system, the duke primarily employed young performers. Meiningen productions were also admired for their historically accurate settings and costumes.

The duke's theatrical innovations became well known throughout Europe because his company toured frequently to other countries, and his influence on future directors of realistic drama has often been cited.

Theater Architecture

Though there were no startling developments in theater architecture between 1800 and 1875, some trends can be discerned. Early in the nineteenth century, as we have already noted, playhouses were enlarged, with increases in size being dictated by the expanding lower-class urban audiences that came with the industrialization of the cities. For a while in England, for example, the influx of working-class audiences resulted in the social elite's abandoning the theaters for the opera houses. The Bowery Theater in New York City—nicknamed the "slaughterhouse" because it offered "blood and guts" melodramas—was an example of a huge nineteeenth-century theater building catering to lower-class audiences. In its initial year of operation, 1826, the Bowery seated 2500 spectators and was the largest playhouse in New York. Nineteen years later, the Bowery was enlarged so that it could accommodate 4000 patrons at each of its presentations of sensational melodrama.

GEORG II, DUKE OF SAXE-MEININGEN
(1826–1914)

Had Georg II been able to choose his own profession, he would have remained in Berlin to pursue a military career. When the Revolution of 1848 broke out in Germany, however, his father ordered him to return to Saxe-Meiningen, and once home, the young duke became involved in the theater.

As the only son of Duke Bernhard II, he had been given an education which prepared him to rule the duchy. Georg's two childhood tutors, a theologian and an artist, instilled in him a love of nature and of art. Art remained a part of his education during his training at the University of Bonn and while he was a lieutenant in the Royal Guards at Berlin. Though he painted with oils, the duke's talent was in drawing and sketching.

When he was called home in 1848, Georg became active in the court, where he found a competent but uninspired theater company. He married Princess Charlotte of Prussia in 1850, with whom he had three children before her death five years later. When she died, he turned for consolation to art and music, traveling to Italy for a year of study. In 1858, he married a German princess who died in 1872.

During the 1850s and 1860s, Prussia was becoming the dominant force in Germany, an influence opposed by Duke Bernhard. Georg, however, favored Prussian and German unification, and in 1866 the Prussian army occupied Saxe-Meiningen and forced Bernhard to abdicate in favor of his son. As ruler of Saxe-Meiningen, Georg II was an enlightened monarch, liberalizing land ownership laws, promoting trade agreements and tariff reforms, and providing health and welfare benefits for the citizens. He also served in the Franco-Prussian War of 1870.

In the evenings, he supervised the activities of the court theater, planning and directing the productions and providing sketches for the scenery and costumes. Ludwig Chronegk, the regisseur, was responsible for the daily operations of the theater. The third person involved in the company's artistic management was the duke's third wife, Ellen Franz, baroness von Heldburg, with whom the duke eloped after the death of his second wife in 1872. She was responsible for the selection of plays and for the stage diction of the actors. The three continued to direct the company until it was disbanded in 1890, after having astounded the world with its acting ensemble and its unified, historically accurate productions. The years before Georg's death in 1914 were tranquil and his third marriage was happy.

𝒞ovent Garden Theater   *In the early nineteenth century Covent Garden held about 3000 spectators. It had a pit, boxes, and galleries for the audience; there were grooves on the stage floor for scene shifting and a large fly space and areas for carpentry and painting. Theaters in this period emphasized detailed spectacle, especially for melodrama. (Photo—Victoria and Albert Museum, London.)*

By the 1860s, however, there was a shift away from the construction of huge theaters. This shift can be explained by the proliferation of playhouses in the European and American urban centers that catered to specific segments of late-nineteenth-century society. In London, for example, the number of theaters staging various types of dramas not covered by the Licensing Act of 1737 increased significantly during the early 1800s. Finally, in 1843, the Theater Regulation Act abolished the monopoly that was supposed to have been in effect but could not be enforced.

The traditional proscenium arch and pit, box, and gallery dominated theater buildings in the nineteenth century. In a few innovative theater buildings before that time, the pit no longer had backless benches but had

*R*ichard Wagner's Bayreuth Festpielhaus   *This theater, completed in 1876, was one of the first modern theaters. Built as the ideal home of Wagner's operas, it has "continental" seating—with no center aisles—and a balcony that set the pattern for modern auditoriums. Also, the sunken orchestra pit has become an integral part of the modern musical playhouse. (Photo—Victoria and Albert Museum, London.)*

instead comfortable individual seats; this area became the equivalent of the modern orchestra, while the galleries gave way to balconies which extended out over the orchestra. Individual seats, of course, allowed for the selling of advance reserved seating.

There were many examples of theater buildings which broke from the traditional architectural pattern established during the Italian Renaissance. In London, the boxes in the Adelphi Theater were raised so that the pit could be extended to the side walls, thus making the tiers more like balconies; later, in the same theater, individual, comfortable armchairs were put into the pit. In the late nineteenth century, the English architect C. J. Phipps (1835–1897) popularized the balcony and orchestra configuration in many London theaters. By the late 1800s, engineering advances allowed for the construction of balconies without supporting columns.

In America, the Booth Theater, completed in 1869 for the renowned American Shakespearean actor, is often cited as the first modern theater in New York City. Instead of a pit and galleries, the theater contained a modern orchestra area and balconies. The seating consisted of individual armchairs, although there were boxes in the proscenium arch. The stage in Booth's theater was also revolutionary since it was not raked and contained no grooves. Scenery could be raised from the basement by elevators or dropped in ("flown in") from above, and scenic pieces were often supported by braces. The fly space in Booth's theater was high enough to accommodate scenic drops without their being rolled up. By 1875, with theaters like Booth's, the modern proscenium-arch theater had been established.

Another innovative nineteenth-century theater building, the Bayreuth Festspielhaus, built for the German opera composer Richard Wagner, opened in 1876, after four years of construction. This theater also broke with the earlier tradition of the pit, box, and gallery house. Wagner wanted a theater in which seating did not emphasize class distinctions. There were thirty raked rows of individual seats, accommodating 1300 spectators and forming a fan-shaped auditorium. The rows became larger the farther away they were from the stage, and audiences exited at the ends of the rows. This type of arrangement is known as *continental seating*. There was a small box at the rear of the house as well as a 300-seat balcony. All seats in this opera house cost the same price. While the stage of the Bayreuth Festspielhaus, modeled along traditional Italianate lines, was not as revolutionary as the auditorium, it did have a few innovations. The theater contained a double proscenium arch as well as a sunken orchestra pit which separated the audience from the stage and which Wagner referred to as his "mystic gulf." For special effects, steam jets were built into the forestage.

SCENERY, COSTUMING, AND LIGHTING

The eighteenth-century experiments with realistic devices and conventions in scenery and costuming were carried even further in the nineteenth century. Historical accuracy in sets and costumes became more common with the increasing availability of works of historical research, such as J. R. Planché's *History of British Costume* (1843). This new knowledge about the past, combined with the fascination with antiquity that characterized the nineteenth century, led various theater artists to mount historically accurate productions. These artists included the English actor-manager Charles Kemble (1775–1854), William Charles Macready, and Charles Kean (1811–1868), as well as the American actor-manager Edwin Booth and the duke of Saxe-Meiningen. In the Saxe-Meiningen presentations, costumes were carefully researched, and authentic materials were purchased, regardless of the cost or difficulty in obtaining them; moreover, performers were not allowed to alter their

RICHARD WAGNER
(1813–1883)

Wilhelm Richard Wagner was important not only as an opera composer but as a stage theorist. One of his theories was that a production, whether opera or theater, should be a *Gesamtkunstwerk*, which means a masterwork in which all elements—music, words, action, scenery, lighting—are integrated "total theater." One man, Wagner argued, should serve as writer, composer, and director.

Throughout the many reversals in his life, Richard Wagner held fast to his vision of what opera should be. Wagner was egocentric, forceful, and convinced of the superiority of his own theories. Though his personality was sometimes his greatest hindrance, it helped him realize his goal of creating a new version of opera.

Wagner's stepfather was a painter and a singer-actor. As a result, he was acquainted with opera and theater from his earliest years. Even as a child, growing up in Leipzig, Germany, he was impulsive and self-willed, neglecting all studies except for music. At seventeen, Wagner had an overture performed in the Leipzig Theater. He enrolled in the University of Leipzig for a brief but wild time, and for the next several years worked as a conductor for a series of third-rate provincial orchestras while composing his earliest operas. Shortly thereafter, he was forced to flee his debtors and went to Paris, hoping to dazzle the operatic establishment with his greatness.

In 1842, after three poverty-stricken years in Paris, Wagner gladly returned to Dresden, where his opera *Rienzi* was a resounding success. He then received a post at the court opera. The works that followed—*The Flying Dutchman* (1843), *Tannhauser* (1845), and *Lohengrin* (1848) —were popular with audiences, though the critics disapproved of their employment of total theater and other techniques. In 1849, Wagner was forced to flee again, this time as a wanted criminal for taking part in the Revolution of 1848.

During his twelve years in exile, Wagner developed his theories and began composing the individual works that formed his great operatic cycle, *The Ring of the Nibelung*. For these operas, he selected a national myth that he hoped would serve as a unifying force for Germany.

Wagner did not get a chance to test his theories until 1876, when he staged the *Ring* cycle at his new theater in Bayreuth, built with the help of his patron, Louis II of Bavaria. Several times in the years of struggle he was nearly ruined because of debts or adulterous relationships, but he persisted and overwhelmed his critics with his music until his death in 1883. His second wife, Cosima Liszt Wagner, and after that his sons and grandsons, carried on his work. His ideas on a combined art work controlled by one person influenced theories of "total theater" expounded in the twentieth century.

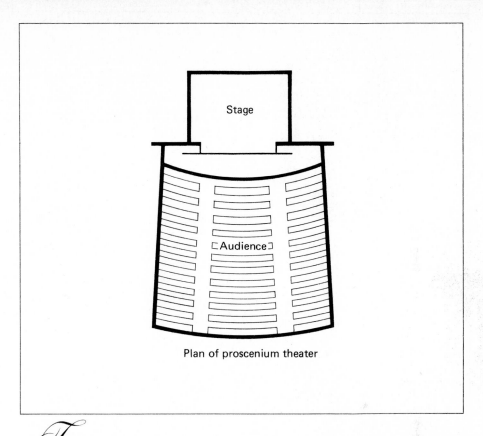

Stage

Audience

Plan of proscenium theater

The modern proscenium arch theater By the end of the nineteenth century, the modern proscenium theater, still widely in use today, was well established. All seats, including balcony seats, face the stage with its picture-frame opening. Behind this, scenery is placed and stage machinery concealed. This arrangement is particularly important for the box set which is placed in back of the proscenium opening.

stage garments. The same careful attention was given to the settings the duke designed.

The Box Set

Even more important than the introduction of historical accuracy in scene design was the gradual disappearance of wing-and-shutter settings shifted by pole-and-chariot or groove systems. This type of setting did not suddenly disappear, and it continued to be employed for some time. However, throughout the first seventy-five years of the nineteenth century, alternatives to the painted wing-and-shutter sets were introduced. The most significant alternative was the *box set*. As noted in the

MADAME VESTRIS
(Lucia Elizabeth Bartolozzi)
(1797–1856)

Theatrical management was an unusual profession for a woman in 1830 and a financially unstable profession for anyone, given the disorder and chaos of the London stage. In spite of these difficulties, Madame Vestris not only was able to make major innovations in staging but also made a profit as proprietor of the Olympic Theater.

By the time she opened her theater, Madame Vestris had had fifteen years of theatrical experience. The daughter of a London engraver, she married Auguste Armand Vestris, a dancer and member of a famous family of ballet performers, when she was only sixteen. Two years later, she made her stage debut. After her husband left her, she continued acting on the stage, playing in both Paris and London. With her excellent singing voice, she might have had a career in opera but instead played in burlesques, extravaganzas, and comedies. She was much admired for her beautiful figure, sparkling eyes, and dark hair.

Madame Vestris opened the Olympic Theater with *Olympic Revels*, an extravaganza written by J. R. Planché, the best writer of burlesques, extravaganzas, and farces in England at that time. Planché was to be her resident dramatist at the Olympic and later at the Lyceum Theater.

Though she presented only light entertainment at the Olympic, Madame Vestris produced the plays with a degree of care that was usually reserved for the classics, paying close attention to every element of the production and coordinating them into a unified whole. She is credited with introducing the box set to England around 1832. She dressed all her settings with real properties—doorknobs, dishes, rugs, tables, chairs, curtains—instead of following the usual method of painting them on the set. Her care extended to costuming, where she replaced the exaggerated costumes of extravaganza and burlesque with clothes from everyday life.

In 1838, Madame Vestris married Charles Mathews, a light comedian in her company. After an American tour, they managed Covent Garden for three years, using the same staging practices used earlier at the Olympic. Though their production of *The London Assurance*, Dion Boucicault's first play, was a success, the managerial venture ended in failure in 1842. The couple took over the Lyceum Theater in 1847, but their insistence on quality led to another failure. Madame Vestris died in 1856, in the midst of the Lyceum's bankruptcy proceedings.

preceding chapter, some historians believe that the box set may have been introduced in the late eighteenth century. In any case, between 1800 and 1875, many theatrical artists employed this type of setting, which consists of flats hinged together to create the representation of a room. In many instances, the box set was furnished with practicable elements, such as doors and windows, which could be used during the course of the presentation.

Madame Vestris, an English actress-manager, is frequently credited with introducing the box set during her management of London's Olympic Theater in the 1830s. While Vestris was probably not the first to introduce the box set, she did fill her settings with many realistic accouterments. In America, Edwin Booth is often credited with popularizing the box set. Booth also broke with the traditional wing-and-shutter set by placing scenic pieces wherever he wished on the stage floor and supporting them with braces.

New Technology

During the nineteenth century, the technology of the industrial revolution was introduced into the theater. The *moving panorama*—painted settings on a long cloth which could be moved across the stage by turning spools—created the illusion of movement and changing locales. A popular American play, William Dunlap's *A Trip to Niagara* (1828), employed this device for the presentation of a voyage from New York City to Niagara Falls. (Today, in film, a similar technique, known as *rear projection*, is used to create the illusion of movement. Behind a stationary object—such as the interior of a car—a film of changing backgrounds and locales is projected. The stationary object and the projected material are then filmed, creating the illusion of complete movement.)

New means of scene shifting were needed for the new types of settings. We have already noted that elevators and equipment for flying scenery were employed at the Edwin Booth Theater. By the close of the century, the elevator stage and the revolving stage were perfected. The elevator stage allows sections of a stage floor, or even the entire floor, to be raised or lowered. One of the century's innovative theater technologists was Steele Mackaye (1842–1894), an American dramatist, manager, acting teacher, and inventor. In 1880, at the Madison Square Theater in New York, Mackaye employed two stages, one above the other, which could be raised and lowered; while one stage was in view of the audience, the scenery on the other, which was either in the basement or in the fly area, could be changed. The revolving stage is a large turntable on which scenery is placed; as it moves, one set is brought into view as another turns out of sight.

Lighting

Nineteenth-century technology revolutionized stage lighting, which until then had been a primitive art. The introduction of gas lighting was the first step. In 1816, Philadelphia's Chestnut Street Theater was the first gaslit playhouse in the world. The use of gas allowed control of the intensity of lighting throughout the theater. By the middle of the century, the "gas table," the equivalent of a modern dimmer board, enabled control of all of the stage lighting by one stagehand. The control of lighting made special effects possible; for example, it allowed Richard Wagner to extinguish the lights in the auditorium of the Bayreuth Festspielhaus.

Thomas Edison's incandescent lamp, invented in 1879, further revolutionized stage lighting. By 1881, London's Savoy Theater was employing the new source of lighting, though it may be that some other playhouse was the first to utilize the innovation. Electricity, of course, is the most flexible, controllable, and safe form of lighting and has made twentiety-century stage-lighting design truly a theatrical art.

Summary

The transformations in the theater between 1800 and 1875 prepared the way for the modern theater. In drama, the romantics broke away from the neoclassical rules and argued that all subject matters—the grotesque as well as the ideal—were appropriate for the stage. Melodrama was the popular nineteenth-century genre and continues to be popular in modern films and television. The well-made-play structure, refined by the French writers Scribe and Sardou, is still employed by many twentieth-century dramatists.

The business of acting was transformed in the nineteenth century by the star system, the combination company, and the long run. While the classical, romantic, and melodramatic acting styles were predominant, many performers, including William Charles Macready, the Bancrofts, Mikhail Shchepkin, and Eleonora Duse, strove for greater realism. The director became the overseer of the production process, following the lead of Richard Wagner and the duke of Saxe-Meiningen.

The modern, comfortable proscenium-arch theater became a reality. Two of the era's most innovative playhouses were Booth's Theater in New York and Richard Wagner's Bayreuth Festspielhaus. Historical accuracy became more commonplace in scenery and costuming, and the box set began to replace painted scenery. In lighting, gas and then electricity provided a controllable source of light.

By 1875, the elements that would form the foundation for the realistic revolution were in place, including the emergence of the director, more realistic acting, and the box set. What was missing was serious realistic drama, and that began to emerge in the 1870s.

Part Four

THE MODERN THEATER

The period beginning in 1875 and continuing to the present is called *modern*, not just because it is close to us in time but because it has characteristics and a shape that are unique.

Forces that had begun to emerge in the nineteenth century surfaced at its end. Charles Darwin's theory of evolution was a direct challenge to the centuries-old biblical concept that all creatures, including human beings, were created by God. The German philosopher Friedrich Nietzsche (1844–1900) went so far as to declare that God was dead. Just as Darwin's theory challenged religion, so the theories of Karl Marx (1818–1883) challenged traditionally accepted political beliefs, especially theories of capitalism. At the end of the century Sigmund Freud (1856–1939) declared that people are ruled as much by subconscious thoughts and desires as by their conscious ones, and in the early twentieth century, Albert Einstein (1879–1955), in his theory of relativity, pointed out that certain elements of the universe that were thought to be fixed were changeable.

All of this added up to a drastic shift in the way human beings regarded themselves and the world around them. This is one mark of the modern period—the upheaval in long-held beliefs. Another has to do with advances in technology and communications.

The past 100 years have seen the invention of radio, films, and television, and in travel, of the propeller airplane, the jet plane, and rockets into outer space. These many inventions have brought the world closer together: news travels around the globe instantaneously, and people can travel from continent to continent in a matter of hours. This has brought advantages to people everywhere, but it has also increased the possibilities for horror. The wars in the twentieth century have been *world* wars, and mass murder—of Jews by the Nazis and of political prisoners in Soviet Russia—has occurred on a scale never known before. The turmoil in the modern world has included not only the two world wars but the Russian Revolution, the great depression, the Vietnam War, terrorist assassinations of political leaders, and wars in the Middle East and the Falkland Islands in the early 1980s.

The worldwide upheavals of the last century have been mirrored in the theater, which has been fragmented by numerous movements and trends, especially avant-garde movements. Some historians divide the theater of the past century into two camps: the realists and the antirealists. The realists include Henrik Ibsen, August Strindberg, George Bernard Shaw, Anton Chekhov, the Moscow Art Theater, and the Group Theater; among the antirealists were the symbolists, the expressionists, the futurists, the dadaists, and the surrealists, Vsevolod Meyerhold, Antonin Artaud, Bertolt Brecht, the absurdists, and Jerzy Grotowski. Other analysts point to the sharp division between commercial artists, such as those who work in New York's Broadway theater, and the noncommercial practitioners who initiated such idealistic ventures as the little theaters, off-Broadway, and off-off-Broadway. All of these movements are proof of the fragmentation of the modern theater.

Which theatrical trends of the last 100 years will prove to be historically significant is difficult to predict. What is certain is that the modern theater will be remembered for spawning a great many revolutionary movements.

Chapter Eleven

THE THEATER FROM 1875 TO 1915

The radical transformation of western society between 1875 and the outbreak of World War I in 1914 was mirrored in the theater; trends of the first part of the nineteenth century, such as nationalism, imperialism, and urbanization, continued to transform European and American societies. The further development of industrialization, for example, resulted in the organization of huge industrial monopolies that controlled specific businesses. This had its counterpart in the theater. In 1896, for example, the American theater became dominated by six producers who banded together to form the Theatrical Syndicate. The syndicate controlled the

Modern realistic drama   *In the late nineteenth century several playwrights fashioned forms of dramatic realism that set the pattern for this type of play for the next 100 years. Chief among them were Ibsen, Strindberg and Chekhov. Seen here are the main characters from one of Chekhov's realistic masterpieces:* The Three Sisters. *(Photo—Diane Gorodnitzki, The Acting Company.)*

The Theater between 1875 and 1915

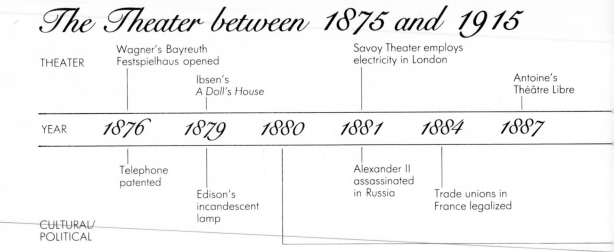

THEATER	Wagner's Bayreuth Festspielhaus opened	Ibsen's A Doll's House		Savoy Theater employs electricity in London		Antoine's Théâtre Libre
YEAR	*1876*	*1879*	*1880*	*1881*	*1884*	*1887*
CULTURAL/ POLITICAL	Telephone patented	Edison's incandescent lamp		Alexander II assassinated in Russia	Trade unions in France legalized	

best playhouses throughout the nation and produced the most noteworthy touring shows.

CHANGES IN LATE–NINETEENTH–CENTURY SOCIETY

Possibly the most significant development was the rise of the working class. As indicated in the preceding chapter, industrialization resulted in urbanization; the working class, throughout the nineteenth century, grew in size. Politicians, social scientists, and artists focused on the concerns of the lower classes. An indication of the increased political power of the working class was the trend, throughout Europe, to allow larger numbers of people to vote. The growing suffragette movement, which sought voting rights for women, was tied to this political transformation. Furthermore, workers gained economic and political power by unionizing. Some of the early American theatrical unions, for example, were founded during this era.

Scientific advances continued to alter radically western life-styles. Advances in medicine increased the average life expectancy. The work of Freud, Einstein, and Nietzsche, following the writings of Darwin and Marx earlier in the century, added up to an assault on accepted beliefs in religion, science, and politics. In the area of psychology, Sigmund Freud established psychoanalysis. Psychological motivations, Freud maintained, could be discovered; seemingly illogical subconscious processes, such as dreams, could be analyzed and explained. In physics, the work of people like Einstein altered our understanding of the universe. Many philosophers point out that the growth of modern scientific knowledge

Strindberg's
Miss Julie

Brahm's
Freie Bühne

Grein's Independent Theatre;
Wedekind's *Spring's Awakening*

Lugné—Poë's
Théâtre
de l'Oeuvre

Shaw's
*Arms and
The Man*

Chekhov's *Seagull;*
Jarry's *Ubu Roi;*
revolving stage in Munich

1888   1889   1891   1893   1894   1896

Dreyfus Affair in France

Height of Imperialism (1880–1914)

resulted in western society's becoming more atheistic as God and religion became less important in daily life.

Einstein's term "relativity" provides a key: things that were thought to be fixed became relative. Not only God and religion were questioned, but the supposed "natural order" of the universe and even the workings of human beings—their conscious control of their actions—were challenged. It was a time of intellectual and moral upheaval, and this was reflected in the drama of the period.

There were radical changes, as well, on the technological front. Inventions, including Alexander Graham Bell's telephone, Thomas Edison's incandescent lamp, Wilbur and Orville Wright's flying machine, and the early automobile, made daily life easier. Some of the inventions of this period, such as recording devices, film, and radio, resulted in new electronic art forms. They also influenced the emerging modern theater.

REALISM

In the theater between 1875 and 1915 one can see the emergence of two artistic impulses that have stood in sharp contrast throughout the twentieth century.

On one hand, realistic artists attempted to create the illusion of everyday life onstage. At the same time, abstract theatrical artists created seemingly illogical stage pictures that were rooted in the subconscious or dream world.

Realism ushered in the modern theater. The Norwegian playwright Henrik Ibsen is often cited as the "father" of realism. *A Doll's House,*

The Theater between 1875 and 1915

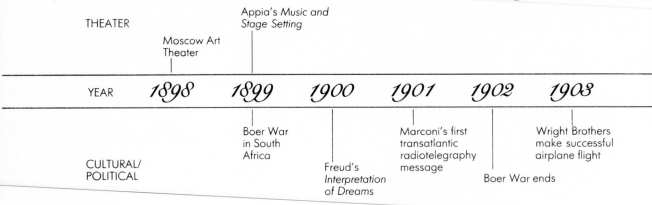

THEATER		Moscow Art Theater	Appia's Music and Stage Setting				
YEAR	*1898*	*1899*	*1900*	*1901*	*1902*	*1903*	
CULTURAL/ POLITICAL		Boer War in South Africa	Freud's Interpretation of Dreams	Marconi's first transatlantic radiotelegraphy message	Boer War ends	Wright Brothers make successful airplane flight	

Ghosts, and *An Enemy of the People* are among his dramas which epitomize the form. It should be pointed out that Ibsen was not a realist throughout his career. As a young playwright, he wrote romantic dramas; near the end of his career he experimented with the abstract symbolist form of drama. Another prominent realistic dramatist was the Swede August Strindberg; the preface to his play *Miss Julie* (1888) is a theoretical manifesto for the realistic movement.

Realists sought to convince their audiences that the stage action in their dramas represented everyday life. While this is not a revolutionary concept for contemporary audiences, many late-nineteenth-century theatergoers and critics were scandalized by realism in the theater. The reasons should be apparent. In the attempt to portray daily life, realists argued, no subject matter should be excluded from the stage. Among the taboo subject matters dramatized by realists were economic injustice, the sexual double standard, unhappy marriages, venereal disease, and religious hypocrisy. Many realists believed that the purpose of drama was to call audience attention to social problems in order to instigate change.

Furthermore, realists refused to make simple moral judgments or to resolve their dramatic action neatly. Unlike popular melodramas, realistic plays frequently implied that morality and immorality were relative and not clearly distinct or easily defined. Rather than employ stock characters, realists created complicated personalities who had been molded by their heredity and environment. The language of these characters was colloquial and conversational. (In contemporary realistic drama the dialogue has included obscenities, again shocking the sensibility of some audiences.) Not surprisingly, then, realists were confronted

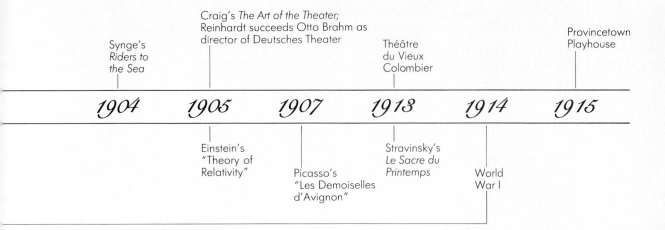

Synge's
*Riders to
the Sea*

Craig's *The Art of the Theater*;
Reinhardt succeeds Otto Brahm as
director of Deutsches Theater

Théâtre
du Vieux
Colombier

Provincetown
Playhouse

1904   *1905*   *1907*   *1913*   *1914*   *1915*

Einstein's
"Theory of
Relativity"

Picasso's
"Les Demoiselles
d'Avignon"

Stravinsky's
*Le Sacre du
Printemps*

World
War I

with a great deal of opposition to the producing of their plays. Censorship problems constantly plagued them.

Turning to production, the scenery used in late-nineteenth-century realistic drama was most often the box set. As was noted earlier, this was closed in on three sides—sometimes with a ceiling—and was meant to be as lifelike as possible.

Ibsen's *Ghosts*

A realistic play that created a great deal of furor was Ibsen's *Ghosts*. The negative critical commentary that followed its initial London presentation in 1891 was typical of the criticism of the play. William Archer, an English critic as well as an Ibsen supporter and translator, published a summary of these critiques. They included such statements as: "An open drain; a loathsome sore unbandaged; a dirty act done publicly . . . Candid foulness . . . Revoltingly suggestive and blasphemous. . . . If any repetition of this outrage be attempted the authorities will doubtless wake from their lethargy. . . . As foul and filthy a concoction as has ever been allowed to disgrace the boards of an English theater."[1] These attacks came a decade after Ibsen wrote the play.

The subject matter of Ibsen's *Ghosts* must have been startling to Victorian audiences. The action revolves around the character of Mrs. Alving. Many years prior to the time when the action of the play begins, she had wanted to leave her philandering husband. When she had visited Manders, her pastor, at that time, she was attracted to him. Manders,

[1]Henrik Ibsen, *Ghosts and Three Other Plays*, tr. Michael Meyer, N.Y., Doubleday–Anchor, 1966, pp. 115–116.

An early automobile assembly line   *The automobile was just one of the many inventions that transformed early twentieth-century life. The assembly line developed by Henry Ford in 1913 resulted in mass production. Many artists depicted the problems created by the emergence of mechanization in their works. A famous comic example was Charlie Chaplin's* Modern Times. *(Photo—The Ford Motor Company.)*

however, persuaded her to remain with her husband.

When the play begins, Mrs. Alving's husband is dead, and she and Manders are preparing to dedicate an orphanage to his memory. Mrs. Alving reveals to Manders that her husband had not changed his ways even after she returned to him and that he had died from the ravages of venereal disease. Furthermore, Mrs. Alving reveals that Regina, her servant, is her husband's illegitimate daughter.

The dramatic action is complicated by the fact that Mrs. Alving's son Oswald, who has recently returned home, is unaware that Regina is his half-sister. Oswald wishes to marry Regina, but before Manders and Mrs. Alving can reveal the truth to him, the orphanage—which has not been insured because of Manders's fear that insurance would suggest his lack of religious faith—burns down. Manders is convinced by Engstrand, a drunken carpenter and Regina's supposed father, that he, Manders, is

Modern realism   *Henrik Ibsen's plays addressed serious themes in the format of the well-made play.* Ghosts *is a powerful drama of family relationships where past actions—adultery, deceit, hypocrisy—affect such victims as Mrs. Alving on the left, played by Liv Ullman, and her son, played by Kevin Spacey. This recent production was at the Kennedy Center, Washington, D.C. (Photo—Jack Buxbaum.)*

responsible for the fire. In order to avoid scandal, Manders agrees to use the remaining funds in the estate to help Engstrand establish a home for sailors in Captain Alving's memory. It is obvious, however, that the home will, in reality, be a brothel.

In the final act, Oswald confesses that he is suffering from venereal disease. Mrs. Alving then reveals the truth about their father to Regina and Oswald. Oswald begs his mother to promise to assist him in committing suicide when the venereal disease incapacitates him mentally. At the close of the play, Oswald deteriorates completely; at daybreak, as he goes blind, he calls for his mother to give him "the sun." The curtain closes without Ibsen's revealing whether or not Mrs. Alving will carry out the mercy killing.

Ghosts touches on many subjects which were, and might still be, considered offensive by some. A sexual double standard, for instance, is

Courtesy of the Norwegian Information Service

HENRIK IBSEN
(1828–1906)

The Norwegian playwright Henrik Ibsen is known as the "father" of modern realism, but he also wrote important poetic and symbolic plays. Ibsen is known for his mastery of dramatic technique, his psychological insights into human nature, and his poetic symbolism.

For much of his life, Ibsen was an outcast from the society that he dramatized. When he was born in Skien, Norway, in 1828, his father was a prosperous businessman, but in 1834 the business failed, and the family was forced to move outside of the town. At 15 the dramatist left home to work as a pharmacist's apprentice; later he tried to qualify for the university. In 1852, he became producer at the theater in Bergen and was commissioned to write one play a year for the theater's anniversary. While he was a producer at Bergen he took a study tour of the German and Danish theaters. He moved to Christiania in 1857 to become artistic director of the Norwegian Theater. When it went bankrupt he secured a small government grant and, in 1864, left Norway, living in Rome, Dresden, and Munich for the next twenty-seven years. Ibsen returned to Norway in 1891. He continued to work in his careful, methodical way, allowing two years to write and polish a play. Incapacitated by a stroke in 1900, followed by another stroke the following year, he was a nearly helpless invalid until his death in 1906.

Ibsen's earliest plays, based on Norwegian history and mythology, are romantic verse dramas examining the extremes of the Norwegian national character. These include *Lady Inger of Ostraat* (1855), *The Vikings at Helgeland* (1858), *The Pretenders* (1863), and *Peer Gynt* (1867).

The middle plays—the realistic social dramas for which he is best known—explore the interaction of people with society. Among these plays, which deal with such problems as unhappy marriages, the sexual double standard, infidelity, and the position of women, are *A Doll's House* (1879), *Ghosts* (1881), and *An Enemy of the People* (1882). Because of their frank treatment of controversial subject matter, these plays often provoked angry debates when they were first presented.

While still working in a realistic Norwegian setting, Ibsen moved toward symbolism and mysticism in his later plays. The dramas in this group include *The Wild Duck* (1884), *Rosmersholm* (1886), *The Master Builder* (1892), *John Gabriel Borkman* (1896), *The Lady from the Sea* (1888), and *When We Dead Awaken* (1899). Regardless of the period or style, there is a common theme throughout all of Henrik Ibsen's plays: the exploration of self amidst conflicting social pressures.

questioned when Mrs. Alving asks Manders why only women must be virginal on their wedding nights. Ibsen also suggests that the women of his era have been forced to sublimate their sexuality; Mrs. Alving, for example, recognizes that she brought "no joy of life" into her marriage. Furthermore, the institution of marriage is derided. Oswald tells Manders that while he was in Paris he knew couples who lived together and had children but due to financial hardship were unmarried. The young Alving argues that these relationships are more honest than most conventional marriages.

Ibsen also satirizes religious hypocrisy. Pastor Manders's wish not to insure the orphanage, his inability to see through Engstrand, and his attacks on books he has not read illustrate his foolishness. The references to venereal disease, incest, and euthanasia were, of course, all controversial. Still, as Ibsen frequently pointed out, *Ghosts* is not a play about syphilis, but about persons who are haunted by their pasts.

The realistic qualities of Ibsen's *Ghosts* are typical of realistic drama. The characters are not stereotypes; there are no heroes or villains, for example. The audience is made to understand each character's psychological, social, and economic motivations: how personalities have been shaped by environment and heredity. Just as there is moral deformity in this universe, there is also physical deformity. Engstrand's "left leg is slightly crooked; under the sole of his boot is fixed a block of wood." The language is colloquial. The setting for the play is a box set representing "a spacious garden room."[2]

In an attempt to make the dramatic action believable and logical, Ibsen employs crisis and well-made-play structures. Like a Greek tragedy, *Ghosts* observes the unities of time, place, and action, and much of the action has occurred prior to the beginning of the play. This dramatic structure is well suited to a play in which the characters are haunted by the ghosts of their pasts. The technique by which the past is slowly revealed is reminiscent of Sophocles's *King Oedipus.* The influence of the well-made-play form perfected by Scribe and Sardou in France earlier in the nineteenth century is apparent. Each of the three acts concludes with a climax: Oswald chasing Regina at the end of Act I, the burning of the orphanage at the end of Act II, and the mental deterioration of Oswald at the close of the play.

All of the action is carefully prepared for and foreshadowed. In the first act, Mrs. Alving casually remarks that a fire had been extinguished in the orphanage, preparing the audience for the eventual catastrophe of the fire. The plot of the play revolves around two central secrets: the identity of Regina's true father and the origin of Oswald's disease. Despite his use of well-made-play devices, the Norwegian playwright breaks one of the fundamental rules of the Scribean formula: *Ghosts* does not resolve neatly; the audience does not know whether or not Mrs. Alving will give

[2]Ibid., p. 131.

her son the morphine. This change from past formulas was part of Ibsen's creativity in giving more substance and meaning to his plays than his predecessors had to theirs.

As we have indicated, Ibsen, later in his career, turned from realism to the more abstract form of symbolism. Even in his realistic plays, however, we can see Ibsen's dramatic use of symbols. The orphanage, symbolizing Captain Alving's reputation, burns down. Engstrand's brothel is a more fitting memorial for the dissolute husband. The gloomy weather symbolizes the pall hanging over the Alving household. Eventually, Ibsen would shift his focus from creating a realistic world to drawing a universe in which symbolic elements predominated.

NATURALISM

Related to realism is *naturalism*, a movement that began in France in the nineteenth century and spread to other European countries. Naturalism can be looked on as a subdivision of realism: an extreme form of realism. As a pure movement it did not last long, but certain of its ideas have shown up frequently in later dramas as well as in films and television.

The "father" of naturalism is said to have been the Frenchman Emile Zola (1849–1902), who formulated the concept of "scientific objectivity," which suggests that the artist should present a picture of the real world without making his own presence felt. The best-known naturalistic dramas from this era are Gerhart Hauptmann's *The Weavers* (Germany, 1892) and Maxim Gorki's *The Lower Depths* (Russia, 1902).

The naturalists argued that what should be presented on the stage was a "slice of life." Because the naturalists wanted the controlling hand of the artist to remain unseen, they argued against stage contrivances. Instead, the artist should function as an objective scientist; everything on stage—characters, language, properties, settings, costumes—should seem to have been lifted directly from everyday life. Authenticity was the basic requirement.

Many of the naturalists believed that the most appropriate subject matter for drama was the lower class. The naturalists frequently focused on the sordid and seamy aspects of society in their day. They did so in order to call their audiences' attention to social problems and to instigate reforms. Gorki's *The Lower Depths* presents characters who have sunk to the lowest depths of Russian society. In most naturalistic dramas we see a series of episodes that demonstrate the control that environment and our own animal desires have over us. For this reason, naturalistic works seem more loosely structured than realistic ones. A modern parallel to this kind of naturalism is provided by filmed documentaries, sometimes called *cinema verité*, of people who live wretched lives in squalid

axim Gorki's *The Lower Depths*
*A scene from the Moscow Art Theater's
original production of Gorki's famous
naturalistic drama. In the center is the
renowned actor, director, and theorist of
realistic acting Konstantin Stanislavski.
The Lower Depths, set in a
turn-of-the-century Russian flophouse, is an
example of naturalism as defined by the
French theorist Emile Zola.
(Photo—Sovfoto.)*

conditions: a film about derelicts, for example, who sleep in flea-bag hotels and exist on cheap wine, or one about people in a desert country suffering the effects of drought and famine.

Naturalism is a more stringent form than realism. One reason is its insistence on showing the stark side of life; the other is its attempt to be like a documentary, which means that the action cannot be shaped by the same kind of artistic techniques as realism. The latter can employ symbols and can structure events in a way that often is more aesthetically satisfying. The extreme point of view of the naturalists ultimately prevented the movement from being more influential, and realism was seen as a more viable theatrical form. Nonetheless, the naturalist movement helped to further the development of a theatrical art dedicated to reproducing life on the stage, and its influence can still be seen in such contemporary plays as Eugene O'Neill's *The Iceman Cometh* (America, 1939) and David Storey's *The Changing Room* (England, 1971).

INDEPENDENT PRODUCERS OF REALISM AND NATURALISM

As we have noted, realistic and naturalistic works were perceived by the establishment as too controversial for production. In those countries where the theatrical art was subject to censorship, realists could not get their dramas staged. In England, the lord chamberlain refused licenses to many of these controversial works. Even in those countries where official censorship did not exist, such as the United States, these dramas were not considered commercially viable. (A 1905 Brooklyn production of George Bernard Shaw's realistic *Mrs. Warren's Profession* led to the arrest of the entire cast.)

In order to produce realistic and naturalistic dramas, a number of independent theaters were established throughout Europe. These theaters were exempted from government censorship because they were organized as subscription companies, with theatergoers being treated almost like members of a private club. These theaters, which were not striving for commercial success, presented their plays to small audiences interested in the new dramatic forms. Some of them also popularized realistic production techniques. The four major independent theaters were France's Théâtre Libre, Germany's Freie Bühne, England's Independent Theatre, and Russia's Moscow Art Theater.

Antoine's Free Theater

The Théâtre Libre, or Free Theater, was founded in 1887 by André Antoine. At the time he founded his independent company, Antoine was a gas clerk and a member of an amateur theater group. When he recommended that his fellow amateurs produce a one-act adaptation of a Zola short story, the group refused. Undaunted, Antoine rented the theater and organized a subscription company to produce the work. While the Théâtre Libre began inauspiciously, it revolutionized the French theater. Antoine's company introduced Parisian audiences to the major realistic and naturalistic playwrights; these dramatists included Zola, Ibsen, and Henri Becque (1837–1899). By applying to these dramas many of the illusionistic stage practices previously employed by Madame Vestris and the duke of Saxe-Meiningen, Antoine popularized theatrical realism.

Antoine strove to create the illusion of the fourth wall so that his audience would believe that they were peeking in on everyday life. His stage settings, individually designed for each production, were box sets filled with practicable elements. Concerned with the illusion of stage lighting, Antoine employed *motivated lighting* in his productions; this means that the light which illuminated the stage picture seemed to come from actual onstage sources, such as a table lamp. Like Richard Wagner in the Bayreuth Festspielhaus, Antoine extinguished the houselights in order to focus his audiences' attention on the stage.

 EORGE BERNARD SHAW
(1856–1950)

Had George Bernard Shaw died before his fortieth birthday he would have been remembered as a somewhat eccentric ne'er-do-well who let his mother support him, published five unsuccessful novels, and was a vegetarian and a Fabian socialist. It was only after his friend, the critic William Archer, got him jobs as a book reviewer and an art critic that Shaw was able to make use of his writing ability.

Shaw's years of unemployment were spent in developing his intellect and writing ability. Born in Dublin, Ireland, of English parents, he was an indifferent student who wanted to pursue his own interests in music, art, and literature. At 16 he was working as a clerk in a land agent's office. His mother had left his alcoholic father and was living in London, teaching music. Shaw joined her in 1876. He read widely, wrote extensively on political issues for the Fabian Society (a socialist organization), and became a noted political speaker.

By 1895, Shaw had become the theater critic for the *Saturday Review*. His commentaries, later published as *Our Theater in the Nineties*, set new standards for excellence in dramatic criti-

cism. In his writings, he championed the new realistic theater, particularly the plays of Ibsen, and condemned the stale commercial theater of his time. Not finding any English plays that fit his theatrical views, he began writing his own, using them to transmit his ideas on political and social reform.

His first plays were privately produced for limited audiences to avoid the censor, but in 1898 he published them as *Plays Pleasant and Unpleasant*. With this volume, Shaw began the practice of writing long introductory prefaces discussing the issues raised in the plays. He also provided detailed descriptions of settings and stage directions so that readers might be able to visualize his plays better. Though most of his plays discussed social problems or philosophical ideas, they were also witty, engaging comedies with lively dialogue and unusual, well-drawn characters. They could be characterized as realistic comedies of manners. Some of his best-known plays are *Candida* (1895), *Caesar and Cleopatra* (1899), *Major Barbara* (1905), *Man and Superman* (1903), and *St. Joan* (1923).

Shaw was awarded the Nobel Prize for literature in 1925. In his later years, his plays became more filled with philosophy and were less interesting dramatically. He was also in disfavor socially and politically for his view of war as a useless enterprise, and for his occasional praise of Mussolini and Hitler. Greatly saddened by the death of his wife in 1943, he lived for seven more years. On October 31, 1950, he announced "I am going to die," and three days later he did.

Antoine also transformed French stage acting. Arguing against the star system as typified by the careers of Sarah Bernhardt and Benoît Coquelin (1841–1909), Antoine organized a company of amateur actors who worked to create ensemble performances. Ensemble acting, which requires balanced casting and the integration of all of the performances, does not allow an individual star to overshadow the supporting players. In striving for an ensemble, Antoine again was emulating the duke of Saxe-Meiningen. The French director, believing that the actor should appear to be living, not acting, on the stage, also opposed the employment of conventional gestures, vocal patterns, and blocking practices.

The impact Antoine had on the modern French theater can be seen in his later career. He left the financially troubled Théâtre Libre in 1894 and three years later founded the Théâtre Antoine. More significantly, in 1906 he was appointed head of the Odéon, France's second national theater. Obviously, then, by the first decade of the new century, realism had become an accepted movement in the French theater. Antoine's influence could also be seen on the German and English independent theaters.

The Free Stage of Berlin

Two years after the founding of the Théâtre Libre, the Freie Bühne, or Free Stage, began operating in Berlin. Like Antoine's company, it was a subscription theater dedicated to the introduction of realism and naturalism. The Freie Bühne was noted for its productions of the plays of Ibsen and the German naturalist Gerhart Hauptmann (1862–1946). It was operated by a board of directors, with Otto Brahm as the elected leader. Antoine, on the other hand, had been the dictatorial director of his company. Since the Freie Bühne employed professional actors, the company was able to perform only on Sundays, when its performers were not otherwise engaged. While the Théâtre Libre rented small, out-of-the-way Parisian theaters, the Freie Bühne rented professional houses. Both groups were noncommercial operations.

For several reasons—because the theater produced only on Sundays, used professional actors who were employed elsewhere during the remainder of the week, and rented theaters occupied from Monday to Sunday—the productions of the German independent theater were not as carefully realized as those of the Théâtre Libre. Still, the goal of this theater was not to introduce realistic production techniques but to introduce realistic drama. The Freie Bühne ceased regular operations in 1891 but occasionally continued to produce noteworthy dramas that the German government refused permission to stage. For example, in 1892, the independent theater was revived in order to produce Hauptmann's *The Weavers*.

The Independent Theatre in London

The English Independent Theatre, founded in 1891 by the Dutch-born critic Jacob Thomas Grein, was organized as a subscription company in order to circumvent censorship by the lord chamberlain. The Independent Theatre, which operated in London for six years, produced in a fashion similar to the Freie Bühne. Professional actors were employed, professional theaters leased, and performances staged on Sundays. The goal of Grein's theater was to introduce the realists and naturalists, including Ibsen and Zola, to the English public. The company's first production was *Ghosts*; the disparaging reviews cited earlier were of this production.

In 1892, the Independent Theatre introduced the Irish-born George Bernard Shaw to the London public by producing his first play, *Widower's House*. Shaw, who as a theater critic defended fellow realists and naturalists, believed that drama should inspire social reform. Unlike the works of other realists, however, many of Shaw's socially conscious dramas are comedies. In Shaw's hands, subjects that most realists saw as gloomy and tragic were perfect for satirical ridicule. When the Independent Theatre ceased operating in 1897, Shaw's works were staged by other independently organized English companies.

The Moscow Art Theater

Possibly the most influential of the late-nineteenth-century theaters dedicated to realistic productions was the Moscow Art Theater. Founded in 1898 by Konstantin Stanislavski and Vladimir Nemirovich-Danchenko (1858–1943), the Moscow Art Theater continues to produce drama today. The production style of the Russian theater was at first influenced by the duke of Saxe-Meiningen. The turning point in the company's initial season, however, was the production in 1898 of Anton Chekhov's *The Seagull*, a play that had failed dismally in its premiere presentation in 1896. The first company to produce the play had not understood Chekhov's complex dramatic form. Chekhov wrote three additional realistic plays—*Uncle Vanya*, *The Three Sisters*, and *The Cherry Orchard*—for the Moscow Art Theater. Chekhovian drama, with Stanislavski's carefully realized realistic productions, established the company's reputation.

Chekhov's plays are not significant simply for the realistic universes they present but also because they are perfect examples of modern tragicomedy. We have already seen that in some periods of theater history, such as the Elizabethan, comic scenes occurred in tragic plays. These scenes, such as the grave-diggers' episode in *Hamlet*, are separated from the serious scenes. In modern tragicomedy, however, the tragic and comic are blended; the plays are bittersweet. The comedy does not

A Moscow Art Theater Production of *Uncle Vanya*   *The Moscow Art Theater, famous for its realistic production technique, is also known as the home of Anton Chekhov. This is a 1948 production photo of* Uncle Vanya *done for the company's fiftieth anniversary; the play, one of Chekhov's realistic tragicomedies, was first produced by the Moscow Art Theater in 1899, where it was directed by Konstantin Stanislavski. (Photo—Sovfoto.)*

provide a contrast but increases our awareness of the tragic circumstances. Heightening the sense of tragedy is the fact that Chekhov's tragicomic characters are unable to fulfill their basic desires.

In Chekhov's *The Cherry Orchard* Madame Ranevsky and her family lose their beloved country home with its orchard to Lopakhin, whose father had been a serf. In this play, Chekhov is mirroring the changing class structure in turn-of-the-century Russia. The once-aristocratic family members are often comic in their inability to save the orchard. For example, Varya, Ranevsky's oldest daughter, and Lopakhin seem destined to marry, which would keep the orchard in the family. In the final act Varya and Lopakhin are left alone so that he can propose. Instead, they are unable to discuss their feelings. The "nonproposal scene" is quite funny, because she is fumbling with luggage while he is discussing the weather, but after it is over we realize that the last chance to save the beloved cherry orchard has been lost. The genius of Anton Chekhov is that he makes us see that underneath comedy there is often tragedy.

ANTON PAVLOVICH CHEKHOV
(1860–1904)

When he first visited St. Petersburg in 1885 to finish his medical studies, Anton Chekhov was astonished to discover that he was a famous writer. The short stories that he had been casually writing to support his family and pay for his education had been highly acclaimed. As a result, he resolved to improve his work habits and concentrate on literature as a career.

As a schoolboy in Taganrog, Russia, Chekhov had acted and written for the local theater. His father, a grocer, had gone into bankruptcy during the writer's last years in school and the family fled to Moscow to escape the creditors. His literary sketches, written for Moscow and St. Petersburg magazines, helped Chekhov support his family and continue his studies for a medical degree. Though he finished medical school, he never entered active practice because of his literary career.

In 1887 Chekhov's first successful play, *Ivanov*, was produced in Moscow. An earlier drama, *Platonov*, written while he was a student, had been rejected by the Moscow theaters. His third play, *The Wood Demon*, written under the influence of Tolstoy's philosophy,

was a failure in 1889. He also wrote several short farces, or "jokes" as he labeled them, in his late twenties. Though the structure and actions of these plays are very different from his later dramas, the early works show Chekhov's interest in the ordinary incidents of middle-class, provincial life and in the outside forces that change people's lives. Particularly in the farces, he was able to swiftly and insightfully draw characters and to intertwine comedy and tragedy.

It was seven years before Chekhov's next play, *The Seagull*, was produced. During this time, he perfected his dramatic techniques, relying on indirect action and character development to create the tensions in his plays. Like a complex musical score, the plays have a variety of themes that are developed through many characters and images.

Though the initial production of *The Seagull* was not a success, the Moscow Art Theater, headed by Konstantin Stanislavski, produced it successfully in 1898; it also produced Chekhov's next three plays, *Uncle Vanya* (1899), *The Three Sisters* (1900), and *The Cherry Orchard* (1904). Despite their success, Chekhov berated Stanislavski for neglecting the humor in his plays.

The playwright contracted tuberculosis when he was 23 and in the last years of his life was forced to leave his estate outside of Moscow and move south to Yalta for his health. In 1901, he married Olga Knipper, an actress with the Moscow Art Theater. He was elected to the Russian Academy of Science, but resigned when his friend, the writer Maxim Gorki, was expelled. He died in 1904 at Badenweiler, Germany, where he had gone in an attempt to regain his health.

The Stanislavskian Acting Technique

Along with productions of dramatists like Chekhov, the Moscow Art Theater is also renowned for Stanislavski's techniques for training actors. Much of contemporary American acting training, for example, is influenced by Stanislavski's system. Stanislavski worked very intensively with his actors, spending extensive amounts of time on rehearsal. The Russian actor-director focused on developing methods of internally based psychological realism. According to Stanislavski the actor must do a great deal of script analysis. The performer must be aware of the character's background, environment, and relationships, as well as any additional information the dramatist provides; these are the given circumstances of the play.

The actor, in order to place himself in his character's situation, employs the "magic if," asking what he would do *if* he were confronted by similar circumstances. Furthermore, the performer must ascertain what motivates his character. The super-objective, also referred to as the *spine* or *throughline*, is the "active verb" that defines the character's overall goal in the play. For each scene, the actor must also be able to identify his character's specific objective.

Concentration is also central to the Stanislavskian system; the actor must listen to and observe the stage action as if it had never occurred before. The American actor-playwright William Gillette (1855–1937), who also sought to define the characteristics of a realistic performance, referred to this technique, in a 1915 essay, as "the illusion of the first time."

To assist the actor in portraying emotions realistically, Stanislavski devised an exercise known as *emotional recall* or *affective memory*. The performer is called upon to remember an event in his own life that parallels the emotional situation in the play. (As an experiment, think about the last event in your own life that caused you, for example, to cry. Do not think about the feeling itself but about all the specifics of the occasion: where you were, what you were wearing, who you were with, the time of day, and so forth. As you mentally reconstruct the specific circumstances, notice how the emotion begins to well up.)

Stanislavski cautioned against excessive use of emotional recall. According to the Russian theorist, if a performer is immersed in the given circumstances of the drama, the desired emotions will develop out of the dramatic action. Emotional recall was to be employed only for particularly difficult situations. Also, it must be remembered that traditional training in vocal techniques and bodily movements was taken for granted by Stanislavski—a fact often overlooked by his twentieth-century imitators.

The influence of Konstantin Stanislavski on the modern theater cannot be overstated. Most actors in America today are trained with a variation of the Stanislavskian system. There have been alterations and adaptations of his system, but through it all, his work remains pervasive.

KONSTANTIN SERGEEVICH STANISLAVSKI
(1863–1938)

The most famous system for training performers to act realistically—that is, to be believable—was developed by the Russian actor and director Konstantin Stanislavski. In his recollection of his early career, chronicled in *Art Notes*, Stanislavski wrote: "herein lies the problem, to bring life itself upon the stage." His system of acting was developed as a response to the problem of making characters live on the stage, particularly in the realistic dramas of the late nineteenth century.

Though his father was an industrialist, his grandmother had been a French actress, and at 15 Stanislavski founded the Alekseev Circle, an amateur group consisting of many of his family members (Alekseev was his family's surname). He studied at a theatrical school and observed the actors of the time before studying with F. P. Komissarzhevsky, a dramatist and producer.

Together, he and Komissarzhevsky founded the Society of Art and Literature in 1888, another amateur group which became noted for its productions of the works of Tolstoy and Dostoyevsky. Fascinated by the realistic staging of the Meiningen players, Stanislavski modeled his productions after theirs, but he sought to substitute realism in acting for their declamatory, or oratorical, style.

The playwright V. I. Nemirovich-Danchenko, director of the drama school of the Moscow Philharmonic Society, invited Stanislavski to form a new theater in 1898: the Moscow Art Theater. Nemirovich-Danchenko was responsible for the literary and administrative duties while Stanislavski handled the staging and production. With the Moscow Art Theater, he was able to refine his system of realistic acting. Virtually every modern approach to realistic acting stems from this system.

The Moscow Art Theater had early successes with productions of Tolstoy, but it became most famous for its productions of Chekhov's plays. Stanislavski created many of the leading roles in these plays, including Dr. Astrov in *Uncle Vanya* and Gaev in *The Cherry Orchard.*

Though most of his work was with realistic dramas, Stanislavski also staged the symbolist plays of Maeterlinck and Andreyev and worked with the designer Gordon Craig on an experimental production of *Hamlet*. The leaders of the Russian avant-garde theater of the 1920s, Meyerhold, Vakhtangov and Tairov, all worked with the Moscow Art Theater early in their careers. After the Russian Revolution, the Moscow Art Theater confined itself to realism. Stanislavski, though he no longer acted because of poor health, continued to develop his system of acting until his death in 1938.

ANTIREALISTIC THEATER

As noted, one could argue that the two basic theatrical trends of the last 100 years have been realism and deviations from realism. Between 1875 and 1915 there were many antirealistic experimenters who attacked the attempt to put "slices of life" on the stage.

Symbolism was the leading antirealistic movement between 1880 and 1910. While the major proponents of the movement were French, symbolism influenced playwrights and practitioners throughout the world. The symbolists believed that drama should present the mystery of being and the cosmos, the infinite qualities of the human spirit, not mundane, day-to-day activities. They called for a poetic theater in which symbolic images rather than concrete actions are the basic means for communicating with the audience. Frequently symbolist plays appear to take place in a dream world, with the evocation of atmosphere and mood the major dramatic goals instead of telling a story.

As for characterization, the symbolists, unlike the realists, did not strive to create individual characters but rather representative figures of the human condition. The symbolists also argued against realistic scenic detail, believing that the stage picture should contain only the bare essentials necessary to evoke the dramatic universe. Probably the most renowned symbolist dramas were Maurice Maeterlinck's (1862–1949) *Pelléas and Mélisande* (1892) and Paul Claudel's (1868–1955) *The Tidings Brought to Mary* (1912).

Like the realists, the symbolists also needed independently organized theater companies to produce their plays. In France, two independent theater companies were dedicated to antirealistic drama and production style. In 1890 Paul Fort organized the Théâtre d'Art. When this theater closed three years later, Aurélien-Marie Lugné-Poë, who had acted for André Antoine at the Théâtre Libre and for Paul Fort, established the Théâtre de l'Oeuvre. Both Fort's and Lugné-Poë's companies were dedicated to the symbolist theories of stage production. They deemphasized scenery, experimented with stylized vocal and physical techniques, and presented avant-garde antirealistic drama.

Possibly the most notorious presentation staged by Lugné-Poë was of Alfred Jarry's (1873–1907) *Ubu the King* (1896), a comic-book-style takeoff on Shakespeare's history plays, *Julius Caesar* and *Macbeth*. The farcical plot details how the bungling and gluttonous Ubu conspires to take over as ruler of Poland and is later dethroned by the assassinated king's only surviving son. The play's opening line, "merdre," a takeoff on the common French term for feces, created an immediate furor, as did many of its other scatological references. Jarry's cynical and absurdist view of political leaders makes *Ubu the King* a shockingly prophetic work in light of twentieth-century history.

Ireland's Abbey Theater is often associated with early symbolist drama. The founders of the Abbey, in the first decade of the twentieth century, wanted to establish a company which would deal with the national concerns and myths of the Irish people. The three playwrights initially associated with the Abbey were William Butler Yeats (1865– 1939), Lady Augusta Gregory (1863–1935), and John Millington Synge (1871–1909). Yeats, who was opposed to realism, created symbolist plays which treated Irish myth. Later in his career, he experimented with the stylized conventions of Japanese noh drama. The works of Lady Gregory and Synge were more realistic; Synge, however, in a play like *Riders to the Sea* (1904), created a poetic drama in the realistic form. The Abbey Theater, which today is Ireland's national theater, also introduced the works of Sean O'Casey (1884–1964) in the 1920s.

Ibsen and Strindberg as Antirealists

It is difficult to categorize all of the authors who wrote antirealistic dramas between 1880 and 1910. Most of the symbolists were highly individual in style. Some playwrights wrote in both realistic and antirealistic forms, and even mixed the two. Two playwrights who were influenced by symbolism but whose antirealistic works defy facile categorization are Henrik Ibsen and August Strindberg.

While both Scandinavian authors are remembered for their realistic plays, late in their careers they moved away from the realistic mode. In *The Master Builder, Little Eyolf, John Gabriel Borkman*, and *When We Dead Awaken*, Ibsen follows many of the tenets of symbolism.

August Strindberg's later antirealistic dramas have been more influential than the antirealistic plays of Ibsen. The two best known are *A Dream Play* and *The Ghost Sonata*. As the title of the earlier play indicates, the dramatic action evokes the world of a dream. We see the Christ-like goddess, the Daughter of Indra, journeying through a variety of human situations and experiencing continual suffering. The scenes are not always causally related but rather are a series of stages or, to emphasize the Christian imagery, stations in the Daughter of Indra's journey. Places, time, and characters transform suddenly and unexpectedly. Characters such as the Officer, the Attorney, the Poet, He, She, and the Dean of Philosophy are more representative of prototypes than individuals; thus they are referred to by titles rather than by names.

Symbols abound: a castle grows out of a dung hill, a shawl contains all human suffering; two lands are referred to as Foulgut and Fairhaven, and an Attorney's face has become hideously lined by the torment of those who have engaged him. In *A Dream Play*, Strindberg deals with many of the concerns found in his realistic dramas—the destructiveness of marriage, materialism, and the class struggle—but he dramatizes these concerns, as he says in the play's preface, in "the disconnected but apparently logical form of a dream. Anything can happen; everything is possible and probable."[3]

[3]August Strindberg, *Six Plays of Strindberg*, tr. Elizabeth Sprigg, N.Y., Doubleday–Anchor, 1955, p. 193.

AUGUST STRINDBERG
(1849–1912)

Swedish playwright August Strindberg is one of the towering figures of the modern theater. He set standards in both realism—the theater resembling everyday life—and antirealism. In the latter form he experimented with many styles, including dream plays and works that anticipated expressionism.

Strindberg had an unhappy, insecure childhood as the son of a steamship agent and a former waitress and servant. His youthful unhappiness was a prelude to a troubled adulthood, including frequent bouts with mental illness, but he was able to take these experiences and use them as the basis of his writing.

After some intermittent study at the University of Uppsala, Sweden, Strindberg returned to Stockholm and worked as a teacher, librarian, and journalist while revising *Master Olaf*, his first play. In 1875, he met Siri von Essen, a soldier's wife, whom he married in 1877. Their stormy marriage, which lasted until 1891, provided many situations for his novels and plays, particularly the dramas *The Father* (1887) and *Miss Julie* (1888). Both were naturalistic works examining the battle between the sexes. In his preface to *Miss Julie*, he describes the realism in characterization and in production methods that he wants for the play.

In 1884 Strindberg was prosecuted for blasphemy. This increased his feelings of paranoia and his dislike for Sweden, and as a result he spent much time abroad, particularly in Paris, until 1897. When his second marriage failed in 1895 he went through a period of severe stress and mental instability before undergoing a conversion to religious mysticism. His plays written after 1897—such as *To Damascus* (1898) and *A Dream Play* (1902)—are expressionistic in form, employing symbolism and unrealistic shifts in action, and are steeped in his new beliefs. The plays from this period were to be influential on the surrealist movement and, after that, on the theater of the absurd.

Several of his later plays cover events in Swedish history, a possible reflection of his return to Stockholm in 1899. Here Strindberg, who had reembraced the radical ideas of his youth, wrote many social and political treatises for the press. In 1902 he married Harriet Bosse, a young actress, but the marriage failed in 1904.

Some of Strindberg's most experimental and influential plays were written for the Intimate Theater in Stockholm, which he and August Falck ran for a time. His chamber plays, like *The Ghost Sonata* (1907), reflected his interest in music, particularly Beethoven, and showed his preoccupation with the removal of facades to reveal grotesque elements beneath the surface. When he died in 1912, the Swedish Academy ignored him, as it had always done, but his countrymen mourned him as their greatest writer.

𝒜dolphe Appia: father of modern scene design *Appia's ideas of lighting and scenery were revolutionary. He moved away from realistic settings to the use of shapes and levels which would serve the performers as acting areas. An example is this design for* Iphigenia in Aulis. *He was also among the first to realize the vast possibilities of modern lighting techniques. (Photo—Cleveland State University, Theater Arts Area.)*

Appia and Craig: Antirealist Designers

Swiss-born Adolphe Appia and Englishman Gordon Craig are often described as symbolist designers because they were able to present visually many of the symbolists' stage theories. Ironically, most of their ideas remained in the form of sketches or drawings, since neither was given much opportunity to put his ideas into practice. Their theories, however, have had great influence on many twentieth-century scene designers.

While these two designers worked independently, they arrived at many similar conclusions. Both attacked the realistic theater, arguing against photographic reproduction as the basic goal of scene design. Appia's disregard for the realistic fourth-wall convention resulted in his designing a German theater building which was the first in the modern era not to contain a proscenium arch. Both men believed that settings should suggest, not reproduce, locale. Appia and Craig, employing levels and platforms, designed spaces that were functional for the actor. Moreover, taking full advantage of the introduction of electricity, which made it possible for stage lighting to develop as an art, both designers used light as an integral visual element. Most of their designs are extremely atmospheric, stressing the contrast between light and dark.

It should not be imagined, however, that Appia and Craig were in total agreement. Craig believed that the theatrical art needed a master-artist who could create all of the production elements. Appia believed that the regisseur, or master director, fused the theatrical elements, and that the designer was an interpretive artist, bringing an author's work to life and providing a functional environment for the performers. Craig, believing that the star system made acting the weakest of the theatrical elements, argued that the best performer would be like an *Übermarionette*, a super-puppet, who would allow the director to control totally the performance. Craig's designs were frequently conceived on a more grandiose scale than those of Appia. Appia's designs usually required set changes for each of a production's locales. Craig, on the other hand, was the father of the modern unit setting. The *unit set* is a single setting that can represent various locales through movement of its basic elements along with slight additions of properties.

Appia and Craig influenced many leading twentieth-century American designers, including Robert Edmond Jones (1887–1954), Lee Simonson (1888–1967), Norman Bel Geddes (1893–1958), Donald Oenslager (1902–1975), Boris Aronson (1900–1980), and Jo Mielziner (1901–1976). Most of these designers, working in the theater between the world wars, proved the practicality of Adolphe Appia's and Gordon Craig's theories.

Meyerhold and Russian Theatricalism

The reaction against realism also influenced a number of Russian artists who rejected the guiding artistic principles of Konstantin Stanislavski and the Moscow Art Theater. Possibly the most influential was Vsevolod Meyerhold. Ironically, Meyerhold had been an original member of the Moscow Art Theater, playing the part of Konstantin in *The Seagull*. Between 1905 and 1939, Meyerhold was the leading Russian antirealist, frequently experimenting with *theatricalism*. Theatricalists expose the devices of theater, such as the way stage machinery works, to make their audiences aware that they are watching a theatrical performance; they also borrow techniques from the circus, the music halls, and similar entertainments.

The list of Meyerhold's innovations and experiments is astounding.

𝒜DOLPHE APPIA
(1862–1928)

ℰDWARD GORDON CRAIG
(1872–1966)

Modern stage design begins with two men: Swiss-born Adolphe Appia and the Englishman Gordon Craig. Among other innovations, they saw the tremendous possibilities of using light for scene changes and striking effects, and of moving away from the realistic box set.

Adolphe Appia was the first to develop a theory of antirealistic staging. Trained in music, he was an admirer of Wagner's operas but felt that realistic staging detracted from their effect. Instead, in 1891, he proposed the use of simple, symbolic sets that would work with the actor. He also advocated the use of multidirectional, colored lighting to paint the stage and to move in harmony with the production.

Appia had a few opportunities to demonstrate his ideas. For some years he worked at Émile Jaques-Dalcroze's theater school in Hellerau, Germany, designing experimental and dance productions. He also designed sets for Wagner's operas at La Scala and in Basle, Switzerland. His second book was published in 1921. A simple, shy man, he shunned publicity, preferring to let his work speak for itself.

Gordon Craig, by contrast, delighted in the limelight and sometimes was deliberately provocative in order to make his theories known. The son of the actress Ellen Terry and Edwin Godwin, an architect and scene designer, Craig had been an actor in Henry Irving's company before turning to design. Though he designed several productions for the Purcell Operatic Company and for his mother's theater, he failed to find financial support for his ideas in England.

In 1904, Craig was invited to go to Germany, and there he published his essay "The Art of the Theater." Craig wanted to free the theater from its dependence on realism, literature, and the actor, and to create a unified art work—with light as a key element—under the control of one person. His magazine *The Mask* (1908–1928) was an influential publication for the avant-garde theater. For a few years before World War I, Craig ran a theater school in Italy. After the war, he lived in both Italy and France, writing steadily, wittily, and sometimes acidly about his theories until his death in 1966.

Meyerhold: a directing genius   One of the giants of twentieth century theater is the Russian director Vsevelod Meyerhold, who carried out many experiments in antirealism. He used commedia and circus techniques with his actors, created "constructivist" stage sets, and reinterpreted the classics. In the scene from The Inspector General *shown here, he crowds the stage with a wild assembly of character types. (Photo—Novosa from Sovfoto.)*

Much of what was labeled avant-garde in the theater of the 1960s, for example, can be traced back to Meyerhold's early-twentieth-century experiments. Meyerhold's theater was a director's theater; as director, he literally authored his productions. Meyerhold frequently restructured or rewrote classics. He searched for suitable environments for his presentations, arguing that *found spaces*—that is, spaces not originally meant for theatrical productions—should be employed. Examples include streets, factories, and schools. Meyerhold wished to shatter the fourth-wall convention. On occasion he left the houselights on, extended the stage apron into the audience, or stationed performers in the house. He experimented with, and theorized about, the employment of multimedia in stage productions. He attempted to train his actors physically by employing commedia dell'arte, circus, and vaudeville techniques.

Meyerhold's most-remembered experiments were undertaken in the 1920s, immediately following the Russian Revolution. He devised an acting system known as *biomechanics*, which emphasized external, physical training and performance style for the actor. Biomechanics suggested that the actor's body could be trained to operate like a machine. Furthermore, Meyerhold argued that through physical actions a performer could arouse the necessary internal responses in himself and audience members. In his early biomechanical experiments, Meyerhold had his performers create outlandish physicalizations to represent emotional states; later he moved to more natural physicalizations.

Meyerhold's settings known as *constructivist* settings, provided machines for his performers to work on. The settings frequently looked like huge tinker toys, consisting of skeletal frames, ramps, stairways, and platforms. The constructivist set was highly theatrical; it was not meant to indicate a specific locale, such as a room in a house, but was a practical apparatus for the actors.

Meyerhold made use of a constructivist design for his 1922 production of *The Magnificent Cuckold*. The setting, according to Meyerhold's biographer Edward Braun,

consisted of the frames of conventional theater flats and platforms joined by steps, chutes, and catwalks; there were two wheels, a large disc bearing the letters "CR-ML-NCK," and vestigal windmill sails, which all revolved at varying speeds as a kinetic accompaniment to the fluctuating passions of the characters. Blank panels hinged to the framework served as doors and windows.[4]

A description of the production's opening scene reveals how the set was employed:

You heard an exultant voice ring out offstage, full of joyful strength and happiness; and then up the side ladder to the very top of the construction flew—and "flew" is the word—[Igor] Ilinsky [Meyerhold's leading actor] as Bruno [the "magnificent cuckold"]. His wife Stella . . . ran to meet him and stood, indescribably youthful, lithe, and athletic, with her straight legs apart like a pair of compasses. Without pausing, Bruno hoisted her onto his shoulder, then slid down the highly-polished chute and gently lowered his weightless load to the ground.[5]

In the 1930s, Meyerhold's work was attacked by the Soviet government. The Soviets officially supported "socialist realism" as the only appropriate theatrical form, arguing that the theater should present realistic portrayals of the socialist struggle. Meyerhold's antirealistic work was attacked for being obscure and, therefore, anti-Soviet. When the

[4]Edward Braun, *The Theatre of Meyerhold*, London, Eyre Methuen, 1979, p. 170.
[5]Ibid., pp. 172–173.

Sovfoto

$\mathcal{V}$ SEVOLOD EMILIEVICH MEYERHOLD
(1874–1940)

If Konstantin Stanislavski was the most influential twentieth-century theorist of psychologically based realistic acting, Vsevolod Emilievich Meyerhold was his counterpart in the external, antirealistic school.

Meyerhold was born outside of Moscow in 1874. In the second year of his law studies, he was admitted into the Moscow Philharmonic Society's drama school, where he studied with Nemirovich-Danchenko. As one of the original members of the Moscow Art Theater, Meyerhold played the role of Konstantin, the frustrated young writer, in the company's production of Chekhov's *The Seagull*. However, during the next four years, Meyerhold's position in the Moscow Art Theater became less prominent. In 1902, he left Stanislavski's company to work as a director.

Between 1902 and the Russian Revolution, Meyerhold experimented with antirealism, staging a number of symbolist dramas. In 1905, he was invited to direct at an experimental studio in the Moscow Art Theater; this association did not last out the year. Meyerhold was then invited to direct the Russian actress Vera Komissarzhevskaya's company.

After two seasons, he was forced to leave because of his belief that the director, not the star performer, was the primary theater artist. During the next ten years, when he worked at the Imperial Theater in St. Petersburg, his productions became increasingly stylized and theatrical. He also staged studio productions employing commedia, vaudeville, and circus techniques.

Meyerhold's importance to the Russian theater became apparent following the Russian Revolution. Between 1919 and the mid-1930s he was the leading Russian theatricalist. In 1920 he was appointed the deputy commissar of the theatrical department of the Commissariat for Education, and for three years he was involved in the government's organization of the theatrical arts.

During the 1920s Meyerhold undertook his renowned antirealistic experiments. He developed his theories of biomechanics and experimented with constructivist scene designs. Meyerhold's best-known productions during this period were *The Magnificent Cuckold* (1922) and *The General Inspector* (1926).

In the early 1930s, Meyerhold was attacked by the leaders of the Soviet government for his failure to produce socialist realism. (His work was always bold and experimental.) Ironically, after his theater was taken from him, Meyerhold was invited to work in the Opera Studio of the Moscow Art Theater, where he staged *Rigoletto* in 1938. In June 1939, he was invited to address the All-Union Conference of Stage Directors. It was expected that he would recant his stylistic experimentation, but instead he attacked the Soviet-controlled theatrical art and was arrested. Most historians believe that Meyerhold died in a Soviet labor camp in 1940. His wife, Zinaida Raikh, who was his leading actress, was found brutally murdered in their apartment.

government closed his theater in 1938, Stanislavski invited Meyerhold to work at his Opera Theater. (In 1905, Stanislavski had briefly engaged Meyerhold to work on antirealistic projects at a Moscow Art Theater studio.) In 1939, almost a year after Stanislavski's death, Meyerhold was arrested; he died in prison in 1940.

Meyerhold, of course, was not the only Russian theater artist to champion antirealism. Alexander Tairov, for example, between 1914 and 1950 also experimented with various nonrealistic techniques at his Kamerny (Chamber) Theater. After the revolution, he too was harrassed by the Soviet regime.

The Eclectics

Some early-twentieth-century theater artists attempted to bridge the divergent views of the realists and antirealists. These practitioners were not doctrinaire in their practices and, instead, argued that each play should define its own form. These directors, known as *eclectics*, included the Austrian Max Reinhardt (1873–1943) and the Russian Yevgeny Vakhtangov (1883–1922).

Max Reinhardt, who began his career as an actor with the Freie Bühne, was a major director in the Austrian and German theater from 1905 until 1933, when, because he was a Jew, he was forced to leave Hitler's Germany. Reinhardt's productions were particularly noteworthy because of his innovative use of theater spaces. He employed a converted circus building to stage *King Oedipus* and *Lysistrata* and directed a modern adaptation of the medieval morality play *Everyman* outside of the Salzburg Cathedral. Reinhardt experimented with adaptations of the Elizabethan stage for productions of Shakespearean dramas, and for productions of a drama entitled *The Miracle* he had theaters remodeled to look like the interior of a cathedral. The German director also experimented with theatrical conventions from the orient and from other periods of western theater history. Throughout his career Reinhardt was the total regisseur, or director-designer, overseeing all aspects of his productions.

Another eclectic, Yevgeny Vakhtangov, staged most of his significant works for studios of the Moscow Art Theater. In 1921 and 1922, Vakhtangov directed his four best-known productions: Maeterlinck's *The Miracle of St. Anthony*, Strindberg's *Erik XIV*, S. Anski's *The Dybbuk*, and Carlo Gozzi's *Turandot*. Vakhtangov was able to synthesize Stanislavski's psychological realism with Meyerhold's theatricalism and thus brought a theatrical truthfulness to his productions.

A leading performer with Vakhtangov was Mikhail Chekhov (1891–1955), Anton Chekhov's nephew, who developed a system of acting training based on what he called the *psychological gesture*. According to Chekhov, a performer could create a realistic stage portrayal by finding

The Miracle directed by Reinhardt *A twentieth-century director who liked to present plays on a vast scale was the Austrian, Max Reinhardt, who used a circus building for one play and the outside of a cathedral for another. For* The Miracle, *shown here, he converted the inside of a theater to look like an enormous cathedral. (Photo—The New York Public Library at Lincoln Center, Astor, Lenox, and Tilden Foundations.)*

physical characteristics for his role that would then trigger internal responses. Again, one can see the influence of Stanislavski and Meyerhold. Chekhov left Russia in the 1920s and taught acting in England and America.

𝒮𝓊𝓂𝓂𝒶𝓇𝓎

The beginning of the modern theater was marked by the advent of realism and naturalism. The most noted realistic playwrights were Henrik Ibsen, August Strindberg, George Bernard Shaw, and Anton Chekhov; among the naturalists were Émile Zola, Gerhart Hauptmann, and Maxim Gorki. The controversial plays written by these playwrights were produced by the independent theaters, which included André Antoine's Théâtre Libre, Otto Brahm's Freie Bühne, J. T. Grein's Independent Theatre, and Konstantin Stanislavski's Moscow Art Theatre.

One of the earliest reactions against realism was symbolism, and theaters like the Théâtre d'Art and the Théâtre de l'Oeuvre were independent producers of these plays. Among the designers who broke with the conventions of the realistic theater were Adolphe Appia and Edward Gordon Craig; directors who experimented with antirealistic staging techniques included Vsevolod Meyerhold and Alexander Tairov. Eclectics, such as Yevgeny Vakhtangov and Max Reinhardt, strove to bridge the contrasting styles which were emerging in the early modern theater. Some writers, like Ibsen and Strindberg, wrote in both realistic and nonrealistic forms.

Later when we note the revolutionary theatrical developments of the mid-twentieth century, the strong influence of all of these trends and innovators will be apparent.

Chapter Twelve

The period from 1915 to 1945, from the year after the start of World War I to the end of World War II, was a time of unusual unrest for the western world. On the one hand the world was being brought closer together through the communications provided by radio, telephone, and motion pictures. On the other hand, nations were jealously guarding their independence and sovereignty, as other nations attempted to take them over. These drastic political and economic changes led to instability, and the theater during these three decades mirrored the unrest. Many of the theatrical movements we are going to discuss were defined by their relationship to emerging political, social, or economic ideologies.

Cross-currents in theater   In the period from 1915 to 1945, strong forces of both realism and antirealism were at work. Among the major antirealistic dramatists was the German Bertolt Brecht, whose The Good Woman of Setzuan *is shown here. Among the play's antirealistic devices are a narrator and songs. Seen here is Shen Te, a prostitute who befriends a small, abandoned boy. (Photo—Percy Paukschta, The Berliner Ensemble.)*

The Theater between 1915 and 1945

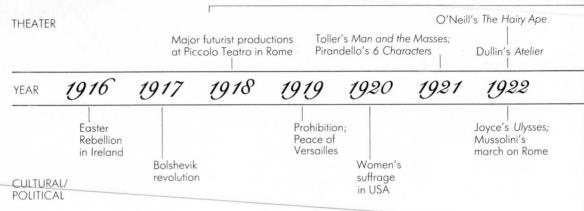

THEATER			Major futurist productions at Piccolo Teatro in Rome		Toller's *Man and the Masses*; Pirandello's *6 Characters*	O'Neill's *The Hairy Ape* Dullin's *Atelier*	
YEAR	*1916*	*1917*	*1918*	*1919*	*1920*	*1921*	*1922*
CULTURAL/ POLITICAL	Easter Rebellion in Ireland	Bolshevik revolution		Prohibition; Peace of Versailles	Women's suffrage in USA		Joyce's *Ulysses*; Mussolini's march on Rome

THE WEST IN THE TIME OF WORLD WARS I AND II

This era of unrest was ushered in by the First World War, which resulted in nearly 8.5 million deaths. The ultimate cost of the conflict, which American President Woodrow Wilson termed "the war to end all wars," was not, however, immediately apparent. When the war ended in 1918, most people believed President Wilson's idealistic pronouncements and attempts were made to organize a workable League of Nations and World Court. Unfortunately, America's isolationist policy—that is, the determination to stay out of foreign affairs—prevented the United States from becoming a League member and kept the organization from being a viable international force. Furthermore, fervent nationalism kept many countries from giving the League any real power.

The unrest in Europe also contributed to the Russian Revolution in 1917, which led to the establishment of the Soviet government. Before it took control, however, the new Communist regime was forced to fight a costly civil war.

Throughout Europe and America economic problems developed. In the 1920s rampant inflation and the depression that followed proved to be the cost of the previous political turmoil. Many nations' economies were destroyed; monetary systems were devalued. A famous photograph of the period shows a German pushing a wheelbarrow full of paper money to purchase a loaf of bread.

Many historians believe that the political and economic unrest set the stage for the rise of totalitarianism in Europe. Totalitarianism is a form of government under which the individual is totally subservient to

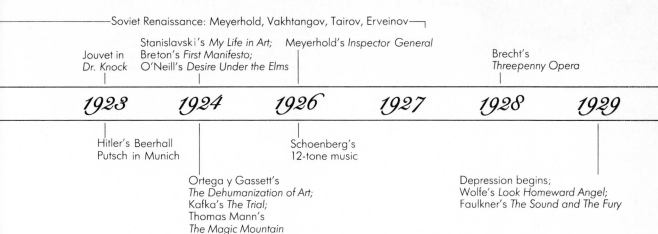

Soviet Renaissance: Meyerhold, Vakhtangov, Tairov, Erveinov

Stanislavski's *My Life in Art*; Meyerhold's *Inspector General*

Jouvet in
Dr. Knock

Breton's *First Manifesto*;
O'Neill's *Desire Under the Elms*

Brecht's
Threepenny Opera

1923   **1924**   **1926**   **1927**   **1928**   **1929**

Hitler's Beerhall
Putsch in Munich

Schoenberg's
12-tone music

Ortega y Gassett's
The Dehumanization of Art;
Kafka's *The Trial*;
Thomas Mann's
The Magic Mountain

Depression begins;
Wolfe's *Look Homeward Angel*;
Faulkner's *The Sound and The Fury*

the state; in most cases, totalitarian states are controlled by dictators. Between the world wars, there were fascist totalitarian dictatorships in Italy and Germany, nationalist dictatorships in several other countries, and a Communist totalitarian dictatorship in the Soviet Union. The fascists—believing in dictatorial government and forcible suppression of opposition—argued that nation and race were more important than the individual and formulated extreme economic and social regimentation. The leading fascist leaders were Adolf Hitler, whose Nazis dominated Germany beginning in 1933, Benito Mussolini, who took control of Italy in 1922, and Francisco Franco, who ruled Spain from 1939 until his death in 1975.

The extremes of fascism were horribly illustrated in Adolf Hitler's Nazi Germany. Political opposition was totally supressed, and those opposed to the Third Reich were imprisoned in concentration camps. Nazi repression of individual liberties resulted in the imprisonment of Jews, gypsies, and homosexuals, as well as pacifist Jehovah's Witnesses. Adolf Hitler used nationalistic arguments as a pretext for the takeover of Austria and the dismemberment of Czechoslovakia; his invasion of Poland on September 1, 1939, began World War II. The "Aryan race"—an unscientific grouping of non-Jewish, Nordic Europeans championed by Hitler—was exalted, and "non-Aryans" were persecuted. During World War II, the Nazis turned some of their concentration camps, such as Auschwitz in Poland, into extermination centers. Altogether, the Third Reich murdered 6 million Jews and 1 million gypsies, claiming that they were racially inferior.

Similar abuses occurred in the other fascist regimes as well as in the

The Theater between 1915 and 1945

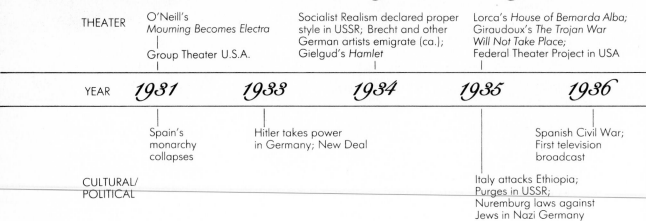

THEATER	O'Neill's *Mourning Becomes Electra*		Socialist Realism declared proper style in USSR; Brecht and other German artists emigrate (ca.); Gielgud's *Hamlet*		Lorca's *House of Bernarda Alba*; Giraudoux's *The Trojan War Will Not Take Place*; Federal Theater Project in USA
	Group Theater U.S.A.				
YEAR	*1931*	*1933*	*1934*	*1935*	*1936*
	Spain's monarchy collapses	Hitler takes power in Germany; New Deal			Spanish Civil War; First television broadcast
CULTURAL/ POLITICAL				Italy attacks Ethiopia; Purges in USSR; Nuremburg laws against Jews in Nazi Germany	

Communist dictatorship of Josef Stalin, who ruled Russia from 1928 until his death in 1951. Stalin suppressed individual freedoms and imprisoned opponents to his regime, dispatching several million people to their deaths in the slave-labor camps of Siberia's Gulag Archipelago. As noted in the preceding chapter, the Russian director Meyerhold, because he opposed socialist realism, was executed in a Soviet prison in 1940.

Given the nationalistic fervor of the totalitarian dictators, the chaotic economic situation, and the widespread political instability, many historians believe that the Second World War was inevitable. The six-year war was more horrible than any of its predecessors, with over 35 million people losing their lives. The concentration camps became mechanized death factories, used to exterminate innocent victims of anti-Semitism and of the war. The atomic bomb proved that humanity was capable of developing weaponry that could annihilate the human race. World War II posed unanswerable questions: How could civilized, rational societies wreak such irrational destruction? Were individuals responsible for societal actions? How could the genocide of the Second World War be explained?

A THEATER OF UNREST

These thirty years were also turbulent ones for the theater. Theatrical innovators reacted to the popular commercial theater as well as to the tumultuous world situation. Those artists who revolted against the

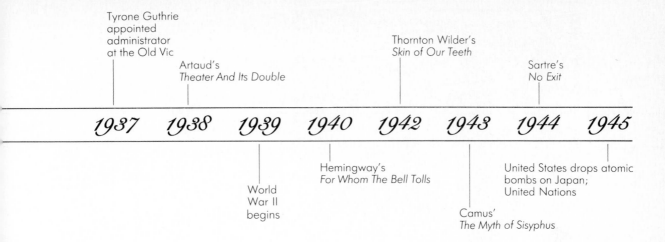

Tyrone Guthrie
appointed
administrator
at the Old Vic

Artaud's
Theater And Its Double

Thornton Wilder's
Skin of Our Teeth

Sartre's
No Exit

1937   *1938*   *1939*   *1940*   *1942*   *1943*   *1944*   *1945*

World
War II
begins

Hemingway's
For Whom The Bell Tolls

Camus'
The Myth of Sisyphus

United States drops atomic
bombs on Japan;
United Nations

commercial theater, particularly in the United States, England, and France, did not equate financial success with artistic accomplishment. As the cost of mounting productions increased due to factors such as inflation, depressed economies, and unionization, innovative artists searched for noncommercial outlets.

Many of the theatrical innovators between the wars revolted against realism, which by then had become the most popular form of theater. Several antirealist practitioners discussed in the preceding chapter, such as Meyerhold and Tairov, continued to be productive. The eclectics who worked in many different forms of theater, such as Vakhtangov and Reinhardt, also introduced experimental production techniques. For most of the avant-garde artists and theorists, realism was too simplistic and too limited in its potential. In America, realistic and naturalistic spectacle became so commercialized that audiences expected authentic settings for trite melodramas. The turn-of-the-century American producer David Belasco (ca. 1854–1931), for example, popularized naturalistic settings and lighting, authentically recreating on stage a Child's Restaurant in a 1912 melodrama.

Most of the movements and artists we are going to discuss reacted to the chaotic world scene. Some movements, such as expressionism and epic theater, supported socialism. Others, such as futurism, supported fascism. Many of the era's playwrights, including Ernst Toller (Germany, 1893–1939), Stanistaw Ignacy Witkiewicz (Poland, 1885–1939), Karel Capek (Czechoslovakia, 1890–1938), Jean Giraudoux (France, 1882–1944), and Bertolt Brecht, dealt with specific political concerns.

*P*ablo Picasso's *Harlequin With Violin* (1918) *Picasso's cubist painting of the commedia dell'arte character is an abstraction of the recognizable figure. Cubism, which is characterized by sharp edges and angles, reflected the artist's subjective view of the dynamic contemporary world. The antirealistic techniques in the visual arts were paralleled in the theater. (Photo—The Cleveland Museum of Art, Purchase, Leonard C. Hanna, Jr., Bequest.)*

American Innovation: The Reaction to Commercialism

The American theater between the world wars was probably the most commercially oriented in the world. The Theatrical Syndicate, a group of businessmen who controlled the theater in the United States, was toppled in 1915 by Lee Shubert (1875–1954) and his brother Jacob J. Shubert (1880–1963), who developed their own theater monopoly, owning or controlling almost 75 percent of all theater buildings in the country. The Shubert organization heirs, in the form of a foundation, still control nearly 50 percent of the Broadway theaters in New York.

Possibly the most commercially successful theatrical form during this period was the musical. In the 1920s and 1930s, revues—productions composed of skits and musical numbers—were extremely popular. The Broadway producer Florenz Ziegfeld (1869–1932) made a reputation for producing annually the spectacular Ziegfeld Follies. More importantly, the modern American musical comedy was born during this era. Beginning with *Showboat* (1928), by Oscar Hammerstein II and Jerome Kern, the music, song, and dance of the musicals were more carefully integrated with plot and character development. *Oklahoma!* (1943), by Richard

𝒯he American Musical *An important step in the development of this uniquely American form was the production of* Showboat *in 1927. Shown here in a revival,* Showboat *had a glorious musical score, but also a more serious book than previous musicals, dealing with black-white relations and eliminating the chorus line. (Photo—The New York Public Library at Lincoln Center, Astor, Lenox, and Tilden Foundations.)*

Rodgers and Oscar Hammerstein, with choreography by Agnes DeMille, is often said to be a landmark step in this development. The musical remains an important commercial form in the American theater.

The commercial theater faced troubles, however. The economic unrest in the 1920s as well as increased production costs lessened the number of commercial shows produced annually. Another factor that hurt the commercial theater was the growing popularity of movies, especially after the introduction of sound in 1929.

Between 1915 and World War II, there were attempts, however, to establish noncommercial theaters in the United States. While these ventures, usually referred to as *little theaters*, introduced new artists, plays, and production techniques, most were unable to withstand the ravages of the depression as well as the beckoning of financial security in the commercial theater for their most promising talents.

THE LITTLE THEATER MOVEMENT

The little theater movement flourished in the second decade of the twentieth century. Among these theaters were the Provincetown Playhouse, the Neighborhood Playhouse, and the Washington Square Players. All of these theaters were founded in 1915 as alternatives to the commercial theater. Many historians claim that they also inspired the post–World War II off-Broadway movement.

The Provincetown Playhouse

An examination of the Provincetown Playhouse provides general insights into the little theater movement. The company was organized in 1915 in Provincetown, Massachusetts, by vacationing artists. The two founding members were George Cram Cook and his wife, playwright Susan Glaspell (1882–1948). After presenting a series of plays in Massachusetts, the playhouse moved, in the following year, to a small Greenwich Village theater, outside the Broadway district in New York City. In 1923 the company split into two separate producing agencies, and in 1929 the depression brought this noncommercial venture to an end.

The Provincetown was an extremely influential theater. The company, in its earlier years, was dedicated to presenting new American dramas. The Provincetown helped to establish Eugene O'Neill as America's leading playwright by producing such works as *The Emperor Jones* (1920) and *The Hairy Ape.* New production styles were also introduced by the Provincetown, particularly through the designs of Robert Edmond Jones. Jones was a leading figure in the "new stagecraft" movement in America. This design movement put into practice many of the theories of Adolphe Appia and Edward Gordon Craig, in particular their emphasis on lighting. The "new stagecraft" designers also strove for "simplified realism," using only those details needed to suggest the specific locale as well as to reinforce characterization and dramatic action.

The Theater Guild

Another little theater, the Washington Square Players, which operated in Greenwich Village from 1915 through 1918, evolved into the Theater Guild. The Guild, a subscription-based professional organization—which eventually built its own theater in the Broadway district—introduced in the 1920s many of the leading experimental European and American playwrights as well as new production techniques. The Guild also

The Group Theater's *Awake and Sing, Clifford Odets' play, produced in 1935 and featuring Stella Adler, Luther Adler, Morris Carnovsky, and John Garfield, is an example of a realistic social drama dealing with American concerns of the 1930s. The play—an intense family drama set in a Bronx apartment during the Depression—required the realistic ensemble acting for which the Group Theater was noted. (Photo—Vandamm Collection, The New York Public Library at Lincoln Center.)*

attempted to establish a permanent acting company. The depression, coupled with the Guild's attempts to expand into other American cities, so hurt the organization that it eventually became simply another commercial producing entity. During its most active period the Theater Guild supported the initial production of the Group Theater.

The Group Theater

The Group Theater, a noncommercial company which produced its plays in the Broadway district, was dedicated to introducing Stanislavskian acting technique to America and to producing socially relevant dramas. The political leanings of the company were left-wing, and its members hoped to motivate political and social action through their theatrical presentations.

The founding members of the Group Theater were Lee Strasberg (1901–1982), Cheryl Crawford (b. 1902), and Harold Clurman (1901–1980), and members of the acting company included Franchot Tone, Morris Carnovsky, Stella Adler, Luther Adler, and John Garfield. The company's resident playwright was Clifford Odets (1906–1963). Dissen-

STELLA ADLER
(born 1902)

Konstantin Stanislavski's theories of acting did not come to the United States until the 1920s, when some members of the Moscow Art Theater emigrated to New York and began teaching his methods. It was not until 1931, however, that the Group Theater was founded to explore the Stanislavski system of acting. One of its founding members was Stella Adler, an actress with twenty-five years of stage experience.

In the Yiddish theater, an important part of New York City theater at the turn of the century, the name of Adler was synonymous with excellence in acting. Stella's father, Jacob Adler, was the premier actor of the Yiddish stage, famed for his portrayal of King Lear. She made her stage debut in 1906 as a member of her father's Yiddish company, in which she performed for several years. In 1919 she made her London debut, and in 1922, her Broadway debut. Her three sisters and two brothers were also actors.

Stella Adler and her brother Luther studied the Stanislavski system under Maria Ouspenskaya and Richard Bole-

slavsky, both of whom had come to this country after distinguished theatrical careers in Europe. The two Adlers became original members of the Group Theater, and in 1934, Stella and Harold Clurman, one of the Group's principal directors, went to France to study with Stanislavski. When they returned to America, they reported that Stanislavski placed more emphasis on the study of text and character than on the actor's emotional memory. This led to dissension with Lee Strasberg, the Group's other director, who left the company. The Group disbanded in 1941.

Though Adler has had an active career as an actress and director since 1941, she has primarily been interested in the teaching of acting. After teaching in the Dramatic Workshop of the New School for Social Research, she opened the Stella Adler Theater Studio in New York City in 1949. Following her own interpretation of Stanislavski's method, she emphasizes the text of the play and encourages students to explore the many possibilities of the characters.

sion over the correct interpretation of Stanislavski's system developed in the Group Theater in the mid-1930s, with the result that Lee Strasberg left the Group after being criticized by Harold Clurman and Stella Adler for overemphasizing emotional recall, the technique of calling on past experiences to create present emotions. In contrast to Strasberg, Adler called for a greater emphasis on analysis of the script's given circumstances. The Group Theater disbanded in 1941.

The influence of the Group Theater, however, continued to be strong in the American theater. Harold Clurman, until his death in 1980, was a leading director and critic; Lee Strasberg, beginning in the late 1940s at the Actors Studio, trained many well-known actors, including Marlon Brando (b. 1924); and Stella Adler has remained a leading acting teacher. Two other Group Theater members, Elia Kazan (b. 1909) and Robert Lewis (b. 1909), are leading directors.

The Federal Theater Project

One additional experiment in the American theater between the wars should be noted. During the depression, President Franklin Delano Roosevelt established the Works Progress Administration (WPA), which organized governmentally subsidized agencies to put America's unemployed back to work. The Federal Theater Project, headed by Hallie Flanagan Davis (1890–1969), a university professor, was one of the agencies. For four years, the Federal Theater Project supported theatrical ventures throughout the United States and helped to revitalize interest in theater outside of New York City.

One of the most popular forms developed by the Project was the "living newspaper"; these were dramatizations of current events, such as breadlines and rising unemployment. The Federal Theater also assisted aspiring black theaters and artists, supporting, for example, Orson Welles's all-black production of *Macbeth*. The government, for political reasons, discontinued funding the project in 1939. Many Congressmen claimed the project was sympathetic to Communism. While today federal, state, and local governments provide some support to theater companies, the Federal Theater Project was the closest the American government has come to establishing a national theater.

Though we have focused on the noncommercial theater, it should be noted that a number of significant plays by important playwrights were produced on Broadway during this period. In addition to several plays by Eugene O'Neill, these include *The Adding Machine* (1923) by Elmer Rice (1892–1967), *Winterset* (1935) by Maxwell Anderson (1888–1959), *Awake and Sing* by Clifford Odets, *Our Town* (1938) by Thornton Wilder (1897–1975), and *The Little Foxes* (1938) by Lillian Hellman (b. 1905). There were also notable comedies by Philip Barry (1896–1949), George S. Kaufman (1889–1961), and Moss Hart (1904–1961).

*I*nnovative work by the Federal Theater Project   *A theater funded by Congress during the Depression to give work to those in the theater profession, it spawned a great deal of talent and achieved important productions. One was an all-black version of* Macbeth, *shown here. Set in Haiti, it was conceived and directed by Orson Welles. (Photo—The New York Public Library at Lincoln Center, Astor, Lenox, and Tilden Foundations.)*

GREAT BRITAIN: EXPERIMENTATION WITH TRADITION

The British theater between the world wars was, like the American theater, highly commercial. As a reaction to growing commercialization, little theaters arose. There were also individual actors and directors, most of them renowned for their work with Shakespeare, whose focus was on the artistic rather than the business side of theater.

Britain's most noteworthy directors during this era were Harley Granville Barker (1877–1946) and Tyrone Guthrie (1900–1971). Barker, who was also a playwright and critic, is most remembered for his approach to staging Shakespeare. He focused on making the poetry of the plays come alive and remaining faithful to the spirit of the scripts. Since acting, for him, was the central element in his productions, settings were simple and suggestive, and the costumes not lavishly detailed.

Tyrone Guthrie is remembered in America for founding the Guthrie Theater in Minneapolis in 1963, but between the wars in London, he developed a reputation at the Old Vic, which was the home of Shakespearean productions. Guthrie broke with traditional staging by interpreting the classic dramas imaginatively and by developing unique concepts for his productions. He often presented Shakespeare in modern dress. Guthrie's influence is still felt on those directors who attempt to direct Shakespeare's works in ways that make them more accessible to contemporary audiences. Many of the productions staged for the summer New York Shakespeare Festival in New York's Central Park—such as the musical version of *Two Gentlemen of Verona* and A. J. Antoon's *Much Ado About Nothing*, with its use of Mack Sennett's silent-film comedy techniques—are descendants of Guthrie's experiments to find ways to make Shakespeare contemporary.

The British theater between the wars also introduced many stars who developed international reputations. Most are noted for their Shakespearean work, but their amazing versatility should not be overlooked; many, for example, have also had successful film careers. They include John Gielgud (b. 1904), Laurence Olivier (b. 1907), Michael Redgrave (b. 1908), and Alec Guinness (b. 1914). The acting technique employed by these world-acclaimed performers has often been contrasted to the technique employed by American realistic performers. Olivier, for example, claims that he begins to work on a character by discovering his external makeup before attempting to discover any internal characteristics. Gielgud and Olivier were also innovative directors who kept alive the British tradition of the actor-manager.

Many of the British playwrights who were considered significant during this era are no longer as admired as they were formerly. Noël Coward (1899–1973), in such witty works as *Private Lives* (1930) and *Blithe Spirit* (1941), continued the tradition of the comedy of manners by satirizing the social pretensions of theater people and the English upper class. While T. S. Eliot (1888–1965) was an American by birth, he spent most of his life in England. A renowned poet, Eliot attempted to revive verse drama in such works as *Murder in the Cathedral* (1935) and *The Family Reunion* (1939).

While the British theater between the wars was less avant-garde than the continental theater, British experimentation with traditional forms and classic plays foreshadowed similar undertakings in the last two decades.

THE ANTIREALISTIC THEATER CONTINUES IN EUROPE

In the early years of the twentieth century, many new antirealistic movements developed in the continental European theater. Going by

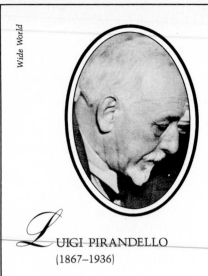

*L*UIGI PIRANDELLO

(1867–1936)

Italian playwright Luigi Pirandello was a master of theatricality. In his plays he experimented boldly with theatrical techniques in an attempt to dramatize the ideas that fascinated him. "My art is full of bitter compassion for all those who deceive themselves," he wrote, "but this compassion cannot fail to be followed by the ferocious decision of destiny which condemns man to deception." Deception, illusion, and the subjectivity of truth were the concepts Pirandello explored in his plays, novels, and short stories.

As the son of a sulfur merchant, Pirandello received private tutoring at home in Agrigento, Sicily, before attending universities in Palermo, Rome, and Bonn, where he received his doctorate in 1888. His father had wanted him to become a businessman, but Pirandello chose literature as a career and by 1893 had settled in Rome. He was married the following year to a girl he barely knew, an arranged marriage to unite two families of sulfur merchants. When the sulfur mines were flooded in 1904, the family fortune was lost, and his wife became mentally ill for the rest of her life.

This economic and personal disaster forced Pirandello to supplement his earnings from writing by teaching at a girls' school. By the beginning of World War I, he had become a respected novelist and short story writer, but had done little playwriting. After the success of his play *Right You Are If You Think You Are* in 1916, he began to concentrate on drama.

In that play, as in his other famous plays, *Six Characters in Search of an Author* (1921) and *Henry IV* (1922), Pirandello explores the distinctions between illusion and reality, truth and fiction, madness and sanity. *Six Characters* uses the novel theatrical device of dramatic characters interrupting a rehearsal to ask the performers to play out their story. Pirandello's other plays are more realistic in form, but all present his philosophical ideas through debates among the characters.

Pirandello ran the Teatro d'Arte from 1925 to 1928, touring its productions in Europe and America. The need for state subsidies might have been part of the reason that the author joined the Fascist party in 1924, but Pirandello's political views were conservative and he often praised Mussolini in his newspaper articles. He even donated his 1934 Nobel Prize for literature to the government during its invasion of Ethiopia. Pirandello's private life was brightened by his love for Marta Alba, an actress, to whom he willed nine of his plays. He died in Rome in 1936, leaving a document requesting that his death be ignored and his body burned.

such names as expressionism, futurism, dadaism, and surrealism, they were primarily movements in the visual arts. Nevertheless, they did have an important influence on avant-garde theatrical practices. An influential nonrealistic playwright whose work did not fit any of the usual categories was the Italian Luigi Pirandello, whose plays often questioned the relationship of appearance to reality and incorporated highly theatrical devices.

Expressionistic Theater

Expressionism, which originated in Germany in 1905, was a movement in art and literature in which the representation of reality is distorted in order to communicate inner feelings. In a painting of a man, for example, the lines in his face would be twisted to indicate the turmoil he feels inside. Expressionism in drama incorporated well-defined characteristics: the dramatic action of an expressionist play is seen through the eyes of the protagonist and, therefore, frequently seems distorted or dreamlike. Expressionist plays are often highly subjective and opposed to society and the family.

The protagonist in a typical expressionist play is a Christ figure who, during the course of the drama, journeys through a series of often non-causally-related incidents. Expressionist dramas, therefore, are said to be structured as station plays, emphasizing the parallels between the protagonist and Christ. (Expressionism is a first-cousin to symbolist drama, discussed in Chapter 11.)

The characters in expressionistic plays are representative types, often given titles, such as Man, Woman, or Clerk, rather than names. The language of the plays is telegraphic, with most speeches consisting of one or two lines. These speeches alternate with long lyrical passages. Many of the expressionist playwrights are politically motivated, supporting socialist and pacifist causes, though some expressionists were apolitical. The major German expressionist playwrights were Georg Kaiser (1878–1945) and Ernst Toller.

Shortly after expressionism flourished in Europe, its influence was felt in America. It can be found, for example, in some of the plays by the American dramatist Eugene O'Neill. O'Neill's *The Hairy Ape* contains many expressionistic qualities. After the protagonist, Yank, a stoker on a ship, is ridiculed by a wealthy woman, he begins to see himself as an impotent hairy ape. Later in the drama Yank punches a wealthy man strolling on Fifth Avenue, but the man shows no effects: he is unharmed. When the stoker is imprisoned for attacking the man, he acts like a caged animal. This action is all presented from Yank's point of view. Furthermore, *The Hairy Ape* is constructed of eight scenes, and most of the characters are representative types. O'Neill's drama is an attack on the depersonalization of twentieth-century society.

Expressionistic drama Expressionism first took hold just after the turn of the century; the movement was short-lived, but many of its techniques and ideas continued. Among the dramatists experimenting with these techniques was Eugene O'Neill in such plays as The Hairy Ape *and* The Great God Brown *(1926). In this latter play, shown here, characters used masks to indicate their different personalities. (Photo—Van Williams, Phoenix Theater.)*

In its pure form, the expressionistic movement was short-lived lasting only about fifteen years. Many expressionistic techniques, however, found their way into the mainstream of modern experimental theater. Even today dramatists employ a number of nonrealistic devices labeled expressionistic.

Futurism and Dadaism

Futurism and dadaism had less of an impact on the theater; later, however, the aesthetic principles of these movements influenced avant-garde theater artists in the 1960s. *Futurism* originated in Italy in 1909; its leading exponent was Filippo Marinetti (1876–1944). The futurists, unlike the expressionists, idealized war and the developing machine age.

PART FOUR · THE MODERN THEATER

316

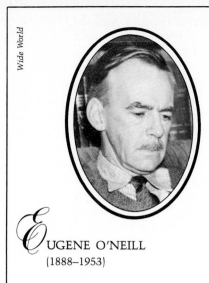

*E*UGENE O'NEILL
(1888–1953)

The man generally conceded to be America's greatest playwright is Eugene Gladstone O'Neill. The reputation rests in part on his ambition and persistence. He attempted almost every form of drama—realism, expressionism, modern versions of Greek tragedy—in an attempt to bring the American theater to maturity. In a large measure, he succeeded.

As the son of James O'Neill, an actor famous for playing the Count of Monte Cristo, Eugene O'Neill spent his childhood in hotels and on trains before being sent to a series of boarding schools. His mother, Ella, suffered from recurrent bouts of drug addiction, and his older brother, James, was an alcoholic who introduced young Eugene to a loose, bohemian life-style.

After being expelled from Princeton for a prank, the dramatist spent six years leading a haphazard, alcoholic existence, often working as a sailor. After a suicide attempt, he pulled himself together and worked as a reporter on a newspaper for six months but had to leave when he contracted tuberculosis. Confined to a sanitorium, he became an avid reader and began to work seriously on his writing, spending a year at Harvard in George Pierce Baker's playwriting course. In 1916 an experimental theater group in Provincetown, Massachusetts produced his one-act play, *Bound East for Cardiff.*

The Provincetown Players reappeared that fall in Greenwich Village, New York, where O'Neill then lived. Several of his early plays were produced there before being transferred to Broadway. In 1920 he won his first Pulitzer Prize for *Beyond the Horizon.*

O'Neill experimented with a variety of forms and styles throughout his career. His early plays, like *Anna Christie* (1921), are realistic, and many of them deal in some way with the sea. He experimented with expressionism in *The Hairy Ape* (1922), with characters speaking subconscious thoughts in *Strange Interlude* (1928), and with masks in *The Great God Brown* (1926). A three-part drama, *Mourning Becomes Electra* (1931), combines Greek myth with Freudian psychology. Though he planned an eleven-part saga covering one family's life in America, he finished only a portion of it. His last plays are tied closely to his own experiences, especially the powerful realistic drama *Long Day's Journey into Night* (1957), in which he finally comes to an understanding of his family.

In 1936 O'Neill became the first American dramatist to win the Nobel Prize for literature. After that year, however, he wrote less, though the plays he did write are among his finest. In his final years he became depressed and was hampered by a nerve disorder that eventually made him an invalid. His first two marriages ended in divorce, and his third, to Carlotta Monteray, was often stormy. When he died in a Boston hotel in 1953, his plays were considered outmoded, but he is now recognized as America's finest dramatist.

Italy, in the first decade of the twentieth century, was the least industrialized nation in western Europe, which may explain the futurists' fascination with machinery and war. The futurists attacked past artistic ideals, ridiculing "museum art" and arguing that new forms had to be created for new eras. They sought a "synthetic" theater of short, seemingly illogical dramatic pieces, and believed that audiences should be confronted and antagonized. The futurists also argued against the separation of performers and audience in the theater and fought for the incorporation of the new electronic media into the theatrical art.

Dadaism, which originated in Switzerland in 1916, was a short-lived movement that never really caught on. A reaction to the insanity of World War I, dadaist art, its proponents argued, would mirror the madness of the world. Like the futurists, the dadaists railed against museum art and strove to confuse and antagonize their audiences, but the pacifistic dadaists were not concerned, as the futurists were, with glorifying war and mechanical inventions. They concentrated instead on nonsense and the irrational, and questioned conventional definitions of art suggesting that almost anything could be art.

Surrealism

In 1924, out of the dadaist movement, surrealism developed. The major exponent of surrealism was André Breton (1896–1966). (The term *surrealism*, however, had been used previously in 1917 by the French playwright Guillaume Apollinaire to describe his play *The Breasts of Tiresias* and the ballet *Parade*.)

The surrealists argued that the subconscious was the highest plane of reality and attempted to recreate its workings dramatically. Many of their plays seem to be set in a dream world, mixing recognizable events with fantastic happenings. While the center of surrealism was France, the movement had an international impact. Stanistaw Ignacy Witkiewicz was a noted Polish surrealist whose dramas include *The Water Hen* (1921), *The Cuttlefish* (1922), and *Gyubal Wahazar* (1921).

ARTAUD AND BRECHT

The two most influential theatrical theorists in Europe between the world wars were Antonin Artaud and Bertolt Brecht. Artaud, like Adolphe Appia and Edward Gordon Craig, was given few opportunities during his lifetime to put his theories into practice. Brecht, on the other hand, was a successful playwright and director.

Antonin Artaud and the Theater of Cruelty

Artaud, who had originally been associated with the surrealists, theorized about a "theater of cruelty" in the 1930s. According to the French theorist, the western theater needed to be totally transformed. He believed that its literary tradition, with an emphasis on language, was antithetical to the ritualistic origins of the theater. Artaud argued that western theater artists should study the stylized oriental theaters.

Renouncing the literary tradition, Artaud asserted that there were "no more masterpieces." By this he meant that classics should not be produced solely for the sake of producing historically significant works but only if they were still relevant to contemporary audiences. Furthermore, he did not believe the text was sacred; the script could and should be reworked in order to point up its relevance.

If theater for Artaud was not a literary event, it was a sensory experience. His emphasis on the sensory is what characterizes the theater of cruelty. Artaud did not literally mean that theater artists should "manhandle" their audiences—although some avant-garde theater artists in the 1960s interpreted cruelty as actual physical confrontation with spectators—but rather that the viewers' senses should be bombarded. Contemporary multimedia presentations strive for such a sensory involvement.

Artaud, as did many of the antirealists who preceded him, called for a restructuring of the theatrical event. He wanted, for example, to reorganize the theater space and make the audience the center of attention. He argued that productions could be staged in "found spaces," spaces that had not originally been intended for theatrical presentations. Artaud also attacked Stanislavskian acting technique, arguing instead for stylized, ritualized performances.

Artaud believed that humanity's natural inclination toward violence and aggression—manifested in Europe in the mid-1930s by the rise of fascism and Stalinism—could be purged in the theater of cruelty. For Artaud, the theater could act like a "plague" cleansing modern society of all that was ugly.

Bertolt Brecht's Epic Theater

Bertolt Brecht developed the conventions of what he termed "epic theater," though he was not the first to employ epic techniques. The German director Erwin Piscator (1893–1966), with whom Brecht worked in the 1920s, established many of the conventions later borrowed by the German playwright. Brecht's major plays, including *Mother Courage, Galileo,* and *The Good Woman of Setzuan,* were written between 1933 and 1945 while Brecht was in exile from Hitler's Germany. As a director Brecht made an international impact with East Berlin's Berliner Ensemble from 1947 until his death in 1956. His theories, most of which were formulated in the 1930s but frequently revised, have influenced many contemporary playwrights and directors.

Epic theater, as the term implies, is epic in scope. Brecht's plays are

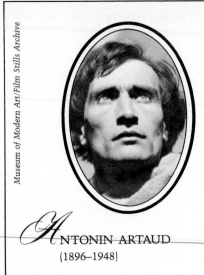

ANTONIN ARTAUD
(1896–1948)

Antonin Artaud's *The Theatre and Its Double*, a series of essays and manifestos published in 1938, is one of the twentieth century's most influential books of theatrical theory. In it Artaud called for a "theater of cruelty" to assault the senses of the spectator in order to free the inner self, and advocated "total theater" where the audience is assaulted from all sides by sounds, performers, film, and lights. The French theorist also called for experimentation with the actor-audience relationship in the playhouse, placing them in different physical arrangements or closer together. His plays *Spurt of Blood* (1924) and *The Cenci* (1935) illustrate some of his theories.

Artaud, who was born in Marseilles, France, went to Paris in 1920 and became an actor, working with many important directors: Lugné-Poë, Charles Dullin, Georges Pitoëff, and Louis Jouvet. He also acted in films, where his most notable role was the monk in Carl Dreyer's *The Passion of Joan of Arc*. For Dullin he also directed and designed Calderón's *Life Is a Dream*. Some of his poems were also published.

From 1924 to 1926 Artaud was involved with the surrealist movement in the theater, which stressed the importance of the subconscious. Together with Roger Vitrac and Robert Aran he founded the Théâtre Alfred Jarry, which produced four programs between 1927 and 1929, including Strindberg's *A Dream Play*. André Breton, the leader of the surrealists, expelled Artaud from the movement because of his interest in the occult, oriental religions, and mysticism. Artaud, who had suffered physical as well as mental disorders all his life, also experimented with various drugs, chiefly morphine.

Artaud was extremely influenced by a Balinese dance group he saw in Paris in 1931; he was impressed by their use of song, dance, and pantomime in a physical, nonverbal form. Artaud went to Mexico in 1936 to search for an authentic primitive culture. He lived among the Tarahumara Indians and experimented with peyote. Convinced that unidentified forces were seeking to destroy him, he returned to France the following year and spent the next nine years in mental institutions. He was released in 1946, through the efforts of his theatrical associates, and died of cancer two years later.

His books and theories, though overlooked in his time, became major influences in the experimental theater, particularly in the 1960s. The experiments of Jerzy Grotowski and the Living Theater were, in part, inspired by Artaud's theater of cruelty.

episodic in structure. They usually deal with history or foreign lands, cover a great deal of time, shift locale frequently, have intricate plots, and contain large number of characters. The goal of epic theater is to instruct. Brecht, an ardent socialist, believed that theater could create the intellectual climate for social change. In the early 1930s he wrote short dramas he labeled *Lehrstücke*, "learning pieces." The German dramatist attacked theatrical works created purely for mass consumption and entertainment, referring to them as "culinary art."

Brecht felt that in order for a theater production to succeed at teaching, the audience should not be emotionally hypnotized but intellectually involved. Brecht believed that the production should force the audience to remain emotionally detached—that is, alienated—from the dramatic action. In order to do this, the German dramatist argued, epic theater had to break with the Wagnerian goal of the *Gesamtkunstwerk*, the unified work of art. Each production element should independently indicate the political message to the audience.

Brecht's works, in order to prevent emotional involvement, are also highly theatrical; the audience members are always made aware that they are in the theater. Narrators are frequently employed in Brecht's plays to comment on the dramatic action. When instructing actors, Brecht warned them against Stanislavskian techniques; he believed that the audience needed to be aware that they were watching an actor play a character. Multimedia was often employed in Brechtian productions to heighten the theatricality.

In order to alienate the audience, Brecht also employed a technique he referred to as "historification." Many of Brecht's plays, such as *Galileo*, are set in past periods of history, but it is apparent that the German playwright is really concerned with contemporary events which parallel the historic occurrences. The technique of placing the events of the play in the past distances the audience from the dramatic action. In a similar fashion, Brecht often set his plays in fictitious foreign lands.

Brecht employed many other epic techniques in his plays and productions. In order to prevent the audience from becoming too involved in the dramatic action, scenes in Brecht's plays have opening titles which indicate what is to happen. Songs in Brechtian dramas, rather than revealing more about plot and character, usually underline the political message.

Epic Theater: *Mother Courage and Her Children*

Possibly Brecht's best-known work is *Mother Courage and Her Children*, which is set in the period between 1624 and 1636 during the Thirty Years' War. An episodic play, containing twelve scenes with many shifts in locale, the epic drama chronicles the losses of Anna Fierling, known as Mother Courage, who operates a traveling canteen. During the course of the dramatic action—sometimes because of her own greed and

Courtesy of the German Information Center

BERTOLT BRECHT
(1898–1956)

Bertolt Brecht—a significant theorist and playwright between the two world wars—established many of the conventions of what he called "epic theater," a sweeping, panoramic theater intended to teach political and moral lessons. The German playwright's basic goal was to point up the need for social change; in particular, he propagandized for socialism. Brecht believed that the members of the audience should be intellectually, not emotionally, involved in a stage production and should be aware of the fact that they were in a theater. For example, he wanted lighting instruments and other theatrical elements made visible to the audience.

Attacking the Stanislavski system of realistic acting, Brecht instructed actors to present their roles as if telling a story so that the audience would not identify too closely with the characters. Nevertheless, the major characters in his plays are so full of life that it is difficult not to sympathize with them.

Educated in his native Bavaria, Brecht was bored by regular schooling but loved to write. When he graduated from college in 1917 he began to study medicine in Munich before being drafted as an orderly in 1918. Brecht's father offered to publish his first play, *Baal* (1918), but only if the Brecht family name was not mentioned, a condition the playwright refused. In 1922, Brecht's play *Drums in the Night* was awarded the Kleist Prize, one of Germany's highest literary honors.

Brecht settled in Berlin in 1924, where he worked for a time with directors Max Reinhardt and Erwin Piscator, but mostly with smaller experimental groups. One of Brecht's friends was the composer Kurt Weill, with whom he wrote *The Threepenny Opera* (1928), a modern version of *The Beggar's Opera*. During the time he was in Berlin he became a Marxist. At this same time he began to develop his theories of theater. Forced by the Nazis to flee Germany in 1933, he lived in Denmark, Sweden, and the United States, where he did some filmwriting in Hollywood.

During his years of exile, Brecht had the time to refine his ideas on epic theater and wrote such noteworthy plays as *Mother Courage* (1938), *Galileo* (1938–1939), *The Good Woman of Setzuan* (1938–1940), *The Resistible Rise of Arturo Ui* (1941), and *The Caucasian Chalk Circle* (1944–1945). In 1947 Brecht was called before the House Committee on Un-American Activities for his leftist ideas and left the United States shortly after his appearance there.

He settled in East Berlin, where the government gave him his own theater, the Berliner Ensemble, which opened in 1949 with *Mother Courage*. For the next seven years he and his wife, Helene Weigel, worked to develop epic theater, and when Brecht died in 1956 his wife took over the company, which had developed into one of the foremost acting troupes in the world.

*B*recht's *Mother Courage* This play, about a woman during the Thirty Years War who survives by selling goods to soldiers, is an example of what Brecht termed "epic drama." There are a number of episodic scenes and songs that interrupt the action to teach a lesson. In the end, Mother Courage loses her three children: the two sons shown here pulling her wagon and her daughter. (Photo—Berliner Ensemble.)

opportunism—Mother Courage loses her two sons and her deaf-mute daughter.

Mother Courage teaches a political lesson. Courage is an ironic title for Brecht's protagonist. As Eric Bentley, a leading Brecht critic and translator, points out: "Valor is conspicuously absent at those times when Mother Courage (however unwittingly) seals the fate of her children. At moments when, in heroic melodrama, the protagonist would be riding to the rescue, come hell or high water, Mother Courage is in the backroom concluding a little deal."[1] Ultimately, Brecht presents a protagonist and a war which are created and controlled by the profit motive. Thus, the German dramatist is arguing for a change in the capitalist economic system.

Many of the epic techniques are found in *Mother Courage and Her Children*. The use of historification is apparent. While the play is set during the Thirty Years' War—which has been characterized as a seventeenth-century world war—parallels can be drawn to political developments at the time of its conception. Written in 1938, the drama

[1]Bertolt Brecht, *Mother Courage and Her Children*, tr. Eric Bentley, N.Y., Grove Press, 1966, p. 10.

was later revised by Brecht in the early 1940s. The world premiere took place in 1941. The reverberations of World War II are quite obvious.

Titles preceding each scene reveal the coming action, thereby forcing the audience to think about the political and economic implications. Scene 1, for example, opens with a title that reads: "Spring 1624. In Dalarna, the Swedish Commander Oxenstierna is recruiting for the campaign in Poland. The canteen woman Anna Fierling, commonly known as Mother Courage, loses a son."[2] There are a number of songs which comment on the thematic implications of the dramatic action. The most famous is "The Song of the Great Capitulation," in Scene 4, which describes a person who begins life with high ideals but quickly learns to compromise. The representative nature of Brecht's characters is illustrated by the fact that they are frequently referred to by titles rather than names (e.g., Chaplain, Cook, Recruiting Officer).

TOTALITARIANISM, THE SECOND WORLD WAR, AND THE THEATER

As might be expected, the rise of totalitarianism and the outbreak of World War II in 1939 curtailed the development of European theater and drama. This is not to suggest that theatrical activity ceased to exist. In the totalitarian societies, particularly in Stalin's Russia and Hitler's Germany, government-supported theaters were employed as instruments of propaganda, while daring artists attempted to attack the regimes. For the most part, though, experimentation and freedom of expression were suppressed.

The Soviets immediately recognized the propagandistic value of the theater. After the revolution, mass spectacles—usually expensive outdoor events with casts composed partially of amateurs—were organized. In the 1930s the Soviets established "socialist realism" as the only acceptable theatrical form. Plays were to be written in the realistic mode with obvious socialist messages. In Nazi Germany, similar theatrical forms were supported. During the Third Reich numerous melodramas were staged exalting the Nazi point of view. Early in Hitler's rule mass spectacles known as *Thingspielen* were presented. An example of this form was Richard Euringer's *Deutsche Passion: 1933*, which presented Hitler as a Christ figure, adorned with a crown of thorns made of barbed wire, gathering his apostles and converts to save Germany from the evil Weimar Republic. After rescuing the fatherland, the crucified Nazi dictator ascended to heaven amid organ music and a chorus of singing angels.

Obviously, theater artists who opposed the totalitarian regimes were suppressed. In Spain, the playwright Federico García Lorca (1898–1936), author of *Yerma* (1934), *Blood Wedding* (1933), and *The House of*

---

[2]Ibid., p. 23.

he House of Bernarda Alba   Garcia Lorca, a Spanish playwright and poet, wrote about repression in Spain, and opposed the political party later headed by Franco. He died during the Spanish Civil War. In this play, the mother, on the left, keeps her four daughters completely under her domination. Her youngest daughter, on the right, opposes her and ends by committing suicide. (Photo—Fred Fehl.)

Bernarda Alba (1935), was killed by Franco forces during the Spanish Civil War. Productions of Lorca's works, which dramatized the oppression of Spanish women, were allowed only after Franco's death.

In the Soviet Union playwrights whose works were viewed as politically dangerous were censored and not allowed to be staged. Recently one of these dramas, Nikolai Erdman's *The Suicide* (1928), which presents suicide as an act of political resistance, was produced in London, Chicago, and New York. We have already noted that the director Vsevolod Meyerhold—who attempted unsuccessfully to stage *The Suicide* in 1929—was imprisoned and executed for his opposition to socialist realism.

Numerous German theater artists, because of either religion or politics, were forced to flee Germany after Adolf Hitler's takeover in 1933. They included the directors Max Reinhardt and Erwin Piscator as well as the playwrights Bertolt Brecht and Ernst Toller. Many artists who opposed the Third Reich but did not leave were interned in the Nazi concentration camps.

Nonetheless, theatrical artists did resist the rise of totalitarian regimes. During the 1940s, for example, the exiled Bertolt Brecht authored *The Resistible Rise of Arturo Ui*, which characterized the Nazi dictator as a Chicago gangster. The use of theater as a form of resistance to these regimes and the horrors of World War II was most vividly illustrated by the theatrical activities organized by inmates of the Nazi concentration camps. In the mid-1930s, the Nazi guards at the Oranienburg and Dachau camps forced internees to stage productions. Surviving accounts reveal that these presentations satirized the camps, yet the artists were not punished.

In the concentration camps in the conquered territories during World War II, such as Auschwitz, there were surreptitious entertainments in the barracks. These improvised presentations consisted of literature and drama recited from memory, satirical skits, and traditional songs. In the camp at Theresienstadt, in Czechoslovakia, satirical plays, operas, and cabaret entertainments were written and staged. Such entertainments were possible because the Nazis employed Theresienstadt as a "model" camp to which they brought the Red Cross and foreign officials in order to discredit the rumors of atrocities. Most of the artists who passed through Theresienstadt were then sent to the extermination centers.

Summary

The theater between World War I and World War II mirrored the social upheavals of the three decades. In America, little theaters, such as the Provincetown Playhouse and the Washington Square Players, reacted against commercial Broadway fare and introduced new playwrights. The Theater Guild and the Group Theater also produced new dramas using innovative production styles. The latter organization is often referred to as America's Moscow Art Theater. During the depression, the Federal Theater Project was an experiment with government-subsidized theater.

In Europe, many antirealistic movements developed, including expressionism, futurism, dadaism, and surrealism. Possibly the two most influential European theorists were Antonin Artaud and Bertolt Brecht. While Artaud was given few opportunities to realize his theater of cruelty, Brecht developed his epic style in the plays he authored and, later, those he directed at the Berliner Ensemble after World War II.

The rise of totalitarianism affected the theaters in Italy, Russia, Germany, and Spain. While the theater was employed by the governments of these countries for propaganda, courageous artists used it as a means of resistance.

The theater between the world wars illustrated the significance of the theater to western society. The drama and theater of this era served as an escape from harsh realities, a mirror of social upheavals, propaganda, and political resistance. The theater between 1915 and 1945, in many ways, indicates why dramatic art has survived the transformations and ravages of history.

Chapter Thirteen

THE THEATER FROM 1945 to 1980

It is difficult to assess the many social, political, and economic upheavals of the thirty-five years from 1945 to 1980; we are too close to these historical events to evaluate their significance in the development of western society. We can, however, look at certain key events.

POST–WORLD WAR II SOCIAL UPHEAVALS

The Second World War, as indicated in the preceding chapter, posed many haunting questions. How could the civilized world engage in a war that resulted in over 35 million deaths? How could rational societies undertake genocide? Would the atomic bomb lead to the annihilation of the

New Interpretations of old plays   *One hallmark of the period from 1945–1980 was the reinterpretation by stage directors of works from the past. Polish director Jerzy Grotowski and British director Peter Brook were among the leaders of this movement. Shown here is a scene from Brook's modern version of Shakespeare's* A Midsummer Night's Dream, *which, among other devices, had actors caught in coiled wires and swinging on trapezes. (Photo—Max Waldman.)*

The Theater between 1945 and 1980

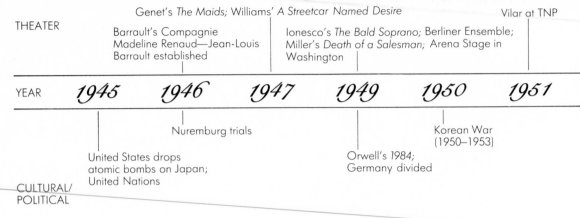

THEATER	Genet's *The Maids*; Williams' *A Streetcar Named Desire*					Vilar at TNP
	Barrault's Compagnie Madeline Renaud—Jean-Louis Barrault established		Ionesco's *The Bald Soprano*; Berliner Ensemble; Miller's *Death of a Salesman*; Arena Stage in Washington			
YEAR	*1945*	*1946*	*1947*	*1949*	*1950*	*1951*
	United States drops atomic bombs on Japan; United Nations	Nuremburg trials		Orwell's *1984*; Germany divided	Korean War (1950–1953)	
CULTURAL/ POLITICAL						

human race? Such questions forced western society to reevaluate its most cherished beliefs.

Is humanity as rational and civilized as proclaimed by eighteenth- and nineteenth-century philosophers? Could God exist and allow the destruction of so many innocent human beings? Are individuals responsible for group actions? These questions formed the basis of philosophies, such as existentialism, which rejected traditional beliefs.

The end of World War II did not mark the disappearance of conflict. Possibly the most destructive battle was psychological. In the 1950s, the United States and the Soviet Union engaged in a cold war during which both superpowers strove to establish military superiority and extend their respective spheres of influence. The toll of this psychological war was great, with both sides fearful of nuclear holocaust. The cold war came to a head in 1962, when President John F. Kennedy threatened to blockade Communist Cuba if Russia did not remove its missiles. A policy of detente and disarmament was undertaken by President Richard Nixon in the 1970s, but the Soviet intervention in Afghanistan in 1980, the suppression of the Polish labor union Solidarity at the close of 1981, and other events threatened the easing of the cold war.

The United States, in the past thirty-five years, has been involved in several military conflicts. In the early 1950s the Korean War was an attempt to prevent Communist North Korea from invading South Korea, and in the late 1960s and early 1970s the United States fought in the Vietnam War. This controversial war resulted in peaceful as well as violent antiwar activities, including draft resistance and sit-ins. Many Americans felt that the United States was protecting a corrupt regime in South Vietnam and should not be involved in a civil war. The United

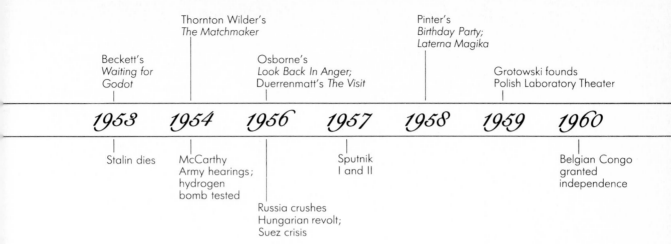

Beckett's
*Waiting for
Godot*

Thornton Wilder's
The Matchmaker

Osborne's
Look Back In Anger;
Duerrenmatt's *The Visit*

Pinter's
Birthday Party;
Laterna Magika

Grotowski founds
Polish Laboratory Theater

1953 1954 1956 1957 1958 1959 1960

Stalin dies

McCarthy
Army hearings;
hydrogen
bomb tested

Russia crushes
Hungarian revolt;
Suez crisis

Sputnik
I and II

Belgian Congo
granted
independence

States pulled out of Vietnam in 1972, and eventually all of the southeast Asian country became Communist. The reverberations of the war are still apparent, with the ambivalence of the American conscience being mirrored in such films as *The Deer Hunter* and *Apocalypse Now*. Furthermore, the continued political turmoil throughout southeast Asia confuses any final analysis of the American involvement.

There were also during this period a series of wars in the Middle East following the founding of the state of Israel. The wars were a product of Israeli and Arab nationalism, complicated by geography, oil resources, and competition between the superpowers.

The desire for peace in this thirty-five-year period was strong. The institution that represented the idealistic desire for worldwide peace was the United Nations, founded immediately following World War II, but the elusiveness of peace and nationalistic fervor kept the U.N. from being able to resolve international conflicts.

The continued growth of nationalism was illustrated in the rise of third world nations. Countries in Africa, for example, broke from colonial rule and asserted their independence. While many of the third world nations in Africa and Asia have valuable natural resources, they still struggle to develop economies that will allow them to be self-sustaining. The third world nations which prospered most were the oil-rich middle eastern countries.

Unfortunately, many third world nations were wracked by political turmoil: two examples were Uganda, which, after deposing dictator Idi Amin, was unable to establish a stable government, and Iran, which, after deposing the shah, was controlled by the unstable Moslem regime of Ayatollah Khomeini.

The Theater between 1945 and 1980

| | Café LaMama founded; Albee's *Who's Afraid of Virginia Woolf?* | | National Theater under Laurence Olivier | New York Shakespeare Festival (Joseph Papp) produces *Two Gentlemen of Verona, Sticks and Bones* and *That Championship Season* in New York City | | |
| | | | | Elder III *Ceremonies in Dark Old Men* | | |

YEAR	*1961*	*1962*	*1963*	*1964*	*1969*	*1972*	*1974*
	Berlin Wall	Cuban missile crisis		Krushchev resigns	Man on Moon		Nixon resigns

CULTURAL/
POLITICAL

Warfare escalates between North and South Vietnam;
Martin Luther King arrested in Birmingham;
John F. Kennedy, President of the United States, assassinated.

This thirty-five-year period was a time of general social unrest. In the United States, an epidemic of assassinations claimed the lives of John F. Kennedy, Robert Kennedy, Martin Luther King, and, twelve years later, John Lennon. Throughout the western world political terrorist organizations used violence as a means of publicizing their discontent.

There were also radical transformations between 1945 and 1980. The civil rights, gay rights, and feminist movements forced people to reevaluate their perceptions of minority or oppressed groups. The sexual revolution forced a reevaluation of traditional morality, including the questioning of such institutions as marriage and the family.

Twentieth-century society continues to be technologically innovative: television joined film as theater's major competitor; medical advances resulted in the eradication of polio and in genetic experimentation; nuclear energy became a controversial power source; and space exploration culminated in Americans walking on the moon.

POSTWAR EXPERIMENTAL THEATER

The thirty-five years from 1945 to 1980 were also turbulent ones for the theater. There was an explosion of experimentation with new avant-garde trends springing up one after another. The proximity of these movements to our own lifetimes prevents us from conclusively evaluating their historical significance. It is clear, however, that established theatrical and

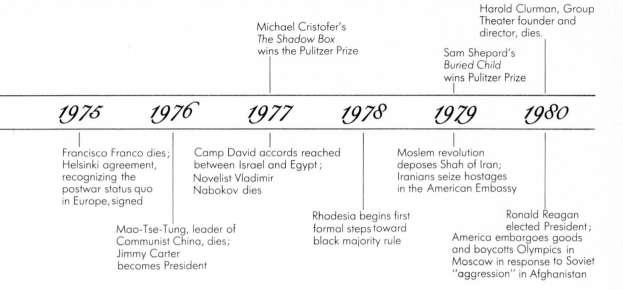

Michael Cristofer's
The Shadow Box
wins the Pulitzer Prize

Harold Clurman, Group
Theater founder and
director, dies.

Sam Shepard's
Buried Child
wins Pulitzer Prize

1975   1976   1977   1978   1979   1980

Francisco Franco dies;
Helsinki agreement,
recognizing the
postwar status quo
in Europe, signed

Camp David accords reached
between Israel and Egypt;
Novelist Vladimir
Nabokov dies

Moslem revolution
deposes Shah of Iran;
Iranians seize hostages
in the American Embassy

Mao-Tse-Tung, leader of
Communist China, dies;
Jimmy Carter
becomes President

Rhodesia begins first
formal steps toward
black majority rule

Ronald Reagan
elected President;
America embargoes goods
and boycotts Olympics in
Moscow in response to Soviet
"aggression" in Afghanistan

dramatic forms were questioned and restructured, and that movements such as absurdism and environmental theater forced people to redefine their perceptions of drama and theater.

Existentialism

Existentialism is a philosophy most clearly articulated by two Frenchmen, Jean-Paul Sartre (1905–1980) and Albert Camus (1913–1960). Most historians point to the obvious impact of World War II on these thinkers. Existentialists believe that there is little meaning to existence; God, for these philosophers, does not exist, and therefore humanity is alone in an irrational universe. The only significant action an individual can take is to accept responsibility for his or her actions.

Camus and Sartre wrote plays which illustrated their beliefs. The best known are Sartre's *The Flies* (1943), an adaptation of the Greek *Oresteia,* and *No Exit* (1944), in which hell is presented as other people. While the philosophical outlook of these dramas is revolutionary, their dramatic form is fairly conventional. The plot structures follow a traditional cause-and-effect logic, while the characters are recognizable, fully developed human beings.

Theater of the Absurd

After World War II, a theatrical approach emerged which combined existentialist philosophy with a revolutionary, avant-garde dramatic

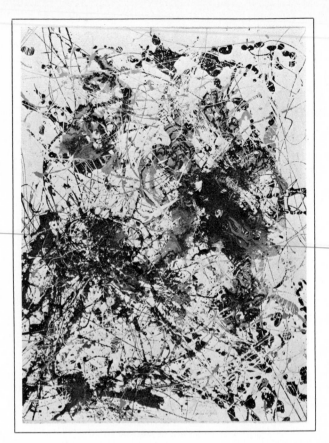

*G*reater abstraction in contemporary art *This Jackson Pollack painting, titled* Number 12, 1949, *is an example of the abstract, antirealistic work done by many painters in the post-World War II period. Drama, too—in plays by writers like Samuel Beckett and Eugène Ionesco—moved toward greater abstraction and antirealism. (Photo—Museum of Modern Art, Gift of Edgar Kaufmann, Jr.)*

form. Although not a movement, it was labeled *theater of the absurd* by the critic Martin Esslin. Though they differ markedly from one another, there are certain qualities that playwrights in this group share in common. One is the notion that much of what happens in life cannot be explained logically; it is ridiculous or absurd. These playwrights also feel that this ridiculousness or absurdity should be reflected in the dramatic action of their plays. Among the writers with this approach are Samuel Beckett, Jean Genêt (a Frenchman born in 1910), Eugène Ionesco, Harold Pinter, and Edward Albee (an American born in 1928).

The dramas of these playwrights present human existence, including such aspects as relationships and language, as futile or absurd. In order to reinforce this thematic statement, the dramatic techniques employed also seem illogical. Plots follow neither the traditional crisis structure nor the episodic. Frequently nothing seems to happen, because the plots move in a circle, concluding the same way in which they began. The characters are not created in a realistic fashion and little expository information is provided about them. The settings are frequently strange, unrecognizable locales or ostensibly realistic worlds that suddenly be-

$\mathscr{E}$UGÈNE IONESCO
(Born 1912)

Eugène Ionesco is one of the most productive of the playwrights who are grouped together as absurdists. In his dramas, Ionesco often turns his characters into caricatures and pushes the action to the point of the ridiculous. Since Ionesco is particularly concerned with the futility of communication, the language of his plays often seems nonsensical. He dramatizes the absurdity of the human condition by presenting comic characters who lose control of their own existences.

As a child, Ionesco was enchanted by Punch and Judy puppet shows and enjoyed performing in plays. Though born in Romania, when he was young he lived with his mother in Paris for thirteen years. Returning to Romania, he had to learn his "native" language. At the University of Bucharest, he studied French and occasionally wrote poetry. When he finished college, he taught French in high school. He married in 1936 and in 1938 returned to France on a government grant, supposedly to write a thesis on Baudelaire. He has not yet written a word of the thesis.

Ionesco became a playwright by accident. As a reader in a legal publishing firm, he decided to learn English and began by using a simple primer. He took the empty and illogical phrases he was learning in the primer and turned them into the dialogue for his first play, *The Bald Soprano* (1949). It was somewhat ironic that he wrote a play because, at that time, he claimed he disliked the theater. Ionesco's dislike of the theater was rooted in his feeling that the reality of the live actor clashed with the fictional world of the stage.

Ionesco followed his first play with several other one-act works, including *The Lesson* (1951) and *The Chairs* (1952). His full-length plays include *Amédée* (1954), *Rhinoceros* (1959), and *Exit the King* (1962). He has also written several volumes of sharp, sometimes argumentative, criticism and some political works. He remains adamantly opposed to the notion of didactic drama, feeling that the purpose of the theater is not to teach a lesson, but to present a vision of life that is enlightening or entertaining, or both.

amuel Beckett directs Waiting For Godot *One of the plays that most typifies the spirit of alienation and loneliness found in dramas after World War II is* Waiting For Godot, *about two men waiting to be saved by someone who never comes. Shown here is the playwright, Samuel Beckett, at a rehearsal for a production which he directed. (Photo—Ilse Buhs.)*

come topsy-turvy. The language of the play is often telegraphic and sparse; the dialogue seems to make little sense, and the characters fail to communicate. An example of absurdist dialogue is the following exchange from Ionesco's play *The Bald Soprano:*

MR. SMITH: Take a circle, caress it, and it will turn vicious.
MRS. SMITH: A schoolmaster teaches his pupils to read, but the cat suckles her young when they are small.
MRS. MARTIN: Nevertheless, it was the cow that gave us tails.[1]

Waiting for Godot

Samuel Beckett's *Waiting for Godot* is probably the most famous of these

[1]Eugène Ionesco, *Four Plays*, tr. Donald M. Allen, N.Y., Grove Press, 1958, p. 38.

Eve Arnold/Magnum Photos

HAROLD PINTER
(born 1930)

Harold Pinter is the leading English-language absurdist playwright. In his dramas, he feels no need to explain why something happens or who a character is; it is enough that they exist within the world of the play. Characteristic elements of Pinter's works are the lack of explanation of backgrounds or motives, the introduction of menacing outside forces which upset a seemingly stable environment, and dialogue which captures the pauses, evasions, and incoherencies of modern speech. Pinter acknowledges Franz Kafka, Samuel Beckett, and American gangster films as his greatest influences. Unlike Beckett and Ionesco, however, the world of his plays seems to be somewhat realistic.

Though he began writing poetry while still in school in London's East End, Pinter's first career choice was acting. He attended the Royal Academy of Dramatic Art for a time but faked a nervous breakdown when he found the other students to be too sophisticated. He completed his studies at the Central School of Speech and Drama and, under the name of David Baron, acted professionally.

Pinter's debut as a playwright was accidental. He had mentioned an idea for a play to a friend in the drama department of Bristol University. The friend wrote that he was interested in the play but needed the script within a week if the school was to produce it. Pinter wrote back "no," but finished the play in four days, and *The Room* was performed in May, 1957. Two of his other plays, *The Dumbwaiter* and *The Birthday Party*, were also produced in 1957.

The term "comedy of menace" is sometimes applied to such plays as *The Birthday Party*, *A Slight Ache* (1958), and *The Homecoming* (1965) because they frighten and entertain at the same time. The term is not as applicable to Pinter's later plays, such as *Old Times* (1971), which, though uncomfortably funny, deal more realistically with failed human relationships and do not contain unexplained menacing forces. In a later work, *Betrayal* (1978), he experiments with form, reversing time in order to trace a relationship from its end back to its beginning.

Pinter also writes for television, radio, and film, adapting his own plays and the works of others as well as writing original scripts. Occasionally he also directs for the theater. Pinter's creativity and adaptability in several media make him one of the most vital forces in the English theater today.

enigmatic or nontraditional dramas. (This is the play, mentioned in Chapter 1, that was presented at San Quentin Prison). The setting is "A country road. A tree." In the second act, four or five leaves are added to the tree. The two central characters, Vladimir and Estragon—also known as Didi and Gogo—are tramplike clowns who are waiting for Godot. Godot's identity is never revealed nor does he ever appear. Instead, a young messenger promises that he will arrive tomorrow. Godot may be God, or he may not even exist. Two additional characters, Lucky and Pozzo, switch roles as master and slave in their two appearances.

Waiting for Godot epitomizes the absurdist form. The characters are absurd, clownlike figures who have problems communicating and dealing with their environment. They contemplate suicide, for example, as a means of relieving their perpetual boredom. The setting represents everywhere and nowhere. Some critics have remarked that the barren, sterile world of the play conjures up the image of the aftermath of a nuclear holocaust. The language is stichomythic (written in brief, alternating lines) and frequently ludicrous. Lucky, in Act II, gives a three-page speech of seemingly unrelated ideas. Like many absurdist dramas, the plot of *Godot* is cyclical. The action appears to start over with nothing having changed. The closing lines and stage direction suggest the absurdity of the universe:

VLADIMIR: Well? Shall we go?
ESTRAGON: Yes, let's go. *(They do not move.)*[2]

The final movement of *Waiting for Godot* underlines the futile, absurdist philosophy of the play. Vladimir and Estragon spend their time waiting. They accomplish nothing, exhibiting their inability to take control of their existences. Lucky and Pozzo have no control over their destinies; fate reverses their roles, transforming one from master into servant and the other from servant into master.

Some critics suggest that Samuel Beckett's *Waiting for Godot* is a modern allegory, much like the medieval *Everyman*. The playwright suggests that we spend our lives waiting for the unknowable. Some analysts suggest that Godot represents God. More generally, Godot is anything and everything that human beings wait for during their lifetimes. Our lives are thus defined by the absurd wait rather than by the actions we take. Beckett refers to *Waiting for Godot* as a "tragicomedy in two acts," and thereby reveals his tragicomic view of the human condition. Human inaction is comical but has tragic consequences.

Directors of Absurdist Drama

Some directors have become renowned for their staging of dramas that reflect absurdity, ridiculousness, or the enigmatic. In France, Roger Blin (b. 1907) is noted for his productions in the early 1950s of Samuel

[2]Samuel Beckett, *Waiting for Godot*, N.Y., Grove Press, 1954, p. 61.

Gisele Freund/Photo Researchers, Inc.

𝒮AMUEL BECKETT
(born 1906)

Samuel Beckett is the most renowned of the absurdist playwrights; in his plays he captures the ridiculous aspects of life in dramatic form. His dramas deal with the dullness of routine, the futility of human action, and the inability of humans to communicate. In Beckett's plays, the plots, language, and characters seem absurd. Thus, his dramatic style underlines his thematic statements.

Samuel Beckett was born April 13, 1906. The day of his birth happened to be Good Friday, which seems quite appropriate, since the notions of sorrow, isolation, and ill luck associated with that day are also important concepts to Beckett. For a man so obsessed with the futility of existence, Beckett had a very normal childhood in a cultured, affectionate, upper-middle-class Irish family. At prep school, he was not only a brilliant scholar but an extremely popular student and an excellent athlete, particularly at cricket. He received his M.A. from the University of Dublin, Ireland, in modern languages. He then taught at schools in Paris and Dublin, wandered around Europe for a while, and finally settled in Paris in 1937.

It was during his first visit to Paris in 1929 that Beckett became acquainted with the writer James Joyce. Joyce encouraged Beckett to write and arranged to have some of his early essays published; in turn, Beckett sometimes assisted Joyce with *Finnegan's Wake*. Their shared Irish background, literary taste, and tendency to depression drew them together. According to one account, they conversed mainly in silences.

Beckett wrote and published essays, short stories, poetry, and novels during the 1930s and the 1940s, but his work was known only to a very small group of the avant-garde. A French translation of his novel *Murphy* sold ninety-five copies in four years. It was not until the early 1950s, with the publication of three novels and the play *Waiting for Godot* (1953), that he came to be considered one of the major writers of the postwar generation.

In *Waiting for Godot*, Beckett uses many of the themes and dramatic techniques that are to recur in his other plays. The futility of action reappears as a theme in *Act Without Words I & II*. The inability of two people who need each other to get along is seen again in *Endgame* (1957); *Happy Days* (1961) and *Krapp's Last Tape* (1958) dramatize our failure to communicate.

Besides writing for the theater, Beckett has written for television and radio and authored a short film starring Buster Keaton. After a spurt of writing in the late 1950s and early 1960s, his output has diminished, but *Not I*, written in 1972, shows that neither his concerns nor his dramatic powers have changed. Beckett received the Nobel Prize in 1969 but did not attend the ceremony.

A study in frustration   *In his plays, Samuel Beckett has found unique ways to dramatize the absurdity and loneliness of modern life. Shown here in a recent production of Beckett's* Happy Days, *is actress Irene Worth playing a woman who is buried in a mound of earth to her waist in the first act, and to her neck in the second. (Photo—George E. Joseph, The Public Theater.)*

Beckett's dramas. The reputation of the American director Alan Schneider (b. 1917) is based on his productions of plays by Beckett, Albee, and Pinter. The English director Peter Hall (b. 1930), first as a director with the Royal Shakespeare Company in the 1960s and later in the 1970s with the National Theater, established his reputation with productions of Harold Pinter's works. Many dramatists of the so-called absurdist school, including Beckett, Pinter, and Albee, direct their own plays.

Directors like Blin, Schneider, and Hall are all dedicated to being truthful to the text. Furthermore, their basic goal is to illuminate the enigmatic plays through their staging. Alan Schneider, for example, when undertaking *Godot*, wrote to Beckett asking the perplexing question, "Who is Godot?" Beckett responded that if he wished him to know he would have revealed the answer in the text.

*S*elective realism *Arthur Miller's* Death of a Salesman *is the story of Willy Loman, an unsuccessful salesman, shown here with his wife on the left, and his two sons on the right. The play mixes realistic scenes with antirealistic devices such as flashbacks and fantasy scenes from Willy's imagination. (Photo—The New York Public Library at Lincoln Center, Astor, Lenox, and Tilden Foundation.)*

REALISTIC DRAMA

The hold that the realistic form exerts on the theater, while constantly questioned in this thirty-five-year period, is still apparent. A good indication is the fact that the majority of dramas that have won the Pulitzer Prize in recent years have been realistic. These include *The Subject Was Roses* (1965) by Frank D. Gilroy, *That Championship Season* (1973) by Jason Miller, and *The Gin Game* (1978) by D. L. Coburn.

Selective Realism

America's leading post–World War II playwrights, Arthur Miller and Tennessee Williams, have written in the realistic form but have also been successful with *selective realism*, a type of realism that heightens certain details of action, scenery, and dialogue while omitting others. For example, in Miller's *Death of a Salesman*, which presents the tragic demise of salesman Willy Loman, the playwright highlights selected elements of Willy's world which symbolize his downfall: the refrigerator in need of repair, the tape-recorder in his boss's office. Rarely is the setting completely realized in a naturalistic fashion; frequently scenes from the past are presented from Willy's point of view. Nonetheless, Miller's play is set in a recognizable, realistic world in which elements have been carefully selected to underline thematic concerns. Tennessee Williams employs a similar stylistic technique in such plays as *The Glass Menagerie* (which employs a narrator) and *A Streetcar Named Desire*.

Angry Young Men

In England in the 1950s, a group of antiestablishment playwrights known collectively as the "angry young men" dealt with the problems of the dissolving British Empire, social class, and political disillusionment. The most notorious of these plays was John Osborne's (b. 1929) *Look Back in Anger* (1956). Most of the "angry young men" dramas employ traditional realistic forms, modifying them slightly. Some critics suggest that England's most successful contemporary playwright, Peter Shaffer (b. 1926), in such works as *The Royal Hunt of the Sun* (1964), *Equus* (1973), and *Amadeus* (1980), continues the traditions of the "angry young men" movement. His plays, particularly *Equus*, mix realistic characteristics and causally related plots with highly theatrical devices. *Equus*, for example, employs actors costumed in metallic kothornoi (platform shoes) and head coverings to represent horses.

Documentary Drama

A German movement in the 1960s, referred to as *documentary drama*, proved to be influential. Documentary dramas, by such playwrights as Peter Weiss (b. 1916), Rolf Hochhuth (b. 1931), and Heinar Kipphardt (b. 1922), for example, are based on historical documents. Thus the plays are given an air of authenticity. The basic goal of the documentary dramatists was to convince audiences that they were watching history unfold in front of their eyes. The dramatists, however, did modify the documents for dramatic effect. Peter Weiss's *The Investigation* (1965) dramatizes the Frankfurt war-crimes tribunal which tried former Nazi extermination-camp guards. While Weiss's play is based on transcripts of the proceedings, he has made specific changes and has employed Brechtian epic techniques. His witnesses are given numbers, not names; this parallels the camp process of stripping prisoners of their identities. His stage directions require that the actors be unemotional in the delivery of their testimony so that the audience focuses on the facts

ARTHUR MILLER
(born 1915)

Arthur Miller is regarded as one of the three most outstanding American dramatists of the twentieth century. Using the ideas of failure, guilt, responsibility for one's actions, and the effects of society on the individual, Miller repeatedly tries to make his audiences examine their own lives. His most successful dramas are reminiscent of Ibsen's well-made problem plays. It is not surprising, then, that in the early 1950s, Miller authored an adaptation of the nineteenth-century Norwegian playwright's *An Enemy of the People.*

As the son of a garment manufacturer who lost his business in the depression, Miller understands failure. After high school, the playwright worked as a shipping clerk in a warehouse before attending the University of Michigan. There he won a Hopwood Award for playwriting. He worked for ten years at a variety of jobs, including one at the Brooklyn Navy Yard, and wrote at night, until he became a successful dramatist.

Though his first Broadway play, *The Man Who Had All the Luck* (1944), was a failure, *All My Sons* (1947), the story of a wartime manufacturer, established Miller as a promising new dramatist. With the Pulitzer Prize–winning *Death of a Salesman* (1949), he became one of the most renowned American playwrights. The play is often characterized as a modern tragedy of the common man. His next play, *The Crucible* (1953), is about witchhunting in seventeenth-century Massachusetts and also a commentary on the investigations of the McCarthy era. Miller returned to contemporary America in his next two plays, *A View from the Bridge* and *A Memory of Two Mondays* (1955). In *After the Fall* (1964), he gives a thinly disguised account of his marriage to Marilyn Monroe.

Miller's later dramas, except for *The Price* (1968), were unfavorably received by the critics. His two plays of the 1970s, *The Creation of the World and Other Business* (1972) and *The Archbishop's Calling* (1979), were failures, though *The American Clock*, which opened in 1980, was better received. Several of his early plays have recently had successful revivals, and his television adaptation of an account of a female musician's life in a concentration camp, *Playing for Time* (1980), was critically acclaimed. Miller has also written short stories and screenplays.

TENNESSEE WILLIAMS
(Thomas Lanier Williams)
(born 1911)

Tennessee Williams is one of America's leading twentieth-century playwrights. He had a series of critical and popular successes from the 1940s through the 1960s, including *The Glass Menagerie* (1945), *A Streetcar Named Desire* (1947), *Summer and Smoke* (1948), *The Rose Tattoo* (1950), *Cat on a Hot Tin Roof* (1954), *Sweet Bird of Youth* (1959), and *The Night of the Iguana* (1961). Both *Streetcar* and *Cat* won the Pulitzer Prize.

A common thematic thread running through these works is the plight of society's outcasts, trapped in a hostile environment. Though these outsider characters usually are victims with an inability to comprehend the world, Williams, through the use of lyrical and poetic language as well as symbolism, is able to create compassion for them. While his most popular plays are fairly realistic, in many of his later dramas Williams has increased the use of nonrealistic techniques, as in *The Seven Descents of Myrtle* (1968).

Williams had a long wait for his critical and commercial success. The son of a traveling shoe salesman, the playwright was born in Columbus, Mississippi and grew up in St. Louis. He entered the University of Missouri in 1929, but financial difficulties forced him to leave school. After several years and many jobs, he received his B.A. from the University of Iowa in 1938.

In 1939, Williams received a citation from the Group Theater for his collection of one-act plays, *American Blues*. The Theater Guild production of his full-length drama *Battle of Angels* closed in Boston in 1940 after a brief run. He spent six months as a contract writer for MGM in 1943 and while in Hollywood wrote the first draft of *The Glass Menagerie*.

In recent years, Williams has become somewhat of an outsider to the theater. His latest full-length plays have been failures, though some of his shorter plays like *Small Craft Warnings* (1973) have had extended runs off-Broadway. Williams still continues to write, however, and his work continues to be performed frequently and to influence other American playwrights.

Experimental theater productions   One of the most innovative directors of the 1960s was Jerzy Grotowski, founder of the Polish Laboratory Theater. Grotowski stressed physical and vocal flexibility in his performers. Also, he shunned traditional actor-audience relationships and created a unique physical environment for each production. For The Constant Prince, *shown here, he built a low fence around a central stage space for spectators to sit behind. (Photo—Max Waldman.)*

presented. The victims are not referred to as Jews, nor is the camp specifically identified, since Weiss wishes to universalize the Holocaust so that it represents all barbaric historical events.

Documentary dramas were also written in America during the 1960s. Many of them mirrored the social upheavals in this country, including the civil rights movement and the Vietnam War. Among these plays were *The Pueblo, The Trial of the Catonsville Nine,* and *Are You Now or Have You Ever Been* (a play about the McCarthy era).

EXPERIMENTAL THEATER

Turning from plays to production, following absurdism there were further attempts to supersede traditional theater practices. These experiments, carried out in Europe and the United States in the 1960s and 1970s, went in many directions—a reflection, no doubt, of the sense of fragmentation experienced in modern life. The experiments included environmental theater, happenings, and multimedia.

Environmental Theater

The term *environmental theater* was coined by the American director-teacher Richard Schechner (b. 1934), in the 1960s, though many of the characteristics of environmental theater developed out of the work and theories of earlier twentieth-century avant-garde artists, including Vsevolod Meyerhold and Antonin Artaud. Environmental theater holds that the entire theater space is performance space, thereby suggesting that the division between performers and viewers is artificial. For every production, spatial arrangements are transformed. For Schechner the script is not an essential nor a sacred element, and both improvisation and the reworking of an existing drama are permissible.

The major influence on Schechner's theories is the Polish director Jerzy Grotowski. The works he staged with the Polish Laboratory Theater from its founding in 1959 until 1970 exhibit many of the characteristics of environmental theater. For each production the theater space and the actor-audience relationship were arranged to conform to the play being presented. In Grotowski's production of *Kordian* the space resembled the world of a mental institution, with audience members scattered among beds and patients (the actors). In his version of *Dr. Faustus*, the theater space was filled with two large dining tables at which audience members sat as if attending a banquet given by Faustus. And in *The Constant Prince*, a small fence was built around the playing area and the audience sat around it as if watching a bullfight.

For most of Grotowski's productions, existing scripts were radically modified by the actors and director. The acting style was externally based, with the emphasis on the actor's control of body and voice rather than inner emotions. According to Grotowski, he was attempting through his productions to ascertain the essential elements of the theatrical art. He concluded that the essence of theater was the interaction between live performers and audiences. Hence his emphasis on reorganizing the spatial arrangements. (His stress on the importance of the theatrical environment and the nonverbal aspects of performance has a strong affinity with the ideas of Antonin Artaud.)

Since 1970, Grotowski has stopped producing and has been involved in "paratheatrical" experiments. These experiments require that members of his company and participants take part together in the rituals of daily life in order to rediscover the origins of the theater. Many critics question whether this is not closer to therapy—sociodrama or psychodrama—than theatrical activity.

Grotowski's experiments influenced a number of American theater practitioners in the 1960s. In order to understand this influence, however, we need to examine the transformations in the American theater since World War II.

Happenings and Multimedia

Two other developments of the 1960s and 1970s were *happenings* and experiments with *multimedia*. Happenings were what the name suggests: They were supposed to be nonstructured events that occurred with

ℐERZY GROTOWSKI
(born 1933)

In modern times, one of the people who has tried to answer the endlessly debated question "What is theater?" is Jerzy Grotowski. Grotowski's notion of "poor theater," which he developed while working with his Polish Laboratory Theater, stems from his belief that the only two essentials for theater are the actor and the audience. The script, scenery, and other elements are considered not as important; hence the term poor theater. To intensify the actor-audience relationship, he experimented with various spatial arrangements to intertwine the actors and audience, though he did not advocate eliminating the barrier that separates them.

The plays Grotowski produced were reduced to essential ideas; they were cut, rearranged, or rewritten to serve his purposes. The actor, the core of his productions, is trained so that nearly every muscle of the body is under complete control and can be moved at will.

The son of a painter-sculptor and a schoolteacher, Grotowski was born in Rzeszów, Poland. His family was well educated, and both of his parents were interested in the orient, an interest that he shares. Grotowski became gravely ill at the age of 16 and spent an entire year in the hospital, much of it in the ward for terminal patients. Instead of following the doctor's advice and remaining under indefinite care, he returned home and began to lead a normal life. He also began to meditate and to read extensively.

Though his family objected to his career choice, Grotowski entered the Advanced School of Dramatic Art in Cracow in 1951, first to study acting and then directing. He became interested in Stanislavski's work, admiring it because he felt that the Russian director had asked the right questions about acting. The work of another Russian, Meyerhold, was also an important influence on him. During a trip abroad, Grotowski was impressed by the Berliner Ensemble's production of Brecht's *Mother Courage*. In 1959, he became director of a theater in Opole, where he began his Polish Laboratory Theater. In 1965, the Laboratory Theater, now the Institute for Research in Acting, moved to Wroclaw, Poland.

The productions for the Polish Laboratory Theater, particularly *Akropolis* (1962–1967), *The Constant Prince* (1965–1968), and *Apocalypsis cum Figuris* (1968), attracted great attention throughout the world. The group performed in New York in 1969 to small, select audiences. Since 1970, Grotowski has moved from theatrical production and actor training to an activity which involves personal exploration and the communal sharing of mystical experiences by a group working together, not unlike certain consciousness-raising activities in the United States. Grotowski has returned to American several times to discuss this new turn in his work.

a minimum of planning and organization. The idea—quite popular in the 1960s—was that art should not be restricted to museums, galleries, or concert halls, but can happen anywhere: on a street corner, in a grocery store, at a bus stop. Theatrical happenings were closely allied with the work of abstract painters, and they usually occurred only once. The originator with a few colleagues would set up a situation and then act it out in an improvisatory fashion.

Multimedia is the joining of theater with the other arts—especially dance, film, and TV. Work of this sort still goes on in which live performers interact with sequences on film or television. The idea here is to fuse the art forms or to incorporate new technology into a theatrical event.

RECENT DEVELOPMENTS IN THE AMERICAN THEATER

At the close of World War II, there were limited outlets for experimentation in the American theater, particularly because of the high cost of commercial productions. The commercial Broadway theater, located on the west side of midtown Manhattan in New York City, was, and still is, traditionally oriented. The theaters are large proscenium-arch playhouses, and the types of plays presented usually appeal to popular tastes. For example, among the most popular productions since World War II have been musicals and the comedies of Neil Simon (b. 1927), including *The Odd Couple* (1965), *The Sunshine Boys* (1972), *California Suite* (1976), and *Chapter Two* (1978). Of course, significant serious dramas have also been produced on Broadway, including Arthur Miller's and Tennessee Williams's major works as well as more recent plays of a serious nature. Nonetheless, the commercial nature of the Broadway theater leads primarily to the production of popular entertainments.

Off-Broadway

The off-Broadway movement developed in the late 1940s as a reaction to Broadway commercialism. The primary goal was to provide an outlet for experimental and innovative works unhindered by commercial concerns. The off-Broadway movement was dedicated to introducing new playwrights or reviving plays that had been unsuccessful in initial Broadway productions. For example, the Circle in the Square, a noted off-Broadway playhouse, revived Tennessee Williams's *Summer and Smoke* in 1952 and Eugene O'Neill's *The Iceman Cometh* in 1956, both of which had failed in their initial runs. In the 1960s, the plays of several young American playwrights, including Israel Horowitz (b. 1939), John Guare (b. 1938), and Lanford Wilson (b. 1934), were produced off-Broadway. The movement also introduced new actors, directors, and designers. Among the performers who debuted off-Broadway were Jason Robards, Colleen

A new life in revivals   *Eugene O'Neill's* The Iceman Cometh, *was originally done on Broadway, but was not successful until revived off-Broadway at the Circle in the Square in 1956. Shown here are Fredric March and Robert Ryan in a still later revival. In recent years, both new plays and revivals have often been most successful in non-Broadway theaters. (Photo—United Press International.)*

Dewhurst, Dustin Hoffman, and Al Pacino, all now recognized as significant acting professionals. The director José Quintero (b. 1924) established his reputation as America's leading interpreter of Eugene O'Neill's dramas at the Circle in the Square Theater.

Finally, the off-Broadway movement popularized the use of intimate, non-proscenium-arch houses. Many of the off-Broadway theaters, each seating about 200 spectators, are thrust or arena stages. While such theaters had been employed in America earlier, many off-Broadway playhouses, along with many regional theaters, proved the viability of open spaces. Even those off-Broadway playhouses which contain proscenium-arch stages are much more intimate than their Broadway counterparts, because of their smaller size.

The off-Broadway movement, in the 1960s and 1970s, became more commercial and, therefore, less experimental. As production costs rose, the types of productions staged became more conventional. In the last two decades, many productions, such as the enormously popular musical *Grease*, were moved from off-Broadway to Broadway, illustrating the blurring of distinctions.

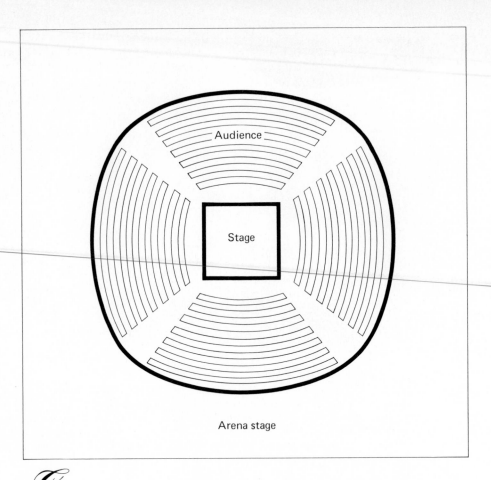

*G*round plan for the arena stage. The arena (also known as theater-in-the round) is either square-shaped or round, and has the stage in the center with the audience surrounding it. This is one of the most ancient audience-performer relationships and became popular again after World War II. It provides maximum intimacy and is economical because it requires very little scenery.

Off-Off-Broadway

In recent years, off-off-Broadway has replaced off-Broadway as the center for experimentation in New York. Off-off-Broadway is dedicated to introducing and showcasing new talent, experimenting with new styles of production, and avoiding the limitations of commercialism. Possibly the most important playwright produced off-off-Broadway is Sam Shepard (b. 1943), whose *Buried Child* won the Pulitzer Prize in 1979. Many off-off-Broadway groups perform in *found spaces*, that is, spaces such as factory lofts, churches, and warehouses not originally intended for theater production. The environmental experiments in America have frequently been undertaken off-off-Broadway. Some of the experiments with participatory theater—in which audience members are asked to take an active part—have been staged off-off-Broadway.

The number of experimental off-Broadway and off-off-Broadway groups which attempted to transform accepted theatrical conventions is staggering. Many of these companies flourished in the turbulent 1960s and were highly political, attacking American involvement in Vietnam, capitalism, and traditional values. Three such groups that deserve to be singled out are the Living Theater, founded in 1946 by Julian Beck and Judith Malina, the Open Theater, founded in 1963 by Joseph Chaikin (b. 1935) and Peter Feldman, and the Performance Group, founded by Richard Schechner in 1968.

Although these groups went through a variety of phases and were distinct in style, they all experimented with improvisation, restructuring of texts, environmental staging, and external acting style. Another influential off-off-Broadway figure is Ellen Stewart, who founded the

*G*round plan of the thrust stage. *One of the most popular stage configurations of all time is the thrust in which the stage juts into the audience and is surrounded on three sides by audience seating. Used by the ancient Greeks, the Romans, and the Elizabethans, it has been revived in recent years. It allows focus for the players and a scenic background, and also creates intimacy for the audience surrounding the action.*

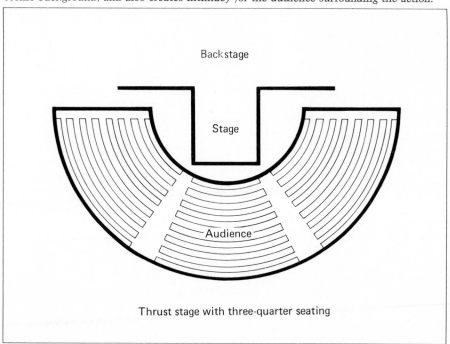

Thrust stage with three-quarter seating

THE LIVING THEATER
(founded 1946)

The Living Theater, founded in 1946 by Julian Beck (b. 1925) and Judith Malina (b. 1926), was a particularly influential avant-garde company of the later 1950s and the 1960s. The group's transformations mirrored the changes in American society and experimental theater.

Initially, the Living Theater performed poetic dramas and plays by earlier avant-garde dramatists. Among the authors the Living Theater staged were Bertolt Brecht, García Lorca, Gertrude Stein, W. H. Auden, August Strindberg, Jean Cocteau, and Jean Racine. The group also experimented with production styles. Its members used masks, stylized gestures and vocalizations, and theatrical conventions from past eras. In the late 1950s, they also became interested in the theories of Antonin Artaud.

The two productions that established the Living Theater's reputation were Jack Gelber's *The Connection* (1959) and Kenneth Brown's *The Brig* (1963). *The Connection* presents dope addicts waiting to make a connection for a fix. *The Brig* dramatizes the daily routine in a Marine Corps prison. Both productions tried to make the audience believe they were watching actual occurrences.

In the 1960s, because of tax problems, the Living Theater became nomadic, presenting many of its productions in Europe. In 1971, members of the company were arrested in Brazil for political activities. The Living Theater's problems in the 1960s were due to the political activism of its members, particularly their opposition to the Vietnam War and capitalism, as well as their belief in anarchy. During this period they also developed the production style for which the group was noted. Many of the works they staged were created by the group through improvisation. Rather than play characters, the members portrayed themselves confronting societal institutions and norms. Their best-known work of this period, *Paradise Now* (1968), included audience participation and confrontation in order to arouse spectators to the call for social revolution. The other two noteworthy works by the Living Theater in the mid-1960s were *Frankenstein* and *Mysteries and Smaller Pieces.*

The Living Theater has undergone numerous personnel changes. One early member, Joseph Chaikin, left the group and organized the Open Theater. Prior to the Brazilian tour, the company broke up into three groups. While Beck, Malina, and the Living Theater have not been highly visible since the early 1970s, they continue to produce; they staged *Prometheus* in London in 1979. In this production, audience members were invited to help stage the Communist revolution. At the close, spectators were asked to join the Living Theater in a march outside a nearby prison. The production was a continuation of the Living Theater's experiments in the 1960s.

Children of a Lesser God This play by Mark Medoff illustrates a notable trend of the last twenty years: a play having its initial success away from Broadway. The story of a deaf woman and her husband, played here by Phyllis Frelich and John Rubenstein, it was first produced by the Mark Taper Forum and directed by Gordon Davidson in Los Angeles and then became a hit on Broadway. (Photo—Martha Swope.)

Café LaMama in 1961, and has been instrumental in introducing new playwrights and directors. Recent artists like Richard Foreman, Robert Wilson, and the Mabou Mines Company have experimented with a style some critics label the "theater of images." Their emphasis is not on text or social activism but on the aesthetic impact of the stage picture.

Joseph Papp (b. 1921) is an off-off-Broadway producer who has had a strong impact on the American theater. In 1954, he opened the New York Shakespeare Festival, which gives free Shakespearean productions every summer in New York's Central Park. He has operated the Public Theater, which is a series of theater spaces in a converted library, since 1967. At the Public and for the Shakespeare Festival, he has produced a number of successful shows which have been moved to Broadway in order to help underwrite production costs for the off-off-Broadway spaces. These include *Hair, Two Gentlemen of Verona, That Championship Season, A Chorus Line*, and *Runaways*.

Papp has introduced a number of significant young playwrights, among them David Rabe, the author of the Vietnam War dramas *The Basic Training of Pavlo Hummel* (1971), *Stick and Bones* (1971), and *Streamers* (1976). In the summer of 1980, he presented Gilbert and Sullivan's operetta *The Pirates of Penzance* in Central Park, with pop star Linda Ronstadt, a show that moved successfully to Broadway.

Regional Theaters

Professional regional theater companies transformed the American theater. The regional theater movement, in which a permanent company operates in one community, began in the late 1940s. Among the most notable regional companies are the Alley Theater in Houston (1949), the Arena Stage in Washington, D.C. (1949), the Tyrone Guthrie Theater in Minneapolis (1963), the Actors Theater of Louisville (1964), the Long Wharf in New Haven (1965), and the Mark Taper Forum in Los Angeles (1967).

The regional companies attempt to present theatrical art relevant to the community in which they are located. Their playhouses are usually innovative in terms of architecture; many are thrust and arena spaces. In addition to presenting the classics, the regional theaters often discover new talent. A few of them have resident companies, that is, acting troupes which remain together for an extended period of time. One mark of the success of the regional theater movement is the number of dramas it has originated that have been transferred to Broadway, including Howard Sackler's *The Great White Hope*, Preston Jones's *The Texas Trilogy*, Michael Cristofer's *The Shadow Box*, G. L. Coburn's *The Gin Game*, and Mark Medoff's *Children of a Lesser God*.

THE POSTWAR ECLECTICS

To cite every postwar European theatrical innovator would be impossible. There are numerous directors whose productions borrow from the theatrical experiments previously discussed. They are eclectics who incorporate varied avant-garde techniques into their presentations.

French director Jean-Louis Barrault (b. 1910), who between the world wars worked with director Charles Dullin (1885–1949) and Antonin Artaud, has employed many Artaudian and environmental staging techniques. These were particularly evident in his production of *Rabelais* in 1968.

English director Peter Brook (b. 1925) is a more renowned contemporary eclectic. Brook, in staging Peter Weiss's *Marat/Sade* (1964), employed concepts borrowed from Artaud's theater of cruelty. His production of Shakespeare's *A Midsummer Night's Dream* (1970) was clearly influenced by Meyerhold's experiments with biomechanics and the circus arts; for example, the fairy gods appeared on trapezes. Since 1971, when he became the director of the International Center for Theater Research, Brook's work has exhibited the influence of Grotowski's innovations. Like the Polish director, Brook has become more concerned with the theatrical process, that is, how things are done, than with the product or the end result. As he indicates in his theoretical work *The Empty Space* (1968), Brook strives to avoid the "deadly" commercial theater, which does not allow for experimentation.

THE NEW TECHNOLOGY

Any discussion of the postwar theater must take into account the introduction of new technology into scene and lighting design. The Czechoslovakian designer Josef Svoboda (b. 1920), for example, has experimented with such elements as projections, multimedia, movable platforms, and new materials, including plastics.

Computer technology has been incorporated into many modern theater buildings. Lighting, for example, can now be computer controlled. Some critics, however, argue that the human factor, such as the live actor, which is the basic element of the theatrical art, will not allow for excessive computerization.

Summary

A number of theatrical movements were in evidence between 1945 and 1980. The absurdist dramas of Samuel Beckett, Eugène Ionesco, and Harold Pinter have had a profound influence on contemporary playwriting, along with such movements as the British angry young men and documentary drama. America's two leading dramatists, Arthur Miller and Tennessee Williams, continue to work in the more conventional realistic style.

Environmental staging, as seen in the works of Jerzy Grotowski's Polish Labortory Theater, Julian Beck and Judith Malina's Living Theater, Joseph Chaikin's Open Theater, and Richard Schechner's Performance Group, have forced theatergoers to reevaluate their traditional expectations of the actor-audience relationship. The avant-garde artists now working in the theater—such as the Americans Richard Foreman, Robert Wilson, and the Mabou Mines—have attempted to work with visual images. It is difficult to predict what lasting impact their efforts will have.

In America, there have been attempts by Off-Broadway, Off-Off-Broadway, and regional companies to break the stranglehold of the commercial Broadway theater. Regional professional theaters have become firmly established in many American cities in the past thirty years. Producers such as Joseph Papp and Ellen Stewart have introduced new playwrights and practitioners. The influence of these movements has resulted in new scripts and production styles being introduced into the commercial theater.

Chapter Fourteen

THE CONTEMPORARY THEATER

What is the state of the theater in the 1980s, and where is it headed in the future? We cannot be certain about the answer to the second part of the question, but we can reach reasonable conclusions about the first. A good way to examine the theater in the 1980s is to look at examples of contemporary theater experiences. Because we cannot cover all of Europe and America, we will look at a variety of theater activities in the United States which will serve as an indication of what is happening throughout the western world.

THE BROADWAY THEATER

We begin our survey on Broadway. It is a raw December day in 1981 in New York City. A group of college students and faculty members have

The eclectic quality of contemporary theater *Much of recent theater has drawn from a number of styles from the past. A prime example was the production of* Nicholas Nickleby *by Britain's Royal Shakespeare Company. This dramatization of Charles Dickens' novel successfully combined elements of Shakespeare, Bertolt Brecht, story theater, and nineteenth century melodrama. Shown here is Nicholas comforting his friend Smike while theater manager Mr. Crummles looks on. (Photo—Martha Swope.)*

gathered outside the Plymouth Theater on 46th Street, west of Broadway. It is just before 2 P.M., and they are preparing for a nine-and-one-half-hour theater experience. As they enter the Plymouth, they see a proscenium theater that has been transformed: ramps, platforms, and catwalks made of weather-beaten wood, wrought iron, and rope cover parts of the stage and also reach out into the auditorium to encircle the boxes and the front edge of the balcony. Performers in early-nineteenth-century British attire—the men in frock coats and top hats, the women in bonnets and long dresses—are walking in the aisles chatting with audience members. Soon, after everyone is seated, the performers gather on stage in a tableau—as if posing for an old-fashioned picture—and the performance of *The Life and Adventures of Nicholas Nickleby* begins. The play is an adaptation by David Edgar of the early-nineteenth-century novel written by Charles Dickens, directed by Trevor Nunn and John Caird.

The first part of the play will go for four hours with one intermission. Then, after an hour for supper, the play will continue for four and one-half hours more. In all, some forty performers will play 250 roles.

The story concerns Nicholas Nickleby and his sister Kate. When their father dies, they come to London with their mother, hoping to find a way to sustain themselves financially. They hope to enlist the aid of their rich uncle Ralph, but he acts contemptibly toward both of them. During the play Nicholas and Kate go through a series of episodes—in and out of London, some adventures happy, some unhappy—until they finally find good fortune.

In presenting the story of Nicholas Nickleby, the Royal Shakespeare Company (RSC) of Great Britain uses acting and production techniques that typify the eclecticism of theater in the 1980s. Eclecticism implies drawing from many sources, and that is exactly what the RSC has done. First, the performers are trained—as so many British performers are—to be able to speak language clearly, forcefully, and in a variety of accents. They also move well: with grace, precision, and economy. Directorially, this production adopts the fluidity of style used by most modern Shakespeare companies, not only in Britain but in Canada and the United States. This style—bringing a new scene onstage simultaneously with the end of the previous one—is consistent with the requirements of episodic drama as written by Shakespeare and his contemporaries. It is also reminiscent of modern cinematic techniques of cutting from one scene to the next.

Charles Dickens, the author of the novel *Nicholas Nickleby*, was enormously fond of the theater; he wrote several plays himself and served for a time as manager of a theater company. In the 1800s a number of his novels, including the popular *A Christmas Carol*, were adapted for the stage. An important section of *Nicholas Nickelby* deals with the Crummles theatrical troups, which Nicholas joins for a short time as an actor. The Crummles company gives us a marvelous insight into nineteenth-century theatrical practice. Companies toured small towns in the provinces, putting on all kinds of plays, but especially melodramas and domestic comedies. Actors and actresses played set parts: there was a leading man and a leading lady, an ingenue, a villain, an old character actor, and so forth. The playing style was broad, with lots of posturing and pompous elocution. As for the plays, the companies would think nothing of changing a script to suit their own ends, and the close of the first four hours of *Nicholas Nickleby* is a rousing rendition of Shakespeare's *Romeo and Juliet*, rewritten so that Romeo and Juliet return to life and are reunited at the end.

Throughout the production there are blends of old and new theatrical practices. The emphasis on the physical environment in the theater—the catwalks of old wood and wrought iron—is derived from the theories of Meyerhold in the 1920s, Antonin Artaud in the 1930s, and Jerzy Grotowski in Poland and a number of American groups in the 1960s.

Acting devices, too, come from ideas made popular in the 1960s—ideas developed in "story theater" and children's theater. At times the performers in *Nicholas Nickleby* use pantomime, pretending that physical scenes and props are present when they are not. They turn a bare stage into a field or a country road. At other times they use props in an imaginative way: creating a stagecoach, for example, out of wicker hampers and leather trunks.

Another technique is reminiscent of the work of the German playwright Bertolt Brecht. At certain points, performers step forward to narrate the story—speaking of their characters in the third person—and then move back to play a scene in the first person. The actor playing Nicholas, for example, will say, "Nicholas moved toward Portsmouth, where he and his friend were forced to stop at an inn." And a moment later, the actor will be in the midst of a scene with the innkeeper.

The remarkable thing is that these many elements—Shakespeare, nineteenth-century melodrama, Artaud, Brecht, and so forth—have been blended into a seamless whole. This is the theater of the 1980s at its best: a synthesis of many traditions from the past blended into a single experience.

When the nine and one-half hours are over, audience members are reluctant to leave. As they emerge into the cold, night air, they experience a form of culture shock because for an entire afternoon and evening, they have been living in England in the early part of the 1800s.

A Modern Broadway Musical

Two blocks away from *Nicholas Nickleby*, in December of the same year, a new musical called *Dreamgirls* opened on Broadway. This experience, too, tells us a great deal about the theater of the 1980s. First, it takes place in the Imperial Theater, which, like virtually every playhouse in the

A 1980s musical   *Typical of today's splashy Broadway musical is* Dreamgirls, *about a black singing group modeled on the Supremes. Shown here are Loretta Devine, Sheryl Lee Ralph and Deborah Burrell.* Dreamgirls *features flashy costumes and impressive sets. Recent musicals like* Dreamgirls *appear to stress such production elements more than the story emphasized by musicals of the past. (Photo—Martha Swope.)*

Broadway area, has a proscenium, or picture-frame, stage. The site of *Dreamgirls*, therefore, is part of a tradition in theater architecture that goes back to the Renaissance.

The musical form itself is also time-honored. As we have seen throughout our survey of theater history, music has often been an integral element of the theater. Music, for example, was one of Aristotle's six elements of the dramatic art. Furthermore, there have been many forerunners of the musical theater form, including opera, ballad opera, and the burletta, all of which mix songs with drama. This particular production, however, is part of the recent tradition of the American musical, a form that came to full flower in the decades of the 1940s, 1950s, and 1960s.

The new production tells us something about where musicals are today. The story concerns a group of popular singers and is loosely based on the Supremes, the black musical group that emerged in the 1960s and successfully made the transition from an ethnic sound into a style that was accepted by the full spectrum of audiences of popular music. In the story, one singer, who is overweight and refuses to change her singing style, is callously dropped from the group as it becomes ever more successful.

With *Dreamgirls*, however, the story, or book, is not the main thing: the book cannot compare with the ones in musicals like *My Fair Lady* (1956), *West Side Story* (1957), and *Fiddler on the Roof* (1964). Rather, the emphasis is on dazzling visual effects. The women singers appear in a spectacular array of gowns—purple, red, yellow, and white—made of satins and silks and covered with sequins. They disappear behind a beaded curtain, for instance, and a moment later magically reappear in another outfit.

The scenery and lighting are equally impressive. The scenery consists of long towers and bridges made of metal pipes. These skeletal constructions—which have lighting instruments in them as well—twist and turn, moving up, down, forward, and backward, to create a kaleidoscopic picture. Frequently—with the lighting effects changing constantly, too—they create cinematic frames, and many scene changes are like cuts in film, changing perspective, for example, from backstage to frontstage.

Dreamgirls illustrates a significant shift in large-scale musicals that had taken place by the early 1980s: the substitution of visual and technical effects for material of substance—characters, plots, and themes. *Nine*, another musical of that season, is an example of the same approach. Just how long and how far this trend will continue is difficult to predict.

The lack of new material in musicals has had another effect, however, in bringing about an increasing number of revivals of well-known musicals of thirty or forty years ago. This, of course, is another hallmark of theater in the 1980s: the availability of theater of the past—not only musicals but straight plays and not just on Broadway but in theaters across the United States.

Before we leave Broadway, it should be added that *Dreamgirls*, like all Broadway musicals, was expensive. The prices of tickets escalated in the early 1980s, and had it not been for half-price ticket booths and discount tickets distributed to schools and other groups, these large, professional productions would have been beyond the reach of many people.

PLAYS FROM THE PAST

A continent away from Broadway in Oregon, off Interstate 5 just north of the California border, lies the small town of Ashland. This is the site of the Oregon Shakespeare Festival, founded in 1935. In the summer, families and couples gather in the early evening at Lithia Park, just below the theater, for picnic suppers. When dusk comes, they wander up the hill to the theater itself. An outdoor amphitheater surrounded by the verdant Oregon hills, the theater at Ashland harks back to the Elizabethans and, beyond them, to the Middle Ages and the Greeks. These early theaters, too, were outdoors. The one important difference, perhaps, is that with modern lighting performance can now be held at night, whereas in former ages outdoor performance always took place during the day. The experience, though, of seeing theater created not in the closed, artificial environment of a theater building but with a playing space open to the skies can be exhilarating.

Though the stage architecture at the Oregon Shakespeare Festival does not conform strictly to the Elizabethan or the ancient Greek, it has a strong affinity with both. The seating area spreads in a fan shape around an open stage that projects slightly into the audience. The stage house behind—where performers make their entrances and exits—is in the Tudor style and is fashioned from plans of the Fortune Theater built in London in Shakespeare's day.

The play tonight is *Romeo and Juliet*, the story of Shakespeare's "star-crossed" lovers. As the tragedy unfolds, scenes of the two young people thwarted in their attempts to get together and the sounds of the magnificent poetry—"But soft! What light through yonder window breaks? It is the East, and Juliet is the sun!"—offer the same sights and sounds that have been heard by audiences since Shakespeare wrote the play at the end of the sixteenth century. The people seated under the stars in Ashland join a tradition that stretches back nearly 400 years.

The scene in Ashland is repeated throughout North America and in other countries as well: summer festivals of plays from the rich heritage of western theater.

A Modern Repertory Company

South of Ashland, a third of the way down the California coast, is San Francisco. Here, one of the country's premiere resident theater companies, the American Conservatory Theater (ACT), is also active in presenting plays from the past. Most of ACT's productions are in the Geary Theater, a typical indoor proscenium house, and are performed by a permanent company of carefully trained, thoroughly professional actors and actresses.

A look at the offerings in a recent season will indicate the diversity of plays from the past that are presented: two plays from the Elizabethan period (*Richard II* by Shakespeare and *Volpone* by Jonson); *The Three Sisters* by Chekhov; a nineteenth-century French farce, *Cat Among the Pigeons*, by Georges Feydeau; and two American classics, *Mourning Becomes Electra* by Eugene O'Neill and *Another Part of the Forest* by Lillian Hellman. The variety of this list—representing plays from many countries and periods—is an example of the range of drama available to audiences in many parts of the United States and Europe on a regular basis.

What makes ACT so significant is that it is one of the few American theaters that operates in a true repertory fashion. Its year is divided into two seasons, with four plays rotating nightly in performance during each. As we have already noted, the repertory setup was central to the English-language theater from the Elizabethan era through the nineteenth century. Actors were expected to revive dramas on a moment's notice and stage new ones very quickly. While we today view eight plays in a year as a large repertoire, it is minuscule in comparison to earlier eras. (We might note that there are more active repertory companies in Europe; still, the commercialization of theater worldwide precludes a significant number from developing.) As indicated, many analysts are concerned about the disappearance of the repertory company because it was an ideal training ground for actors, a place for revivals of classics, and a home for new playwrights.

MANY PLAYWRIGHTS: FEW OUTSTANDING PLAYS

Every year, on a weekend in March in Louisville, Kentucky, critics from all parts of North America and Europe (and some from Africa and Asia) gather at the Actors Theater of Louisville (ATL) for the theater's annual festival of new plays. During the year, over 4000 new scripts have been submitted to the theater; from these, eight new plays are chosen for production. Over a three-day period, visitors will see all eight. (Local subscribers to the theater can see the plays at a more leisurely pace.) From mid-morning to late at night, spectators move between a downstairs theater seating 500 to a smaller, 150-seat house on the third floor of an old warehouse building in which part of the theater is located. In the first few years of the festival, a number of new playwrights were given their first major productions. Two of these plays won Pulitzer Prizes: D. L. Coburn's *The Gin Game* and Beth Henley's *Crimes of the Heart.*

This emphasis on new plays points to a paradox in the contemporary theater in the United States, and in many other countries of the world. On one hand, there is a great emphasis on developing new plays. Many theater institutions in the United States—the O'Neill Playwrights Conference in Waterford, Connecticut, Playwrights Horizons in New York City, and the Cricket Theater in Minneapolis—devote their full energies to presenting new plays. In the process, literally thousands of new scripts are read each year. In other words, there is no shortage of plays being written which are also given some form of reading or production. Despite this unprecedented encouragement, though, the present age is not bringing forth major plays.

It is difficult to say what the reasons are—an increasingly fragmented and confusing age which makes it difficult for writers to have a clear vision, a lack of outstanding talent, or some other cause. But it is clear that our age is not producing superior playwrights like those who appeared throughout the modern era until now, such as Ibsen (Norway), Strindberg (Sweden), Chekhov (Russia), Pirandello (Italy), Brecht (Germany), Lorca (Spain), Yeats and O'Casey (Ireland), Giraudoux, Anouilh, and Beckett (France), Shaw (Great Britain), and O'Neill, Williams, and Miller (the United States). The 1980s is not an age of such dramatists. It should be added, however, that although the current plays fall short of being masterpieces, they nevertheless are often provocative, revealing, and moving.

FINE PERFORMERS BUT FEW STARS

Just as there is a great deal of playwriting activity but little outstanding drama, so the modern period is one in which we find many competent, well-trained actors and actresses but few "superstars" of the theater. There are many theater-training programs in the United States, such as the ones in colleges described in the next section. And there are acting schools in the major cities of the country.

The level of acting on Broadway and in the regional theaters ranges from outstanding to mediocre. But the 1980s is not an era of box-office idols such as were found in earlier centuries. In the theater, this is not a time when the actor is glorified to the exclusion of all else, as was the case in the Hellenistic period of ancient Greece or during much of the nineteenth century. There are no Edwin Booths or Sarah Bernhardts on the stage today. The worship of actors and actresses in our day is reserved largely for film and television stars. There is so much recognition value in films and TV—performers are seen by so many people, often as larger than life—that this is where adoration occurs. Even so, the general level of acting is high.

SPECIAL–INTEREST THEATERS

In the previous chapter we referred to the Off-Off-Broadway theater movement in New York City and elsewhere around the country. This movement has continued with great vigor into the 1980s and has become a recognized part of the total theater scene. Theaters of this kind are found in places like Chicago, Atlanta, Seattle, San Francisco, and Los Angeles as well as New York. They have several things in common: they generally operate on a very limited budget and in a small playhouse, which seats anywhere from 50 to 200 people; the theater space itself has usually been converted from a warehouse loft, an old factory, or an abandoned church to serve as a theater; the actors and actresses frequently perform for little or no money.

One important feature of these theaters is that they often serve special-interest groups. By operating on a low budget in a theater with a limited seating capacity, they can survive with audiences who share their interest in a special subject or view of life. Accordingly, there are small theaters of this sort dedicated to many ideas and causes: feminism, radical political philosophies, homosexuality, ethnic cultures, and so forth. Of course, there are also small theaters concentrating on new plays, as mentioned above, and on reviving the classics. Whatever the focus of the individual theater, however, the overall effect is of a rich mixture of theatrical offerings, giving audiences a wide choice of materials. This, too, is a continuing aspect of theater in the 1980s.

COLLEGE, COMMUNITY, AND CHILDREN'S THEATERS

A survey of contemporary theater would not be complete without looking at the vast number of activities that occur among nonprofessionals: those who are training for future careers in the theater; those who participate for their own pleasure or fulfillment but not as their primary career; those who wish to bring theater to groups such as young people and the elderly. We will begin our look at this important segment of theater with a visit to the University of Minnesota.

On a clear, crisp November night, just before Thanksgiving, students and faculty from the University of Minnesota in Minneapolis make their way to the Rarig Center on the west bank of the Mississippi River. This is the theater complex for the University. Off the atriumlike lobby are several theaters: a 500-seat thrust stage, a 500-seat proscenium stage, and a seven-sided arena theater that seats 200. Downstairs is a fourth theater: an experimental space with flexible seating that can accommodate anywhere from 50 to 150 people.

Tonight, members of the college community, as well as local townspeople, have come to see George Bernard Shaw's *Misalliance,* a play written in 1910, about a wealthy manufacturer who feels he gets no respect from his family. He is entertaining the son of his best friend when a Polish woman aviator crashes through the roof of his greenhouse. The men in the play, young and old, proceed to fall in love with the woman, but she gets the best of all of them.

Taking part in the play are students from the University of Minnesota's theater program. In all, about 300 undergraduates and about 100 graduate students are enrolled in one degree program or another.

The acting students have had to work very hard on their British accents and their stylized, well-mannered movements for this production. Other students, in design, have worked on scenery, lights, and costumes, while still others have concentrated on the business side of things: publicity, box office, ticket sales, and ushering. The entire process is a training ground both in theater practices and in the mounting of a polished production for public performance.

College and university theater Theater departments at colleges and universities are a vital segment of contemporary theater in America. These theaters—which serve as a training ground for future artists—are particularly noted for their presentations of the classics. The scene here is from a production of Shaw's comedy Misalliance at the University of Minnesota at Minneapolis. (Photo—Department of Theatre, University of Minnesota.)

This arrangement is typical of colleges and universities throughout the United States. They now provide a major training ground for future performers, directors, designers, technicians, critics, playwrights, and theater administrators. Some programs offer theater as part of an overall liberal arts degree; other institutions have special programs—the bachelor of fine arts degree, for instance—that concentrate heavily on theater courses and practical experience. The most concentrated of all are conservatories that focus entirely on such training. Among these are the American Conservatory Theater mentioned above, the Juilliard School in New York, and the North Carolina School of the Arts in Winston-Salem.

Such programs serve a number of important purposes. As suggested above, they provide fundamental training for future theater professionals. In addition, they help students to cultivate a meaningful interest in theater and provide them with the opportunity to take part in artistic enterprises, an experience that will serve them well in other endeavors in later life.

The use of the university as a training ground for the dramatic arts in the 1980s is an interesting contrast to the training procedures in most other periods of theater history. In the past the most significant means of training the actor was through actual experience as an apprentice or minor performer in a repertory company; actual experience provided the basic lessons. Even the great acting schools were affiliated with theater companies, such as the Paris Conservatoire de Musique, which in the nineteenth century functioned as the training institution for the Comédie Française. Today, with the disappearance of the repertory company, there is little opportunity for the young artist to learn through practice. Universities and colleges, in the United States, are the places that now provide the training and onstage experience, and in many communities they function as significant theatrical institutions.

Children's Theater

Across town from the University of Minnesota, in the southern part of Minneapolis, is the Children's Theater Company (CTC). On an icy January day, a couple of months after *Misalliance* opened, the snow is piled high. It is one of the coldest winters on record in the American mid-west; 40 inches of snow is already on the ground and another 17 inches have fallen during the night. By 10 A.M., however, buses carrying 700 schoolchildren have arrived at the CTC, a modern theater building adjacent to the Minneapolis Institute of Arts.

Inside, they take their places in the 746-seat proscenium theater and wait for the curtain to go up on a production of *Puss in Boots*. The play is a musical adaptation by Sharon Holland of the familiar children's tale. Holland has transposed it from France to New Orleans in the early 1900s. The opening scene is a full-scale musical number called "The Jazziest, Snazziest Cat in Town." The eleven adults in the permanent acting company of the CTC, plus other adults and ten to fifteen children, are onstage for this big number, set in a graveyard. In the story, a man has just died and left all his money to his two oldest sons; the youngest son, Merlis, gets only a cat—but it turns out to be a remarkable cat named Puss. During the course of the show, Merlis and Puss have many adventures in New Orleans: at Mardi Gras, with a voodoo queen, and in a gambling hall. This last is the scene of another large number called "Catmandou."

During the performance the schoolchildren have forgotten the snow and cold outside. They are held spellbound, not only by the performances and musical numbers, but also by the elaborate scenery and costumes, and the striking lighting effects.

The production is an excellent example of a theater phenomenon

*I*mpressive children's theater   *An important segment of theater today is that produced for young audiences. One of the best known producing organizations is the Children's Theater Company of Minneapolis. Shown here is a large production number from a recent production of* Puss In Boots. *This scene—with elaborate sets, costumes, and props—takes place during Mardi Gras in turn-of-the-century New Orleans. (Photo—George Heinrich, courtesy of The Children's Theater Company.)*

found throughout the United States: children's theater. It is presented primarily for young audiences (though in Minneapolis many adults attend too) and performed either by adults or by children themselves. Sometimes, as with CTC, the performers are both adults and children. The CTC has a school in which children of elementary and high school age are enrolled. Many of them take part in the company's productions, but most do not intend to pursue theater as a career. They find it rewarding enough to experience the camaraderie and discipline of putting on productions.

Another form of participatory theater across America is community theater: amateur performances organized to give pleasure to those who take part, strictly as an avocation, and also to provide inexpensive entertainment for audiences.

WESTERN THEATER OUTSIDE THE UNITED STATES

We are concentrating on theater in the United States in this chapter, but this might be an appropriate place to see how our observations apply to theater in the rest of the western world. Though it is rarely on the scale of Broadway—with fewer large theaters filled simultaneously—all the capitals and large cities of Europe and the west have active professional theaters. Some of these are national theaters, such as in London and Paris. Usually there is a mixture of nonprofit theaters—with institutions like the Royal Shakespeare Company—and commercial theater.

In most nations of the western world there are also the equivalent of America's regional theaters: companies in the major and middle-sized cities that produce both new and classic works. In many cities in Europe, there is a tradition of city or state support for such theaters.

In other western countries, too there seems to be the same lack of outstanding drama being written. In some cases, the emphasis on scenic and lighting effects parallels that in the United States. Also, among performers, the most popular stars are from film and television, though in Europe and Great Britain there is frequently more crossover between theater and the other media than there is in the United States. A film or television star will also be a stage star.

There is one important difference between theater in the United States and in other western countries. Programs to encourage new plays and the teaching of theater at regular colleges and universities are far more extensive in the United States than elsewhere. In fact, such programs do not even exist in a number of other countries. Instead, there are acting academies and other institutions devoted exclusively to theater training, but they are not part of a college program.

LIVE THEATER SURVIVES

In the twentieth century the theater has been subjected to a series of unprecedented challenges. First came silent films, then radio, next talking pictures, and finally television. With each new challenge it was assumed that theater would suffer an irreparable setback. After all, each of these media offered drama, and in a form that was much more accessible than in the traditional theater setting.

When talking pictures emerged, for example, it was argued that anyone who went out for entertainment would go to the movies rather than the theater; movies would be cheaper and would offer glamorous stars besides. With television, it was argued that people did not even need to leave their homes to see drama.

Inevitably there have been changes in audience habits. For most of the eighteenth and nineteenth centuries, the theater was the main source of escapist dramatic entertainment: both farce comedies and suspense melodramas. In the 1980s, television, with its situation comedies, provides much of the light entertainment formerly offered by theater, and movies provide horror and suspense stories. Despite these shifts, though, the theater has not suffered in the way predicted. Much to the surprise of the prophets of doom, there is probably more theatrical activity in the United States now, as the survey in the past few pages shows, than at any time since the advent of the movies.

Why is this so? First, because in spite of their similarities, there is a basic difference between theater on the one hand and films and television on the other. This is the presence in theater of the live performer. Both film and television provide *images* or pictures of people, not the real thing. The human contact between the audience and the performers answers a need so profound and so fundamental that it is doubtful that the large screen in the movie theater or the small screen in our living rooms could ever substitute for it. The electricity that flows back and forth between actors and audience—the laughter at comic moments and the hushed silence at serious ones—is irreplaceable.

In Chapter 1 we described the universal impulse that leads every society, where it is not expressly forbidden, to create its own theatrical activity. This need and desire will continue into the future, throughout Europe and the Americas, as well as other parts of the world. It will perpetuate a theater that will exist alongside others, such as the Asian and black theaters to be discussed in Part V.

THE FUTURE

Where will the theater go from here? It is impossible, of course, to answer with any sure knowledge. We can assume, though, that the trends described in this chapter will continue. The theater of the future will no doubt follow the practice of presenting new works alongside a rich mixture of plays from the past. In both writing and production, the theater will take from many sources. It is questionable whether the plays that will be written will match the greatness of the recent past, but playwrights show no sign of abandoning the theater completely, despite the larger financial rewards of films and television.

The theater will survive in a vigorous form despite the challenges posed by the electronic media. At the same time, modern technology will play an important role: in lighting effects, with the use of computer lighting boards, in the shifting of scenery, and in other ways. There will continue to be multimedia experiments, fusing theater with film, television, and dance.

With all the innovations, however, certain things about the theater of the future will be an extension of the theater of the past—the theater we have traced in this book. Theater will be enacted by women and men in person before an audience. The plays they perform will deal primarily with the hopes, fears, agonies, and joys of the human race. That is what theater has focused on from the start, and what it will always focus on; and that will be the source of its appeal as far ahead as we can see.

Summary

The contemporary theater is eclectic. It combines styles and techniques from many sources: the Elizabethan theater, the realistic acting of the late nineteenth and early twentieth century, the ideas of Antonin Artaud and Bertolt Brecht, to name a few. Today's writers and directors take from all these sources when they write or direct a play.

There is a rich storehouse of theater available today: regional professional theaters, college theaters, and other groups perform a wide range of classics from the past on a regular basis. There are also programs to encourage dramatists and to train performers, designers, and administrators. These programs ensure that there will be people to continue the tradition into the future.

The present age is not one of great new drama or of performers who are idolized by the public. Rather it is a period of tremendous activity in writing and producing, in avant-garde, experimental work, and in the revival of classics.

Part Five

The main portion of this volume has been concerned with western theater, from the Greeks to the present. This is the tradition out of which most theater in the United States has grown. Our playwrights, our theater buildings, our acting methods, and our staging techniques derive from the western tradition, as do the plays we still produce. Shakespeare is the most widely produced playwright in America, more so than contemporary dramatists like Tennessee Williams.

Despite the predominance of the western tradition, there are other theaters of importance and sophistication that have grown up independently of western theater, or alongside it. Chief among those that have developed outside the west are the theaters of Asia. In the Introduction we discussed the universal tendency toward theater and observed that it is likely to take hold in any civilization where it is not expressly forbidden by religious or other laws. This was the case in India, China, and Japan, the countries we will focus on in Chapter 15, and also in other Asian countries like Indonesia.

Each of the Asian theaters is unique, but they also have things in common that set them apart from western theater. To name two: they rely much more on dance than our theaters (in many instances Asian theatrical presentations could be called dance-dramas), and they emphasize symbolism. During the past century, a number of western playwrights, directors, and designers have been heavily influenced by the styles and techniques of Asian theater. Among them are the Russian directors Vsevelod Meyerhold and Yevgeny Vakhtangov, the Irish poet and playwright William Butler Yeats, the German dramatist Bertolt Brecht, and the French theorist Antonin Artaud.

The other theater discussed in this section, the black theater, has inherited traditions from Africa and the Caribbean and has combined these with elements of western theater. It is also noteworthy for having a succession of outstanding performers. No knowledge of theater in the United States is complete without an awareness of the important role of black theater.

Chapter Fifteen

THE ASIAN THEATER

The thrust toward theater is so universal that whenever a culture develops, theater is likely to follow. Strong evidence for this is found in Asia. Different forms of theater have grown up throughout the continent, but in this chapter we will look at the theater that evolved in India, China, and Japan. There are similarities among them, but each has its own characteristics.

Anyone who reads about or, better still, is fortunate enough to experience in performance any of the major dramatic forms of Asia will come to realize how varied and how profound the human theatrical experience has been. All of the three great Asian traditions, the Indian, the Chinese, and the Japanese, have created and sustained one form or another of what has been called "total theater." In this type of theater the

Kabuki—stylized Japanese theater *Most Asian theaters, in contrast to those in the west, are highly stylized: some use masks and many incorporate dance. Actors in Japanese kabuki use exaggerated movements and all parts are played by men. Shown here is a demon figure from a kabuki play: note the wild wig, the detailed makeup, and the elaborate robe. (Photo—United Press International.)*

The Asian Theater—*India*

THEATER	Sanskrit drama highly developed	*Natyasastra*, principal critical work on Sanskrit drama; *The Little Clay Cart*		King of the Dark Chamber, Rabindrath Tagore (1861–1941)
	Shakuntala, Kalidasa, best known Sanskrit playwright	Decline of Sanskrit drama	Indian dance drama, puppet and folk plays	

YEAR	*320*	*400*	*600*	*800/900*	*1150*	*1192*	*1526*	*1790*	*1914*

	Gupta dynasty reunites Northern India after 500 years division; golden age of classical Sanskrit			Mogul Empire (until 1761)	
CULTURAL/ POLITICAL		Earliest known use of the zero and decimal	Beginning of Muslim rule		British power established in India

many facets of theatrical art—acting, mime, dancing, music, and text—combine to produce a totality greater than any single element. Western theater in certain phases of its history has known such a synthesis, and many of the modern innovators in Western theater, such as Artaud, Meyerhold, and Brecht, have gone to the Asian theater in order to find techniques that would enable them to move away from modern realistic theater, which is not so all-embracing.

One reason for the development and continued support for this synthesis in Asian theater lies in the fact that the religious roots of the theater are still kept alive in Asia. All three traditions reached a high point of artistic excellence at a time when religion and philosophy were central in each culture, and this level of excellence has kept the focus of the traditional theater at least allied to these realms, even when the societies themselves modernized and changed. The early development of the theater in each of these three great cultures often remained rather obscure until the rise of these high points, which usually came about when writers of poetic and intellectual ability began to create a dramatic tradition in which the text assumed a central place.

In later years, it was usually the word, not the production style, that remained. Japan is unique in that it has preserved many of the ancient acting, dancing, and singing techniques of its traditional theater. In the case of China and India, however, little is known of early performance practice. Still, it is the ancient traditions, interpreted and reinterpreted as the cultures have developed and changed, that have continued to color and shape many later experiments. Each of the three theatrical traditions is unique and self-contained, but all have aspects that may seem most familiar to western spectators who have been exposed to opera where a colorful synthesis of ideas, art, and technique is crucial.

In the nineteenth and twentieth centuries, each of these traditional forms came under the influence of western theater. Ibsen, Strindberg, and Chekhov had as powerful an effect in Bombay, Shanghai, and Tokyo as in Paris, London, and New York. As a result of this influence a modern, spoken theater has developed in each of the three traditions that, as in the west, can hold up a mirror to contemporary consciousness: personal, political, and philosophical.

INDIAN THEATER

The Indian theater represents the most ancient of all the traditions of Asia, and in some ways, it remains the most difficult for modern western audiences to grasp. One of the reasons for this is that almost nothing is reliably known about the way ancient Sanskrit drama was produced. Another is that the metaphysical basis of classical Asian drama is, from a western point of view, more lyrical than dramatic—it is easier to understand as poetry than as theater.

Indian history has been characterized as a succession of immigrations into the Indian subcontinent. Early traces of civilization go back to 3000 B.C. The Aryans, who came into southern India a thousand years later, left behind them works in Sanskrit that constitute the basis of the great Indian literary traditions. By 1000 B.C., scholars believe, such fundamental aspects of Indian civilization as the caste system were already established. Under the caste system, people are classified by heredity. A person must remain in the caste to which he or she was born, and people are forbidden to change occupations or social classes.

Around 400 B.C., Buddhism, the religion of eastern and central Asia that follows the teachings of Buddha, reached a high peak of development. King Asoka, who ruled arout 240 B.C., managed to unite the whole nation under Buddhist rule, but a period of disorder and confusion followed until the Gupta dynasty, around A.D. 320, began to unite the nation again. Hindu culture entered its golden age at this time, and it was during the following centuries that the great Sanskrit dramas were written and performed. Hinduism stresses the belief that soul or spirit is the essence of life. The goal of all people is to achieve a oneness with the supreme World-Soul, known as Brahman. The things of this life do not exist in the same way as Brahman, who is eternal, infinite, and indescribable.

Sanskrit Drama

What remains from the tradition of this Golden Age is a group of plays written in Sanskrit, the language of the noble classes, composed to be performed in various court circles. There are between fifty and sixty plays that can be reliably assigned to this period, and the greatest of them are among the finest works of classical Indian literature.

Although the texts have been preserved, no information remains on how the plays were acted. We do have descriptions of a typical theater in which the plays were performed. It was 96 feet long and 48 feet wide, divided equally into stage and auditorium. The seating capacity was probably about 400. There were four pillars in the auditorium—colored white, yellow, red, and blue—indicating where members of different castes were to sit. A curtain divided the stage into two parts: one part for the action, and the other for dressing rooms and a behind-the-scenes area.

Scenery was evidently not used, although elaborate costumes probably were. Dance, symbolic gesture, and music played an important part in the productions, but again, no specific information concerning performance practices is known. The plays often make use of fixed characters, such as a narrator and a clown. Details concerning how these performers appeared onstage are not available.

The plays themselves usually draw on themes from Indian epic literature. The greatest of all the playwrights from the classic period is doubtless Kalidasa, whose play *Shakuntala* is usually considered the finest drama in classical Indian literature. The play might be described as a lengthy love idyll on various classic themes. It has been known in the west through a variety of translations beginning in the eighteenth century, when Goethe found himself profoundly inspired by Shakuntala. Another play, *The Little Clay Cart*, the authorship of which is uncertain, was composed about 900, and concerns the love between a ruined merchant and a courtesan. Here, politics and humor enliven the style of playwriting, enriching it even further.

These plays were written in the Sanskrit language (although the "lower" characters sometimes speak in a hybrid of local dialect and the classical tongue) and so had little following among the general public, who could not understand them. From the few records available, most performances were given by troupes invited to perform at the courts of noblemen, and performing spaces were arranged in courtyards and similar areas.

Indian Dramatic Criticism

Along with playwriting, dramatic criticism also reached a peak during the great period of the Sanskrit theater. The fact that the ideas and ideals of that period were written down in a definitive form established an important link with later traditions. The greatest work of dramatic criticism of the period is doubtless the *Natyasastra*, often attributed to the early dramatist Bharata but actually of a later date, probably the eighth or ninth century A.D. Indeed, many Indian critics have said that the

$\mathcal{K}$ALIDASA
(A.D. 373?–415)

While the Roman empire was beginning its final decay, the thriving civilization of India was producing a highly sophisticated and poetic Sanskrit drama. The most renowned of the Indian dramatists was the poet Kalidasa, author of the most famous Sanskrit play, *Shakuntala.*

Though his play is acknowledged to be a masterpiece of Indian drama, almost nothing is known about Kalidasa's life. Many scholars have attempted to establish his date of birth and to learn details of his life, but they have had little success. At one point, it was thought that he lived in the ninth century A.D., but recent studies have placed his writings in the late fourth and early fifth centuries. It is possible that he lived at the court of King Chandragupta II, in the city of Uj Jain.

There is no doubt, however, that *Shakuntala* is a masterwork of Sanskrit drama. In seven acts, the play recounts the romance of King Dushyanta and Shakuntala, the foster daughter of a hermit, who secretly marry and then are subjected to a long separation brought about by the curse of an irate sage. After many trials, the lovers are reunited and the king finally meets his son and heir.

Subtitled *The Recovered Ring*, the play features story elements similar to Wagner's *The Ring of the Nibelung*: a private marriage, forgetfulness caused by a curse, and a magic ring. The drama also has elements of Indian philosophic, religious, aesthetic, and psychological thought. Like all Sanskrit dramas, it mixes serious and comic elements and includes a large number of locations and characters. Kalidasa's power as a lyric poet is shown in the description of the king's journey in his chariot and in the account of Shakuntala caring for her plants and pet fawn.

While *Shakuntala* follows the traditional patterns of Sanskrit drama, it is set apart from other plays by Kalidasa's delicate lyricism. He also wrote several poems which mingle love, nature imagery, and religion, and two other plays: *Malavike and Agnimitra*, a courtly comedy; and *Vikrama and Urvashi*, a heroic mythological drama.

Natyasastra represents a perfect philosophical description of Kalidasa's dramas. In the course of this complex treatise, the author defines the quality refered to as *rasa*, or a "flavor," which permits the spectator to surrender himself in sympathy to a dramatic situation that corresponds to a particular powerful feeling that the spectator possesses within himself. The theater thus can serve as a means toward enlightenment; art becomes a way to move toward metaphysics and the divine.

The *Natyasastra* also serves as a kind of dictionary on theatrical practice. In an abstract way, every element of the complex ancient theater is treated, from gesture and posture to music, dance, voice, and so forth. Types of characters and categories of plays are discussed, and all this specific information is related in turn to a series of metaphysical principles which, although perhaps difficult for the modern reader to grasp, are nevertheless challenging, even humbling, to read. At its best, the *Natyasastra* is one of the finest works of theatrical theory and criticism ever written.

The Theater Following Sanskrit Drama

The period of Sanskrit drama—the plays themselves and the dramatic criticism—had faded by the end of the ninth century. By the twelfth century, the Arabs had begun to invade India, and in 1206 they established the Delhi sultanate. With this latest series of invasions, the Hindu Sanskrit traditions disappeared. Under Islamic rule, theatrical activities were not encouraged, and the old ways of performing were no longer maintained among educated people.

Folk dramas, however, had always been popular in the many vernacular languages, and the continued performance of such works, while never on a high artistic level, helped to keep certain traditions alive. Many of these folk plays have continued to the present day. They used the same traditional epic materials found in the Sanskrit dramas, but they were usually composed by groups of anonymous dramatists, and the scripts, assuming that they were even written down, have not been preserved. Such plays were extremely eclectic and emphasized spectacle rather than metaphysical profundity.

Also popular among the wide public were dance dramas that took up aspects of the Indian myths. In the performance of such dramas, movement, rather than the spoken word, was strongly emphasized. An interesting form of dance drama prominent in southwestern India during the past three centuries is *kathakali*. Presented on a stage approximately 16 feet square covered with a canopy of flowers, it is produced at night by torchlight. It heightens elements of Sanskrit drama, with violence and death being presented onstage in dance and pantomime. The stories revolve around clashes between good and evil, with good always winning. Featured are the passions of demons and gods, as well as extraordinary

athakali—Indian dance drama *Much of Asian drama contains a large element of dance. A prime example is Kathakali, a dramatic form found in southwestern India. In Kathakali, stories of strong passions, the furies of the gods, and the loves and hates of extraordinary humans are told in dance and mime. Notice the heavy makeup and stylized headresses and costumes. (Photo—Clifford R. Jones, The Asia Society.)*

human beings. A language of 500 or more gestural signs has been developed to tell the stories.

In the sixteenth century, India was forced to endure still another set of conquests, this time by Europeans. This period of conquest began with the Portuguese and continued through the British, who, under Robert Clive, established British rule in India in 1757. It was during the time of British colonial domination in the nineteenth century that a resurgence of Indian drama began. The British, so fond of the drama, had opened theaters of their own, and the Indians were eventually able to observe troupes of British and European actors, whose work served as a model for creation of their own modern, spoken theater. Also, a number of Indian intellectuals thought that they could employ traditional Indian themes as a way to increase a sense of nationhood among the population.

By the turn of the century, Ibsen and Chekhov began to have the same power over Indian intellectuals that they were to have in China and Japan. Perhaps the greatest of the Indian writers influenced by modern

$\mathcal{R}$ABINDRANATH TAGORE
(1861–1941)

The most noted of India's modern playwrights, Rabindranath Tagore blended the Indian and western traditions in his fifty plays. Though his methods were eclectic, Tagore's plays reaffirm the traditional values of Indian life.

As the youngest of the fourteen children of Debendranath Tagore, a prominent philospher and social reformer, the playwright received an excellent education, particularly in Hindu philosophy. He began writing verses while still at home and published his first important collection of poetry, *Manasi*, in 1890. In 1891, Tagore became the manager of his father's estates in Shileida and Sayadpur. Through close contact with the villagers he learned of their lives and problems and also of the traditions of the Bengali folk drama.

Tagore's plays were written in Bengali and cover a wide variety of styles and subjects. *Nature's Revenge* (1884) uses the nature imagery of Sanskrit poetry. *The King of the Dark Chamber* and *Rakta Karaui* (1924) are allegories. In *Vis Barjan* (1890) he invents a myth to focus on the issue of nonviolence. *Last Cause* (1904) and *The Bachelors' Club* (1904)

show his ability to write realistic comedy and satire. Many of his later works, such as *Chitrangada* (1936), are dance dramas, a form Tagore came to favor in later life. His works contain song, mime, dance, and lyrical verse, and are tinged with mysticism. Because of these elements, English translations of his plays, even those Tagore did himself, seem stilted and unnatural.

At his school in Santiniketan, Tagore directed and acted in his plays. Much of his international reputation comes from his numerous collections of poetry and short stories and his lectures in Europe, America, and Asia. Tagore received the Nobel Prize for literature in 1913 and was knighted in 1915, but he surrendered the title in 1919 to protest the Amritsar massacre, in which British troops killed nearly 400 Indians during an outbreak of rioting and mass demonstrations. In 1924 he founded the Visva-Bharati University in Santiniketan as a center for Indian and international culture. Since his death in 1941, Tagore's reputation in India as a dramatist has grown.

European theater and traditional Indian theater was Rabindranath Tagore, whose fifty plays, some in modern style and some in a more traditional mode, formed the basis and inspiration for much of the best work that has followed. While his plays had only a certain vogue in the west, Tagore is regarded as a classic writer in Indian, and attempts to stage his elusive and poetic dramas—which theatrical practitioners in the west have difficulty with—have continued year after year.

After World War I, Mahatma Gandhi, an Indian leader, initiated a campaign of passive resistance against the British, at which point British censors became increasingly strict in their suppression of any suggestion of anti-British sentiment expressed on the stage. Few serious dramas were composed during the 1930s and 1940s. With the coming of independence in 1947, however, a wide variety of plays of all types, ranging from avant-garde experiments to a series of attempts to revive the ancient traditions of Sanskrit drama (presented, of necessity, in various modern versions), have made the contemporary world of Indian theater a complex and intense one. In all of this activity, the influence of the dance remains paramount, and it is perhaps to the dance that Indian theater will always look for its ultimate inspiration.

CHINESE THEATER

The civilization of China can be traced back to at least 2000 B.C., when a unified culture spread over large parts of the area we now refer to as the People's Republic of China. The Shang dynasty (ca. 1500 B.C.–1000 B.C.) represents the first period of rule that can be authenticated through artifacts and documents. During the succeeding turbulent Zhou dynasty (ca. 1000 B.C.–250 B.C.), Confucius, Laozi, and Mencius, three of the greatest Chinese philosophers, lived and wrote. By 200 B.C., the centralized imperial system had been developed, and China was provided with a central government that continued to remain effective through many long periods of stability down to modern times.

The early development of the theater, like many other forms of art in China, was linked to the patronage of the imperial court. Popular forms of theater may have flourished as well, of course, but no records of early folk performances survive. Records of court entertainments, however, go back as far as the fifth century B.C., and such diverse activities as skits, pantomimes, juggling, singing, and dancing are frequently mentioned in ancient chronicles. The court of the emperors during the Tang period (A.D. 618–906) was one of the high points of world culture. At this time there was a kind of actors' training institute in the capital referred to as the "Pear Garden." Details of activities and performances there have not been preserved, but a tradition of training theatrical performers was firmly established with the Pear Garden.

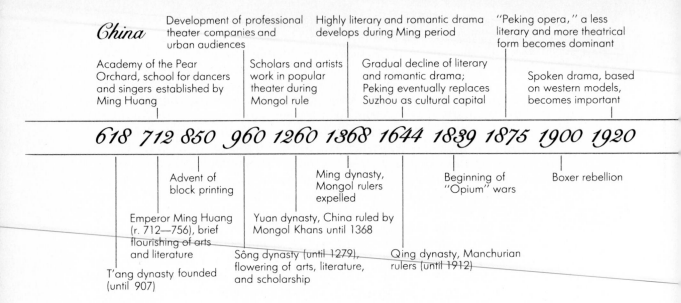

China

Development of professional theater companies and urban audiences

Highly literary and romantic drama develops during Ming period

"Peking opera," a less literary and more theatrical form becomes dominant

Academy of the Pear Orchard, school for dancers and singers established by Ming Huang

Scholars and artists work in popular theater during Mongol rule

Gradual decline of literary and romantic drama; Peking eventually replaces Suzhou as cultural capital

Spoken drama, based on western models, becomes important

618 712 850 960 1260 1368 1644 1839 1875 1900 1920

Advent of block printing

Ming dynasty, Mongol rulers expelled

Beginning of "Opium" wars

Boxer rebellion

Emperor Ming Huang (r. 712—756), brief flourishing of arts and literature

Yuan dynasty, China ruled by Mongol Khans until 1368

T'ang dynasty founded (until 907)

Sông dynasty (until 1279), flowering of arts, literature, and scholarship

Qing dynasty, Manchurian rulers (until 1912)

In the Sông dynasty (960–1279), which preceded the coming of the Mongols, various court entertainments contributed much to the development of the so-called variety plays. In addition to the court records, there are other documents recording the existence of traveling theatrical troupes, some fixed playhouses, and theatrical activity that involved not only actors, dancers, and singers but shadow puppets and marionettes. Low comedy was popular, and the effect must have been, in Chinese terms, something akin to vaudeville. The synthesis of art and the popular tradition was to come in the dramas of the Yuan period (1280–1368), which followed the Sông.

Theater in the Yuan Dynasty

The Yuan dynasty, well-known in the west through the writings of the great Italian explorer Marco Polo, was ruled over not by a Chinese emperor but by the Mongol Kublai Khan, whose grandfather Genghis Khan had conquered China. The Mongol rulers, although tolerating many Chinese customs, nevertheless dismantled much of the traditional bureaucracy. Ironically, this turned out to be an important asset in the development of the Chinese theater. Until this time, the highly educated literati (literary intellectuals) composed essays and poetry of the highest quality but disdained the composition of plays as beneath their dignity. With the coming of the Mongols, many of the literati were no longer employed by the government and took up literary and theatrical pursuits as a way of making a living. In this way, high art and the popular theatrical tradition could meet. Modern scholars have often compared the Chinese theater in this period to the Elizabethan theater in England, for in both cases a complex mixture of cultural influences produced a rich outpouring of theatrical accomplishments.

The plays perfected in the Yuan dynasty were usually written in four acts, or, perhaps more accurately, in four song sequences, since the plays used a great deal of music. Rather than writing specifically for the dramas, however, playwrights composed their texts to suit the rhythms and meters of popular music already known to the audience. (This was similar to the way in which John Gay composed his ballad opera, *The Beggar's Opera*, in eighteenth-century England.) Usually the protagonist sang all the music in any given act. The poetic content of the plays was considered the central element in their success.

Because of the lyrical nature of these dramas, a small number of characters was employed, and subplots and other complexities were avoided. Unfortunately, none of the music has survived. Accounts from the Yuan period show that the topics chosen by the playwrights ranged from stories about love and romance to religious and historical dramas, plots with domestic and social themes, crime and lawsuit dramas, and themes involving bandit-heroes, in a Robin Hood vein.

Perhaps the most famous of the plays from this period that have survived is *The Romance of the Western Chamber*, actually a whole cycle of plays, by Wang Shifu (fl. late thirteenth century). These dramas chronicle the trials of two lovers—a handsome young student and a lovely young girl of good family—who became in turn the models for thousands of imitations down to the present century. The plays contain a certain amount of adventure and a good deal of superlative poetry.

Another exceedingly popular play that has survived is called *The Orphan of Chao*, which deals with matters of vengeance, sacrifice, and loyalty. *The Orphan of Chao* was one of the first Chinese plays known in the west, as a version of it was translated into French in 1735 and was adapted for the French stage by Voltaire.

Another well-known Yuan drama, *The Story of the Lime Pen*, is a great example of the lawsuit-and-trial genre in which a clever judge, in Solomon-like fashion, frees an innocent person accused of a crime. When the modern-day German playwright Bertolt Brecht saw a version of the play (freely adapted and translated into German), he was so intrigued with the theme that he produced his own version in *The Caucasian Chalk Circle*.

Despite the fact that many of these texts survive and have been admired down to the present day, relatively little is known concerning the way in which they were performed. Contemporary spectators left few records of their reactions, perhaps because theatergoing was regarded as an activity beneath the notice of the highly educated. Nevertheless, in recent years, careful scholarship has managed to piece together a certain amount of information on theater presentations. Professional actors and actresses performed, and each played both male and female roles on occasion. Some of the actresses even performed for private entertainments at the palace, and the stories of their various affairs in high society were as eagerly sought out as the stories about the activities of film and television stars today. The actors were organized into troupes, some of which were run by women.

There is some variance among the meager bits of information that remain concerning the theaters used for these performances. Most seem to have been built for outdoor use and were not roofed over. Curtains and such properties as swords and fans were employed, but there is no evidence that any scenery was provided. Much of the color of the performances came from the use of elaborate costumes. Some of the stylized robes, which are illustrated in art works of the time, resemble those used in the Peking opera even now. Makeup was also important and was evidently applied in a heavily stylized fashion.

Theater in the Ming Dynasty

By the end of the Yuan period, the level of accomplishment in the theater was very high and drama had become firmly established as a respectable artistic form. With the overthrow of the Mongols, however, and the establishment of the Ming dynasty (1368–1644), a Chinese emperor was restored to the throne. At this point, the traditional patterns of social behavior were restored; highly educated scholars were still able to write plays, but they tended to confine their efforts more and more to the composition of dramas that would please the elite. The theater, because of its very legitimacy, tended to become ornate and artificial; it lost contact with the broad mass of the public, which had originally supported it.

What had in the Yuan dynasty been an active theater, responsive to general audiences, now became a kind of "literary drama," which revealed an emphasis on poetry and an aversion to sustained and powerful dramatic action. The structure of the plays often became far more complex than that of the Yuan dramas; while only one actor sang in each act of the Yuan plays, several actors were now permitted to sing during an act, and the instrumental accompaniments became very elaborate.

One of the earliest and best plays written in this expanded form was the drama *Lute Song* by Gao Ming (ca. 1301–1370), which dealt with questions of family loyalties in a woman those husband had abandoned her for political reasons. The play shows strong characterizations and beautiful poetry. *Lute Song* has been popular ever since its composition, and the story of this faithful wife even managed to reach Broadway in a musical comedy version, also called *Lute Song*, written for Mary Martin in 1946.

Various attempts during the Ming dynasty to create drama of distinction climaxed in the works of Li Yu, a scholar who, having failed his examinations, became instead a playwright, theater critic, and impresario. His writings on the theater—in which he dealt with such matters

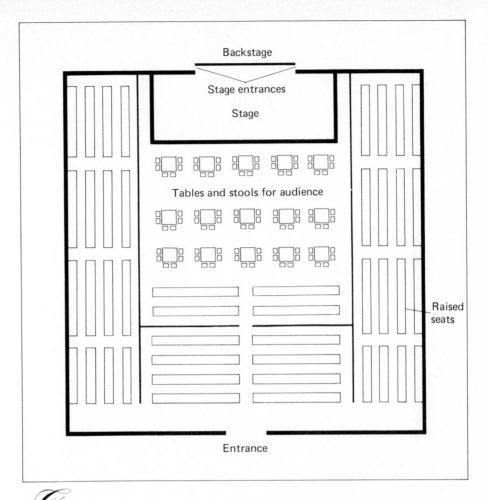

Backstage

Stage entrances

Stage

Tables and stools for audience

Raised seats

Entrance

$\mathcal{G}$round plan of traditional Chinese theater *Diagrammed here is the arrangement for seating in Chinese theater for the period from the seventeenth through the nineteenth centuries. Before that, performances were held in teahouses and when permanent theaters were built tables with chairs around them were retained in the section nearest the stage. Women and commoners sat at the sides and back.*

as plot construction, dialogue, music, and versification—are considered the greatest in the history of Chinese dramatic criticism. His interest was basically in entertainment for the upper classes, and in these terms his plays succeeded brilliantly. During this period, however, the theater, which was heavily patronized by the rich, began to lose all real contact with the larger public, and its vitality seeped away.

By the middle of the sixteenth century, the Manchu peoples had begun to advance southward into northern China, and in the middle of the next century, like the Mongols before them they conquered the

$\mathcal{L}$I YU
(1611–ca. 1680)

China's first important drama critic, Li Yu, believed that a playwright should write clearly, with the mass audience in mind, and should be well versed in practical stage knowledge. These conclusions were based on his own experience as a popular playwright.

Li Yu had turned to the theater to earn his living after several failures to pass the provincial examinations for government service. To support his forty wives and his numerous concubines and children, he and his company of singing girl-actresses traveled around the country, seeking the patronage of local mandarins. Often, his troupe was charged with corrupting the morals of young men because of the beauty and skills of the young actresses. Though he was a friend of many influential men, he was forced to sell his home and worked as a landscape gardener several times to pay his debts.

As a playwright, Li Yu was criticized by contemporary Chinese literary figures for his dramatic style. He wrote his plays for entertainment and placed little emphasis on the poetic songs that the other playwrights favored. Instead, he developed well-made comedies of situation with intricate plot structures and sophisticated dialogue. Rather than borrow his material from standard literary sources, Li created original plots based on the lives of the common people. He was particularly skilled at writing strong female characters for his girl-actresses. Most of his notable plays, including *Ordained by Heaven*, *Be Circumspect in Conjugal Relationships*, and *The Error of the Kite*, revolve around romantic themes.

In his dramatic criticism Li championed the methods and knowledge he gained as a practicing playwright but exerted little influence on his fellow dramatists. He was also supposedly an expert on painting, music, poetry, architecture, feminine charm and the sexual arts, travel, recreation, diet, hygiene, and furniture. Li Yu's plays and his extensive knowledge made him a popular author in both China and Japan.

he Peking Opera   A highly formalized type of theater, Peking Opera was developed in China in the nineteenth century. It is not like western grand opera, but is popular entertainment that offers plays filled with song, dance, and acrobatics. It makes wide use of symbols—with a table standing for a mountain—and is performed in costumes such as those in the scene shown here. (Photo—Wide World.)

country and set up a period of foreign rule that lasted until the dissolution of the empire in 1912. The Manchu rulers enjoyed Chinese culture, including theater, and continued to support the sort of lavish literary productions that had become the tradition among the elite. On the other hand, popular theater was often suppressed, and the scripts destroyed, for political or moral reasons.

The Peking Opera

In the nineteenth century, elements of the folk theater and other genres close to the ordinary people formed the basis for the development of a truly popular theater called in the west the Peking opera, one of the most colorful and striking theatrical forms now practiced in Asia. Though referred to as opera, this form is not like western grand opera, but combines music, theater, and dance in its own unique way. Because of its origins in popular entertainment, the Peking opera has little to offer in terms of high literary merit or philosophical speculation. The long traditions, however, of popular singing, acrobatics, and acting preserved in this form do give insight into the high development of performance techniques in traditional Chinese theater. The plays or skits involve elaborate and colorful conventions of makeup, movement, and voice production.

In staging, the Peking opera stresses the symbolic. The only furniture on the stage is usually a table and several chairs, but these few items are used with imagination. Depending on the way they are arranged or referred to, the table and chairs may represent a dining hall, a court of justice, or a throne room. The table may stand for a cloud, a mountain, or any high place. A tripod on the table holding incense indicates a palace. When the script calls for a long journey, the performers walk in a circle about the stage. This creative way of using the stage has impressed many western dramatists, among them Bertolt Brecht, mentioned above, and the American playwright Thornton Wilder, author of *Our Town*.

Well before the turn of the century, the vitality of the Peking opera had made it the most popular form of traditional theater in China, and the stars of this genre, notably the great Mei Lanfang, became stars of enormous reputation not only in China but in the west.

The Modern Chinese Theater

It was also at this time that increased contact with the west by Chinese scholars and intellectuals led eventually to the development of a great curiosity concerning western drama. Realizing that the theater could deal with ideas as well as portray sentiment, young students in urban centers began to translate and stage plays by Ibsen, Chekhov, and Shaw as a means of educating the public in regard to social and political problems. Many of the writers and actors interested in this "spoken drama," as they called it, had been impressed by the possibilities of such theater while living in Japan, where an interest in European theater had developed even earlier. With the help of Japanese colleagues, Chinese students living in Tokyo staged versions in modern Chinese of *La Dame aux Camélias* by Dumas fils and of *Uncle Tom's Cabin*.

After the 1911 revolution, when the Qing Dynasty was overthrown, Shanghai, the most westernized of the large cities, became the focal point for a growing interest in creating a tradition of modern Chinese spoken drama. Many of the playwrights were leftist in political orientation and wrote on social themes. The greatest of the playwrights in this period was doubtless Cao Yu, whose dramas were written before the Second World War. *Thunderstorm* and *Peking Man* both show a good grasp of modern dramaturgy and a burning sense of social injustice. Novelists and other

*M*EI LANFANG
(1894–1961)

Mei Lanfang, the most renowned modern performer of Peking opera, preserved and expanded its traditions in his work. Acclaimed throughout the world for his portrayals of female characters, he was one of the first oriental theater artists to influence the development of western theater.

Like most actors of Peking opera, Mei came from a family of performers. Both his father and his grandfather had specialized in the *tan*, or female roles. Mei began his acting training at eight, and when he was ten he made his stage debut. Through his technical perfection and precise characterizations, he enhanced the importance of the female roles, which had been considered secondary, in Peking opera. Mei worked with the playwright and theater scholar Qi Rushan to expand and revise the traditional repertoire and to introduce historical accuracy in the costumes and dances.

In 1919 and 1925, Mei toured Japan, where his performances and innovations were greatly admired. When he performed in the United States in 1930, he was the guest of Douglas Fairbanks and Mary Pickford in Hollywood. He also met Charlie Chaplin, whose comic abilities he enthusiastically admired. During his tour of Russia in 1935, Mei met both Konstantin Stanislavski and Bertolt Brecht. Mei's acting was one of the most important influences on the development of Brecht's acting theories.

After the Japanese invasion of China in 1937, Mei refused to act and grew a mustache so that it was impossible for him to perform the female roles. Though it meant financial hardship he continued his retirement until the Japanese surrendered in 1945. After the war, when he returned to performing, he made several films, including *Bitter Life and Death* (1947). Throughout his career, he trained many performers, including some of the first actresses to appear in Peking opera. Mei continued to perform until 1959 and died two years later.

Eastfoto

*C*AO YU
(born 1910)

The pioneers of a western-style "new drama" in China had to rely on translations and adaptations of foreign plays because of the lack of native modern playwrights. With his play *The Thunderstorm* (1933), Cao Yu became the most important Chinese writer of the new drama.

Cao Yu's interest in theater went back to his high school years in Hupei province, where he was active in experimental theater groups. As a university student in Peking he studied English and read much western drama, including the plays of Aeschylus, Euripides, Shakespeare, Ibsen, Chekhov, and O'Neill. He also did some acting and once played Nora in Ibsen's *A Doll's House*.

The Thunderstorm was finished before Cao Yu graduated from the university. Although the play was influenced by O'Neill's *Mourning Becomes Electra* and Aeschylus's *The Oresteia*, Cao's play is Chinese in character and action. In skillful dialogue, he tells of a complex series of family relationships that result in suicide and madness. The play also shows the disintegration of the traditional social and family structure and the conflicts between the rich and the poor. Initially produced at a university in Shanghai, the play became a popular success in 1936 with its production by the China Traveling Drama Troupe.

Cao's next play, *Sunrise* (1935), dealing with sex and the conflict between honest workers and dishonest speculators, won China's annual literary prize. During the next ten years, he wrote a series of plays which dealt with contemporary problems and the conflict between the old and new standards of society, dramas that enhanced his reputation as one of China's leading playwrights.

At the invitation of the State Department, Cao visited the United States in 1946. The political turmoil in China after World War II prompted him to quit writing, and it was five years before he returned to teaching at Shanghai's Experimental Drama School. His first play for the People's Republic was *Bright Skies* (1956), the story of how the doctors at the Peking Medical College serve the people and root out American subversive influences. Though his later works, including several plays on ancient Chinese history, are not as forceful as his first dramas, Cao Yu is still a leader of the modern Chinese theater.

writers also began to compose plays, among them Mao Dun and Lao She, whose play *Teahouse,* written in 1957, provides a series of remarkable glimpses into the social deterioration of China before the Communist victory in 1949.

After the civil war and the coming to power of Mao Zedong, spoken drama continued to be written, but additional emphasis was given to the traditional forms of popular theater. These were familiar in the country-side and served as a means of carrying the message of the government to remote corners of the country. During the cultural revolution, which began in 1966, theatrical activities were more restricted, particularly in the area of spoken drama; increasing emphasis was placed on a few dance-dramas, elaborately staged and danced, that had a heavy ideological or propaganda content. At present, however, in the current period of liberalization, both the spoken drama and traditional theater are again flourishing, and their hold on the public and the professional theater world remains unshaken. If all goes well, the years to come should show a new flowering of both the new tradition and the old.

JAPANESE THEATER

While the civilization of Japan is younger than that of China, her heritage is a long and complex one. The origins of the Japanese people are obscure, but anthropologists have found artifacts suggesting migrations from such diverse areas as Siberia, Korea, south China, and southeast Asia. We know that by the fifth century A.D., the southern portions of the country were consolidated and a series of capitals were established in the vicinity of present-day Kyoto. At the time, the Japanese followed a religion closely allied to nature and spirit worship called Shinto, or the Way of the Gods. With the growing influence of the Tang dynasty in China (A.D. 618–906) on the Japanese aristocracy, the Buddhist religion, which was more sophisticated than Shinto in both ritual and doctrine, became a prevailing influence first in court circles, then in the country as a whole. Influences of both Shinto and Buddhism were strong in the development of the theater in Japan.

The earliest recorded theatrical activities are the court entertainments of the Heian period (A.D. 794–1195). These entertainments were influenced by Chinese models, thus providing the only link—and a very remote one—between the two traditions. Later, somewhat similar sorts of performances formed part of annual Shinto and Buddhist ceremonies. These were usually of a popular nature and included such activities as juggling, skits, and dancing.

The first great period in the history of the Japanese theater occurred in the fourteenth century, not long after similar developments in China. The sudden and remarkable development of the *noh* theater, one of the three great traditional forms of Japanese theater, came about when

The Asian Theater — Japan

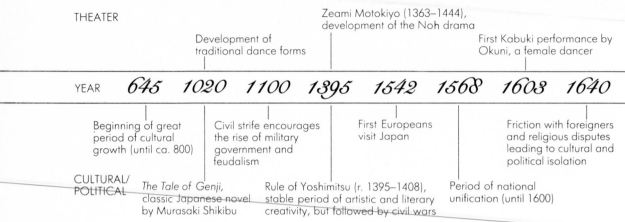

THEATER		Development of traditional dance forms		Zeami Motokiyo (1363–1444), development of the Noh drama			First Kabuki performance by Okuni, a female dancer
YEAR	645	1020	1100	1395	1542	1568	1603 1640
		Beginning of great period of cultural growth (until ca. 800)		Civil strife encourages the rise of military government and feudalism	First Europeans visit Japan		Friction with foreigners and religious disputes leading to cultural and political isolation
CULTURAL/ POLITICAL		The Tale of Genji, classic Japanese novel by Murasaki Shikibu		Rule of Yoshimitsu (r. 1395–1408), stable period of artistic and literary creativity, but followed by civil wars	Period of national unification (until 1600)		

popular stage traditions and high learning joined forces. Despite similarities in theatrical developments, however, there were no direct connections between Japan and China at this time, and there were significant differences in the ways theater emerged in the two cultures. For example, whereas the Chinese upper classes in the Yuan period often disdained theater, well-known, powerful personalities, both political and artistic, shaped the noh theater in Japan. For this reason the documentation concerning the development of the noh is far more complete than that for the development of the Yuan drama.

The Noh Theater

In the fourteenth century in Japan there were a number of roving troupes of actors who performed in a variety of styles, some of which were vulgar and popular, some of which showed certain artistic pretensions. One of the latter troupes was directed by the actor Kan'ami (1333–1384), whose son Zeami was one of the finest child actors in Japan. A performance by the troupe was seen by Ashikaga Yoshimitsu (1358–1408), the shogun of Japan, a man of wealth, prestige, and enormous enthusiasm for the arts. Fascinated by what he saw, he arranged for Zeami to have a court education in order to improve the quality of his art. When Zeami succeeded his father as head of the troupe, it remained attached to the shogun's court in Kyoto. With a patron of this caliber, Zeami was able to set aside problems of finance and devote himself to all aspects of theater: the composition of plays, training of actors, and the constant refining of his own acting style, the outlines of which had been inherited from his gifted father. Under Zeami's direction, the noh became the dominant

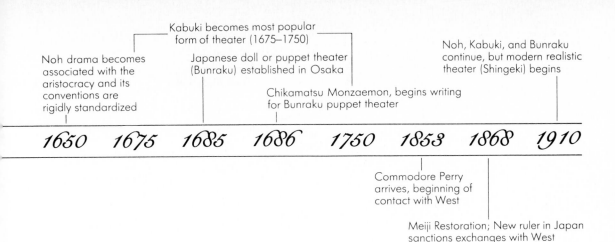

Noh drama becomes associated with the aristocracy and its conventions are rigidly standardized

Kabuki becomes most popular form of theater (1675–1750)

Japanese doll or puppet theater (Bunraku) established in Osaka

Chikamatsu Monzaemon, begins writing for Bunraku puppet theater

Noh, Kabuki, and Bunraku continue, but modern realistic theater (Shingeki) begins

1650   1675   1685   1686   1750   1853   1868   1910

Commodore Perry arrives, beginning of contact with West

Meiji Restoration; New ruler in Japan sanctions exchanges with West

form of serious theater in his generation, and it retained that role well past 1600, when it was supplanted in the popular tastes by *bunraku* and then *kabuki.*

The noh, as perfected by Zeami, was and is a remarkably sucessful attempt to create an integrated synthesis of various theatrical forms into one total experience. Actors (there were no actresses in Zeami's theater), trained from childhood, became adept in singing, acting, dancing, and mime. The plays they performed were remarkably sophisticated in language and content, and all were constructed around a definite series of organizational principles based on musical, psychological, and mimetic (or imitative) movements which move gradually from a slow to a fast tempo as a play progresses. Many of the greatest noh plays were written by Zeami himself, and a number of these are still being performed in the active repertory.

The stories deemed appropriate for noh plays often came from literary or historical sources, particularly the famous novel of Heian court life, Lady Murasaki's *The Tale of Genji,* written around 1220. Another important source is *The Tale of the Heike,* a chronicle of the devastating civil wars that destroyed the power of the aristocracy in Japan at the end of the Heian period in 1185. Either literary or historical characters were generally chosen from the many characters already familiar to the audience. The play reveals some working-out of the various passions felt by that character, who often appears as a ghost or spirit.

Roles in noh are divided into that of the *shite,* or main character, who is often masked, the *waki,* or explainer, and the *tsure,* or accompanying role. There are various types of smaller parts as well, including a *kyogen,*

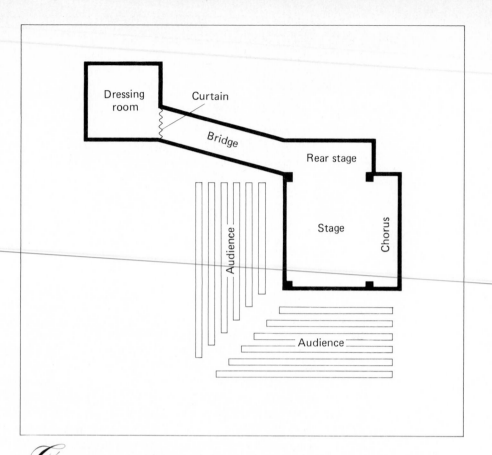

*G*round plan of traditional noh theater *The noh theater of Japan—the stylized theater originally for the upper classes—began nearly 600 years ago. It was performed outdoors; a ramp at the left led from a dressing room to the wooden platform stage. Spectators sat on two sides of the stage, to the left and in front.*

or comic character. A typical play is divided into two parts. In the first part, for example, a Buddhist priest, on a pilgrimage, will visit a famous site, such as a tree or a gravestone, related to the life of the main character. The priest may find there some old person who will say something of the legend of the chief character and then disappear. In the second part of the play, the chief character will appear, reveal to the priest that the old person in the first part had actually been himself in disguise, and then go on to describe some profound experience in his or her life, usually ending this recitation with a dance or other powerful conclusion. Generally the latter half of the finest plays provides an unusual opportunity to combine great poetry, stirring movements, and moving music.

The elegance, mystery, and beauty of the noh have fascinated the

ZEAMI MOTOKIYO
(1363–1443)

Over 500 years after his death Zeami Motokiyo is still considered to be the most important figure in the history of the Japanese noh theater, a complex form of classical dance drama favored by the aristocracy. A gifted actor, Zeami brought new prestige to noh, and his plays are still an important part of the noh repertory. He was most influential, however, as a theorist, for in his writings he established the aesthetic and philosophical basis of noh theater.

His father, Kan'ami, was a talented noh actor and manager, known for his improvements in production methods and for his plays. Zeami began his training to be an actor while he was still a child, and when he was 11 attracted the attention of the shogun. Thereafter he enjoyed the shogun's patronage and protection.

Zeami became the director of the troupe following his father's death in 1384. He continued to improve noh, borrowing elements of other, earlier, forms of dance drama. His 200 plays, 124 of which remain in the noh repertory, incorporated his innovations. He also began writing on the theory and philoso-

phy of noh, ideas that were heavily influenced by his study of Zen.

In his several volumes of theoretical works, Zeami developed the concept of *yugen*, the mysterious, inner heart or spirit behind the outward form, which is the aim of noh performances. (Another definition of *yugen* might be philosophical and physical gracefulness.) These theoretical writings remained secret, however, for they were written to instruct his son and pupil, Motomasa.

Though Zeami was at the height of his acting power in 1408, he and his troupe lost the court patronage when his friend, the shogun Yoshimitsu, died. Zeami continued to perform and to write until 1422, when he gave the troupe to his son and became a Buddhist monk.

A new shogun made Zeami chief court musician in 1424, but he lost that post to his nephew in 1429 when another shogun took office. Motomasa died young leaving Zeami with no direct heir to inherit his writings on noh theory. At the age of 72, he was exiled to the island of Sado for political reasons, but three years later he returned to Kyoto, where he died in 1443.

A noh performance today   The traditional noh theater is still performed in Japan today. The original outdoor theater has been moved, intact, indoors. There is still the entry ramp at the left, the platform stage with a pine tree painted at the back, and the spectators at the left and in the center. (Photo—Todashi Kimura, The Japan Foundation.)

Japanese since the time of Zeami, and the tradition, passed on from teacher to disciple, has been carried on to this day. In most of the larger Japanese cities, noh can be seen in excellent performances by troupes whose traditions go back to the fourteenth century, surely a remarkable legacy. There have been changes in performance practice since the time of Zeami (for one thing, scholars have established, performances now are much more stately and take a good deal more time than in Zeami's day), but the general effect of a modern performance is certainly in consonance with Zeami's original intentions.

Even the noh stage has remained roughly the same since the time of Zeami and his successors. The stage has a bridge, called the *hashigakari*, which leads from the actors' room offstage to the stage proper. The bridge, anywhere from 20 to over 40 feet long depending on the size of the theater, leads onto the main playing space, about 18 feet square, which is roofed and has a ceremonial pine tree painted on the rear wall. At the back of the playing space is a narrow section for four or five musicians who accompany the play. The theaters were originally outdoors, but the modern noh theater is placed inside a larger shell as though it were a giant stage set itself.

The noh actors move in a highly stylized fashion that involves important elements of both dance and pantomime. During the performance of a noh text, the actors alternate sections of chanting with a kind of heightened speech that might best be compared to recitative in western opera. The costumes made for the noh are usually of great elegance, and the masks worn by the *shite* are among the most beautiful, subtle, and effective created for any theater.

The noh has always had a powerful attraction for western writers, who have found in its austere poetry an element congenial to them. Yeats wrote a number of plays in the noh style using Irish legends; Bertolt Brecht and Kurt Weill actually made a short opera from a noh play, which they called *Der Jasager*; and Benjamin Britten adapted another play for his striking opera *Curlew River*, which uses Christian monks instead of Buddhist ones. All of these works are highly successful in their own right and serve as fascinating examples of how one culture can inspire another.

The occasional comic elements in noh eventually developed in an independent theater form, in which the *kyogen* actors performed whole plays by themselves. These comic plays, which use a good deal of folk humor and slapstick, are still highly appreciated today.

The Bunraku (Puppet) Theater

The noh remained the most popular theatrical form during Japan's long medieval period. Civil wars and other disturbances caused political disarray of an increasing gravity, however, until in 1600 a general, Tokugawa Ieyasu, unified the country. All through the long Tokugawa period (1600–1868), which bears his family name, Japan was unified and at peace, but this period of calm was purchased at a price. Alarmed at the political maneuvering of Japan's growing number of Christians, converted by European missionaries, the Tokugawa family outlawed the Christian religion and cut Japan off from any extensive contact with either China or Europe until the middle of the nineteenth century.

Peace did bring, however, a rapid development of commerce and trade that led to an increasingly sophisticated level of urban life. As the merchant class grew, the wealth and increasing leisure time of its members allowed them to patronize various sorts of entertainments. The aristocracy and the Tokugawa family continued to support the noh as a kind of private state theater, but the merchants supported theatrical arts that more closely mirrored the world in which they lived. These entertainments flourished in large cities, particularly Osaka.

The puppet theater, now usually called *bunraku*, the first of the new popular forms, developed in a most unusual way. One of the widespread forms of entertainment in the medieval period was the art of the traveling chanter, who, with his *biwa* (a kind of large lute), would travel around the countryside chanting the medieval chronicles of the wars and the tales of romantic heroes and heroines. By around 1600, it became customary to add to these performances, as a kind of additional attraction, companies of puppeteers, who would act out the stories as a kind of "illustration" to the music of the chanter. These chanted texts are referred to as *joruri,* and their performers, down to the present day, are looked on with the same kind of awe reserved for opera singers in the west. The chanters perform all the voices in a play, as well as the narration, and set the general mood. Originally, they also wrote their own scripts. Eventually, however, it became useful to ask others to write the texts.

Chikamatsu

The first and undoubtedly the best of the writers for the bunraku puppet theater, Chikamatsu Monzaemon, contributed enormously to the transformation of this popular art into a vehicle for great art. In Chikamatsu's art, the text remained central: the puppets (less elaborate at this time than the magnificent ones now used) and scenery remained subservient to the art of the chanter. Chikamatsu wrote both history plays and domestic dramas dealing with life in his own time. The history plays, originally highly esteemed, have not kept their popularity, but the domestic plays are still staged regularly, and one of them, *The Love Suicides at Amijima,* is doubtless his masterpiece. Chikamatsu spoke of maintaining "what lies in the slender margin between the real and the unreal" in his dramas, and this particular quality, plus his remarkable ability as a poet, have kept his plays popular since they were written. His emphasis on oridinary people, too, was not only something new to the Japanese stage but foreshadowed later developments in European theater.

Kabuki

By the beginning of the eighteenth century, a new form, kabuki, had emerged and Chikamatsu therefore tried writing on occasion for troupes of kabuki actors. He soon abandoned the attempt, however, since the live performers, unlike the chanters, tended to change his lines. These groups of all-male kabuki actors had replaced earlier groups of female performers, who had first presented dances, skits, and other entertainments at festivals in Kyoto and elsewhere early in the seventeenth century. (An actress, Okuni, is credited by some with first creating kabuki.) Members of the female troupes also worked as prostitutes, and the government banned their activities. They were replaced by troupes of boy actors, who met the same fate, and by 1652, only male adult troupes were permitted to perform.

As puppet performances were already highly popular, the kabuki actors found themselves in competition with puppets for any commercial success. Often actors and puppets alike performed in the same repertory,

Sketch of Chikamatsu Monzaemon

CHIKAMATSU MONZAEMON
(1653–1725)

The most famous playwright of Japan, Chikamatsu Monzaemon was born to a provincial samurai family in 1653 and became the first important Japanese dramatist since the great period of noh drama 300 years earlier. His family apparently had literary interests because in 1671 they published a collection of haiku poetry which included some pieces by the future dramatist.

Chikamatsu wrote of his early life: "I was born into a hereditary family of samurai but left the martial profession. I served in personal attendance on the nobility but never attained the least court rank. I drifted in the market place but learned nothing of trade." Though he did not succeed at these varied occupations, he gained valuable insights into all classes of Japanese society that he would later use in his plays.

Chikamatsu did not begin to write plays until the age of 30. Most of his dramas were written for the puppet theater (bunraku), the favorite form of theater in Japan during that period. He is the only major world dramatist to write primarily for that form. He also wrote for the kabuki theater, and many of his puppet plays were later adapted for the kabuki.

As a playwright, Chikamatsu was able to use his knowledge of Japanese life to create vivid, detailed, and accurate pictures of the society of his time. His history plays were loosely constructed stories about the nobility. They feature military pageantry and supernatural apparitions. In his domestic dramas he explored the problems of the middle and lower classes. Several of these plays are based on actual happenings. Often the domestic plays feature unhappy lovers who are sometimes driven to suicide by the problems they face.

Both categories of plays—history and domestic drama—are known for the beauty of Chikamatsu's poetry, which elevates the incidents and the characters. He was a firm believer in the ancient Japanese code of honor, a code he often incorporated in his plays and which sometimes makes them appear unconvincing and moralistic to western audiences.

A prolific writer, Chikamatsu has been compared to both Shakespeare and Marlowe by western critics for the quality of his verse and for his knowledge of society. His most famous history play is *The Battles of Coxinga* (1715). Noted domestic dramas are *The Love Suicides at Sonezaki* (1703), *The Uprooted Pine* (1718), *The Courier for Hell* (1711), and *The Love Suicides at Amijima* (1721).

The beginnings of kabuki *According to legend, kabuki was developed around 1600 by a woman named Okuni. Formerly a Shinto priestess, she began performances, so the story goes, in a dried river bed in Kyoto. In this old Japanese painting, Okuni is shown on a stage playing a warrior, leaning on a sword. Many scholars feel that this was not actually kabuki, but a forerunner of the art form.*

and the use of exaggerated gestures in kabuki is often attributed to the fact that, in the early stages of the development of the actors' art, a conscious attempt was made to imitate the puppets. Though the gestures are exaggerated and stylized, kabuki was less formal and distant than noh, which remained largely the theater of the court and nobility.

Of the plays taken over by the kabuki actors from the puppet repertory, the most famous is surely *Chushingura*, or *The Forty-Seven Ronin (1748)*, perhaps Japan's most popular traditional play; it still draws tremendous crowds even today. Based on an actual historical incident in which a provincial lord was falsely accused and forced to commit ritual suicide, the play, which traces the vendetta or revenge of the forty-seven retainers left behind, is a remarkable blend of adventure, pathos, and romance. Ghost stories, too, were popular dramas in the kabuki repertory, and *Yotsuya Kaidan* (*A Ghost Story of Yotsuya*) by Tsuruya Namboku (1755–1829) is considered the finest of an important genre.

By the late eighteenth century, kabuki had attracted a number of fine playwrights, but by the latter part of the nineteenth century, the last of the great writers, Mokuami Kawatake (1816–1893), found it more and

OKUNI OF IZUMO
(ca. 1596)

According to Japanese legends, credit for developing kabuki, the most popular form of traditional Japanese theater, belongs to a Shinto priestess, Okuni of Izumo. Though little is known of her life and of the circumstances that led to the development of kabuki, tradition states that in 1596 the priestess began by dancing in the dried bed of the Kamogawa River in Kyoto.

Okuni's early dances were probably works of Buddhist origin that had been secularized by being intermingled with folk dances. It is said that Nagoya Sanzaemon, a samurai warrior and alleged lover of Okuni, taught her adaptations of dances from the noh, the court drama of the period. She might have used the noh dances in her performances as well as elements of popular dances, but no detailed descriptions of her performances survive.

That her dances were popular, however, is shown by the tour of Japan that Okuni and her troupe took in 1603, which culminated with a performance at the imperial palace in Kyoto. The following year she built a semipermanent theater in Kyoto similar in structure to the noh stage of the period. Her theater opened on October 23, 1604, with a five-day performance to raise money for her shrine in Uzumo.

Dance was the basis of the early kabuki performances, and the musical dance-dramas that developed revolved around stories that were romantic and often erotic. Both women and men occasionally played characters of the opposite sex. Most of the early performers were women, but prostitution became common among the performers of women's kabuki, a fact that irritated the shogun.

As a composite entertainment appealing to the townspeople, kabuki also was seen as an unsettling influence on the rigid social and artistic structure. In 1629 the shogun banned women's kabuki. Following that, young boys performed kabuki, but the shogun also banned these troupes in 1652. All-male troupes then became the rule, a custom that remains to the present day. Though the remaining men's troupes were heavily regulated, kabuki, the form of Japanese theater started by Okuni, flourished in the following centuries.

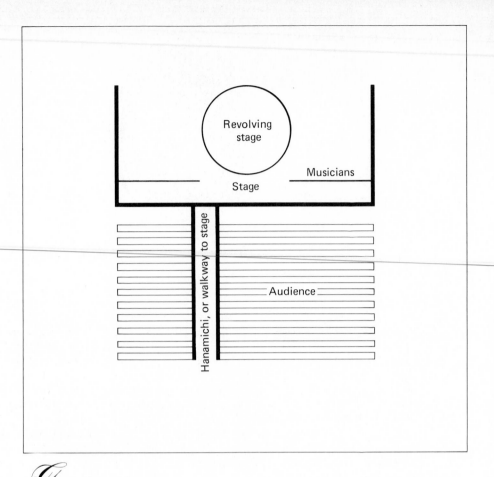

*G*round plan of modern kabuki stage   *Kabuki, the 400-year-old Japanese theater, is performed today in an elaborate theater which, among other stage devices, has turntables on stage for shifting scenery. As shown here, the stage covers the entire front of the theater and is approached by a ramp, called a hanamichi, on which performers make dramatic entrances and exits.*

more difficult to reconcile the conventions of kabuki with the changing social needs of the day. By the time of Mokuami's retirement in the late nineteenth century, kabuki had changed from a contemporary to a classic theater, but it remains extremely popular.

Kabuki actors are trained from childhood in singing, dancing, acting, and feats of physical dexterity. The male actors who play women's parts (called the *onnagata*) are particularly skillful in their ability to imitate the essence of the feminine personality through stylized gestures and attitudes. Costumes and makeup alike in kabuki are elegant and gorgeous. The effect of an actor's performance is always highly theatrical and a bit larger than life.

$\mathscr{K}$INOSHITA JUNJI
(born 1914)

One of the most prominent figures in contemporary Japanese theater, Kinoshita Junji is important as both a playwright and a dramatic theorist. His plays cover historical and contemporary events and use elements drawn from both traditional Japanese sources and western theater. Through the challenges he has issued to modern Japanese theater, he has stirred a debate over its ethics and aesthetics.

Kinoshita's familiarity with two different theater traditions may have come from his education. His family left Tokyo and returned to their traditional home in Kyushu when the writer was 9. After completing high school and college, Kinoshita returned to Tokyo in 1936 and entered the Imperial University to study Elizabethan literature.

While completing his degree in English theater history, Kinoshita began writing plays. His early *minwa-geki*, plays based on folktales, were produced by a drama study group that followed Stanislavski's principles. One historical play, *Turbulent Waves* (1939), was also among his early dramas. When he began to write professionally after the war, he developed a working relationship with the actress Yanamoto Yasue, an association that still exists.

Kinoshita's folktale plays, which he wrote until the late 1950s, established his reputation throughout Japan. One, *The Twilight Crane* (1949), was also produced in the noh and kabuki theaters and as both a Japanese and English opera. The folktale plays weave elements of traditional Japanese literature and theater into a modern form. In his historical dramas, he is concerned with a socialist interpretation of history, as seen in *Between God and Man* (1970), a study of war crimes.

Kinoshita lives in Tokyo and has been active in promoting theatrical exchanges between Japan and the People's Republic of China. A translator of Shakespeare and Somerset Maugham, he studies folktales and the Japanese language in addition to continuing his writing. Both *The Twilight Crane* and *Between God and Man* have been translated into English.

A kabuki actor in a woman's part   *In Japanese kabuki men play women's parts. The actors who perform in kabuki often are descended from many generations of kabuki actors and train for years for their roles. Shown here in the play* Masakado *is Utaemon, one of the most famous modern actors in women's parts. He has been designated a Living National Treasure in Japan. (Photo—The Shochiku Company.)*

The stage used for kabuki performances underwent various changes during the history of the art, but the same principles were observed after the middle of the eighteenth century. The stage is long and has a relatively low proscenium. Musicians generally accompany the stage action, sometimes onstage, sometimes offstage. Kabuki features elaborate and beautiful scenic effects, including the revolving stage which was developed in Japan before it was used in the west. Another device used by kabuki is the *hanamichi*, or "flower way," a raised narrow platform connecting the rear of the auditorium with the stage. Actors often make their entrances on the hanamichi and occasionally perform short scenes there as well.

The Modern Theater in Japan

With the coming of western influence to Japan after 1868—when the house of Tokugawa was overthrown—young Japanese intellectuals began traveling abroad. Among them were a number of gifted men who developed a strong interest in the theater and saw it as a way to express social concerns. The work of Ibsen became a particularly strong force. These men, feeling that the traditional kabuki had nothing to contribute to such a movement, decided to create a means of performing spoken drama in the western manner.

In 1909, Osanai Kaoru (1881–1928) presented the first professional production of a modern play in Japan with specially trained actors. A remarkable pioneer in the development of western-style theater, Osanai continued his experiments until 1923, when with the help of a wealthy colleague, Hijikata Yoshi, he was able to build the Tsukiji Little Theater, which served as the center for the development of modern Japanese drama until its destruction during the World War II bombing of Tokyo.

By the 1930s, two kinds of modern drama were important in Japan. The first was political drama of a leftist persuasion, usually based on German or Russian models, and the other was a drama strongly literary in flavor, using French drama and Chekhov as models. Probably the finest literary playwright during the period was Kishida Kunio (1890–1954), whose work as a critic, playwright, and producer did much to bring mature standards to the theater of his time. Kishida studied with Jacques Copeau in Paris, a leading early twentieth-century director.

As a critic, Kishida was convinced that Japanese writers must learn western dramatic principles by producing foreign plays and then, after absorbing these ideas, use them to create a modern Japanese drama. In his own plays, like *Diary of Falling Leaves* and *A Space of Time*, Kishida used poetic dialogue and a central organizing symbol to describe Japanese attitudes. To speed the development of his idea, Kishida helped to found the Literary Theater in 1937. It was the only modern Japanese company that was permitted to perform during the war and became a major theatrical force after the war.

During the war years, the government suppressed most theatrical activity, particularly the work of artists of socialist or communist leanings. Since the end of the war, however, the contemporary theater in Japan has been in a healthy state. A number of truly gifted playwrights have emerged, chief among them Kinoshita Junji, whose work combines social concerns with humor and, when appropriate, elements from the Japanese folk tradition.

During the 1960s, an avant-garde theater developed as well. Some actors and directors felt that the spoken theater itself had become "establishment." They decided to strike out toward other kinds of theatrical experience, some of them drawing on the abstraction and exaggeration long a part of traditional kabuki and noh. Thus arose the unusual situation of the old becoming the means of radicalizing the new. Today, the modern spoken theater is as active in Tokyo as it is in London and New York. Acting techniques have improved, and staging is certainly on a par with other major centers around the world. What remains remarkable about the Japanese theater is that old traditions are preserved even as new traditions are developed. Thus, a visitor to Tokyo can have the enviable choice of, say, a noh play, a kabuki play, a puppet play, or a new Japanese drama, all on the same evening.

Summary

The traditional theaters of Asia originated out of religious ceremonies and ideas. Most are highly theatrical and stylized, and include a fusion of acting, mime, dance, music, and text. The Sanskrit drama of India, the Chinese Peking opera, and Japan's noh, kabuki, and bunraku are complex theatrical forms which require that audiences be aware of their intricate conventions in order to understand the presentations.

The influence of the Asian theaters on the modern western dramatic art should not be underestimated. Most artists in the twentieth century who have revolted against the realistic theater have, in some measure, taken their inspiration from Asian forms. Meyerhold, Artaud, Brecht, and Grotowski all expressed admiration for the Asian theater.

Chapter Sixteen

THE BLACK THEATER

Black theater—sometimes called Afro-American theater—is theater written by and for black Americans or performed by black Americans. It is part of two important traditions. One is the western theater tradition in which actors like Paul Robeson and writers like Lorraine Hansberry have made significant contributions. The other is a tradition that traces its origin to theater in Africa and the Caribbean. In this chapter we will study both traditions and also look at the important achievements of black theater.

EARLY AFRICAN INFLUENCES

Although formal Afro-American theater and drama are less than 200 years old, some of the important sources for this theater date back hundreds, perhaps thousands, of years to the world's oldest civilizations.

A powerful black drama   *Produced by the Negro Ensemble Company,* A Soldier's Play *by Charles Fuller, a scene from which is shown here, won the Pulitzer Prize for Drama in 1982. It centers on the investigation of the murder of a black soldier at an army camp in Louisiana in 1944. It contains a number of strong confrontations and forceful scenes. (Photo—Bert Andrews.)*

Black Theater

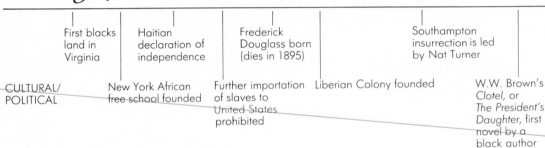

| THEATER | | | | | | African Grove Theater
performs Shakespeare | | *Uncle Tom's*
Cabin produced
in Troy, N.Y. |
| | | | | | | Ira Aldridge arrives
in England | | |

YEAR	*1619*	*1786*	*1801*	*1808*	*1817*	*1821*	*1824*	*1831*	*1852*	*1853*

First blacks land in Virginia — Haitian declaration of independence — Frederick Douglass born (dies in 1895) — Southampton insurrection is led by Nat Turner

CULTURAL/ POLITICAL — New York African free school founded — Further importation of slaves to United States prohibited — Liberian Colony founded — W.W. Brown's *Clotel, or The President's Daughter,* first novel by a black author

Only in recent times have scholars begun to trace which influences were African and which were European, and how these two streams flowed together into an Afro-American theater.

In 1619, twenty African slaves were sold in Jamestown, Virginia, by a Dutch captain. This marked the beginning of a lucrative slave trade which lasted for over 200 years and brought an estimated 15 million Africans to the new world. These people brought their languages, cultures, dances, music, religions, and stories. They brought the knowledge of drums, harps, and pipes. The words *marimba, juke* (as in "juke box"), and *jazz* are all said to derive from African languages. In songs and dances, the Africans brought the ring scout, a circle dance which is the probable source of the minstrel walk-around; the call-response (rhythms and shouts between leader and chorus); and dances in which animals were imitated, such as the buzzard lope, the turkey trot, and the snake hips. They also brought a tradition of satire and ridicule of the pompous and the improper, as well as the ability to be "possessed" by spirits. Many "Africanisms" have continued to evolve: some in dances like the fox trot and the bunny hug, some in the interchanges between preachers and their congregations in church services.

A contribution equal to, if not greater than, particular Africanisms is the philosophy by which Africans viewed themselves in the world. They did not see the universe as a series of dichotomies of good versus evil, or spiritual versus material, but as a vast, intricate harmony of people, nature, and god, each having some element of spiritual as well as material being. Human beings, because they have consciousness and the invoca-

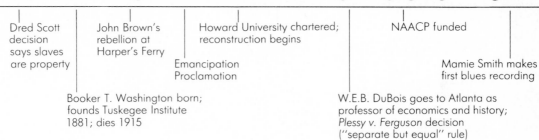

Walker and Williams
introduce the cakewalk
to the stage

Lafayette
Stock Company
opens in Harlem

Brown's *The Escape*,
first play by black author

Callender's Consolidated
Spectacular Colored
Minstrels opens

Bert Williams stars in
The Ziegfeld Follies

1857 1858 1859 1863 1867 1882 1896 1909 1910 1914

Dred Scott
decision
says slaves
are property

John Brown's
rebellion at
Harper's Ferry

Howard University chartered;
reconstruction begins

NAACP funded

Emancipation
Proclamation

Mamie Smith makes
first blues recording

Booker T. Washington born;
founds Tuskegee Institute
1881; dies 1915

W.E.B. DuBois goes to Atlanta as
professor of economics and history;
Plessy v. Ferguson decision
("separate but equal" rule)

tive power of the spoken word, were responsible for maintaining the balance with nature. If this balance was violated through stupidity, greed, or folly, people and nature suffered. One very important means of maintaining the balance was religious ritual, which embraced song, dance, and drama.

Much of Africa's traditional theater has been incorporated in religious or "efficacious" ceremonies. (An efficacious ceremony is intended to achieve results of some kind for the participants.) The theatrical element in these ceremonies has an aesthetic—that is, an artistic—principle different from that of the European theater, which has rested largely on *mimesis* (an imitation or representation of an action). The African tradition lies close to group sharing, or *methexis*. While western theater and drama have emphasized separation of audience and actor, individual creativity, and a set text from which little variation is permitted, African theater has emphasized audience participation, group creativity, and improvisation. The result is that while the purpose of the European theater is to entertain and to teach, that of the African is to embody, to affect, and to be.

Examples of African ritual theater can be found in the Caribbean, where the African gods were integrated with the practices of the Catholic church through religious rituals such as *vodum* in Haiti and *santería* in Trinidad, Puerto Rico, and Cuba. For instance, the Afro-Cuban ritual drama *Shango de Ima*, a mystery play, is a re-creation of the life of the Yoruba god Shango, who is known in Cuba as St. Barbara. This drama, still performed today, contains many Yoruba words and chants; its power

Black Theater

THEATER							

Appearances by Garland Anderson, first play on Broadway by a black author

Othello with Paul Robeson

Shuffle Along reaches Broadway, first of a series of popular musicals

Orson Welles' *Haiti Macbeth* for the Federal Theater Project

The Emperor Jones with Charles Gilpin at the Provincetown

Porgy with Frank Wilson and Rose McClendon

Porgy and Bess; Hughes' Mulatto

Ethel Waters introduced in *Mamba's Daughter*

YEAR   *1920 1921 1922 1927 1929 1935 1936 1939 1940 1943*

Duke Ellington opens at Harlem's Cotton Club

Harlem race riots

Richard Wright's *Native Son*

CULTURAL/ POLITICAL

Marcus Garvey's Universal Negro Improvement Association reaching height of its influence

---

sometimes "possesses" the "performers" so that they "become" *orishas* (gods), thus bringing both worshippers and performers into a community of gods and nature.

Many quasi-religious festivals of the Caribbean reflect a strong African influence. The Trinidadian carnival—for which preparations begin at Christmas and culminate just prior to Ash Wednesday—has all the grand spectacle of theater. It includes costumed parades and calypso contests, skits, and steel bands.

These religious holiday celebrations with their vibrant display of Africanisms are different manifestations from the African cultural assimilation that took place in the United States, where exuberant public song and dance were discouraged by the Protestant church. To circumvent such restrictions, black congregations developed spirituals and call-response between preacher and worshipper, in lieu of being possessed by the god. In secular life, too, when the slave masters suppressed dancing by forbidding slaves to raise their feet off the earth or to cross one leg in front of another, blacks developed the shuffle and the movement of the hips. They borrowed the European marches and reels, turning them into ragtime and, later, jazz, truly Afro-American creations.

BLACK CHARACTERS IN WESTERN THEATER

The figure of the African has been present on the European stage from the time of the Roman playwright Terence. In medieval Christmas pageants, an African figure was present as a magus, one of the three wise men who came to worship the infant Jesus. During the English Renaissance a series

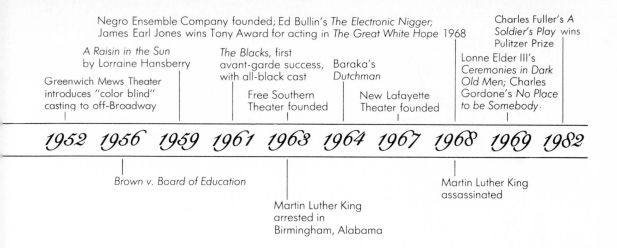

Negro Ensemble Company founded; Ed Bullin's *The Electronic Nigger;*
James Earl Jones wins Tony Award for acting in *The Great White Hope* 1968

Charles Fuller's *A Soldier's Play* wins Pulitzer Prize

A Raisin in the Sun by Lorraine Hansberry

The Blacks, first avant-garde success, with all-black cast

Baraka's *Dutchman*

Lonne Elder III's *Ceremonies in Dark Old Men;* Charles Gordone's *No Place to be Somebody.*

Greenwich Mews Theater introduces "color blind" casting to off-Broadway

Free Southern Theater founded

New Lafayette Theater founded

1952 1956 1959 1961 1963 1964 1967 1968 1969 1982

Brown v. Board of Education

Martin Luther King arrested in Birmingham, Alabama

Martin Luther King assassinated

of tragedies was produced in which a black king, often called a Moor or blackamoor, following capture and humiliation, took bloody revenge. By the late seventeenth century, this noble warrior—depicted by Shakespeare in *Titus Andronicus* and *Othello*—had all but vanished. Slaves, planting tobacco and picking cotton, replaced kings; Othello had become Friday, the loyal servant of Robinson Crusoe.

BLACK THEATER IN AMERICA: THE BEGINNINGS

In early colonial days, nearly all the American drama was either written in imitation of British drama or imported directly from England. American playwrights were not slow to see the comic possibilities of the "darkie" servant, and they set about writing dialogue for this character in a dialect thick with malapropisms (words that are mispronounced or misused in a comic manner so as to distort their meaning). The writers gave the character a slow shuffle, made him stupid, and laughed at the ill-fitting livery they had clothed him in. As a final insult, he was invariably played by white actors in blackface.

There were exceptions. In William Dunlap's play *A Trip to Niagara* (1828), the black character Job Jerryson tells a fellow servant, "If you would like to see our theater, I can give you an order. I am one of the managers. We rehearse every club night—the Shakespeare Club." In all likelihood, Jerryson was referring to the African Grove, a black theater company in New York founded in the season of 1820–21 by William Brown, an Afro-American, in conjunction with the West Indian actor James Hewlett.

African ritual contributes to black theater *The ceremonies of Africa contained highly skilled performances in song and dance. Shown here is an example: a performer from the Watusi tribe in Barundi. Many elements from these rituals found their way into black theater in America, having been brought here via the Caribbean or directly by black people from Africa. (Photo—Thomas D. W. Friedman, Photo Researchers, Inc.)*

The African Grove was the first formal black theater in America. At various times, located at three different sites in Lower Manhattan, it had a capacity of 300 to 400 persons. Newspapers of the period tell of the company's successes, especially its Shakespearean productions. The popularity of the African Grove grew to such an extent that the management "graciously made a partition at the back of the house for the accommodation of the whites."

On the African Grove stage, James Hewlett became the first black man to play Othello. Here, the famous black actor Ira Aldridge made his stage debut in the role of Rolla in *Pizarro*. Here, too, the drama *King Shotaway* (1823)—believed to be the first play both written and performed by Afro-Americans—was performed. The company's repertory, however, was mainly made up of Shakespearean drama and popular plays of the day. The African Grove finally was closed in 1827 by the constable after white rowdies "out for a lark brought disorder and wanton mischief."

With the demise of the African Grove, Afro-American actors were left with the choices of abandoning their profession, accepting roles as stupid "darkies," or going to Europe, where racism against black people was not so virulent. This last choice was elected by many, including Ira Aldridge.

Performing in Europe

Aldridge began a tradition that many other black artists would emulate. Elizabeth Taylor Greenfield, a classical soprano, went to England where in 1854 she gave a command performance at Buckingham Palace. Louis Gottschalk, a Creole and America's first internationally recognized concert artist, traveled extensively in Europe and South America. The Fisk Jubilee Singers, who began their tours to raise money for their college in Nashville, Tennessee, ended by raising the spiritual to international fame. Victor Sejour, another Creole, remained in France as an expatriate for his entire creative life and wrote twenty-four plays for the Paris boulevard theaters.

Another playwright, an ex-slave named William Wells Brown, who had been to Europe and returned, became the first Afro-American to publish a novel, *Clotel*, and a play, *The Escape; or, A Leap for Freedom* (1858). The latter, a melodrama in the style of *Uncle Tom's Cabin*, has an abolitionist theme and is based on the author's own experiences as a slave. Although highly theatrical, *The Escape* remained unproduced until 1971. In place of a production, Brown toured England and America reading from his play.

In the nineteenth century, only one other black playwright published a serious drama. William Easton wrote in the preface to his five-act verse tragedy *Dessalines* (1893): "We have our sketch artists, whose business it has been to supply our burnt-cork artists with ideas. Indeed, we have had excellent caricaturists of the Negro in his only recognized school of legitimate drama, i.e., buffoonery." In other words, there seemed to be no place for serious black drama.

THE MINSTREL SHOW

The buffoonery Easton was referring to was the American minstrel show, a type of production featuring white performers made up in blackface. Before minstrelsy white men had performed in burnt cork with exaggerated lips and eyes. One such performer, Daddy Rice, had captured the nation's fancy in the early 1830s with a grotesque jump-dance that he named "Jim Crow." ("Everytime I wheel about, I jump Jim Crow " was the refrain of his accompanying song.) So popular were his performances that Jim Crow became a generic word for Negro. But it was in the minstrel show that performances by whites in blackface became a commonplace.

The form began in 1843 with a performance by the Virginia Minstrels, a company of four white men in blackface; their evening of so-called Negro songs, dances, and jokes initiated an entertainment that was to be popular on American stages for the next sixty years.

The recipe was simple: a group of men, numbering from six to one hundred and dressed in colorful costumes, with their faces blackened and their eyes and mouths enlarged by white and red lines, formed a

Ira Aldridge as Othello *(Photo—The New York Public Library at Lincoln Center, Astor, Lenox, and Tilden Foundation.)*

IRA ALDRIDGE
(ca. 1806–1867)

One of the leading Shakespearean actors of the nineteenth century, Ira Aldridge performed for forty years, mostly in Europe, where he won wide recognition. The son of the pastor of a Presbyterian chapel in New York City, Ira Aldridge was born around 1806 or 1807 in either Manhattan or Bel-Air, Maryland. He attended the African Free School in New York until the age of 16, when he began acting with the African Grove Theater in New York City, a company of black actors who presented Shakespearean and other classical works. When racial tension in the neighborhood caused the police to close the African Grove, Aldridge took a job at the Chatham Theater, working backstage. He continued to work in amateur productions, playing a number of small roles. His first lead was in Sheridan's play *Pizarro*.

At the age of 17 Aldridge found employment as a steward on a ship bound for England. After studying briefly at the University of Glasgow in Scotland, he went to London and appeared in many plays, including the melodrama *Surinam; or, A Slave's Revenge*. For the next eight years Aldridge toured the British provinces, playing a number of roles and earning a reputation as one of the finest tragedians in England.

He returned to London in April 1833 to perform the title role in *Othello* at the Royal Theater, Covent Garden. The critical praise was overwhelming; one account proclaimed that the production was "the greatest theatrical presentation London has ever witnessed." While in England, Aldridge also appeared as King Lear and Richard II and revived *Titus Andronicus*, which had not been staged in England for almost two centuries.

For the next three decades, Aldridge toured Europe appearing before royalty and winning praise from such figures as novelist Alexandre Dumas, composer Richard Wagner, and tragedian Edmund Kean. He was sometimes billed as "The African Roscius." (Roscius was a famous actor in the ancient Roman theater, and his name was often used as an honorary title for major performers.) The king of Sweden personally invited Aldridge to appear in Stockholm. In 1852 he went to Germany and stayed for three years. While there he was awarded the Gold Medal of the First Class of Art and Science and the Medal of the Order of Chevalier.

Aldridge also visited Russia, where the czar granted him the Cross of Leopold, and the students of Moscow University accorded him their highest honor by unhitching the horses of his carriage and pulling him through the streets. His performances as a slave in a farce delighted Russian audiences, but offended some because his pitifully comic portrayal aroused comparisons with Russia's serf population. Following his performance in *The Merchant of Venice*, a procession of Jews came to thank Aldridge for his very human interpretation of Shylock.

Aldridge died on August 7, 1867, while on tour in Lodz, Poland. Today he is honored by a tablet housed in the New Memorial Theater in Stratford-on-Avon, England, and in 1979 he was inducted posthumously into the New York Theater Hall of Fame. This final honor conferred upon Aldridge a well-deserved respectability in his native land—a respectability he never could have achieved during his lifetime.

semicircle on the stage. At one end of the arc sat Tambo, named for his tambourine; at the opposite end sat Bones, named for the sheep ribs that he played like castanets; in the center stood Mr. Interlocutor, the straight man and master of ceremonies. Burdened with no plot or character development, the minstrel show was a combination of comic and sentimental songs, dramatic and farcical skits, and jigs and shuffle dances—all of it seasoned with a peppering of dialect jokes.

The vast majority of the minstrel shows featured white performers, yet by all accounts, the greatest dancer of the period was a black, William Henry Lane, known as Master Juba, who in 1845 received top billing with a white minstrel troupe. Charles Dickens, who wrote enthusiastically of Juba, called him "the greatest dancer known."

Nonetheless, hundreds of white performers made immense sums of money by mimicking and distorting black music, black speech, black dance, and black culture in a tradition of ridicule that extended through the mid-twentieth century with Al Jolson, Eddie Cantor, George Jessel, and Amos 'n' Andy.

It is true that some blacks founded, operated, and played in their own minstrel companies, most of which originated in the 1870s after the Civil War, when they were able to capitalize on America's interest in seeing "the genuine Negro." To prove that they were not whites in makeup, many did not put on burnt cork. However, black companies soon learned that in order to get bookings in this highly competitive field, they had to work for a white manager.

White culture, fascinated by the black in the post–Civil War period, paid blacks the perverse homage of recognizing the beauty and originality of black songs and dances by adopting them and then corrupting the Africanisms in minstrel shows for racist ends. Nonetheless, minstrelsy provided a meeting ground for the two cultures. In minstrel shows the high-stepping Irish jig gave way to the low-gliding Virginia Essence, which would later become the soft shoe, and white composer Stephen Foster adapted southern plantation melodies that Americans still associate with blacks.

In minstrel shows, many talented black performers also learned and practiced their art. Among them was James Bland, the composer of "Carry Me Back to Old Virginny," the state song of Virginia. W. C. Handy, writer of "The St. Louis Blues," began in minstrels, as did Bert Williams and George Walker, two of the most talented minstrel performers. White America's exploitation of black culture changed the face of American music, dance, and theater. One of the first of the resulting innovations was ragtime.

THE RAGTIME ERA, 1890–1914

The so-called gay nineties, a record-breaking decade for its number of lynchings, saw the Supreme Court, in its *Plessy v. Ferguson* decision, make Jim Crow principles the law of the land by permitting "separate but equal" schools. In this decade the Reverend Thomas Dixon adapted his novel in praise of the Ku Klux Klan for the stage, and later into the film *Birth of a Nation.* Yet the same period encompassed a vibrant series of musical shows written, acted, and produced by blacks.

Rising prices, worn-out jokes, an incipient motion picture industry, and the introduction of women into revues all had contributed to the collapse of the minstrel show. By 1895, the musical theater had developed a new form which had more plot than vaudeville, the revue, and a vigorous new music, the infectious ragtime.

The syncopated rhythms of ragtime had originated in saloons, sawmill camps, and houses of prostitution from the spontaneous talent of unknown black composers and piano players. American daughters and sons, who had been plunked down on piano stools to practice "Whispering Hope," discovered suddenly that it was more fun to play "The Maple Leaf Rag" by Scott Joplin (1868–1917), whose music became, sixty years later, the hit of the musical *Pippin* and the movie *The Sting.* (Joplin, who died in poverty, was buried in an unmarked grave, and his ragtime opera *Treemonisha,* published at his own expense, remained unproduced until 1972.)

As ragtime spread across the nation, it served as a bridge to legitimate musical comedy for a number of talented Afro-Americans. In 1891, *The Creole Show* introduced sixteen beautiful "colored" women into the minstrel. Bob Cole and William Johnson conceived, wrote, produced, and directed the first black musical comedy, *A Trip to Coontown* (1898).

In the same year, William Marion Cook and Paul Lawrence Dunbar wrote "Clorind: The Origin of the Cakewalk." Using the syncopated ragtime, this high-stepping dance was an instantaneous success and the first black dance of many—the turkey trot, the Charleston, the lindy hop, the jitterbug, and the twist—to become popular in America.

Among the great cakewalkers, the comedians Bert Williams (1876–1922) and George Walker (?–1909) and their wives joined composers and writers to produce musicals and operettas that put black performers on Broadway. Their most sucessful shows, *In Dahomey* (1902) and *Abyssinia* (1906), reflect two different but important interests of the time: operetta, with its aristocratic characters involved in romantic plots, and Africa and things African. For the first time Americans saw blacks on the stage without burnt cork, speaking without dialect, and costumed in high fashion.

The Lafayette Players

The success of black writers and producers encouraged the formation of Afro-American stock companies. The first of these was founded in 1904 by Robert Mott on Chicago's South Side. At his Pekin Theater a new show opened every two weeks. In 1914, a second important stock company was founded by a woman who had played with the Williams and Walker shows. Her name was Anita Bush, and her stock company opened at the Lincoln Theater in Harlem. A year later she moved her troupe to the Lafayette Theater, dubbed it the Lafayette Players, and produced a new play every week. By 1932, when the company finally closed in the face of the depression, it had presented over 250 productions and employed a host of black stars, including Charles Gilpin, Evelyn Preer, and Clarence Muse.

The company's repertoire consisted entirely of "white" plays; that is, it brought Broadway to black audiences. One of the great delights for these audiences was to watch Clarence Muse, a very dark-skinned man, in white makeup and wig play *Dr. Jekyll and Mr. Hyde.* Muse later moved to Hollywood and starred in *Hearts in Dixie* (1929), the second talking picture to be made with an all-black cast.

Other contributions of the Lafayette Players included proving to white audiences that black actors were capable of serious dramatic performances and that a black company could sustain itself financially over a long period. Certainly the black dramatic groups that followed—the Negro Art Theater, the Gilpin Players, and the Ethiopian Players—owed their inspiration to Anita Bush's pioneer work.

Vaudeville

Most performers in this era and those to follow made a living not on the legitimate stage but in vaudeville. While a few white circuits like Keith-Albee and Columbia would book blacks, most black vaudeville acts depended on the Negro circuit, which extended from New York to Texas, from Chicago to Birmingham. These bookings were handled by the Theater Owners Booking Association, known as TOBA, an acronym which the actors translated as "Tough on Black Actors." This circuit, founded in 1920 by blacks, was eventually able to book acts in over eighty theaters. According to theater historian Henry T. Sampson, between the years 1910 and 1930, blacks owned and operated 157 theaters.

The black vaudeville acts, like the white, had song-and-dance teams, stunt dancing, cakewalk artists, blues singers, comics, specialty acts, and even dramatic skits. Among the hundreds of talents who made their living in these theaters were Pigmeat Markham, the Nicholas Brothers, Nipsey Russell, Bessie Smith, Butterbeans and Susie, and Sweet Mama Stringbean (Ethel Waters). This lucrative circuit collapsed with the great depression of the 1930s.

THE JAZZ AGE, 1918–1929

During World War I, thousands upon thousands of rural blacks emigrated to find work in the war industries of the north. With them, they brought their folk customs, music, religion, and dreams of a better life. When the war ended in 1918, a spirit of unity and hope prevailed.

The "Negro Awakening"

Blacks artists of the period congregated in Harlem. It was a good time to be there: around them lay the wealth of the black heritage. In this atmosphere, the Harlem Renaissance began: the sculptures of Richmond Barthe and Aaron Douglass's drawings evoked a new image; the books of Langston Hughes, Claude McKay, Countee Cullen, and Zora Neale Hurston described the new outlook; jazz, the new music, expressed the new freedom. Professor Alain Locke of Howard University sensed the spirit and proclaimed the twenties to be the decade of the New Negro.

In the arts, the Negro Awakening took two directions: nationalism, with its pride in the folk art and roots, and exoticism, with its image of the New Negro as a creature of natural rhythm and primitive passions. Both influences were felt in the theater.

W. E. B. Du Bois (1868–1963), founder of the NAACP and editor of its magazine, *The Crisis*, believed that the arts, and the theater in particular, had an important role to play in the black struggle. The NAACP had already produced an antilynching drama, but now Du Bois insisted that there should be a theater *by, for, about,* and *near* Negro people. To encourage this vision, *Crisis* magazine held annual playwriting contests and awarded cash prizes. To ensure the production of plays, Du Bois helped organize amateur groups known as Krigwa Players. (Krigwa stood for Crisis Guild of Writers and Artists.) In a broad sense, these small drama clubs were part of the little theater movement in America.

The black drama clubs produced mostly one-act folk plays; nearly eighty were written and staged. At this time, folk drama, with its natural idioms of speech and its honest, down-to-earth characters, received encourgement from black intellectuals who hoped to emulate the success of the Irish folk movement in Dublin. Although most of the black folk plays were produced in churches, schools, and libraries, Willis Richardson's *The Chip Woman's Fortune* (1923) reached Broadway on a double bill with Oscar Wilde's *Salome.* The producing group, the Ethiopian Players, called themselves a "a folk theater," and many of those who wrote plays for them were poets, schoolteachers, and other amateurs. Among them was a bellhop named Garland Anderson, who, by persistence and an unshakable belief in his talent, managed to put his play *Don't Judge by Appearances* (1925) on the Broadway stage twice.

Commercial Success

While the amateur theater developed its folk roots, blacks in the commercial theater found a temporary place in the sun. In this decade, twenty plays with Negro themes were presented on Broadway, five of

*B*lack musicals on Broadway *The first black musical to break the color barrier on Broadway was* Shuffle Along *in 1921. The score, which included "I'm Just Wild About Harry," was by Sissle and Blake. In the years since, black writers and performers have become frequent contributors to Broadway musicals. (Photo—The New York Public Library at Lincoln Center, Astor, Lenox, and Tilden Foundations.)*

them written by blacks. The first to break the racial barrier was a musical, *Shuffle Along* (1921). This delightful show was written by two comedians, Flournoy Miller and Aubrey Lyles; the music and lyrics were by Noble Sissle and Eubie Blake. The show starred Florence Mills, and tucked away in the chorus was Josephine Baker, who became a famous performer in Europe. The songs included "I'm Just Wild About Harry" and "Love Will Find a Way." Among its many innovations, *Shuffle Along* presented for the first time to a white audience a serious love story about blacks.

The success of *Shuffle Along* encouraged other bright jazz musicals of the 1920s: *Chocolate Dandies, Runnin' Wild, Seven-eleven, Blackbirds,* and *Rang Tang.* From these shows and others emerged an impressive number of stars—some onstage, some in the orchestras. Among them were Josephine Baker, Florence Mills, Bill "Bojangles" Robinson, Fats

Waller, Moms Mabley, William Grant Still, and many others. These stars toured the country and often traveled to London and Paris.

The Emergence of Serious Black Actors

Some black performers achieved recognition in serious drama. In 1920 Charles Gilpin created the title role in *The Emperor Jones* by Eugene O'Neill and was voted by the Drama League one of the ten people of that season who had done the most for the theater. In 1924, Paul Robeson began his theater career with the lead in O'Neill's *All God's Chillun Got Wings*. Rose McClendon and Frank Wilson found artistic recognition in the Theater Guild's triumph *Porgy* (1927) and Ethel Waters in the musical *Africana* (1927).

Ethel Waters, like many singers, also made "race" records, a term used to identify singers who were black. In 1920, Fred Hager of the General Phonograph Company intended to use Sophie Tucker to record "That Thing Called Love" and "You Can't Keep a Good Man Down" but was persuaded instead to use Mamie Smith, a black woman. The recording was a hit, and by 1929, over 500 blues and gospel recordings were being issued each year. During this decade, the first black-owned record manufacturer, the Pace Phonograph Company, began releasing disks under the Black Swan label.

Although the 1920s provided increased opportunities for Afro-American talent, in most cases black theater performers were still restricted to exotica. An example was the show number "Mozambique" from *Blackbirds of 1930*. This scene featured the song "Jungle Moon" and was set in a jungle painted with touches of Walt Disney. Seventeen women in belly-dance costumes and tail feathers, as in a Las Vegas revue, rolled their bellies, eyes, and palms as they shook their blonde Afro-wigs. Much of this exotica came to an end with the beginning of the Great Depression. Nonetheless, between 1910 and 1940, over 800 musicals featuring blacks had been produced.

THE GREAT DEPRESSION AND THE FEDERAL THEATER: 1930s

The Theater is a mirror of its times, and at no time was this theory borne out more clearly than in the decade of the 1930s. With the stock market crash in 1929, good times for black theater evaporated. The old maxim "last hired, first fired" proved to be true in theater employment. The collapse of commercial opportunities, coupled with the competitive advent of talking pictures and radio, forced black performers either to turn to other means of survival or to invent ingenious ways of creating their own theaters. Among these attempts were the establishment of the Harlem Suitcase Theater in New York and the Negro Theater in Los

ETHEL WATERS

(1896–1977)

The Broadway and motion picture actress and singer Ethel Waters made famous such songs as "Taking a Chance on Love," "Cabin in the Sky," and "Am I Blue." At the height of her popularity she was reported to be worth several million dollars, but at the time of her death in 1977, she was close to poverty.

Ethel Waters was born on October 13, 1896, in Chester, Pennsylvania. Her early years were hard. As she revealed in her 1951 autobiography, *His Eye Is on the Sparrow*, her first job was as a chambermaid at a small Philadelphia hotel, earning $4.75 a week. She also sometimes stole food to keep from going hungry.

Her luck began to change at the age of 17 when she won a talent contest at a local theater. This led to a job singing and dancing at the Lincoln Theater in Baltimore, Maryland. From there Waters began working the TOBA circuit, playing mainly to black crowds in the south. Known to her fans as "Sweet Mama Stringbeans," Waters first began to taste success with her rendition of W. C. Handy's classic, "St. Louis Blues." By the time Waters moved to New York in the early twenties, she was already a star in the south, known for the class and innocence she brought to her repertoire of mostly "blue" material.

In 1924 she substituted for singing sensation Florence Mills in *The Plantation Revue of 1924*. From that point on, Waters became one of New York's brightest stars. Irving Berlin, upon hearing her rendition of "Cabin in the Sky," wrote several songs for her such as "Harlem on my Mind," "Heat Wave," and the poignant lament, "Supper Time." Waters introduced these songs in the Broadway revue *As Thousands Cheer* (1933). She also appeared in several other revues on Broadway: *Africana* (1929), *Blackbirds* (1930), *Rhapsody in Black* (1933), and *At Home Abroad* (1935).

In 1938 Waters received critical acclaim in the Dorothy and DuBose Heyward play *Mamba's Daughter*, her first dramatic performance on Broadway. She returned to the musical stage in 1940 in *Cabin in the Sky*. For this performance, the *Herald Tribune* praised Waters as "one of the great musical comedy stars of her time." Waters later appeared in the movie version of *Cabin in the Sky* (1943), which featured a cast of such notables as Lena Horne, Louis Armstrong, Eddie "Rochester" Anderson, Rex Ingram, and Butterfly McQueen.

Waters appeared in nine motion pictures, starred in several radio and television shows, and performed all over Europe, but her most memorable performance was in Carson McCullers's play *A Member of the Wedding*, at first on Broadway (1950) and then in the film version (1952).

Waters died in Chatsworth, California, of kidney and heart failure. In her final years, she devoted her life to religion, singing in revivals all over the world.

Angeles (both founded by Langston Hughes), the Negro People's Theater, the Harlem Experimental Theater, and the Rose McClendon Players (all in New York), and the Skyloft Players, the Chicago Repertory Group, and the Negro Theater at Chicago's Lincoln Center. Many of these groups were racially integrated and leaned politically to the left.

Such small troupes, however, could not support the 3000 unemployed black actors, directors, and technicians. In 1930, the only major New York production involving blacks was *The Green Pastures*, a Broadway play which retold a series of stories from the Bible in what was thought to be an authentic black folk style. The play was written by a white for an all-black cast of nearly 100, including the famous Hall Johnson Choir and Richard B. Harrison, who portrayed "de Lawd" for 1568 performances. In 1935 came the premiere of *Porgy and Bess*, also written by whites but drawing upon the black musical tradition, especially spirituals, and widely acclaimed as an American folk opera. While both of these plays now are sometimes considered condescending to blacks, they were not racist in intent, nor were they so regarded at the time, and they reflected a growing, if naive, interest in black life among whites.

A few shows by blacks also found their way to Broadway: the folk musical *Run Little Chillun* (1933) by Hall Johnson and *Mulatto* (1935) by Langston Hughes, which ran for 373 performances, a record for a straight play by a black playwright. The actress Rose McClendon, who played the lead in this drama about southern racism, had already established her reputation in *Porgy* and in *Abraham's Bosom*, two folk plays by white authors.

The Federal Theater Project

The most fortunate development for black theater in the 1930s came with the establishment of the Federal Theater Project (FTP) in 1935. For the director of the theater wing of the New Deal's Works Progress Administration, President Roosevelt appointed Hallie Flanagan. She was determined not only to bring work to the 25,000 unemployed theater artists but to bring theater to the ordinary citizen who had never seen a play. In four years the FTP played to 65 million people.

A significant aspect of the FTP was the development of ethnic theater for "hyphenated" Americans—Chinese, Germans, Jews, Italians, and blacks. At the suggestion of Rose McClendon and Dick Campbell, separate black units were formed in twenty-two cities "to provide the literature which will serve as a basis for the full flowering of the Negro theater."

While these black units struggled with bureaucracy and racism, they managed to mount dozens of productions by white and black playwrights and gave employment to hundreds of actors, dancers, and vaudevillians. They trained blacks in the technical aspects of lighting, scene building, and stage management; presented audiences with dozens of new images of black people; and created opportunities for writers and scholars to explore Afro-American life and history. The average salary was $24 a week, which in those days was enough to live on.

Among the truly impressive achievements of the FTP, only a few may be listed here. On the west coast the Seattle company produced Theodore Browne's *Natural Man*, an expressionistic drama about the legendary John Henry. In Los Angeles, Clarence Muse mounted a long-running production of *Run Little Chillun* (1938). Under the direction of Shirley Graham Du Bois, Chicago presented Theodore Ward's *Big White Fog*, a realistic drama about the struggle of a family to survive the depression. The Chicago unit also brought the *Swing Mikado*, a jazz version of the Gilbert and Sullivan operetta, to New York. In Harlem, Orson Welles and John Houseman produced a *Macbeth* set in Haiti. In Boston, Ralf Coleman directed *Stevedore, Bloodstream*, and *Jericho*, the last a musical with 150 performers. Newark, New Jersey, could boast of Hughes Allison, whose racially controversial *The Trial of Doctor Beck* reached Broadway.

In 1939, for political reasons, Congress killed the FTP by refusing to vote it funds. (Members of the House Un-American Activities Committee charged that the FTP was sympathetic to Communism, and Congress was also reacting against New Deal relief programs.) The theater program, however, had already created a new generation of Afro-American theater artists who would develop the theater of the forties and fifties.

BLACK THEATER IN WORLD WAR II AND THE 1940s

Pearl Harbor in 1941 mobilized the nation's and the theater's energies toward winning the war, and achievements for black theater were somewhat fewer, if nonetheless impressive. For the commercial stage, Paul Green and Richard Wright adapted Wright's best-selling novel *Native Son* (1941). Directed by Orson Welles, this Mercury Theater production opened twice on Broadway for a total of 181 performances. Canada Lee, in the role of Bigger Thomas, was unanimously praised, but everything else about the story and show was controversial.

Other important ventures on Broadway were Paul Robeson's record run of 296 performances in *Othello* (1943); choreographer Katherine Dunham's successful *Tropical Revue* (1943), which consolidated her dance company and her influence on American dance; and Theodore Ward's historical drama of the struggle of freed slaves to obtain and hold their own property, *Our Lan'* (1946). The longest-running venture was Abram Hill's adaptation of Philip Yordan's *Anna Lucasta* (1944), which played for three years.

Anna Lucasta originated with one of the most important theater groups in black history, the American Negro Theater (ANT), founded in 1940 by Fred O'Neal, who later became president of Actors Equity, and

Paul Robeson in Othello   One of the most impressive actors of the twentieth century was Paul Robeson. An athlete and singer as well as an actor, he particularly distinguished himself in the role of Othello. Here he is seen with Mary Ure as Desdemona and Paul Hardwick as Brabantio in a scene from a production at Stratford-on-Avon in Great Britain. (Photo—Wide World.)

Abram Hill, a Federal Theater Project playwright. Hill wrote ANT's first successful comedy, *On Striver's Row*, a satire on the black middle class.

Beginning in the 135th Street library in Harlem, ANT created training workshops for actors, playwrights, and technicians. Over the years, more than 200 artists studied or taught there, including Alice Childress, Ruby Dee, Canada Lee, Harry Belafonte, Sidney Poitier, and Earle Hyman.

Another major institution in Harlem, the Apollo Theater on 125th Street, began a policy in the mid-thirties of featuring black entertainers. Relying heavily on vaudeville acts and featured singers, the theater also presented dramatic plays with all-black casts. The big bands of Count Basie and Duke Ellington and singers like Billie Eckstine and Maxine Sullivan performed at the Apollo. Sarah Vaughan and Ella Fitzgerald both began their careers by winning attention in the Apollo's famed amateur night. Comedians like Redd Foxx, Nipsey Russell, Moms Mabley, and Pigmeat Markham, as well as tap dancers, sand dancers, and soft shoe specialists (dancers like Honi Coles, Charlie Arkins, and Earl "Snake Hips" Tucker), performed successfully. The Apollo was part of a black circuit that included the Howard in Washington, D. C., and the Regal in Chicago.

$\mathscr{P}$AUL ROBESON

(1898–1976)

Internationally known as an actor, singer, athlete, scholar, and political activist, Paul Robeson led a controversial and luminous career that spanned fifty years.

Born on April 9, 1898, in Princeton, New Jersey, Robeson was the son of a runaway slave who had become a Presbyterian minister. He attended Rutgers University on an academic scholarship and rose to national prominence as an athlete, winning a total of twelve athletic letters in four different sports and being named an All-American in football two years in a row (1917, 1918).

After graduating Phi Beta Kappa, Robeson attended Columbia University and earned a law degree in 1923. Eugene O'Neill saw Robeson perform in an amateur theater production of *Simon the Cyrene* and offered him the lead in *The Emperor Jones*, which Robeson turned down due to prior commitments. Later, Robeson did perform O'Neill's role of Brutus Jones, on the stage (1924) and in the film version of the play (1933).

It was also in O'Neill's play that Robeson launched his career as a concert singer. Asked by the director to whistle in a scene, Robeson sang instead, and the response was overwhelming. Robeson also appeared in O'Neill's controversial *All God's Chillun Got Wings* (1924). In 1926, following a series of successful performances the year before at the Greenwich Theater, Robeson presented a program of spirituals and work songs at Town Hall in New York City. This was the first program of all-black music ever sung on the New York stage by a solo artist.

From 1927 to 1939, while living in England, Robeson appeared in many productions, including *The Hairy Ape*, *Stevedore*, and *Show Boat*, in which he introduced "Ole Man River," the song that was to become his trademark. But his greatest achievement while in England was *Othello*, in which he headed a distinguished cast that included Peggy Ashcroft, Sybil Thorndike, and Ralph Richardson. Robeson repeated this success on Broadway in 1945 with Uta Hagen as Desdemona and Jose Ferrer as Iago. The play ran for 296 performances, a record for any Shakespearean play on Broadway.

While in Europe Robeson had become very outspoken about the racial situation in the United States, and this, coupled with his strong affection for the Soviet Union, led the State Department to take away his passport in 1950, thereby denying him the right to leave the country. He was blacklisted, and denied the use of recording studios and concert halls, and his annual income fell from $104,000 to $16,000.

In 1958, after an eight-year worldwide campaign, Robeson regained his passport. He gave a triumphant concert at Carnegie Hall and then left the country. In 1959 he appeared as Othello at Stratford-on-Avon and journeyed to Russia to receive the Stalin Peace Prize. In 1963 Robeson returned to the United States and lived the remainder of his life in seclusion, making only a few public appearances. He died January 23, 1976.

Downtown on Broadway, in a production of *Carmen Jones*, Todd Duncan and Camilla Williams made history in 1946 by being the first blacks to sing with the New York City Opera. (In 1955, Marian Anderson made her debut at the Metropolitan Opera House, and in the years that followed, Grace Bumbry, Martina Arroyo, and Leontyne Price appeared there, but in the 1940s, audiences still preferred to hear blacks sing in productions featuring black characters, such as *Carmen Jones*.)

BLACK THEATER IN THE 1950s

The decade of the 1950s included the Korean War, McCarthyism, the Supreme Court decision favoring school integration, Martin Luther King, Jr., and the civil rights struggle; it also saw a black theater that seemed to be marking time, waiting for new developments. Nevertheless, important foundations were laid.

The New York theater remained the only place a young artist might hope to make a living, but around the nation, colleges and regional theaters were training new talent, developing new audiences. Perhaps the first organization to offer blacks solid theater training was Karamu, in Cleveland. Founded as a settlement house in 1916 by Russell and Rowena Jelliffe, this theater presented the premieres of many of Langston Hughes's plays. Among the impressive names of its graduates in professional theater are Ivan Dixon and Robert Guillaume.

In the early 1930s, two schoolteachers and a federal employee decided that black children needed plays and skits about their own history and heroes. The three, May Miller, Willis Richardson, and Randolph Edmunds, wrote a total of 100 plays and published six books. In addition, Edmunds founded the second-oldest drama organization in America, the National Association of Dramatic and Speech Arts, to establish a drama curriculum in southern colleges.

The seminal college for training black artists, Howard University, under the director-playwright Owen Dodson, premiered James Baldwin's first play, *Amen Corner*, in 1954. The commercial staging did not take place until 1965.

Another bright spot of the fifties was Louis Peterson's *Take a Giant Step* (1953), a play about a teenager growing up in an integrated neighborhood. Among significant performances on Broadway were those by Eartha Kitt and Avon Long in *Mrs. Patterson*, Lena Horne in *Jamaica*, and Sammy Davis in *Mr. Wonderful*.

At this time, too, the Greenwich Mews Theater, an Off-Broadway house, began casting plays without regard to race. Two history dramas were staged there: William Branch's *In Splendid Error*, a portrayal of the struggle between John Brown and Frederick Douglass, and Loften Mitchell's *Land Beyond the River*, a story about a black minister's efforts to end

A Raisin in the Sun—a theatrical landmark *Lorraine Hansberry, the playwright, was the first black writer, and the youngest American playwright, to win the Drama Critics Circle award for best play. Also, the director, Lloyd Richards, was the first black director on Broadway. Shown here are two performers from the original production: Sidney Poitier and Claudia McNeil playing a son and his mother. (Photo—Friedman-Abeles Collection.)*

school segregation. The Greenwich Mews also produced *Trouble in Mind* by Alice Childress. Although by this time there had been approximately 125 plays written by Afro-American women, *Trouble* was the first to receive professional staging. Three years later, Lorraine Hansberry became the first black woman dramatist to have a play on Broadway.

Hansberry's play, *A Raisin in the Sun*, tells the story of a black family in Chicago—held together by a strong, God-fearing mother—who plan to move into a predominantly white neighborhood where they are unwelcome. The young man in the family loses money in a get-rich-quick scheme but later assumes responsibility for his family and his career. *A Raisin in the Sun* was an important step for black playwrights,

𝓛ORRAINE HANSBERRY
(1930–1965)

Lorraine Hansberry's first play, *A Raisin in the Sun*, is considered by many critics to have been a turning point in the history of the American Theater. To quote James Baldwin: "Never before in the entire history of the American theater has so much of the truth of Black people's lives been seen on the stage."

Born on May 19, 1930, into an upper-middle-class family in Chicago, Hansberry first wanted to be a painter. She studied at the Chicago Art Institute, University of Wisconsin, and in Guadalajara, Mexico. While at Wisconsin, Hansberry saw a production of Sean O'Casey's *Juno and the Paycock*. Inspired by O'Casey's ability to universalize a specific people and their culture—in this case the Irish—she decided to become a playwright.

In 1952 Hansberry journeyed to New York and joined the staff of *Freedom*, a Harlem-based journal created by Paul Robeson. Reacting against what she called "a whole body of material about Negroes. Cardboard characters. Cute dialect bits. Or hipswinging musicals from exotic scores," Hansberry set out to write a play that would be "a social drama about Negroes that will be good art." That play was *A Raisin in the Sun*.

Set in the apartment of the Younger family on Chicago's South Side, *A Raisin in the Sun* takes its title from a poem in which Langston Hughes asks the question, "What happens to a dream deferred?" By including in her play several generations within one household, Hansberry was able to present an across-the-board picture of the changing and conflicting ideologies, dreams, and frustrations of black Americans in the late 1950s.

A Raisin in the Sun opened on Broadway on March 11, 1959. It marked several "firsts": Lloyd Richards was the first black director on Broadway, and Hansberry was the first black writer, as well as the youngest American playwright to that date and only the fifth woman, to win the New York Drama Critics Circle Award for Best Play of the Year.

Hansberry's work set the stage for the black theatrical explosion that was to occur on the New York stage in the sixties and seventies. Her second play to be produced, *The Sign in Sidney Brustein's Window* (1964), was about "the Western intellectual poised in hesitation before the flames of involvement," to quote Hansberry. The play, despite very passionate support from the artistic community, ran for only 101 performances, closing on the day of Hansberry's death, January 12, 1965.

Hansberry's other completed works include *The Drinking Gourd*, *What Use Are Flowers*, and *Les Blancs*, which had a short run on Broadway in 1970. *To Be Young, Gifted and Black*, a theatrical collage based on the writings of Lorraine Hansberry, was the longest-running drama of the 1968–1969 off-Broadway season.

and its success was a harbinger of important works by black playwrights in the years to come.

CIVIL RIGHTS, BLACK MILITANCY, AND BLACK BROADWAY: 1960–1980

In the 1960s, black theater was strongly influenced by the civil rights movement that had begun to emerge in the United States in the 1950's. Aimed at improving the rights and opportunities of minorities, it was especially important to black Americans. Throughout the south—and in parts of the north—there were sit-ins, marches, boycotts, and other forms of protest to end racial discrimination. The Reverend Martin Luther King, Jr., a key figure in the movement, led a successful boycott against the Montgomery, Alabama, bus system in 1955 and headed a massive march on Washington, D. C., in 1963. Awarded the Nobel Peace Prize in 1964, King was murdered in Memphis, Tennessee, in 1968.

With the impetus of the civil rights movement, actor and playwright Ossie Davis wrote *Purlie Victorious* (1961), a comedy satirizing the traditional racial stereotypes of the south. Nine years later, the play returned to Broadway as a musical. Another civil rights effort inspired by the sit-ins and the picket lines confronting segregated facilities was the Obie Award–winning *Fly Blackbird* (1960), a musical by C. Bernard Jackson and James V. Hatch. James Baldwin's drama of southern racism, *Blues for Mr Charlie* (1964), was produced but quickly closed.

Perhaps the outstanding example of theater inspired by civil rights at the grass-roots level was the Free Southern Theater, a troupe established in 1963 by Tom Dent, Gilbert Moses, and Richard Schechner. Based in New Orleans, the company toured Louisiana's rural communities with plays and skits about freedom.

In 1964, two plays by new writing talents were produced: *The Dutchman* by LeRoi Jones, also known as Amiri Baraka, and Adrienne Kennedy's *Funnyhouse of a Negro.* Both plays presented images not seen before upon the stage; they portrayed middle-class blacks who, when unmasked, revealed a sensitivity to pain, rage, and anguish that few whites had thought might be hidden there. Both won Obie Awards as the best Off-Broadway plays of the year.

By the end of the 1960s, it was clear that black playwrights had found their voices in both dramatic realism and antirealism. Playwrights like Lorraine Hansberry, Lonne Elder III (in *Ceremonies in Dark Old Men,* 1969), and Charles Gordone (in *No Place to Be Somebody,* 1969) proved themselves masters of realistic theater. They placed their characters in true-to-life settings and reflected in their dialogue and other aspects of their plays accurate observations of everyday life.

Many other black playwrights, though, employed highly inventive and imaginative antirealistic techniques. Douglas Turner Ward, for exam-

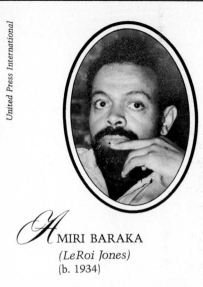

𝒜MIRI BARAKA
(LeRoi Jones)
(b. 1934)

A prolific and provocative dramatist, Amiri Baraka has over thirty plays to his credit. Prior to Baraka, black protest drama had been solely realistic; by infusing allegory and lyricism into his vivid depictions of racially-torn America, Baraka changed the shape of the black protest drama and thereby fathered a whole school of writing.

Born Everette LeRoi Jones on October 7, 1934, in Newark, New Jersey, Baraka attended Rutgers University and then Howard University. After serving briefly in the Air Force, Baraka moved to New York, where he attended Columbia University and earned an M.A. in German literature from the New School of Social Research. It was also during this time that Baraka became associated with the "beat" poets of the fifties. While two of Baraka's earlier plays had been produced, *A Good Girl Is Hard to Find* (1958) and *Dante* (1961), it was *The Dutchman* (1964) that brought him to the forefront of the American theater.

Set in a steaming subway car in New York City, *The Dutchman* is a verbal and sexual showdown between a middle-class assimilated black man and a white temptress. Their battle becomes a metaphor for the political, sociological, and psychological dilemmas which many black Americans were confronting in the early 1960s.

The Dutchman opened in 1964 and earned Baraka a Guggenheim Fellowship as well as an Obie Award for the Best American Play of 1963–64. *The Dutchman* is also credited with beginning the black theater renaissance of the 1960s and 1970s and for setting into motion the need for a new aesthetic for judging contemporary black works.

The Slave and *The Toilet*, a double bill of one-act plays by Baraka, opened off-Broadway in 1965. *The Slave* is a domestic battle involving an interracial couple, set against the background of a race war, and *The Toilet*, set in an inner-city high school bathroom, is an impassioned work in which teenage gang members pummel another boy to death. These plays foreshadowed the urban violence that was to engulf America one year later. Baraka's next notable work was *Slave Ship* (1970).

After Baraka rose to success in the New York theater he left to form his own performing company within the black community. The Black Arts Repertory Theater and School in Harlem was Baraka's first endeavor. He later returned to Newark, where he became founder and director of the Spirit House Movers and Players. In addition to being a dramatist, Baraka is also a poet, novelist, musicologist, essayist, critic, and editor.

*M*odern protest drama   *Amiri Baraka first won praise for his realistic plays like* Dutchman. *Later, he changed his name from LeRoi Jones to Baraka and became increasingly interested in politics. He also became more experimental with dramatic form—an interesting example being* Slave Ship, *a scene of which is shown here. (Photo—Bert Andrews.)*

ple, in his play *Day of Absence* (1970), had black men playing in whiteface—a reversal of the minstrel practice. Baraka, in *Slave Ship* (1970), used a number of ritualistic techniques.

The success of these black writers led other playwrights to speak their minds and hearts, encouraged audiences to demand more black theater, and served as the inspiration for the founding of several theater companies.

Production Organizations

Among production organizations, the Negro Ensemble Company (NEC) holds the contemporary record for survival as a professional black theater company in continuous production. Beginning in 1967, nearly seventy plays, almost all of them original, were produced by NEC on its tiny stage at the St. Mark's Playhouse. Conceived and administered by Douglas Turner Ward, Robert Hooks, and Gerald Krone, the company had a clear concept—a "Negro angle of vision"—that a black repertory company producing original black playwrights and aimed at a black audience, but not excluding whites, would succeed.

The Ford Foundation gave the NEC a grant of $1,200,000 to cover the first three years. The NEC's seasons embraced a variety of playwrights and styles—comedies by Ted Shine and Judi Ann Mason, militant plays by Douglas Ward and Peter Weiss, and ritual by Wole Soyinka and Carter Harrison. Three of its productions moved to Broadway: *The River Niger*, (1973), *The First Breeze of Summer* (1975), and *Home* (1980). In the early 1980s the NEC moved to a larger theater near the Broadway area where it presented Charles Fuller's *A Soldier's Play* (1981) that won the Pulitzer Prize.

The New Lafayette Theater, founded in Harlem in 1966 by Robert Macbeth with help from the Ford Foundation, was also destined to have a far-reaching impact. In this theater, two young and then-unknown playwrights, Richard Wesley and Ed Bullins, brought a new vitality to the seventies. Bullins, in particular, created a series of ghetto and middle-class characters whose driving energy and sense of self-survival electrified the stage. Among the sixteen premieres mounted by the New Lafayette, the presentations of Bullins's *In the Wine Time* (1968), *In New England Winter* (1971), and *The Fabulous Miss Marie* (1971) are landmarks. Several elaborate attempts to conduct ritual theater involved black audience participation that excluded whites. The loss of funding sources and the failure to build audience support were major reasons for the group's disbanding in 1972, but not before it had published six issues of *Black Theater*, a magazine that was important to young black artists across the nation.

The "black is beautiful" spirit of the 1960s, coupled with the willingness of foundations and the federal government to support minority arts programs, accounted for a burgeoning of black theater groups. The Black Theater Alliance listed over 125 groups in 1970. Only a few of these managed to build enough public support to survive the decade; the survivors included the Los Angeles Cultural Center, the Billie Holiday Theater in Brooklyn, and Hazel Bryant's Richard Allen Center in New York.

Black Audiences and Other Developments

In addition to its discovery and development of hundreds of artistic talents, the large grass-roots movement in black theater brought about a major change in American theater: the presence of a large black audience.

This audience provided the impetus for the commercial success in New York of *Don't Bother Me, I Can't Cope, Your Arm's Too Short to Box with God, Bubbling Brown Sugar*, and the Pulitzer Prize–winning *No Place to Be Somebody*. It also rescued the musical *The Wiz* after critics had condemned it. The achievement of an old dream—the establishment of a network of black theater organizations and audiences—was realized with the establishment of the Black Theater Alliance by Joan Sandler and Hazel Bryant, and of Audelco (Audience Development Committee) by Vivian Robinson.

These networks, along with the black theater movement, have produced impressive results: (1) the introduction of black theater history into school curricula and books; (2) the new willingness of producers and directors to cast blacks in ethnic and nonethnic roles; (3) the creation of black television comedies, dramas, and historical epics; (4) the development of a large group of highly skilled and experienced artistic talents who in turn have been awarded recognition nationally with Tonys, Obies, Oscars, and Emmies; and (5) the publication of serious books and articles on the history and development of Afro-American theater.

In addition to these achievements, the two centuries of Afro-American theater have added to the vitality of the American stage by infusing black music, dance, language, and life-styles into its musicals and plays.

Summary

The black theater partakes of an African and Caribbean heritage on one side and of the western tradition on the other. Africa and the Caribbean furnished a background of ritual and theatrical entertainments often closely related to religious ceremonies. The theatrical elements from this tradition include colorful and elaborate costumes, a strong dance component, and a sophisticated use of symbolism.

In nineteenth-century America, there were attempts to develop black theater companies, but due to social and racial pressures none was able to endure. Black actors frequently found that the only place they could perform successfully was in Europe, a prime example being Ira Aldridge.

In the United States, the musical styles of black performers—found in improvised entertainments and church services—were appropriated by white performers and developed as minstrel shows. Gradually, though, black entertainers were recognized in their own right; this was particularly true in the ragtime era (around the turn of the century) with the emergence of artists like the composer Scott Joplin and the comedians Bert Williams and George Walker. Black performers came even more to the forefront in the jazz age (1918–1929), when performers like Ethel Waters got their start.

The debut of actor Paul Robeson in the 1920s marked the recognition of serious black actors on the Broadway stage. Theater companies, too, developed at this time, particularly those sponsored by the Federal Theater Project in the late 1930s.

Following World War II there was a flourishing of black theater on many fronts: performers such as James Earl Jones won wide recognition; Lorraine Hansberry, with *A Raisin in the Sun*, put black playwrights in the mainstream of serious commercial theater; more militant playwrights, led by Amiri Baraka, broke new ground in their dramas of social protest; new theater companies, such as the Negro Ensemble Company, provided permanent homes for the training of black talent and the presentation of black plays.

Appendix I

A GLOSSARY OF THEATRICAL TERMS

(For a more complete discussion of many of the terms discussed below, consult the index and turn to the section of the text indicated.)

Afterpiece A theatrical entertainment staged after the main play in the eighteenth- and nineteenth-century theater.

Agon In classical Greek Old Comedy, a scene with a debate between the two opposing forces in the play, each representing an antithetical side of a social or political issue.

Agonthetes The government official responsible for producing plays for the Hellenistic Greek festivals.

Alienation Bertolt Brecht's theory that the emotional involvement of the audiences at his epic-theater plays should be minimized so that they would instead be involved intellectually with the political message.

Allegory The representation of an abstract theme or themes through the symbolic use of character, action, and other concrete elements of a play. In its most direct form—as, for example, the medieval morality play—allegory uses the device of personification to present characters representing abstract qualities, such as virtues and vices, in an action which spells out a moral or intellectual lesson.

Amphitheater A large oval, circular, or semicircular outdoor theater with rising tiers of seats around an open playing area; also, an exceptionally large indoor auditorium.

Angle perspective   The use of two or more vanishing points, frequently at the sides of a painted design. Ferdinando Bibiena is usually credited with introducing angle perspective early in the eighteenth century.

Antagonist   The character who is the chief opponent of the main character (the protagonist) in a drama. In some cases there may be several antagonists.

Apprentice   A young performer in an Elizabethan acting company who was taught the art of acting through actual experience and who received room and board from a key member of the troupe.

Aposentos   The boxes in the Spanish Golden Age corral.

Apron   The stage space in front of the curtain line or proscenium; also called the *forestage*.

Archon   The Athenian government official appointed to oversee the staging of drama at the classical City Dionysia.

Arena   A type of stage which is surrounded by the audience on all four sides; also known as *theater-in-the-round*.

Aside   In a play, when a character speaks thoughts aloud without others onstage noticing.

Auleum   The front curtain which was raised and lowered on telescoping poles in the Roman theater.

Autos sacramentales   Spanish Golden Age religious dramas which mix the characteristics of mystery and morality plays.

Avant-garde   A term applied to plays of an experimental or unorthodox nature which attempt to go beyond standard usage in either form or content.

Backdrop   A large drapery or painted canvas which provides the rear or upstage masking of a set.

Backstage   The stage area behind the front curtain; also, the areas beyond the setting, including wings and dressing rooms.

Ballad opera   An eighteenth-century English form which burlesqued opera. There was no recitative; songs were set to popular tunes, and characters were drawn from the lower classes. John Gay's *The Beggar's Opera* is the most famous example.

Benefit   A tradition begun in the eighteenth-century theater which required that the profits of an evening's performance be given to a performer or group of performers.

Biomechanics   Meyerhold's acting theory which suggested that the actor's body should be machinelike and that emotion could be represented externally.

Blocking   The arrangement of the actors' movements onstage with respect to each other and the stage space.

Bookholder   The prompter who gave actors their lines in the Elizabethan theater.

Border   A strip of drapery or painted canvas hung across the top of the stage from a batten to mask the area above the stage; also, a row of lights hung from a batten.

Box   A small private compartment for a group of spectators built into the walls of the traditional proscenium-arch theater.

Box set   An interior setting using flats to form the back and side walls and often the ceiling of a room.

Breeches roles   Male roles played by females, particularly popular in Restoration and eighteenth-century English theater.

Bunraku   The Japanese puppet theater. The puppets are two-thirds life-size and are manipulated by men in black robes who are conventionally regarded as invisible by the audience.

Burlesque A ludicrous imitation of a dramatic form or a specific play. Closely related to satire, it usually lacks the moral or intellectual purposes of reform typical of the latter.

Burletta Eighteenth-century English dramatic form resembling comic opera and defined by the lord chamberlain as a play with no more than three acts, each of which had to include at least five songs.

Business Obvious and detailed physical movement of actors to reveal character, aid action, or establish mood (e.g., pouring drinks at a bar, opening a gun case).

Capa y espada Literally "cape and sword"; a full-length Spanish play which revolved around intrigue and duels over honor.

Carros Pageant wagons on which autos sacramentales were staged during the Spanish Golden Age.

Cavea The seating area in the Roman theater.

Cazuela The gallery located above the tavern in the back wall of the Spanish Golden Age theater; the area in which unescorted women were segregated.

Choral Odes In classical Greek drama, the songs chanted by the chorus between the episodes.

Choregus A wealthy person who underwrote most of the expenses for the production of an individual playwright's works at an ancient Greek dramatic festival.

Chorodidaskalos In the ancient Greek theater, the person who trained and rehearsed the chorus.

Chorus In ancient Greek drama, a group of performers who sang and danced, sometimes participating in the action but usually simply commenting on it. Also, performers in a musical play who sing and dance as a group rather than individually.

City Dionysia The most important Greek festival in honor of the god Dionysus; it was staged in Athens in the spring and was the first to include dramatic activities.

Claque People in the audience who are hired to applaud; the tradition of the claque began in the Roman theater.

Comedia Three-act full-length nonreligious plays written during the Spanish Golden Age.

Comedy A category of drama that is generally light in tone; it is concerned with issues that are not serious, has a happy ending, and is designed to amuse and provoke laughter. (See also *Old Comedy, New Comedy, Comedy of humors, Comedy of manners, Farce, Satire, Slapstick.*)

Comedy of humors Developed by Ben Jonson in Elizabethan theater in the early seventeenth century. It is based on Roman comedy and stresses ridicule directed at characters who are dominated by a single trait (or "humor") to the point of obsession.

Comedy of manners A form of comic drama that became popular in the latter half of the seventeenth century in France and among English playwrights during the Restoration. It emphasizes a cultivated or sophisticated atmosphere, witty dialogue, and characters whose concern with social polish is charming, ridiculous, or both.

Commedia dell'arte A form of comic theater which originated in Italy in the sixteenth century in which dialogue was improvised around a loose scenario calling for a set of stock characters, each with a distinctive costume and traditional name.

Compañias de parte Spanish Golden Age acting troupes organized according to the sharing system.

Complication The introduction in a play of a new force which creates a new balance of power and makes a delay in reaching the climax necessary and progressive. It is one way of creating conflict and precipitating a crisis.

Confidant(e) A minor character in whom the protagonist confides.

Conflict Tension between two or more characters that leads to a crisis or a climax. The basic conflict is the fundamental struggle or imbalance underlying the play as a whole. May also be a conflict of ideologies, actions, etc.

Constructivism A post–World War I scene-design movement in which sets were created to provide greater opportunities for physical action. The sets, which were frequently composed of ramps, platforms, and levels, were non-realistic. The Russian director Meyerhold employed many constructivist settings.

Corral Spanish Golden Age theater usually located in the courtyard of a series of adjoining buildings.

Curtain raiser A short play staged prior to the full-length drama in the nineteenth-century theater.

Cycle plays See *Mystery plays.*

Cyclorama A large curved drop used to make the rear and sides of the stage, painted a neutral color or blue, represent sky or open space. It may also be a permanent stage fixture made of plaster or similar durable material.

Dadaism A movement in art between the world wars which was based on the deliberate presentation of the irrational and on attacks against traditional artistic values.

Denouement The moment when final suspense is satisfied and "the knot is untied." The term is from the French and was used to refer to the working-out of the resolution in a well-made play.

Deus ex machina Literally "the god from machine," the convention of bringing in gods on the mechane in the ancient Greek theater. The term now applies to any unjustified or arbitrary dramatic device employed to resolve a plot, usually in the final moments.

Director In American usage, the person who is responsible for the overall unity of the production, coordinating the efforts of the contributing artists. The director is in charge of rehearsals and supervises the actors in the preparation of their parts. The American director is the equivalent of the British producer and the French *metteur en scéne.*

Dithyramb An ancient Greek choral song describing the adventures of a god or heroic figure.

Documentary drama A term which encompasses different types of drama developed during the twentieth century that present material in the fashion of journalism or reporting. The living newspaper drama of the 1930s used signs and slide projections to deal with broad social problems; other documentary dramas use a more realistic approach.

Domestic drama Also known as *bourgeois drama*, domestic drama deals with problems of members of the middle and lower classes, particularly problems of the family and home.

Dominus The leader of a Roman acting troupe.

Double-entendre A word or phrase in comedy that has a double meaning, the second often sexual.

Doubling When an actor plays more than one role in a play. Doubling was common in the Greek and Elizabethan theaters.

Downstage The front of the stage toward the audience.

Drame An eighteenth-century French term usually denoting a serious drama that dealt with middle-class characters; some critics suggest that the drame included such eighteenth-century forms as domestic tragedy, middle-class tragedy, and tearful comedy (comédie larmoyante).

Drolls These short dramas were either excerpts or condensations of longer plays presented in seventeenth-century England during the commonwealth and the beginning of the Restoration.

Drop A large piece of fabric, generally painted canvas, hung from a batten to the stage floor, usually to serve as backing.

Eclectic A theater artist who works in a variety of modes and does not identify with one particular artistic movement.

Ekkyklema The wagon in the ancient Greek theater employed to roll characters onstage—often to reveal the results of violence which occurred offstage.

Emotional recall Stanislavski's exercise which assists the actor in presenting realistic emotions. The actor thinks of an event which led to an emotion similar to that which the character is supposed to feel in the play. By recreating the circumstances in his/her mind, the performer will feel the emotion.

Ensemble playing Acting which stresses the total artistic unity of the performance rather than the individual performances of specific actors.

Environmental theater A type of theater production in which the total theater environment—the stage space and the audience arrangement—is emphasized. A form of it came to the forefront in the experimental theater of the 1960s. Among its aims are the elimination of the distinction between audience space and acting space, a more flexible approach to the interactions between performers and audience, and the substitution of a multiple focus for the traditional single focus.

Epic theater A form of presentation associated with the German dramatist Bertolt Brecht, its chief advocate and theorist, aimed at the intellect rather than the emotions, seeking to present evidence regarding social questions in such a way that they may be objectively considered and an intelligent conclusion reached.

Epilogue A speech addressed to the audience after the conclusion of the play and spoken by one of the actors.

Episkenion The second story of the Hellenistic Greek skene.

Existentialism A set of philosophical ideas whose principal modern advocate was Jean-Paul Sartre. The term *existentialist* is applied to plays by Sartre and others which illustrate these views. Sartre's central thesis was that there are no longer any fixed standards or values by which one can live and that each individual must create his or her own code of conduct regardless of the conventions imposed by society.

Exodos In classical Greek drama, the final scene in which all of the characters exit from the stage.

Exposition The imparting of information necessary for an understanding of the story but not covered by the action onstage: events or knowledge from the past, or occurring outside the play, which must be introduced for the audience to understand the characters or plot. Exposition is always a problem in drama because relating or conveying information is static; the dramatist must find ways to make expositional scenes dynamic.

Expressionism A movement which developed and flourished in Germany during the period immediately preceding and following World War I. Expressionism in the drama was characterized by the attempt to dramatize subjective states through the use of distortion, striking and often grotesque images, and lyric, unrealistic dialogue.

Farce One of the major genres of drama, sometimes regarded as a subclassification of comedy. It aims to entertain and to provoke laughter, and its humor is the result primarily of physical activity and visual effects.

Flat A single piece of scenery, usually of standard size and made of canvas stretched over a wooden frame, used with other similar units to create a set.

Fly loft or flies The space above the stage where scenery may be lifted out of sight by means of ropes and pulleys when it is not needed.

Footlights A row of lights in the floor along the edge of the stage or apron; once a principal source of stage light but now only rarely used.

Forestage See *Apron.*

Found space Space not originally intended for theater which is converted for productions. Avant-garde artists of the 1960s often produced in found spaces.

Fourth-wall convention The pretense that in a proscenium-arch theater the audience is looking into a room through an invisible fourth wall. The term is often credited to the eighteenth-century French philosopher Diderot.

Futurism An art movement begun in Italy about 1905 which idealized mechanization and machinery.

Gallery In traditional proscenium-arch theaters, the undivided seating area cut into the walls of the building.

Gesamtkunstwerk Richard Wagner's theory of the unified operatic work of art, in which all elements—music, words, story, scenery, costumes, orchestra, etc.—form a total piece.

Gradas The benches placed along the side walls of the pit in the Spanish Golden Age corral.

Groove system A system in which there were tracks on the stage floor and above the stage which allowed for the smooth movement of flat wings on and off the stage; usually there were a series of grooves at each stage position. The system was developed during the Italian Renaissance and was employed throughout the nineteenth century in English, American, and Dutch theaters.

Groundlings Audience members who stood in the yard of the Elizabethan theater.

Hamartia An ancient Greek term usually translated as "tragic flaw." The term literally translates as "missing the mark," which has suggested to some scholars that hamartia is not so much a character flaw as an error in judgment made by the protagonist.

Hanamichi The bridge in the kabuki theater from behind the audience (toward the left side of the audience) on which actors can enter to the stage. Important scenes are also played on the hanamichi.

Happenings A form of theatrical event which was developed out of the experimentation of certain American abstract artists in the 1960s. Happenings are nonliterary, replacing the script with a scenario which provides for chance occurrences, and performed (often only once) in such places as parks and streetcorners.

Hashigakari The bridge in the noh theater on which the actors make their entrance from the dressing area to the platform stage.

Hireling An Elizabethan acting-troupe member who was paid a set salary and was not a shareholder.

History play In the broadest sense, a play set in a historical milieu which deals with historical personages, but the term is usually applied only to plays which deal with vital issues of public welfare and are nationalistic in tone.

Hubris An ancient Greek term usually defined as "excessive pride" and cited as a common tragic flaw.

Hypokrite Greek term for "actor."

Inner stage An area at the rear of the stage which can be cut off from the rest by means of curtains or scenery and revealed for special scenes.

Interludes Short dramatic pieces, usually presented between courses of a banquet in England during the Middle Ages.

Intermezzi Between-the-acts entertainments performed during the operas and full-length plays of the Italian Renaissance.

Irony A condition that is the reverse of what we have expected; also, a verbal expression whose intended implication is the opposite of its literal sense. A device particularly suited to theater and found in virtually all drama.

Joruri Chanted texts for the Japanese puppet theater.

Kabuki The most eclectic and theatrical of the major forms of Japanese theater. Roles of both sexes are performed by men in a highly theatrical, nonrealistic style. Kabuki combines music, dance, and dramatic scenes with an emphasis on color and movement. The plays are long and episodic, composed of a series of loosely connected dramatic scenes which are often performed separately.

Katharsis A Greek word, usually translated as "purgation," which Aristotle used in his definition of tragedy. It refers to the vicarious cleansing of certain emotions in the members of the audience through their representation on stage.

Kothornus The platform boot worn by actors in the Hellenistic Greek theater.

Kyogen Farcical interludes presented between plays in the noh theater.

Lazzi Comic pieces of business repeatedly employed by characters in the commedia dell'arte.

Liturgical drama Any religious drama, usually sung or chanted, that relates to the Bible and is presented in Latin inside the church sanctuary. The form was highly developed in the medieval period.

Living newspapers The Federal Theater Project's dramatizations of newsworthy events in the 1930s.

Long run In the commercial theater, when a drama is performed for as long a period of time as it is popular. In the nineteenth-century American and English theater, the long run replaced repertory.

Ludi Romani The Roman festival in honor of Jupiter into which drama was first introduced.

Luñetas The semicircular benches located in the front of the Spanish Golden Age pit.

Magic if Stanislavski's acting exercise which requires the actor to ask, "How would I react if I were in this character's position?"

Mansion Medieval scenic unit, often presented as an individual house or locale.

Masking Scenery or drapes used to hide or cover.

Masque A lavish and spectacular form of private theatrical entertainment which developed in Renaissance Italy and spread rapidly to the courts of France and England. The masque combined poetry, music, elaborate costumes, and spectacular effects of stage machinery,

Mechane   The crane in the ancient Greek theater employed for flying characters into the playing area.

Medieval drama   The range of plays that encompass the religious and folk drama developed during the Middle Ages. (See *Liturgical drama, Mystery plays, Miracle play, and Morality play.*)

Melodrama   Historically, a distinct form of drama popular throughout the nineteenth century which emphasized action and spectacular effects and employed music to heighten the dramatic mood. Melodrama employed stock characters and clearly defined villains and heroes with an unambiguous confrontation between good and evil.

Mime   A form of theatrical entertainment in Greek and Roman times which consisted of short dramatic sketches characterized by jesting and buffoonery.

Minstrelsy   A type of nineteenth-century production featuring white performers made up in blackface.

Miracle play   A medieval drama based on the life of a saint.

Mise-en-scene   The arrangement of all the elements in the stage picture, either at a given moment or dynamically throughout the performance.

Morality play   A medieval drama designed to teach a lesson. The characters were often allegorical and represented virtues or faults, such as good deeds, friendship, avarice, and so forth. The most famous example is *Everyman.*

Multimedia   The use of electronic media, such as slides, film, and videotape, in live theatrical presentations.

Multiple setting   A form of stage setting, common in the Middle Ages, in which several locations are represented at the same time; also called *simultaneous setting.* Used also in various forms of contemporary theater.

Musical theater   A broad category which includes opera, operetta, musical comedy, and other musical plays (the term *lyric theater* is sometimes used to distinguish it from pure dance). It includes any dramatic entertainment in which music and lyrics (and sometimes dance) form an integral and necessary part.

Mystery plays   Also called *cycle plays.* Short dramas of the Middle Ages based on events of the Old and New Testaments. Presented in parts of western Europe and England, many such plays were organized into historical cycles which told the story of human history from the creation to doomsday.

Naturalism   A special form of realism. The theory of naturalism came to prominence in France and other parts of Europe in the latter half of the nineteenth century. The French playwright Emile Zola (1849–1902) advocated a theater that would follow the scientific principles of the age. Drama should look for the causes of disease in society the way a doctor looks for disease in an individual. Theater should therefore expose social infection in all its ugliness. Naturalism attempts to achieve the verisimilitude of a documentary film, conveying the impression that everything about the play—the setting, the way the characters dress, speak, and act—is exactly like everyday life.

Naumachia   Roman sea battles which were staged in a flooded amphitheater or on a lake.

New Comedy   Hellenistic Greek and Roman comedies which deal with romantic and domestic situations.

Noh   Also spelled *no*. A rigidly traditional form of Japanese drama which in its present form dates back to the fourteenth century. Noh plays are short dramas combining music, dance, and lyric with a highly stylized and ritualistic presentation. Virtually every aspect of the production—including costumes, masks, and a highly symbolic setting—is prescribed by tradition.

Objective   Stanislavski's term for that which is urgently desired and sought by a character, the desired goal which propels a character to action.

Obstacle   That which delays or prevents the achieving of a goal by a character. An obstacle creates complication and conflict.

Offstage   The areas of the stage, usually in the wings, which are not in view of the audience.

Old Comedy   Classical Greek comedy which pokes fun at social, political, and/or cultural conditions as well as figures. The only surviving examples are by Aristophanes.

Onkos   The high headdress of the Hellenistic Greek mask.

Orchestra   The ground-floor seating in an auditorium; circular playing space in ancient Greek theaters.

Pageant master   The professional medieval stage-manager who oversaw the production of a cycle of mystery plays.

Pantomime   Orginally a Roman entertainment in which a narrative was sung by a chorus while the story was acted out by dancers. Now used loosely to cover any form of presentation which relies on dance, gesture, and physical movement.

Parabasis   A scene in classical Greek Old Comedy in which the chorus directly addresses the audience and makes fun of them.

Parados   In classical Greek drama, the scene in which the chorus enters. Also, the entranceway for the chorus in the Greek theater.

Parasite   The stock character in Roman New Comedy who is motivated purely by sensual needs (e.g., gluttony).

Paraskenia   The wings of the skene in the ancient Greek theater.

Parterre   The pit in the French neoclassical theater in which audience members stood.

Pastoral   An idealized romantic dramatization of rural life, often containing mythological creatures, popular during the Italian Renaissance.

Patio   The pit area for the audience in the Spanish Golden Age theater.

Peking opera   The popular theater of China which developed in the nineteenth century.

Pensionnaire   A hireling in a French acting toupe.

Periaktoi   Three-sided scenic piece employed in the ancient Greek theater which could be revolved in order to allow the audience to see a different side.

Perspective   The illusion of depth in painting; introduced into scene design during the Italian Renaissance.

Pinakes   Painted flats employed in the ancient Greek theater.

Pit   The floor of the house in a traditional proscenium-arch theater, originally a standing area; later backless benches were added.

Platea   The unlocalized playing area in the medieval theater.

Plot   (1) As distinct from story, the patterned arrangements of events and characters for a drama. The incidents are selected and arranged for maximum dramatic impact. The plot may begin long after the beginning of the story (and refer to information regarding the past in flashbacks or exposition). (2)

Outline of an Elizabethan play's dramatic action which was posted backstage so that actors could refresh their memories during performances.

Point of attack   The moment in the story when the play actually begins. The dramatist chooses a point in time along the continuum of events which he or she judges will best start the action and propel it forward.

Pole and chariot   Giacomo Torelli's mechanized means of changing sets made up of flat wings.

Poor theater   A term coined by Jerzy Grotowski to describe his ideal of theater stripped to its barest essentials. The lavish sets, lights, and costumes usually associated with the theater, he feels, merely reflect base materialistic values and must be eliminated.

Preparation   The previous arranging of circumstances, pointing of character, and placing of properties in a production so that the ensuing actions will seem reasonable; also, the actions taken by a performer getting ready for a performance.

Private theaters   Indoor theaters in Elizabethan England.

Proagon   An initial event of a classical Greek festival at which time performers and playwrights appeared in presentations intended to announce and advertise the upcoming plays.

Producer   The person responsible for the business side of a production, including raising the necessary money. In British usage, a producer is the equivalent of an American director.

Proedria   Front-row seats in the ancient Greek theaters reserved for political and religious dignitaries.

Prologos   In classical Greek drama, the opening scene which sets the action and provides the necessary background information.

Prologue   An introductory speech delivered to the audience by one of the actors or actresses before the play begins.

Props   Properties; objects used by performers onstage or necessary to complete the set.

Proscenium   The arch or frame surrounding the stage opening in a box or picture stage, developed during the Italian Renaissance.

Proskenion   The bottom level of the Hellenistic Greek skene, or stage house.

Protagonist   The principal character in a play, the one whom the drama is about.

Psychological gesture   According to the twentieth-century Russian acting theorist Michael Chekhov, a characteristic movement or activity which would sum up a character's motives and preoccupations.

Public theaters   Outdoor theaters in Elizabethan England.

Pulpitum   The raised platform stage in the Roman theater.

Rake   To position scenery on a slant or angle other than parallel or perpendicular to the curtain line; also, an upward slope of the stage floor away from the audience.

Raked stage   A stage which slopes upward away from the audience toward the back of the set.

Realism   Broadly speaking, the attempt to present onstage people and events corresponding to those observable in everyday life.

Regional theater   (1) Theater whose subject matter is specific to a particular geographic region. (2) Theaters situated outside major theatrical centers.

Regisseur   Continental term for theater director; it usually denotes a dictatorial director.

Repertory or repertoire A kind of acting company which at any given time has a number of plays which it can perform alternately; also, a collection of plays.

Restoration drama English drama after the restoration of the monarchy, from 1660 to 1700. Presented for an audience of aristocrats who gathered about the court of Charles II, drama of this period consisted largely of heroic tragedies in the neoclassical style and comedies of manners which reflected a cynical view of human nature.

Reversal A sudden switch or reversal of circumstances or knowledge which leads to a result contrary to expectations. Called *peripeteia* or *peripety* in Greek drama.

Revolving stage A large turntable on which scenery is placed in such a way that, as it moves, one set is brought into view while another one turns out of sight.

Ritual A specifically ordered religious ceremonial event.

Romanticism A literary and dramatic movement of the nineteenth century which developed as a reaction to the confining strictures of neoclassicism. Imitating the loose, episodic structure of Shakespeare's plays, the romantics sought to free the writer from all rules and looked to the unfettered inspiration of artistic genius as the source of all creativity. They laid more stress on mood and atmosphere than on content, but one of their favorite themes was the gulf between human beings' spiritual aspirations and physical limitations.

Satire Dramatic satire uses the techniques of comedy, such as wit, irony, and exaggeration, to attack and expose folly and vice.

Satyr play One of the three types of classical Greek drama, it was usually a ribald takeoff on Greek mythology and history and included a chorus of satyrs, mythological creatures who were half-man and half-goat.

Scaena The stagehouse in the Roman theater.

Scaena frons The ornate three-dimensional facade of the stagehouse in the Roman theater building.

Scene (1) A stage setting. (2) The structural units into which a play or the acts of a play are divided. (3) The location of a play's action.

Script The written or printed text, consisting of dialogue, stage directions, character descriptions, and the like, of a play or other theatrical representation.

Secrets Special effects in the medieval theater.

Set The scenery, taken as whole, for a scene or an entire production.

Set piece A piece of scenery which stands independently in the scene.

Shareholders In Elizabethan acting troupes, members who received part of the profits as payment.

Shite The leading actor in a noh production.

Shutters Two large flat wings that close off a perspective setting in the back.

Sides An actor's lines and cues; Elizabethan actors learned their roles from their sides.

Simultaneous setting The medieval tradition of presenting more than one locale onstage at the same time.

Siparium The backdrop curtain at the rear of the stage in the Roman theater.

Skene The scene house behind the orchestra in the ancient Greek theater.

Slapstick A type of comedy or comic business which relies on ridiculous physical activity—often violent in nature—for its humor.

Societaire A shareholder in a French acting troupe.

Soliloquy A speech in which a character who is alone onstage speaks inner thoughts.

Sottie A short satirical French farce from the Middle Ages.

Spine In the Stanislavski method, the dominant desire or motivation of a character which underlies his or her action in the play; usually thought of as an action and expressed as a verb.

Stage convention An understanding established through custom or usage that certain devices will be accepted or assigned specific meaning or significance on an arbitrary basis, that is, without requiring that they be natural or realistic.

Stanislavski method A set of techniques and theories about the problems of acting which promotes a naturalistic style stressing "inner truth" as opposed to conventional theatricality.

Stock set A standard setting for a locale used in every play which requires that environment.

Storm and stress An antineoclassical eighteenth-century German movement which was a forerunner of romanticism.

Street theater A generic term which includes a number of groups that perform in the open and attempt to relate to the needs of a specific community or neighborhood.

Subtext Referring to the meaning and movement of the play below the surface; that which is implied and never stated. Often more important than surface activity.

Surrealism A movement attacking formalism in the arts which developed in Europe after World War I. Seeking a deeper and more profound reality than that presented to the rational, conscious mind, the surrealists replaced realistic action with the strange logic of the dream and cultivated such techniques as automatic writing and free association of ideas.

Symbolism Closely linked to symbolist poetry, symbolist drama was a movement of the late nineteenth and early twentieth centuries which sought to replace realistic representation of life with the expression of an inner truth. Symbolism used myth, legend, and symbols in an attempt to reach beyond everyday reality.

Tan A female role in Chinese Peking opera.

Tetralogy In the classical Greek theater, the three tragedies and satyr play written by one author for a festival.

Theater of cruelty Antonin Artaud's visonary concept of a theater based on magic and ritual which would liberate deep, violent, and erotic impulses. He wished to reveal the cruelty which he saw as existing beneath all human action—the pervasiveness of evil and violent sexuality.

Theater of the Absurd A phrase first used by Martin Esslin to describe certain playwrights of the 1950s and 1960s who expressed a similar point of view regarding the absurdity of the human condition. Rational language is debased and replaced by clichés and trite or irrelevant remarks. Realistic psychological motivation is replaced by automatic behavior which is often absurdly inappropriate to the situation. Although the subject matter is serious the tone of these plays is usually comic and ironic.

Theatricalism A style of production and playwriting which emphasizes theatricality for its own sake. Less a coherent movement than a quality found in the work of many artists rebelling against realism, it frankly admits the artifice of the stage and borrows freely from the circus, the music hall, and similar entertainments.

Theatron   The seating area which was carved into a hillside in the ancient Greek theater.

Theme   The central thought of the play. The idea or ideas with which the play deals and which it expounds.

Thespian   A synonym for "actor"; the term is derived from Thespis, who is said to have been the first actor in the ancient Greek theater.

Thingspielen   Massive propagandistic theatrical spectacles staged outdoors in Nazi Germany.

Thymele   The altar in the center of the ancient Greek orchestra.

Thyromata   The large openings into the second story of the Hellenistic Greek skene.

Tragedy   One of the most fundamental dramatic forms in the western tradition, tragedy involves a serious action of universal significance and has important moral and philosophical implications. Following Aristotle, most critics agree that the tragic hero or heroine should be an essentially admirable person whose downfall elicits our sympathy while leaving us with a feeling that there has in some way been a triumph of the moral and cosmic order which transcends the fate of any individual. The disastrous outcome of a tragedy should be seen as the inevitable result of the character and his or her situation, including forces beyond the character's control. Traditionally tragedy was about the lives and fortunes of royalty—kings, queens, and nobility—and there has been a great deal of debate about whether it is possible to have a modern tragedy—a tragedy about ordinary people.

Tragic flaw   The factor which is a character's chief weakness and which makes him or her most vulnerable; often intensifies in time of stress. An abused and often incorrectly applied theory from Greek drama.

Tragicomedy   During the Renaissance the word was used for plays that had tragic themes and noble characters yet ended happily. Modern tragicomedy combines serious and comic elements. Many plays of this type involve a comic or ironic treatment of a serious theme.

Trap   An opening in the stage floor, normally covered, which can be used for special effects, such as having scenery or performers rise from below, or which permits the construction of a staircase which ostensibly leads to a lower floor or cellar.

Trilogy   During the classical Greek era, the three tragedies written by the same playwright presented on one day; they were connected by story or thematic concerns.

Tropes   Lyrics added to musical passages in the religious services of the early medieval church; these interpolations were often structured like playlets and evolved into liturgical drama.

Tsure   A secondary role in the noh theater.

Unities   A term referring to the preference that a play occur within one day (unity of time), in one place (unity of place), and with no action irrelevant to the plot (unity of action). Note: contrary to accepted opinion, Aristotle insisted only upon unity of action. Certain neoclassical critics of the Renaissance insisted on all three.

Vomitoria   The covered-over exits in the Roman theater.

Well-made play   A type of play popular in the nineteenth and early twentieth centuries which combined apparent plausibility of incident and surface realism with a tightly constructed and contrived plot.

Wings   Left and right offstage areas; also, narrow standing pieces of scenery, or "legs," more or less parallel to the proscenium, which form the sides of a setting.

Yard   The pit, or standing area, in the Elizabethan public theater.

Zanni   The comic male servants in the commedia dell'arte.

Appendix II

Below is a list of phonetic spellings to assist in the pronunciation of technical terms, place names, names of theatrical figures—actors, directors, designers, playwrights—and names of characters in plays. (Most pronunciations are based on those found in the unabridged edition of the *Random House Dictionary of the English Language.*)

Abydos	ah-BIGH-dohs
Academia dei Confidenti	ak-uh-DEE-mee-uh DAY cohn-fee-DAHN-tee
Accesi	a-CHAY-see
Aeschylus	EHS-kih-luhs
Aesopus	EH-soh-pus
Agamemnon	ag-uh-MEHM-nahn
agon	AG-ohn
agonthetes	ag-ohn-THEH-tees
Alcestis	al-SEHS-tihs
Aminta	ah-MEEN-tah
Amphitryon	am-FIH-tree-ahn

Andreini	an-DREE-nee
Andromache	an-DRAHM-uh-kee
Andromède	AN-droh-mehd
Antigone	an-TIHG-uh-nee
aposentos	a-poh-SEHN-tohs
archon	AHR-kahn
Aristophanes	ar-ih-STAH-fuh-nees
Aristotle	AR-ih-stah-tuhl
Atipho Phaedria	a-TEE-fo FAY-dree-ah
Atreus	AY-tree-ehs
auleum	AW-lee-uhm
Aulis	AW-lihs
auto sacramentales	AW-tohs- sa-crah-mehn-TAH-lehs
avant-garde	ah-VAHNT-GAHRD
Bacchae	BAK-ee
Bharata	buh-RUHT-uh
biwa	BEE-wah
Bourges	BOORZH
bunraku	buhn-RAH-koo
Calderón	CAWL-deh-ruhn
Capek, Karel	CHAH-pehk, KAR-ehl
Cao, Yu	KOW YOO
carros	CAH-roh3
Castelvetro, Lodovico	kas-tehl-VEHT-roh, loh-duh-VEE-koh
cavea	CAH-vee-uh
cazuela	ca-zoo-EHL-ah
Champmeslé	sham-MAY-zlee
chiaroscuro	kee-ow-roh-SKOO-roh
Chikamatsu Monzaemon	CHEE-kah-MAhT-soo MOHN-zah-eh-MOHN
Choephori	koh-EHF-uh-rih
choregus	koh-REE-guhs
choregoi	koh-REE-gaw-ee
chorodidaskalos	koh-roh-DAHS-kah-lohs
commedia dell'arte	koh-MAY-dee-ah dehl-AHR-teh
companias de parte	cahm-pa-NEE-ahs day PAHR-teh
Coquelin, Benoît Constant	kohk-LAIN, beh-NWAH kawn-STAHN
Corneille	cawr-NAY
Creon	KREE-ahn
denouement	deh-noo-MAHN
deus ex machina	DEH-ews eks MAH-kih-nah
Diderot	DEE-deh-roh
Dionysia	digh-eh-NIH-see-uh
Dionysus	digh-eh-NIGH-suhs
Dithyrambic	dihth-ih-RAM-bik

dominus	DOH-mih-nus
Dottore	doh-TOH-reh
drame bourgeois	DRAM boor-ZHWAH
ekkyklema	eh-KUH-kleh-mah
Epidamnus	eh-pih-DAM-nuhs
episkenion	eh-pih-SKEH-nee-uhn
Erotium	eh-roo-TI-um
Eteocles	ih-TEE-uh-klees
Eumenides	yoo-MEHN-ih-dees
Euripides	yuh-RIH-pih-dees
Francesco	fran-CHEHS-coh
Freie Bühne	FRIGH BOO-neh
Gao Ming	GAH-oh MIHNG
gesamtkunstwerk	geh-samt-KOONST-verk
Gloucester	GLAW-stehr
Godot	guh-DOH
Goethe	GEHR-teh
gradas	GRAH-dahs
Grein	GRIGHN
Gyubal Wahazar	gee-OO-bahl wah-HAH-zahr
hanamichi	hah-nah-MEE-chee
Harlequin	HAHR-luh-kwihn
hamartia	har-MARH-tee-a
hashigakari	ha-shee-gah-KAH-ree
Hippolytus	hih-PAH-lih-tuhs
Hrosvitha	rohs-VEE-tah
hubris	HEW-brihs
I Gelosi	EE jel-OH-see
Ikherofret	ih-KEHR-noh-freht
Ionesco	yuh-NEHS-koh
Iphigenia	ih-fih-jeh-NIGH-uh
Isis	IGH-suhs
Ismene	ihs-MEE-nee
Jocasta	yoh-KAHS-tuh
joruri	joh-ROO-ree
Junji, kinoshita	Juhn-jee kee-NOH-shee-tah
kabuki	kah-BOO-kee
Kalidasa	ka-leh-DAH-sah
Kan'ami	KAHN AHMEE
katharsis	kuh-THAHR-sihs
Kawatake Mokumai	KAH-wah-TAH-kay MOH-koo-MAH-ee

Kitano	kee-TAH-noh
Komachi Sotoba	koh-MAH-chee soh-TOH-bah
kothornoi	koh-THOR-noy
kothornus	koh-THOR-nus
Kunio, Kishida	KOO-nee-oh kee-SHEE-dah
Kwanami	kwah-NAH-mee
kyogen	kee-OH-gehn
Li Yu	LEE YOO
Lope de Vega	Loh-pay deh Vaygeh
Ludi Florales	LOO-dee floh-RAH-lehs
Ludi Romani	LEW-dee roh-MAH-nee
Lugné-Poë	LOO-nee poh-AY
luñetas	LOO-nee-tahs
Lysistrata	lih-sih-STRAH-tuh
Marais	ma-RAY
mechane	MEH-kah-neh
de Medici	deh MEHD-ih-chee
Mei Lanfang	MAY LAHN-fahng
Menaechmus	mih-NEK-mahs
Menaechmi	mih-NEK-mee
Messenio	meh-SEE-nee-oh
Meyerhold, Vsevolod Emilievitch	MIGH-ehr-hohld, ZEH-vee-ohld eh-MEE-lee-eh-vihtch
Miles Gloriosus	MEE-lehs gloh-ree-OH-suhs
Minturno, Antonio	mihn-TOOR-noh, an-TOH-nee-oh
motomasa	moh-toh-MAH-sah
Natyasastra	nat-yuh-SAS-truh
Naumachia	naw-MA-kee-eh
Nietzsche	NEE-sheh
Oedipus	EHD-uh-pus
Oeta	oh-EH-tah
Okuni	uh-KOO-nee
onkos	AHN-kohs
Oresteia	oh-reh-STEE-uh
Osiris	oh-SIGH-rihs
Oxenstierna	UHK-sehn-SHEHR-nah
Pantalone	pan-teh-LOH-nay
parabasis	puh-RAB-uh-sihs
parados	PAR-uh-dohs
paraskenia	pa-ra-SKEE-nee-a
Patelin	pa-teh-LAIN
Peniculus	peh-NIH-koo-luhs

periaktoi	pehr-ee-AK-toy
Peruzzi, Baldassare	peh-ROOT-zee, BAHL-dah-SAH-reh
Philoctetes	fihl-uhk-TEE-tees
Phormio	FOHR-mee-oh
pinakes	pih-NAH-kehs
platea	PLA-tee-ah
Plebeians	pleh-BEE-ans
Plutus	PLOO-tuhs
Polynices	pohl-eh-NIGH-sees
Poquelin, Jean Baptiste	poh-ka-LAIN, ZHAHN bap-TEEST
proagon	proh-AH-gohn
proedria	proh-EH-dree-a
prologos	proh-LOH-gohs
Prometheus	pruh-MEE-thee-uhs
Pseudolus	SOO-dah-luhs
pulpitum	PUHL-pih-tuhm
Qi Rushan	KEE roo-SHAHN
Quem quaeritis	KWEHM KWAY-rih-tihs
regisseur	ray-zhee-SUHR
Roscius	ROHSH-ee-uhs
Salmacida Spolia	sal-mah-SEE-dah SPOH-lee-ah
satyr	SAY-tuhr
scaena	SKAY-nah
Scaliger	SKAL-ih-juhr
Scamozzi	ska-MOH-zee
Shakuntala	shah-KUHN-tah-lah
Shii No Shosho	SHEE-eh NOH SHOH-shoh
shite	SHEE-tay
siparium	sih-PAH-ree-uhm
skene	SKEE-nee
Sophocles	SAH-feh-klees
Tagore, Rabindranath	teh-GOHR, reh-BEEN-dreh-nath
Tasso, Torquato	TAH-soh, tawr-KAW-toh
Téatro Farnese	tay-AH-troh fahr-NEH-seh
Teiresias	tigh-REE-see-uhs
tetralogy	teh-TRAH-luh-gee
Théâtre Libre	tay-AH-treh LEE-bra
theatron	thee-AY-trahn
Thebes	THEEBS
Thérèse Raquin	teh-RAYS, rah-KAIN
Thespian	THEHS-pee-ehn
Thespis	THEHS-pihs
Thyestes	thigh-EHS-tees
thymele	THIGH-meh-lee

thyromata	thigh-ROH-mah-tah
Trachiniae	treh-KIHN-ee-ee
tsure	TSUH-ray
Tsurya Namboku	TSUH-roo-yah NAHN-boh-koo
Turandot	TOOR-rahn-daht
Uruashi	oo-roo-AH-shee
Vikrama	vih-KRAH-mah
	WAHNG SHEE-foo
Wang Shifu	viht-KEH-vihch, stan-IHS-wahv ihg-
Witkiewicz, Stanislaw Ignacy	NATS
Yeats	YAYTS
yugen	YOO-jihn
Zeami	zay-AH-mee

Appendix III

RELATED PLAYS

The following is a list of plays, many of them referred to in the text, that can be read in connection with the study of individual chapters.

CHAPTER TWO—THE GREEK THEATER

Aeschylus: *The Oresteia (Agamemnon, The Libation Bearers, The Eumenides)*
Sophocles: *King Oedipus, Antigone*
Euripides: *The Trojan Women*
Aristophanes: *Lysistrata*
Menander: *The Grouch*

CHAPTER THREE—THE ROMAN THEATER

Plautus: *The Menaechmi*
Terence: *Phormio*
Seneca: *Thyestes*

CHAPTER FOUR—THE MEDIEVAL THEATER

The Second Shepherds' Play
Everyman

CHAPTER FIVE—THE THEATER OF THE ITALIAN RENAISSANCE

Torquato Tasso: *Aminta*
Niccolo Machiavelli: *Mandragola*
Flaminio Scala: *The Portrait*

CHAPTER SIX—THE THEATER OF THE ENGLISH RENAISSANCE

Christopher Marlowe: *The Tragical History of Dr. Faustus*
William Shakespeare: *Hamlet*
Ben Jonson: *Volpone*
John Webster: *The Duchess of Malfi*

CHAPTER SEVEN—THE THEATERS OF THE SPANISH GOLDEN AGE AND NEO-CLASSICAL FRANCE

Lope de Vega: *Fuente Ovejuna (The Sheep Well)*
Calderón de la Barca: *Life Is a Dream*
Pierre Corneille: *The Cid*
Molière: *The Miser*
Jean Racine: *Phaedra*

CHAPTER EIGHT—THE THEATER OF THE ENGLISH RESTORATION

William Wycherley: *The Country Wife*
William Congreve: *The Way of the World*

CHAPTER NINE—THE THEATER OF THE EIGHTEENTH CENTURY

Oliver Goldsmith: *She Stoops to Conquer*
Richard Brinsley Sheridan: *The School for Scandal*
Friedrich Schiller: *Mary Stuart*
Carlo Goldoni: *The Servant of Two Masters*
Carlo Gozzi: *Turandot*

CHAPTER TEN—THE THEATER FROM 1800 TO 1875

Victor Hugo: *Hernani*
George L. Aiken: *Uncle Tom's Cabin*
Eugène Scribe: *A Glass of Water*
Victorien Sardou: *Let's Get a Divorce*

CHAPTER ELEVEN—THE THEATER FROM 1875 TO 1915

Henrik Ibsen: *Ghosts*
George Bernard Shaw: *Candida*
Anton Chekhov: *The Cherry Orchard*
August Strindberg: *A Dream Play*

CHAPTER TWELVE—THE THEATER FROM 1915 TO 1945

Luigi Pirandello: *Six Characters in Search of an Author*
Eugene O'Neill: *The Hairy Ape*
Bertolt Brecht: *Mother Courage and Her Children*
Federico García Lorca: *The House of Bernarda Alba*

CHAPTER THIRTEEN—THE THEATER FROM 1945 TO 1980

Eugène Ionesco: *The Bald Soprano*
Samuel Beckett: *Waiting for Godot*
Harold Pinter: *The Birthday Party*
Arthur Miller: *Death of a Salesman*
Tennessee Williams: *The Glass Menagerie*
Peter Shaffer: *Equus*
Sam Shepard: *Buried Child*

CHAPTER FIFTEEN—THE ASIAN THEATER

Kalidasa: *Shakuntala*
Gao Ming: *Lute Song*
Kanami: *Sotoba Komachi*

CHAPTER SIXTEEN—THE BLACK THEATER

Lorraine Hansberry: *A Raisin in the Sun*
Amiri Baraka: *The Dutchman*

SELECTED BIBLIOGRAPHY

GENERAL THEATER HISTORIES

Berthold, Margot: *A History of the World Theater*, New York, 1972.
Brockett, Oscar: *History of the Theatre*, 4th ed., Boston, 1982.
Nagler, Alois M.: *Sources of Theatrical History*, New York, 1952.
Pickering, Jerry: *Theatre: A History of the Art*, St. Paul, Minn., 1978.
Roberts, Vera M.: *On Stage: A History of the Theatre*, 2d ed., New York, 1974.

CHAPTER ONE—INTRODUCTION

Brown, Ivor: *The First Player: The Origin of Drama*, New York, 1928.
Hunningher, Ben: *The Origin of the Theater*, New York, 1961.
Kirby, E. T.: *Ur-Drama: The Origins of Theatre*, New York, 1975.
Ridgeway, William: *The Drama and Dramatic Dances of Non-European Races*, Cambridge, 1915.
Wilson, Edwin: *The Theater Experience*, 2d ed., New York, 1980.

CHAPTER TWO—THE GREEK THEATER

Arnott, Peter D.: *The Ancient Greek and Roman Theatre*, New York, 1971.
Bieber, Margarete: *The History of Greek and Roman Theater*, 2d ed., Princeton, N. J., 1961.
Butler, James H.: *The Theatre and Drama of Greece and Rome*, San Francisco, 1972.
Flickinger, Roy C.: *The Greek Theatre and Its Drama* , 4th ed., Chicago, 1936.
Pickard-Cambridge, A. W.: *The Dramatic Festivals of Athens*, 2d ed., revised by John Gould and D. M. Lewis, Oxford, 1968.
Webster, T. B. L.: *Greek Theatre Production*, 2d ed., London, 1970.

CHAPTER THREE—THE ROMAN THEATER

Allen, James T.: *Stage Antiquities of the Greeks and Romans and Their Influence*, New York, 1927.
Arnott, Peter: See under Greek Theater.
Beare, William: *The Roman Stage: A Short History of Latin Drama in the Time of the Republic*, 3rd ed., London, 1963.
Bieber, Margarete: See under Greek Theater.
Butler, James H.: See under Greek Theater.
Duckworth, George E.: *The Nature of Roman Comedy*, Princeton, N. J. 1952.

CHAPTER FOUR—THE MEDIEVAL THEATER

Chambers, E. K.: *The Medieval Stage*, 2 vols., Oxford, 1903.
Hardison, O. B.: *Christian Rite and Christian Drama in the Middle Ages*, Baltimore, 1965.
Nagler, Alois M.: *Medieval Religious Stage: Shapes and Phantoms*, New Haven, 1976.
Nelson, Alan H.: *The Medieval English Stage: Corpus Christi Pageants and Plays*, Chicago, 1974.
Wickham, Glynne: *The Medieval Theatre*, London, 1974.
Young, Karl: *The Drama of the Medieval Church*, 2 vols., Oxford, 1933.

CHAPTER FIVE—THE THEATER OF THE ITALIAN RENAISSANCE

Bjurstrom, Per: *Giacomo Torelli and Baroque Stage Design*, Stockholm, 1961.
Ducharte, Pierre: *The Italian Comedy*, translated by R. T. Weaver, London, 1929.
Hewitt, Barnard (ed.): *The Renaissance Stage: Documents of Serlio, Sabbatini, and Furttenbach*, Coral Gables, Fla., 1958.
Mullin, Daniel C.: *The Development of the Playhouse: A Survey of Architecture from the Renaissance to the Present*, Berkeley, 1970.

CHAPTER SIX—THE THEATER OF THE ENGLISH RENAISSANCE

Adams, John C.: *The Globe Playhouse: Its Design and Equipment*, 2d ed., New York, 1961.
Beckerman, Bernard: *Shakespeare at the Globe, 1599–1602*, New York, 1962.
Chambers, E. K.: *The Elizabethan Stage*, 4 vols., London, 1923.
Gurr, Andrew: *Shakespearean Stage, 1574–1642*, Cambridge, 1970.
Hodges, C. W.: *The Globe Restored*, London, 1953.
Nagler, Alois M.: *Shakespeare's Stage*, New Haven, 1958.
Smith, Irwin: *Shakespeare's Blackfriar's Playhouse: Its History and Its Design*, New York, 1964.

CHAPTER SEVEN—THE THEATERS OF THE SPANISH GOLDEN AGE AND NEOCLASSICAL FRANCE

Crawford, J. P. W.: *Spanish Drama Before Lope de Vega*, Philadelphia, 1937.
Lawrenson, T. E.: *The French Stage in the 17th Century: A Study in the Advent of the Italian Order*, Manchester, 1957.
Lough, John: *Paris Theatre Audiences in the Seventeenth and Eighteenth Centuries*, London 1957.
Shergold, N. D.: *A History of the Spanish Stage from Medieval Times until the End of the 17th Century*, Oxford, 1967.
Turnell, Martin: *The Classical Moment: Studies in Corneille, Molière and Racine*, New York, 1948.
Wiley, W. L.: *The Early Public Theatre in France*, Cambridge, Mass., 1920.

CHAPTER EIGHT—THE THEATER OF THE ENGLISH RESTORATION

Hotson, Leslie: *The Commonwealth and Restoration Stage*, Cambridge, Mass., 1928.
The London Stage, 1660–1800, 11 vols., Carbondale, Ill., 1960–1968.
McCollom, John I. (ed.): *The Restoration Stage*, Boston, 1961.
Southern, Richard: *Changeable Scenery: Its Origin and Development in the British Theatre*, London, 1952.
Summers, Montague: *The Restoration Theatre*, London, 1934.

CHAPTER NINE—THE THEATER OF THE EIGHTEENTH CENTURY

Bauer-Heinhold, M.: *Baroque Theater*, New York, 1967.
Burford, W. H.: *Theatre, Drama, and Audience in Goethe's Germany*, London, 1957.

Hughes, Leo: *The Drama's Patrons: A Study of the 18th Century London Audience,* Austin, Texas, 1971.

Pedicord, Harry W.: *The Theatrical Public in the Time of Garrick,* New York, 1954.

Price, Cecil: *Theatre in the Age of Garrick,* Oxford, 1973.

Prudhoe, John: *The Theatre of Goethe and Schiller,* Oxford, 1973.

CHAPTER TEN—THE THEATER FROM 1800 TO 1875

Booth, Michael: *English Melodrama,* London, 1965.

Carlson, Marvin: *The French Stage in the 19th Century,* Metuchen, N.J., 1972.

————: *The German Stage in the 19th Century,* Metuchen, N.J., 1972.

Grimstead, David: *Melodrama Unveiled: American Theatre and Culture, 1800–1850,* Chicago, 1968.

Rowell, George: *The Victorian Theatre: A Survey,* London, 1956.

Vardac, A. Nicholas: *Stage to Screen: Theatrical Methods from Garrick to Griffith,* Cambridge, Mass., 1949.

CHAPTER ELEVEN—THE THEATER FROM 1875 TO 1915

Bentley Eric: *The Playwright as Thinker: A Study of Drama in Modern Times,* New York, 1946.

Garten, Hugh: *Modern German Drama,* London, 1959.

Miller, Anna Irene: *The Independent Theatre in Europe 1887 to the Present,* New York, 1931.

Shattuck, Roger: *The Banquet Years: The Arts in France, 1885–1918,* New York, 1961.

Slonim, Marc: *Russian Theatre from the Empire to the Soviets,* Cleveland, 1961.

Valency, Maurice: *The Flower and the Castle: An Introduction to Modern Drama,* New York, 1963.

Volbach, Walther R.: *Adolphe Appia, Prophet of the Modern Theatre,* Middletown, Conn. 1968.

CHAPTER TWELVE—THE THEATER FROM 1915 TO 1945

Artaud, Antonin: *The Theatre and Its Double,* translated by M. C. Richards, New York, 1958.

Brecht, Bertolt: *Brecht on Theatre,* translated by John Willett, New York, 1964.

Carter, Huntly: *The New Spirit in the European Theatre, 1914–1924,* New York, 1926.

Clunes, Alec: *The British Theatre,* London, 1964.

Houghton, Norris: *Moscow Rehearsals,* New York, 1936.

Rabkin, Gerald: *Drama and Commitment: Politics in the American Theatre of the Thirties,* Bloomington, Ind., 1964.

Willett, John: *Expressionism,* New York, 1970.

CHAPTER THIRTEEN—THE THEATER FROM 1945 TO 1980

Cohn, Ruby: *Currents in Contemporary Drama*, Bloomington, Ind., 1969.
Esslin, Martin: *The Theatre of the Absurd*, London, 1968.
Grotowski, Jerzy: *Towards a Poor Theatre*, New York, 1968.
Poggi, Jack: *Theatre in America: The Impact of Economic Forces, 1870–1967*, Ithaca, N.Y., 1968.
Weales, Gerald: *American Drama Since World War II*, New York, 1962.

CHAPTER FIFTEEN—THE ASIAN THEATER

Arnott, Peter: *The Theatres of Japan*, New York, 1969.
Bowers, Faubion: *Theatre in the East: A Survey of Asian Dance and Drama*, London, 1951.
Ernst, Earle: *The Kabuki Theatre*, New York, 1957.
Gargi, Balwant: *Theatre in India*, New York, 1962.
Scott, A. C.: *The Classical Theatre of China*, London, 1957.
Waley, Arthur: *The Nō Plays of Japan*, New York, 1922.

CHAPTER SIXTEEN—THE BLACK THEATER

Abramson, Doris: *Negro Playwrights in the American Theatre, 1925–1959*, New York, 1969.
Hatch, James V., and Ted Shine: *Black Theater, U.S.A.*, New York, 1974.
Isaacs, Edith J.: *The Negro in the American Theatre*, New York, 1947.
Marshall, Herbert, and Mildred Stock: *Ira Aldridge, the Negro Tragedian*, Carbondale, Ill., 1968.
Mitchell, Loften: *Black Drama: The Story of the American Negro in the Theatre*, New York, 1967.

INDEX

Rice, Tim, 104
Rich, Christopher, 195, 196, 199, 221
Rich, John, 221
Richard Allen Center (New York), 437
Richard II (Shakespeare), 362, 419
Richards, Lloyd, 432, 433
Richardson, Willis, 423, 431
Richelieu, Armand de, Cardinal, 112, 167, 168, 170, 174
Riders to the Sea (Synge), 273, 289
Right You Are if You Think You Are (Pirandello), 313
Ritual, 10–12, 25–27, 81–82, 319, 412–414, 416, 438, 451
Rivals, The (Sheridan), 213, 214
River Niger, The (Walker), 437
Robards, Jason, 349
Robbers, The (Schiller), 215
Robeson, Paul, 411, 414, 428–430, 433
Robinson, Bill "Bojangles," 424
Rodgers, Richard, 60, 306–307
Rodogune (Corneille), 170
Roman festivals, 19, 55–57, 447
Romance of the Western Chamber (Shifu), 385
Romanticism, 181, 215, 230, 242, 244, 251, 255, 265, 451, 452
Romeo and Juliet (Shakespeare), 136, 140, 188, 359, 362
Rope, The (Plautus), 60
Roscius, 67, 419, 459
Rose McClendon Players (New York), 427
Rose Tattoo, The (Williams), 344
Rosmersholm (Ibsen), 276
Royal Hunt of the Sun (Shaffer), 342
Royal Shakespeare Company (RSC), 340, 357–359, 369
Rueda, Lope de, 156
Rules for Actors (Goethe), 231
Run Little Chillun (Johnson), 427

Sabbatini, Nicola, 103, 119
Sabbionetta Theater (Italy), 103, 115
Sachs, Hans, 79, 81
Sackler, Howard, 354
Saint Joan (Shaw), 281
San Francisco Mime Troupe, 107
Sandler, Joan, 438
Sanskrit drama, 376–381, 383, 409
Sardou, Victorien, 235, 238, 247, 250, 265, 276, 463
Sartre, Jean-Paul, 305, 333, 445
Satyr plays, 2, 26, 37, 103, 451, 459

Savoy Theater (London), 264, 270
Saxe-Meiningen, Duke of (see Georg II, duke of Saxe-Meiningen)
Scaena (stage house), 68–70, 451, 459
Scaena frons, 69, 115, 451
Scaliger, Julius Caesar, 110, 459
Scenery, 9, 44–45, 117–122, 144, 151–153, 164–165, 174, 181, 187, 202, 222–225, 233, 256, 259, 261, 263, 265, 280, 291–293, 295–297, 308, 355, 361, 370, 378, 386, 390, 404, 407, 442, 447, 449, 451, 452
Schechner, Richard, 345–347, 351, 355, 434
Schiller, Friedrich, 209, 215, 230, 233, 462
Schneider, Alan, 340
School dramas, 127
School for Scandal, The (Sheridan), 209, 213, 214, 225, 462
School for Wives, The (Molière), 173, 190
Schroeder, Friedrich Ludwig, 226, 228, 233
Scrap of Paper, A (Sardou), 238, 247
Scribe, Eugene, 238, 247, 265, 276, 463
Sea Gull, The (Chekhov), 271, 283, 285, 292, 296
Second Shepherd's Play, The, 78, 85–87, 92, 94, 462
Secrets, 91, 451
Self-Tormentor, The (Terence), 61
Seneca, Lucius Annaeus, 62, 63, 73, 129, 134, 461
Sentimental comedy, 212–215, 233
Serlio, Sebastiano, 102, 117–119, 142
Servant of Two Masters, The (Goldoni), 216, 217, 462
Seven Against Thebes (Aeschylus), 28
Seven Descents of Myrtle, The (Williams), 344
Shadow Box, The (Cristofer), 333, 354
Shaffer, Peter 342, 463
Shakespeare, William, 8, 16, 17, 60, 62, 87, 110, 113, 125, 128–129, 131, 133–138, 140, 144, 146–149, 151, 153, 165, 187–190, 201, 203, 210, 215, 221, 225, 236–238, 241, 244, 252, 254, 255, 288, 297,

Shakespeare, William *(Cont.)*:
310–313, 329, 332, 353, 354, 357–359, 362, 373, 392, 401, 405, 414, 415, 419, 428–430, 451, 462
Shakuntala (Kalidasa), 376, 378, 379, 459, 463
Sharing plans, 107, 145, 165, 176, 195, 444, 447, 451, 452
Shaw, George Bernard, 214, 267, 271, 280, 281, 283, 299, 364–366, 390, 463
Shchepkin, Mikhail, 253, 265
She, Lao, 393
She Stoops to Conquer (Goldsmith), 209, 215, 462
Sheep Well, The (Lope de Vega), 158, 161, 163, 462
Shelley, Percy Bysshe, 242
Shepard, Sam, 333, 350, 463
Sheridan, Richard Brinsley, 199, 209, 213–214, 225, 462
Shifu, Wang, 385
Shine, Ted, 437
Shite, 395, 399, 451, 459
Short View of the Immorality and Profaneness of the English Stage, A (Collier), 187, 190, 194
Showboat (Hammerstein and Kern), 306, 307, 430
Shubert, Jacob J., 306
Shubert, Lee, 306
Shuffle Along, 414, 424
Siddons, Sarah Kemble, 199, 221, 248, 251
Sides, 145, 451
Siege of Rhodes, The (Davenant), 184, 186, 187, 189, 202
Sign in Sidney Brustein's Window, The (Hansberry), 433
Simon, Neil, 8, 348
Simonson, Lee, 292
Siparium (curtain), 69, 451, 459
Six Characters in Search of an Author (Pirandello), 314, 463
Skene (scene house), 1, 2, 43–44, 48, 148, 449, 451, 453, 459
Skin of Our Teeth, The (Wilder), 305
Skyloft Players (Chicago), 427
Slapstick, 107, 451
Slave, The (Baraka), 435
Slave Ship (Baraka), 435, 436
Slight Ache, A (Pinter), 337
Small Craft Warnings (Williams), 344
Socialist realism, 295–297, 304, 324, 325
Sociétaire, 176, 177, 452